Landing a Job For Canadians For Dummies®

by Dawn McCoy, MBA

Cheat Sheet

Six Things an Interviewer [...] ut You

1. **Why do you want to work here in the firs[...]** What is it that attracts you to this employ[...] rather than another one? Have you thought this out? Can you put your answer into words for the interviewer?

2. **What skills can you bring to the table?** The interviewer has established that yes, you have researched the company and you have made a conscious decision that you would like to work for them. The next thing she wants to determine is what you can do for them. What are your hard and soft (transferable) skills and how can these benefit the company?

3. **What kind of person are you, and will you fit into the company culture?** Every organization has its own *culture* (the values and beliefs of the organization) and it is very important that new employees fit into this culture. Is it fast-paced and change-oriented? Does it emphasize teamwork? Whatever the specifics, the inter-viewer wants to find out what kind of personality and work ethic you have so she can determine whether you'll "fit."

4. **Do you have the right attitude?** The interviewer is interested not only in whether you have the ability and skills to do the job, but in whether [...] o the job and, if hired, [...] put 100 percent into the position.

5. **What's different or special about you?** You are most likely one of many candidates. The interviewer wants to find out why she should hire you over all of them. You need to make it obvious.

6. **How much money are we going to have to drop to get you?** What do you expect for a salary? What about benefits? The interviewer wants to hire the best person for the job, but it has to be within her budget. Interviewers will usually wait until the offer stage to raise the issue of salary, but she may ask a few questions toward the end of the interview to try to get a sense of whether they can afford you. Always try to deflect these questions until you get to the offer stage.

If you have a pretty good sense of how you'll answer these six questions before you head in to the interview, you should be able to ace most of the questions they throw at you. For more advice on how to prepare for the big moment, see Chapter 16.

Tips on Keeping That Upbeat Attitude

✔ Stay away from people with negative attitudes.

✔ Realize that being rejected for a job is not a rejection of you as a person.

✔ Use your support network to help you stay positive.

✔ Celebrate small successes.

✔ Set daily goals that are realistic and achievable.

✔ Think of your job hunt as a learning experience.

✔ Accept that your feelings of stress, and possibly panic, are normal.

✔ Seek professional assistance if depression or anxiety begin to affect you.

See Chapter 25.

...For Dummies®: Bestselling Book Series for Beginners

Landing a Job For Canadians For Dummies®

by Dawn McCoy, MBA

Cheat Sheet

Jump-Starting Your Job Hunt the Virtual Way

✔ Log on to the World Wide Web and search for job postings on online job banks, like HotJobs.ca (www.hotjobs.ca), Monster.ca (www.monster.ca), and Workopolis (www.workopolis.com).

✔ Visit company Web sites to find out more about potential employers and job vacancies. Use a search engine, like Google (www.google.ca), to look up individual companies' Web addresses.

✔ Explore industry-specific Web sites to narrow your search to your industry or area of expertise.

✔ Cruise location-specific Web sites for different geographic areas.

✔ Subscribe to newsgroups and e-mail lists to enhance your network and help in your job hunt.

✔ Post your résumé to an online job bank.

See Chapters 12 and 13 for more on making the most of the Internet in your job hunt. And don't forget to check out the Landing a Job For Canadians For Dummies Directory of Job Resources for more employment-related Web sites.

Three Big Questions to Answer Before You Start Pounding the Pavement

1. **What are you good at?** Choose a job or occupation for which you have a natural affinity — that you are good at. You are likely not only to enjoy it, but to be successful at it, too.

2. **What do you like to do?** Choose a job or occupation that you like, and you'll see the same thing happening again: you will probably have a grand time doing the job, and hopefully have a better chance at being successful.

3. **What is important to you?** Do you want to work full- or part-time? What are your values? What kind of company do you want to work for? Choose a job that reflects how you lead your life, to ensure you stay happy in your job.

For 26 more probing questions you can ask yourself about your abilities, passions, and values as they relate to finding the right job, see Chapter 2. It's painless (and fun!).

wiley.com

...For Dummies®: Bestselling Book Series for Beginners

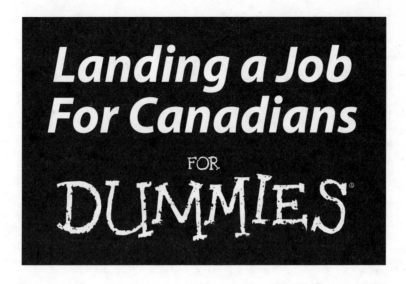

Landing a Job For Canadians

FOR DUMMIES®

by Dawn McCoy, MBA

WILEY

wiley.com

John Wiley & Sons Canada, Ltd

◆ Toronto, ON ◆

Landing a Job For Canadians For Dummies®

Published by
John Wiley & Sons Canada, Ltd
22 Worcester Road
Etobicoke, ON M9W 1L1
www.wiley.ca

National Library of Canada Cataloguing in Publication Data

McCoy, Dawn, 1961–

Landing a job for Canadians for dummies / Dawn McCoy.

Includes index.
ISBN 1-894413-48-2

1. Job Hunting — Canada. I. Title.

HF5382.75.C3M32 2002   650.14'0971   C2002-903679-8

Printed in Canada

1 2 3 4 5 TRI 06 05 04 03 02

Distributed in Canada by John Wiley & Sons Canada, Ltd.

For general information on John Wiley & Sons Canada, Ltd, including all books published by Wiley Publishing, Inc., please call our warehouse, Tel: 1-800-567-4797. For reseller information, including discounts and premium sales, please call our sales department, Tel: 416-646-7992. For press review copies, author interviews, or other publicity information, please contact our marketing department, Tel: 416-646-4584; Fax: 416-236-4448.

For authorization to photocopy items for corporate, personal, or educational use, please contact Cancopy, The Canadian Copyright Licensing Agency, One Yonge Street, Suite 1900, Toronto, ON M5E 1E5; Tel: 416-868-1620; Fax: 416-868-1621; www.cancopy.com

About the Author

Dawn McCoy, MBA, is a regular contributor to Canada's largest online newspaper — CANOE (`www.canoe.ca`), *BusinessWoman Canada* magazine, *Profile Magazine*, and *Canadian Living,* and has been featured in *Alberta Venture, The Edge,* and *Reader's Digest* magazines. She became well known for her inspiring and sometimes controversial column in CANOE Money.

Dawn is a Certified Human Resources Practitioner (CHRP). Her business, E-Lynx Inc., provides human resources and management consulting services to a wide range of clients. In addition, she is a college instructor in Human Resources and Business for Grant MacEwan College, Grande Prairie Regional College, and the University of Alberta. She was the online Business and Technology editor for the U.S.-based information site Bella Online for several years.

Dawn enjoys participating as a keynote speaker in conferences across Canada and the United States. She is the chairperson for the Women at Work Association — an association that helps businesswomen in rural areas network and achieve their full potential. She has spearheaded three national conferences for women in business (`www.womenatwork.ab.ca`). Dawn is also connected to numerous other organizations all over the world via the Internet, and is an active networker.

On a personal side, Dawn loves to travel and combines this passion with her writing career by writing travel columns. She is a single parent and loves to spend time with her 4 children, ages 5 to 11, and her four-legged furry friend, Buddy. She is a prolific volunteer, offering her skills and business savvy to numerous organizations in her community.

She can be reached by e-mail at `e-lynx@shaw.ca` or via her Web site, `www.elynx.ca`.

Dedication

To my children, Ian, Mitchell, Matthew, and Allyson, who tolerated the many work-filled evenings when Mommy had a deadline; who ate pizza for supper too many times to count; and who made me smile when I felt overwhelmed.

To my mom and my brother Darryl for helping when things got to be too much.

Thanks to all of my wonderful family and dear friends for their help and support (and for reading the rough drafts — Carrie and Debbie!).

To you too Buddy, for making me take a break for your walk or just for keeping me company while I worked late into the night.

To my guardian angel, Irene, for making me believe in myself. Till we meet again, my friend.

Thanks to all the wonderful people in my life for always reminding me what is really important!

Author's Acknowledgements

This book was made possible with the help of many individuals. I want to acknowledge my editor at John Wiley & Sons Canada, Ltd., Melanie Rutledge, for her guidance and support all the way along this journey. I also want to thank my technical editor, Karen Girard, who helped me not just with her edit of the book but also with other projects I had going at the same time. I thank Allyson Latta for her fine copy edit of the manuscript. My sister-in-law, Carrie McCoy, also deserves huge thanks for taking the time to review each chapter before I submitted it.

Several individuals also provided reviews of specific parts of the book. I want to thank Tom Carter and Andrew Galeziowski for their review of legal facts.

Thanks to Christiane Coté, at John Wiley & Sons Canada, and to Emma Harrington, at HotJobs.ca.

Many people contributed to the book by completing my "long" questionnaires and responding to my requests for information and stories. Thanks to the following individuals for your input and suggestions: Andrew Galeziowski, Angela Ross, Anna Pranjic-Ross, Anne McCoy, Art Gillies, Barb King, Barbara

Florio Graham, Barbara McCoy, Barry McMahon, Barry Robinson, Bernie Kreiner, Beverly MacDonald, Bob Bettson, Bob Milner, Bob Prescesky, Bonnie Meagher, Brenda Finch, Brenn McCoy, Brian Balkwill, Bruce Basaraba, Caroline Thornton, Carolyn Poulter, Carrie McCoy, Chris Munro, Christine Bulda-Cassidy, Claudette Hargreaves, Colleen Basaraba, Corinne Newman, Craig Lapointe, Curtis Brinker, Cynthia Finch, Dane McCoy, Darren McCoy, Darryl McCoy, Dave Kmet, Debbie McCoy, Debby Mercer, Deborah Rossouw, Diane Zorn, Don Szarko, Donald Diduck, Donna Lazaruk, Donna Messer, Dorothy Spencer, Ed Hanley, Elana Fedorak, Ellen Hearsey, Fiona Ragan-Braun, Fran Hanington, Gail Dunn, Gary Kwasnecha, Glenda Carter, Harry Lasonder, Harry Ullrich, Honey Pell, Jan Paulsen, Jessica Hearsey, John Huey, John Shane, Judi Bachmann, Judy Munson, Julie Dugas, Karen Girard, Karen Graham, Kathy Flynn, Kathy Reimer, Keith Shepherd, Ken Ames, Kim Peters, Kristi Rosko, Laura Leigh White, Laurel Cherman, Laurie Bentz, Liliana Wallace, Linda Hodgson, Linda Maul, Lisa Chell, Lisa Landry, Lisa Risvold, LuAnne Sirdiak, Lyle Benson, Lyn Bilida, Margaret Welwood, Mark Tanguay, Martin Prentice, Martin Sawdon, Melanie Graham, Michelle Olver, Monica Soderstrom, Monika Dery, Noella Kostick, Norm Bates, Pamela Shaw, Pat Moore, Patricia Porter, Paul Folkman, Paula Storie, Paulette Mulcahey, Petula Jurasek, Renée Carmine-Jones, Rhonda Wheele, Richard Pike, Robin Pascoe, Rolf Ullrich, Ron Hordichuk, Rosalie Cederstrand, Shannon Trudeau, Sue Guebert, Tachy Barnett Yapp, Tara Ingram, Terry Scott, Tom Carter, Tom Lakusta, Wendy Kerkhoff. If I missed any contributors, please forgive me and accept my thanks.

Last, but certainly not least, I want to thank my family for recognizing when I needed time to focus on my writing and helping out with my children and my household. I wrote this book during a particularly difficult time in my life and would not have been able to do it without your support. Thank you all.

Publisher's Acknowledgements

We're proud of this book; please send us your comments at canadapt@wiley.com.

Some of the people who helped bring this book to market include the following:

Acquisitions and Editorial

Executive Editor: Joan Whitman

Editor: Melanie Rutledge

Copy Editor: Allyson Latta

Production

Publishing Services Director: Karen Bryan

Layout and Graphics: Kim Monteforte, Heidy Lawrance Associates

Proofreader: Kelli Howey

Indexer: Belle Wong

John Wiley & Sons Canada, Ltd

Bill Zerter, Chief Operating Officer

Robert Harris, Publisher, Professional and Trade Division

Publishing and Editorial for Consumer Dummies

Diane Graves Steele, Vice President and Publisher, Consumer Dummies

Joyce Pepple, Acquisitions Director, Consumer Dummies

Kristin A. Cocks, Product Development Director, Consumer Dummies

Michael Spring, Vice President and Publisher, Travel

Brice Gosnell, Publishing Director, Travel

Suzanne Jannetta, Editorial Director, Travel

Publishing for Technology Dummies

Andy Cummings, Acquisitions Director

Composition Services

Gerry Fahey, Executive Director of Production Services

Debbie Stailey, Director of Composition Services

Contents at a Glance

Cartoons at a Glance

By Rich Tennant

"Frankly? I'd stay away from using 'plucky' as a keyword unless you're looking for a job at a chicken processing plant."

page 143

"I couldn't get this 'job skills' program to work on my PC, so I replaced the mother-board, upgraded the BIOS and wrote a program that links it to my personal database. It told me I wasn't technically inclined and should pursue a career in sales."

page 273

"When choosing a career I ignored my heart and did what my brain wanted. Now all my brain wants is Prozac."

page 7

"I'm sure there will be a good job market when I graduate. I created a virus that will go off that year."

page D-1

"ACCORDING TO THIS RESUME YOU'VE DONE A LOT OF JOB-HOPPING."

page 57

"Very good answer! Now, let me ask you another question..."

page 199

"Well, so much for my lucky hat! I've worn it to five interviews and not ONE call-back!"

page 313

Fax: 978-546-7747

E-mail: richtennant@the5thwave.com

World Wide Web: www.the5thwave.com

Table of Contents

Introduction

Welcome to *Landing a Job For Canadians For Dummies,* the job-hunting book you've been waiting for! I wrote this book for you — the Canadian job hunter. It focuses on Canadian employment issues and Canadian jobs, and it's packed with tips from a Canadian recruiter (that's me!).

In this book, you get the lowdown on what's happening in today's workplace and on how to make the best use of your valuable time when looking for a job. I show you how to jump-start your job hunt and rise above the crowd to land that job you've always dreamed of. (And if you don't have a clue what this dream job is just yet, don't worry, this book gives you some practical tools for figuring that out.)

Landing a Job For Canadians For Dummies is a hands-on, practical guide to finding, applying for, and getting a job in Canada. Whether you are currently employed and considering a career change, or are now graduating from high school or university, this book has something for you. Let's face it: the road to employment can be bumpy. My aim in writing this book is to smooth out some of those bumps, leaving you with a kinder, gentler path to travel in reaching your goal.

About This Book

Sorry, but this book doesn't provide you with a sure-fire formula for getting hired. Know why? Frankly, because such a formula doesn't exist (despite what your math teacher might have said). Instead, this book arms you with the skills and knowledge that will improve your odds of landing a great job. It focuses on the process — what you need to do to be effective and efficient in your job hunt, clearly laying out, in plain English, the steps to complete at each phase of this process — no employment-related jargon in this book! It is, however, up to you to do the work — to take what you read here and apply it.

This book is divided into sections. Each section tackles a different part of the job-hunting process. You can turn right to the part that interests you most (or that you need the most help with), whether it's putting together a knockout résumé, staying as cool as a cucumber during that big interview, or maybe just figuring out which Canadian online job banks are worth your valuable research time, and which aren't worth, well, a hill of beans. You don't need to read the book cover to cover, unless you've got a lot of time on your hands. And one thing I've observed about all people looking for a job is that time is something they *don't* have a lot of.

Conventions Used in This Book

First things first, however. I'd like to fill you in on some of the employment-related terms (not jargon — I promise!) I use in this book:

- A *field* is an overall industry. Law, banking, government, construction, mining, manufacturing, and tourism are examples of industries, or fields.

- An *occupation* is a job classification (for lack of a better word), such as welder, computer programmer, engineer, accountant, lawyer, doctor, teacher, or waitress. You can work in an occupation in numerous fields (such as a computer programmer in the manufacturing or banking fields).

  Choosing an occupation is a key part of your job hunt. The field you work in may also be important to you. But if you don't care which industry you work in, you'll have more flexibility in your job hunt, as long as you're clear on the occupation you want to pursue.

- Your *career* is your work path, or the route you follow in your work life. It includes all of the jobs you have held and will hold, and, by extension, the occupations and fields you work in.

- A *job,* on the other hand, is a specific position in paid employment. Finding a job is the focus of this book.

I'm glad we've cleared that up, because I refer to these terms throughout the book, and I don't want to keep you in the dark. Sometimes I use the word "career" interchangeably with "field," "occupation," and "job."

I also write a lot about recruiters in the book. Just to make sure that we're all on the same wavelength, there are basically two types of recruiters:

- **Corporate recruiters:** Many organizations have their own human resources or personnel departments that are responsible for hiring employees. So they're internal recruiters. They generally have other human resources–related duties as part of their jobs.

- **Third-party recruiters:** Sometimes called *headhunters,* these recruiters help organizations fill their staffing needs, though they aren't employed by the organizations they serve. These recruiters are usually paid a percentage of the new employee's wages as a fee for their services.

When I refer to "recruiters" in this book, I mean the corporate recruiters who work inside organizations, and are on those organizations' payrolls. When I refer to a third-party recruiter, or headhunter, I say so specifically.

Foolish Assumptions

This book is for anyone who is searching for a job or considering a job change. You may be a recent high school or university graduate looking for your first full-time job. Or you may have lost your job recently — a casualty of the "re-engineered workplace" (one of my favourite examples of employment jargon). You may be unemployed or soon-to-be unemployed (a casualty of "right-sizing"), or you may have a job that you just aren't terribly excited about. Some of you might be getting strong messages from your boss that change is in the works within your organization, and you sense you may be somehow pushed into another job. Regardless of your individual circumstances — what *kind* of job you are looking for, how *long* you have been looking, and *why* you are looking — one thing is certain. Job-hunting is a process, and the more methodical and efficient you are in carrying out this process, the more likely you are to succeed.

This is a big-picture book that discusses all aspects of landing a job in Canada (and outside Canada, for that matter, if you're interested). As you read along, you might want to refer to some other useful job-related books in the . . . *For Dummies* series. I recommend *Résumés For Dummies, Cover Letters For Dummies,* and *Job Interviews For Dummies,* all by Joyce Lain Kennedy, and all published by John Wiley & Sons, Inc.

How This Book Is Organized

When writing this book, I broke the job-hunting process down into stages, which translate into the parts in this book. The chapters in each section cover various topics related to the stage of which they're a part. There's also a Part of Tens, a nifty little collection of tips and ideas you won't find elsewhere in the book, and a Directory of Job Resources.

Part I: Job-Hunting Basics

Part I helps you identify your employment goals and shows you how to get organized to best achieve them. Chapter 2 takes you through a fun self-assessment exercise to help you make informed career decisions that are right for you. Chapters 3 and 4 zero in on getting organized for your job hunt, from picking that perfect place at home to set up your Mission Control head-quarters (where you'll conduct your job hunt from), to creating a schedule you can stick with. And let's not forget about downtime! For all you over-achievers out there, it's important to take breaks and celebrate your small successes — even if it's simply identifying a promising lead.

Part II: The Right Stuff: Résumés and Cover Letters

You can't do the job if you don't have the proper tools, right? This part equips you with all the right stuff to put together a winning application package — and to win a place in the memory of the recruiter. Chapter 5 helps you pick the résumé format that shows you and all your irrepressible talent in the best possible light. Chapters 6 and 7 help you craft your résumé. Chapter 9 shows you how to make that same résumé cyber-friendly. Chapter 8 focuses on that important and often overlooked element of the application package, the cover letter. And what do you do after you've signed, sealed, and delivered your application package? No, don't reach for that cold one just yet . . . follow up, of course. Chapter 10 gives you some ideas on how to follow up with a recruiter after you've submitted your application, to win that all-important interview.

Part III: Where the Jobs Are

Having a whiz-bang résumé and cover letter is one thing, but neither will do you any good if you've got nobody to send them to. You need to know how to research jobs effectively — off-line and online. Chapter 11 shows you how to use traditional (off-line) research methods to ferret out job leads (there's still a use for these old-fashioned methods, you know!). Chapter 12 acquaints you with the best search tools on the Web, and offers advice on how to use your time online productively (because it's so easy to get side-tracked on the Internet . . . you know, one link leads to another, which leads to another, and so on). Chapter 13 goes into more detail about Canadian employment sites you should check out. Networking is the topic of Chapter 14.

Part IV: In the Thick of It: Interviews and Negotiations

Part IV is where you pull it all together, land that crucial interview, and make the best impression possible. Chapter 15 gives you an overview of different interview formats and styles you could be faced with. Chapter 16 helps you prepare for your interview. Chapter 17 guides you through game day — listening effectively, answering tricky questions, and ultimately staying in control throughout. When they offer you the job (which they'll be sure to do if you read the first three chapters in this part), you need to know how to negotiate effectively to get what you want, need, and deserve. Chapter 18 covers negotiating offers and employment contracts. Chapter 19 looks at the ins and outs of Canadian employment law, and tells you what you need to be aware of as you scout out that new job.

Part V: Exploring Other Options

If you want to consider employment options available to Canadians other than the traditional 9-to-5 office job, this part is for you. Chapter 20 discusses creative ways to get your foot in the door, such as doing temp work, freelancing, or volunteering. Chapter 21 puts you through your paces to see if you have what it takes to join the growing ranks of entrepreneurs out there and start your own business. And if you want to look further afield for your dream job, Chapter 22 tells you what you need to know as a Canadian who wants to work outside Canada.

Part VI: The Part of Tens

Part VI provides handy at-a-glance lists full of tips and advice to round out your job-hunting skill set. The chapters in this part discuss blips, bloopers, and blunders that you don't want to make when you pound the pavement, ways to keep your spirits bright and your morale high, and a group of *transferable skills,* also called soft skills, which, if you have even a few of them, could help you land a job.

Special Features

The Directory of Job Resources, printed on can't-miss-it yellow paper, contains a wealth of extra information about both online and off-line job-related resources. Check it out!

Icons Used in This Book

As you make your way through this book, you'll notice little pictures — the folks who publish the . . . *For Dummies* books call them icons — to the left of the text. These icons are in the book to help you locate particularly helpful tips and advice quickly. Here is a list of the icons you'll find here:

When you see this icon, you can count on finding insider tips and job-hunting information provided by a seasoned recruitment professional — me.

This icon flags useful bits of information and special tricks that will help you find a better job faster.

This icon alerts you to Web sites that you'll find useful during your job hunt.

This icon lets you know when you should think twice about how you act in a certain situation — that there may be pitfalls if you follow a certain course of action. You know, those times where you should be a little more careful about what you say or do. This icon points out things that might trip you up if you aren't cautious.

These are real-life anecdotes I've culled from people I've worked with over the years. Job hunters' and recruiters' experiences alike appear here. True stories are always fun and help illustrate the points I make in the book.

Where to Go from Here

You can use this book in a number of ways, depending on where you are in your stage of life and your job goals. You can read the book from cover to cover, using the ideas that are relevant to you, photocopying the templates that apply to your situation, and incorporating these ideas into your job hunt.

You can also use this book as a reference tool and quickly find the topic on which you need immediate help. The book is not linear — each topic is self-contained — so you should quickly be able to find ideas, forms, and samples that you can use.

Part I
Job-Hunting Basics

The 5th Wave   By Rich Tennant

"When choosing a career I ignored my heart and did what my brain wanted. Now all my brain wants is Prozac."

In this part . . .

You need to ask yourself some important questions before you begin looking for a job. One of these questions is, "What do I want to do?" Sounds simple enough, right? Well, you'd be surprised how challenging coming up with an answer can be — whether it's a case of your being unable to narrow down your responses, or being unable to muster up even one response. If you can't answer the question, you need to step back and do some background work. In this part, you go through a fun self-assessment exercise to figure out what you are good at, what excites you, and what matters to you. Your answers to these questions will point you in the right direction. This part also helps you get organized for your job hunt, both physically (making sure you have the right tools) and mentally (making sure you have the right attitude).

Chapter 1

The Road to Gainful Employment

● ●

In This Chapter

▶ Navigating the road to employment

▶ Understanding how the pieces of the job-search puzzle fit together

▶ Using this book to help yourself

● ●

*Y*ou are likely reading this book because you're looking for a job. It may be your first job out of university or college, or you may be a stay-at-home parent just re-entering the workforce. You may be a seasoned worker looking for a change of scenery. Whatever the reason, this is an exciting time. It's your chance to make a change, learn new skills, and broaden your horizons. Change can be exciting, but it can also be frightening. Because your job is a major part of your life, job-hunting can cause anxiety for both you and your family.

As you embark on your job hunt, you're probably feeling some or all of the following:

✔ **Excited:** You're psyched about looking for a job, but maybe you need a little guidance to lead you through the process.

✔ **Intimidated:** Who doesn't feel intimidated by the prospect of looking for a new job? Chances are you haven't done this for a while, and things may have changed out there in the marketplace since the last time you were job-hunting. For example, the Internet is now an important tool in your job hunt, but you may not even know how to use it effectively — or at all. The job-hunting process has many parts. Where do you begin?

✔ **Overwhelmed:** You're probably looking at this book, feeling the weight of it in your hands, and thinking that you had no idea there was so much involved in finding a job! The good news is that although it may seem like a lot, it's like putting together a 1,000-piece puzzle. When you first dump everything out on the table, it can seem impossible — where do you start? Once you get a clear picture of the result (look at the cover of the box) and start working toward your goal, your job hunt — like a puzzle — will start to come together.

✔ **Pressured:** It sure would be great if you had the luxury of taking your time to find a job. Unfortunately, that's not the reality for most of us. You may have time restrictions and financial obligations — you need to pay the bills, after all. If you're still living at home, your parents may be pressuring you. Whatever our circumstances, few of us have all the time in the world to make that job move.

Landing a job *does* require some work on your part, but it's not a complicated process. There are some basic steps you need to follow and some basic tools you need to pull together. Once you begin to piece the puzzle together — figuring out where you are going and laying out a plan of how you are going to get there — suddenly it's not so intimidating. In this book, I answer the question "Where do you start," help you gather your job-hunting tools, and show you how to take those crucial steps toward gainful employment.

Before You Get Going

You are embarking on a journey, and there are numerous ways you can get to your destination. But before you start, you have to make sure you know where you want to go.

Ask yourself these three questions:

✔ What are you good at?

✔ What do you like to do?

✔ What is important to you?

Once you answer these questions, you're well on your way to figuring out where you want to go — and, therefore, what type of job you are looking for. Chapter 2 leads you through a self-assessment questionnaire to help you identify your dream job. By the time you finish, you should know yourself a little better. And that's an important place to begin.

The first question in the list above — "What are you good at?" — refers to both your *transferable* or *soft skills* — you know, those skills you use every day and that you can take to any job, and your *technical skills* — your job-specific skills acquired through training. A good way to identify your skills is to sit down with a friend who's known you for some time and who can be somewhat objective, and review your past work experience, education, and interests. Even if you don't have much work experience, recognize that you *do* have skills that are valuable in the workplace. See Chapter 2 for more on identifying your soft skills. You can check out Chapter 24, too.

Transferable (soft) skill sets

Transferable skills can be divided into four sets:

✔ **Communication skills:** Your ability to express, transmit, and interpret information and ideas in both verbal and written form.

✔ **Interpersonal skills:** Your ability to work with, relate to, and help people on the job, and essentially be part of a team. Interpersonal skills also include listening, counseling, delegating, and motivating skills.

✔ **Management and leadership skills:** Your ability to supervise, direct, and guide people toward completing tasks and fulfilling goals. Other important skills include conflict management, decision-making, change initiation, coaching, and training.

✔ **Organizational and planning skills:** Your ability to manage your time, prioritize your workload, and complete projects on or ahead of schedule. Other organizational and planning skills include problem identification, creativity, analyzing, and evaluation.

You have to be well prepared in order to make the journey toward gainful employment as smooth and, in this case, as short as possible. Good preparation is crucial.

You wouldn't start out on any trip without being well prepared, and the same is true with your job hunt. What kind of tools do you need?

First, map your route. You might know where you are going, but how do you plan to get there, and what vehicle do you plan to use? In Chapter 3, I talk about setting up your own version of Mission Control — your job-hunting headquarters — the space in your home from where you'll conduct your job hunt. You could potentially be spending quite a bit of time there, so you want to make your workspace as pleasant and as functional as possible. It's important that it be inviting and comfortable, too. Turn it into a place you actually *don't mind* spending a lot of time in! This will help keep you motivated throughout your job hunt.

You also need some basic hardware to make your job hunt proceed smoothly. By this, I mean things like a telephone, an answering machine or voice mail, and a computer with Internet access, complete with e-mail. You also need a method to keep yourself organized — a manual or computerized system will do — as long as you actually use it! Chapter 3 gives you some ideas to help you get and stay organized.

Once your Mission Control is set up and you get the necessary equipment, it's time to decide on your route. First, you need to map the different ways of reaching your final destination. There are numerous job-hunting tactics you can use:

✔ **Applying to job ads:** You can find them in newspapers, magazines, or trade journals. Chapter 11 talks in more detail about where to find the jobs. You can also find job ads online by exploring online job banks, Usenet, e-mail lists, association Web sites, and company Web sites.

✔ **Making cold calls:** This is where you actually phone, e-mail, or walk in to a company to ask if they have any job openings. Chapter 11 gives you some ideas on how to make cold calls.

✔ **Networking:** Let's face it, the jobs often go, not to the most qualified person, but to the person who "knows someone." Use and expand your networks to help you with your job hunt. Chapter 14 discusses how to network effectively.

First Leg: Developing Your Résumé and Cover Letter

You know where you are going. You've set up your Mission Control centre (see Chapter 3) and you've mapped out your route. This is good preparation. Now the actual journey begins. Don't forget something vital — your résumé and cover letter. On the first leg of your journey, you create your résumé. Then, when you apply for specific jobs, you write a tailored cover letter to show the recruiter why you're the right guy (or gal) for that position.

The résumé format you use varies depending on your level of experience and education in the field where you're seeking work. Your résumé may be functional, chronological, or a combination of the two styles. I walk you through these options in Chapter 5. In Chapter 6, we get into the nitty-gritty of actually developing your base résumé, highlighting what features you have that will give you a competitive edge over other candidates.

Go through the résumé-development exercise in Chapter 6 until you have a résumé you are happy with. Keep in mind that your résumé is a dynamic document. You will adapt your résumé to each job you apply for — not changing fundamentals such as where you worked, but rather drawing out skills you have that are related to the particular position.

The challenge of a résumé is showing yourself in the best possible light, while not stretching the truth. It's important to know how to handle tricky situations like having had time gaps in your work history or having had many jobs in a short period of time. I discuss this in Chapter 7.

Your job hunt has taken on new dimensions with the increasing use of computers and the Internet. The good news is that it is much easier these days to tailor your résumé to each individual job; the bad news is that it has now become expected that you will do so. Employers expect a personalized cover letter that tells them why you are the person for the job — in other words, what you can do for them that the other candidates cannot. Writing a killer cover letter is covered in Chapter 8, with examples and a template to follow.

Adding the Internet to your job hunt also means you need to have your résumé and cover letter in both paper format and virtual format. I cover cyber-résumés in Chapter 9, and I take you a step further in Chapters 12 and 13, where I give you the skinny on using the Internet effectively in your job hunt, as well as where to look online for jobs (without getting lost).

Sending your résumé to an employer or into cyberspace is not the end of your journey, by any means. You need to follow up to make sure it arrived safely and to make sure that the recruiter knows it arrived safely. Following up is a key tactic that can go a long way toward helping you land a job. Check out Chapter 10 for more information on successful follow up.

Second Leg: Researching Potential Jobs, Employers, Occupations, and Industries

Research is a vital component of your job hunt. You research to find out information that will help you land a job. It is one of the most important, yet often overlooked, parts of a job hunt. You need to research jobs, employers, occupations, and even industries. You use this information to make yourself stand out from the crowd — to show the recruiter that you are both willing and able to go the extra mile. So, the second stage of your journey on the road to that dream position is to do your research.

There are lots of sources you can turn to for information relevant to your job hunt:

- Newspaper articles, online or off-line

- Business or industry-specific magazines, online or off-line

- Public information about a company, such as its annual report, online or off-line, or from your local chamber of commerce

- Online job banks, industry- or location-specific employment-related Web sites

- Your own network of family, friends, and colleagues

- The person recruiting for the position for which you're applying

- People who are currently employed in the field you're interested in

You can research the old-fashioned way, using newspapers, trade journals, company annual reports (see Chapter 11), or do this research virtually, on the Net. Chapter 12 gives you some basics on how to use the Internet for your job hunt, while Chapter 13 tells you where to look. Additional resources are also listed in the *Landing a Job For Canadians For Dummies Directory of Job Resources*. You'll likely combine both forms of research, because, while the Internet puts a lot of information at your fingertips (literally), it's not the *only* source of information.

A great tactic to help you get your foot in the door is to identify the jobs you want to apply for, and then find out who has the power to *actually hire* for that position. Most often, it is not the human resources (HR) person who makes the decision about who to interview or hire. His job is to attract qualified applicants, then create a shortlist from the applications he receives. The real power behind the hiring decision is likely to be in the hands of the department manager.

Many people shy away from networking, which is unfortunate, because a large percentage of jobs are not advertised but are filled by word of mouth. Building and maintaining a network has a broader purpose than just helping you look for a job, but it sure can come in handy when you are job-hunting. Nurture and develop your networks and use them to help you get referrals, find out information, and even land a job. Chapter 14 provides tips on how to network effectively and use your network in your job hunt — both online and off.

The Home Stretch: Interviewing for the Job

The moment you land a job interview, it's like rounding that final turn and heading down the home stretch. You want to make sure you handle this part of the trip with care. Be well prepared so you don't drive off the road and have to start over again. In this book, I try to eliminate your fear of interviews by making you comfortable with different interview styles and helping you prepare for and ace the actual interview.

Interviews can involve several different formats, and the questions you are asked can themselves be phrased in several different ways. You may have a panel interview, a telephone interview, or a series of one-on-one interviews. These days, you could even have a virtual interview! Knowing what to expect in each and how you should react will ensure a more successful interview.

Interviewing techniques is a hot research topic for human resources types these days. The style of questioning you'll face in your interview could be simple and straightforward (bless the interviewer!), or weird and weirder, depending on how much of this newfangled research she's read. Two of these new types of questions you could encounter are *situational* and *behavioural* questions. Sound like a foreign language? Once you read Chapter 15, you'll understand and be prepared for questions that ask you to *Describe a time when . . .* or *What would you do if. . . .*

You need to prepare adequately for the interview (see Chapter 16) and, when the time comes, go in there and give a bang-up performance. Preparing for the interview doesn't mean going through a book of 1,000 interview questions and memorizing answers. It really means knowing *six things* about yourself that the interviewer wants to know too, and will almost certainly ask you about in one way or another. Getting these down pat in your own mind will provide you with the foundation to answer virtually any question thrown at you. Acing the interview (see Chapter 17) means knowing how to conduct yourself in the interview, how to answer difficult questions, and how you can make yourself stand head and shoulders above the other candidates.

If you are lucky enough to receive a job offer, you'll want to check out Chapter 18 for some tips on how to negotiate the sweetest deal for yourself, without alienating your future employer. Having successfully completed the negotiations, congratulations! You have reached the end of your job-hunt journey — but just the beginning of a different kind of journey, in a brand-new position!

So why are there more than 18 chapters in the book? Well, you may decide that you want to explore other employment options, such as starting your own business (see Chapter 21) or working outside Canada (see Chapter 22). I cover non-traditional, off-the-beaten-path ways to land a job in Chapter 20, and just in case, I cover the basics of Canadian employment law in Chapter 19.

That Crazy Little Thing Called Luck

You've done everything you can think of to land a job. You've researched employers, networked, made cold calls, followed up, and customized your résumé and cover letter for every job. You've covered the virtual angle as well as the traditional means of job hunting. What else could you possibly need? Well, don't discount the factor of luck! Luck plays a part in all parts of your job hunt. First of all, if you are really lucky, no one else who was qualified for the job actually saw the job ad. You are lucky when your résumé makes it into the shortlist. Landing an interview is great luck too.

Don't discount luck as a factor in your job hunt, but remember that there are ways to improve your luck *and* your chances of landing the job of your dreams. So read on, and good luck!

Is the grass really greener on the other side?

When you are contemplating a change of occupation or change of job, you first need to take a reality check.

Here are some factors you should consider:

✔ **Changes to your income:** You might be contemplating doing something you really like, but will it pay the bills?

✔ **Cost of upgrading your skills:** Are you prepared to shell out if you need a refresher computer course?

✔ **Employee benefits and time off:** Changing jobs could affect the amount of vacation time, and other benefits, you're entitled to.

✔ **Family:** What is important to your spouse and family? Moving to Timbuktu for a great career opportunity may not be exactly what your family had in mind for a change of pace!

✔ **Lifestyle change:** Is your new job going to fit in with your lifestyle? Be aware of the lifestyle changes that may occur as you change jobs or occupations! (Perhaps you want to change your lifestyle altogether.)

✔ **Relocating:** Do you have to move to a new location? This may be positive or negative, depending on your individual circumstances. Some locations are more desirable to some people than others. (I live in the foothills of the Canadian Rockies, a place many people would love to live — unless you are a city person and prefer urban amenities to the great outdoors!) Be sure of your relocation preferences before you jump at that new position.

Chapter 2

What Kind of Job Do I Want, Anyway?

*T*here are people who appear to be born knowing what they want to be when they grow up. My friend Barb, an accountant, told me, "For some crazy reason, I wanted to be an accountant since I was in Grade 8. I had good marks in math, and handled stress well." Barry, another friend from high school, wanted to be a pilot — a goal that seemed rather far-fetched, since he came from a small town in rural Alberta. But low and behold, at our recent high school reunion, it turned out he is indeed a pilot, flying high. Barb and Barry are the fortunate ones. The vast majority of us, though, aren't lucky in this way. (Heck, I have trouble deciding what to eat for breakfast some mornings, let alone figuring out my next career move!)

In this chapter, I provide a painless (and fun) way to assess three things:

✔ What you are good at

✔ What you are passionate about

✔ What is important to you

Once you gain some self-knowledge, I show you how to transform it into job knowledge, which helps you target industries, occupations, and jobs you might be interested in. Barb and Barry are lucky, yes, but sometimes, slowing down and taking a minute to get to know yourself results in your making better job and career choices. We all deserve a job that reflects who we are, what we care about, and what's important to us — and it's not asking too much to have one that makes you want to jump out of bed eagerly every morning, is it? So read on, and identify that dream job!

Three Big Questions You Need to Answer

Few people take the time to figure out what they want to do when they grow up. That's because it's not an easy thing to do. The tasks can involve talking to people — asking them to be honest with you (which can be scary); ignoring people around you who try to give you all sorts of (possibly unwanted) advice about what you *should* be; assessing your wants, likes, characteristics, and talents; and potentially interviewing people in a given field to see if that is really what you would like to do. This is called an *information interview,* and I discuss it in more detail in Chapter 11. You may also want to get some help from an accredited employment counseling professional (see the sidebar, "When to get professional help").

It doesn't have to be tough, though. All you really have to do is keep three central questions in mind. Once you answer them, you can connect what you learn about yourself to potential jobs:

- **What are you good at?** Choose a job or occupation for which you have a natural affinity — that you are good at. You are likely to not only enjoy it, but to be successful at it, too.

- **What do you like to do?** Choose a job or occupation that you like, and you'll see the same thing happening again: you will probably have a grand time doing the job, and hopefully have a better chance at being successful.

- **What is important to you?** Do you want to work full- or part-time? What are your values? What kind of company do you want to work for? Choose a job that reflects how you want to lead your life, to ensure you will stay happy in your new position.

Are aptitude tests apt?

Be cautious in using employment aptitude tests that offer to match you with the ideal job. You know the kind: these are online or off-line tests that state, "Select the traits on this list that most closely describe you" and voilà, you have a list of jobs perfectly suited to you. These test are limited and often generalized. Most of the time, you won't fit one profile exactly. Also, not all possible occupations could be listed in any given program with enough detail to accurately peg your dream job. Barb, an accountant, reports that her aptitude test told her that she should be a bus driver or funeral director. The results

for Lyn, an economic development officer, were similar: they identified careers that would never be appealing to her, such as sheet metal worker.

However, limitations aside, aptitude tests can identify traits that you may not have considered in your self-evaluation. They may even identify jobs that you didn't think about. Used as part of an overall self-evaluation and with the understanding that it is only one of many tools, an aptitude test could be useful in identifying options you may not have considered.

The job you choose should reflect your own goals and desires. But sometimes, it's easy to get sidetracked and select a job or career path for the wrong reasons.

Here are some of the reasons you might choose one job over another, with an explanation of why these reasons aren't always the best:

- **Future earning potential:** Often jobs are chosen because of the large earning potential. This is a bad reason to choose a job because, even if you do hit the high salary range, if you don't like your job, you won't be happy.

- **Prestige and image:** The prestige of certain occupations can be a drawing card to some job hunters. For example, there is a certain level of prestige attached to being a doctor. However, you may not like the hours and working with people. Don't choose a job just for the prestige unless you really like the work.

- **Passion about the work:** What a great reason to choose a job — if you are passionate about something, you are more likely to enjoy your career. A word of caution, however: Be sure the job pays the bills.

- **Parental/family influence:** I've heard these many times: "My dad is paying for my education" or "Each generation has had at least one doctor in my family." Unless you like what you are being influenced to pursue by your parents or family, first take stock of what you really want to do. Being pressured into taking a job often leads to unhappiness.

- **Few options available — need a job!:** In the middle of an economic downturn (and we have had several of those in the past few decades), it can be tough for new grads and experienced workers alike to find jobs of any sort, let alone their dream jobs. In times such as these, it is often best to bite the bullet, take the position, and then, when times get better, move on. Who knows, you may even find that eventually new doors open up to you and you end up in a job you enjoy, after all. You can always start at a lower-level position that could lead to your dream job, so if you have to take a job, take one in an area where there could be room for advancement.

- **Lots of jobs open in that field:** Many people will go into a field simply because there are lots of jobs open at that point in time. This means they will definitely find a job when they are done their training. Well, I hate to break it to you, but the laws of supply and demand say that eventually when too many people enter the field (supply goes up), there are fewer openings available to newcomers. Throw in the possibility of an economic downturn where experienced workers start to get laid off and you are really out of luck. Choose a job because you really want to do it — not because there is a good chance you'll find a job when you graduate!

- **Opportunity for advancement:** Some people choose a job because of the potential to move ahead in the company and industry. If it is a job you really want, this strategy is fine. But remember: Moving ahead in a job you do not really like is not going to make you any happier.

Don't get stuck in a rut

It is important to be sure you are choosing a job that appeals to you. Don't allow your decision to be coloured by the expectations of others. Choosing a job for the wrong reasons could mean you end up doing something you don't really like or that you miss out on your dream job.

I asked Marty, a lawyer who has been practising law for 27 years, if he always wanted to be a lawyer. He explained that when he was a child, a couple of influential uncles often pointed out to him that he would "make a good lawyer." This could have been influenced by his family's keen interest in politics and the fact that "many of the accomplished (and more admired) politicians of the day were lawyers." Noting that he did not really answer my question, I asked him if he could do it all over again, would he choose law? His answer surprised me. "No, I would like to be a photojournalist." You see, Marty not only likes writing and taking photographs, he has a passion for it — while his passion for the

law has faded. Unfortunately, it took seven years of post-secondary training, one year of articling and tens of thousands of dollars in student loans to reach his goal of becoming a lawyer — not to mention the 27 years he has now spent in the field — an investment in money and time that is not easy to walk away from.

My friend and writing colleague, Tom, actually gave up a stress-filled law career to become a writer — writing self-help legal books and articles for legal trade magazines. He is still using his knowledge gained through years of practice but now is actually doing something he really loves. Marty admires Tom's decision: "Tom's desires are probably shared by many lawyers but few of us have his fortitude to make the break." He then goes on to say, "Then again, this occupational ennui (lawyer-talk for being stuck in a rut!) is probably shared by many in our society."

 If you base your decision on any of these reasons, you will have a tougher time giving honest answers to the three big questions I outlined earlier. They can cloud your judgement. You might convince yourself that you want to be a doctor; that you are good at it, that you like medicine, and that it's important to you. But the real reason behind this choice may be that your dad is a doctor and you don't want to let him down. That's fine, I guess, but you'll end up letting yourself down instead. Always return to the three big questions, answer them honestly, and you won't go wrong. In the next section, I give you 26 other questions that help you clarify your answers to the big three.

26 More Questions Worth Answering

The questions in this section are derived from the three big questions I put to you in the last section: What are you good at? What do you like to do? and What is important to you? The idea is to work your way through these questions in order to clarify or pin down your answers to the big three — which is all you really need to know to choose the right job. There are also some bigger-picture questions to help you tie it all together.

Your answers to these questions will suggest a series of what I call *job requirements,* things *you* need or require out of a job. Your job requirements will suggest a series of potential jobs. For example, one of the questions asks you what type of organization you'd like to work in. You might answer that you'd prefer to work in a small or growing organization — or even for yourself. What job requirements do these answers suggest to you? One might be that you do, in fact, need to work for a small organization. Another one could be that you need to work with a lot of *autonomy* (independence). What potential jobs do these job requirements suggest? Perhaps a job as a consultant, office manager, or public speaker.

When you are filling in your answers, make sure you focus on your *job requirements,* what you need or require out of a job, and not your *job wants,* all those things that would be nice to have (like a six-figure salary) but which aren't necessary or realistic. Adding all those "nice-to-haves" to your list will leave you with a list so long that you'll have to go back and redo the exercise just to narrow down your answers.

Try to answer the questions objectively — don't skew your answers to what you're experiencing in your current job or to a job you are contemplating applying for. For example, if you are contemplating a career as a teacher, you might be tempted to say you like kids. But if you really *prefer* working with adults, then you could direct yourself to adult education. Also remember to leave out your parents' expectations ("You'd really make a great engineer, son!"), your spouse's desires ("I'd really like to live in the mountains — can you apply for a job in forestry instead?"), or society's expectations ("A male nurse! Oh my!").

Not all the questions in this section will apply to everyone, so if you think a particular question doesn't apply to you, skip it. If you run into trouble, ask a close friend or family member to go through the questions with you. You may be surprised at how their perceptions differ from, but complement, your own.

Before you begin answering, take out a blank sheet of paper and draw a grid similar to the one in Table 2-1. Record your answers to the questions in the far left column. Your answers in the far left column will suggest a series of job requirements in the middle column, which will in turn suggest a series of potential jobs in the far right column.

Table 2-1	Your Job Requirements and Potential Jobs	
Answers	*Job Requirements*	*Potential Jobs*
1.		
2.		
3.		
4.		
5.		
6.		
Etc.		

What are you good at?

1. **Pick a couple of things from the list below that you think would make a job worth getting up for every morning.**

   Being creative

   Being entrepreneurial

   Being in charge

   Convincing people

   Doing office work

   Helping people

   Making or fixing something

   Reading

   Speaking to groups

   Supervising people

   Teaching people how to do something

   Working by yourself

   Working with data, numbers, or computer code

   Working with people

   Writing

   Something else?

2. **Do you have specific expertise that you know you want to use in your job?** For example, an MBA or Web site design expertise.

3. **Do you have any soft skills or abilities you know you want to use in your next job?** *Soft skills*, or *transferable skills*, are those that you develop as a result of your life experiences, jobs, classes, projects, parenting, hobbies, sports, and so on. Soft skills fall into four categories:

    Communication skills: Your ability to express, transmit, and interpret information and ideas in both verbal and written form.

    Interpersonal skills: Your ability to work with, relate to, and help people on the job, and essentially be part of a team. Interpersonal skills also include listening, counseling, delegating, and motivating.

    Management and leadership skills: Your ability to supervise, direct, and guide people toward completing tasks and fulfilling goals. Other important skills include conflict management, decision making, change initiation, coaching, and training skill.

    Organizational and planning skills: Your ability to manage your time, prioritize your workload, and complete projects on or ahead of schedule. Other organizational and planning skills include problem identification, creativity, analyzing, and evaluation.

4. **Is there anything that comes easily to you?** Some people find book-keeping easy — others find it easy to write or draw. Learning new computer programs or sewing may be a skill you have that others don't find quite as easy.

What are you passionate about?

5. **If you were to write a book, what would it be about?** Does the topic suggest a potential job for you?

    For example, you might want to write a book about gardening, which could suggest a job or career as a landscaper or landscape architect.

6. **What magazine, newspaper, or online articles are you most likely to read carefully?** Do you see a pattern in your reading habits that points to a job requirement or potential job?

    I find that business- or career-related articles always catch my eye. Some people go straight to the sports section, while others opt for the arts section.

7. **Is there a type of organization you'd love to work for?** For example, a world-class ski resort, a large newspaper, a high-tech company, or a charitable organization.

8. **Have you or someone you love faced adversity?** Is there a job in this area that interests you?

My friend Rolf became a quadriplegic in a car accident at the age of 16. His battle to recover, master life in a wheelchair, put himself through university, become a lawyer, and live independently had a strong impact on his siblings. His sister, Irene, got a job helping place disabled adults with residential attendants to allow them to live more independently. This job turned into a career. She later shifted careers and became a social worker, working with disabled children to help them reach their full potential.

9. **Do you have a cause that excites you or something that makes you angry?** Do you want a job that allows you to take up this cause?

For example, you may be concerned about the orphaned children of parents who have died from AIDS in Africa. This could lead you to a job with UNESCO, working with these children directly.

10. **Is there something on this list that you would love to make a part of your next job?** Remember, choose only the things that you are passionate about.

Accounting/taxes	Criminal justice	Investments
Aerospace	Dance	Labour–employee relations
Animals	Educating/training	
Architecture	Electronic equipment	Landscaping
Artificial intelligence	Energy	Law
Aviation	Environmental issues	Machines
Biotechnology/Genetics	Film	Management
Books, magazines	Fitness	Mass transportation
Cars	Food	Mathematics
Computer hardware	Foreign languages	Medicine
Computer programming	Getting a good deal	Music
Computer software	Healthcare	New technology
Construction	Health planning	Newspapers
Consumer advocacy	Helping people	Outdoor recreation
Cooking	History	Outdoors
Counseling	Human rights	Photography
Creating beauty	Insects	Plants
	International affairs	Politics

Public speaking

Real estate

Relationships

Religion/spirituality

Research

Romance

Science

Selling

Sewing

Sex

Sharing knowledge

Sports

Substance abuse

Telecommunications

Television/radio

Theatre

Travel

Urban/regional planning

Web sites

Writing

Something else (specify):

11. **Is there a certain type of person you definitely want to work with?**

Adults

Adults with disabilities

Alone (don't want to work with people)

Children (specify age group if important to you):

Children with disabilities

Creative people

Enthusiastic people

Entrepreneurs

Happy people

Mentally troubled people

Nerds

Older adults

People of a particular race, gender, or sexual orientation (specify):

People of average intelligence

People of high intelligence

People of low intelligence

People who build or fix things

People with a problem (specify):

Physically sick people

Team players

Teens

Something else (specify):

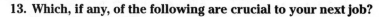

12. Does the idea of being your own boss — self-employment — excite you? If your answer is yes, check out Chapter 21 after you've finished answering these questions.

What is important to you?

13. Which, if any, of the following are crucial to your next job?

Your answers should help you determine some of your job requirements. Remember to focus on what you *need or require* out of your job — not on the "nice-to-haves."

A fast- (or slow-) paced job

A minimum salary of (specify):

A particular location (specify) — such as one of the following: home-based, a specific city, on the coast, in the mountains

A particular work environment (specify) — such as one of the following: at home, in the wilderness, in a luxurious office building, in a big city, in a small town

A prestigious job title

Being self-employed

Culture of the organization (dress, social aspect, open workspace, offices)

Short training time

The opportunity for self-expression/creativity

Working by yourself

Working for a cause (specify):

Working for a certain size organization (small, medium, large) (specify):

Working for a nonprofit organization

Working for the government

Working on a team

Work–life balance (schedule, flexibility)

Something else (specify):

14. In one sentence, describe what you'd most like to accomplish in your work and life. Does this suggest a a job requirement or a potential job? For example, if you'd most like to make a contribution to the welfare of homeless children, this might suggest a job or career as a social worker in the inner city.

Merge your job with your goals and values

If you don't have a job that is compatible with your goals and values, you may end up finding yourself not wanting to get up and go to work in the morning.

A friend of mine in university always wanted to be an architect — he was passionate about creative problem solving and designing almost anything. Once in his mid-thirties, after pursuing his educational goals, he found himself disillusioned as a project manager in a large firm. Far from being happy, he realized he was not designing buildings the way he had envisioned as a young adult. In fact, he did very little design at all, but spent the majority of his time responding to conflicts, hammering out budgets, and trying to squeeze extra time out of already too-tight schedules. All he was doing was managing. He no longer saw himself as leading a creative process or providing value.

He realized that he hadn't achieved his goals, and that, in some cases, he was acting against his core values. He felt that the buildings the firm designed and built were often being done too quickly, influenced by internal fees and budgets, and without adequate concern for their impact on the urban fabric and the environment. He stepped back, reassessed his career, and said goodbye to the corporate world. Now, he takes on smaller projects that are more consistent with his values.

15. **Do you feel you are doing something now that doesn't really fit with your goals and values?** Many people don't act in accord with their own values — in the area of money, work, pleasure, or relationships. If you find this applies to you, write down what it is you are doing that goes *against* your goals.

The bigger picture

16. **What do you consider to be your major accomplishments? What do others consider to be your major accomplishments?** What have you done that has given you a strong sense of achievement — something that required plenty of drive to complete? For example, perhaps you organized a major event or you completed a difficult research project.

    If you can't think of anything from recent adulthood, go back to your younger days or ask family, friends, and co-workers to help.

17. **Describe your dream workday, from the moment you get up until the moment you go to sleep.** Does this suggest a potential job?

18. **What job or career do your parents, partner, or close friends think you should pursue?** If you think it is reasonable and it appeals to you, add it to the Potential Jobs column.

If you don't know what your family and friends think you would be good at, you always have the option of asking them. Remember, you are not looking for them to direct your choice but just to tell you their thoughts. You can (and should) still leave your options open.

19. **If you didn't care what your family and friends thought, what job would you pursue?** Add your answer to the Potential Jobs column.

20. **If you had a twin, what would they tell you to do?** Of course, you have to assume you have a twin that knows you very well and tells you exactly what he or she thinks! This is often not what your parents would suggest, or even what you yourself would think of. If you come up with anything here, add it to the Potential Jobs column.

21. **Do you know anyone high up in a company or well-respected in your community who you could ask for help in finding a job? If yes, what kind of work would you do for that person?** If it appeals to you, add it the Potential Jobs column.

The adage rings true: Sometimes it's not what you know, but *who* you know. What I'm asking you to think about is, of course, networking. If you're uncomfortable about networking — if you can't ever see yourself kissing up to someone for a job — well, you've got networking all wrong. I set the record straight about networking in Chapter 14, where I let you in on why, in today's super-competitive job market, you can't afford *not* to network.

22. **What would you like your life to look like 10 years from now?** Are there any implications that would affect your job choice?

23. **Imagine that years from now, an article announcing your retirement appeared in the newspaper. What would you want it to say about your career?**

24. **Sometimes what you need more than anything else is a change. What job appeals to you that would represent a dramatic change from what you're currently doing?** Add to this to the Potential Jobs column.

25. **If you're contemplating a career change, why do you think it's better to go this route instead of seeking a promotion in your current job or trying to make more of it?** For example, seeking out new assignments or a new boss.

26. **Perhaps you know, deep down, what you'd really like to do. Ask yourself, "What job would I love to do more than any other job in the world?"**

When to get professional help

If you are stuck without any hot ideas, think about seeking the help of an employment counselor or a career coach. *Employment counselors* usually hold a degree in counseling and the level of service they offer depends on the setting and client needs. Employment counselors will help you clarify your job and life goals; administer tests that will assess your aptitudes and skills and identify job options; assist you in developing résumés and teach you job-search strategies. There may or may not be a fee for the services of an employment counselor. All high schools, most colleges, and Human Resources Development Canada (HRDC) offices offer free employment counseling.

Career coaches, on the other hand, charge a fee for their services — anywhere from $150 to $1000 per month depending on the level of service. A career coach takes a different approach from that of an employment counselor. The *synergy* (coach-talk for how well you connect!) between the coach and the client is vital to the success of the relationship. While a counselor may only see you one or two times, you actually develop a longer term relationship with a coach. You have regular sessions and go through the entire self-assessment process in great detail. The coach then continues to work with you as you implement a job-search plan, including developing strategies to overcome or circumvent any obstacles that arise. According to career coach Martin Sawdon, of Coaching Works (www.coachingworks.ca), "The coach's role is to question, challenge, empathize, support, perhaps even provoke, but always with the one intent of supporting the client in reaching the goals which are fully congruent with their values and aspirations."

Choose a career coach wisely — make sure you get along with your coach and feel comfortable. Remember that a career coach won't give you all the answers or find you a job, but instead guides you along the road to self-discovery and to being hired. You will still do the work, but under the direction of your coach.

Making the Connection: From Self-knowledge to Job Knowledge

I have just taken you on a journey of self-discovery, and you should know more about yourself than you did before. You should be somewhat closer to identifying a job you might like to do. Self-knowledge is the first step toward what I call job knowledge. In this section, I will help you take that knowledge and use it to pinpoint the job of your dreams.

Let's walk through what you have already done and pull it together.

1. What are your most significant job requirements?

Go back through your answers to the questions in the previous section and review the most significant job requirements you came up with. For example, perhaps your priority is to make $50,000 a year and have flexible hours. Prioritize your job requirements — this way you can make sure you meet the most important ones.

2. **How many of the potential jobs you identified satisfy your most significant job requirements?**

   Refer to the list of potential jobs that you compiled. Can you eliminate any of those potential jobs? For example, you might not be able to return to school for additional training at this point in your life, so you could cross off jobs that require more education or training.

3. **Do your most significant job requirements suggest other potential jobs to you?**

   Go over your job requirements again. Maybe something will jump out and grab you — or, at least, suggest a job you haven't identified yet. For example, if three of your most significant job requirements include working with children, making a difference in the world, and travelling, you might want to consider a job with a humanitarian organization that provides services for children in Third World countries.

4. **Pick, from your list of potential jobs, one or more jobs that might actually work for you — which feel like they could be a possible fit with your most significant job requirements.**

   These potential jobs now become your *prospective jobs* — jobs you will research and perhaps apply for.

5. **Learn more about your prospective job.**

   One of the biggest mistakes people make is not investigating a job or career thoroughly. Before you take any more steps toward applying for a given job, do yourself a favour and learn more about it. Part III fills you in on researching jobs both online and off-line, going for an information interview, and networking — all great ways to learn more about a prospective job.

Still Not There? A Few More Tips . . .

Are you unable to turn your list of job requirements into potential jobs? If you are having trouble making the connection between self-knowledge and job knowledge, here are a few more tips to help you out.

Here's what you can do if you're having trouble coming up with potential jobs that satisfy your job requirements:

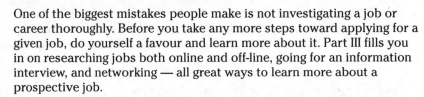

✔ **Investigate the industry.** This tactic works well if you're having trouble transforming your job requirements into potential jobs. If being able to build things is one of your requirements, why not find out more about the construction industry or the aerospace industry in general?

Finding what's out there

An important but difficult part of job-hunting is finding out what different jobs are available — there are many occupations out there that you don't even know exist. There are thousands of different jobs in hundreds of occupations and dozens of different fields, and most of us are only aware of a small number.

To find out what jobs are available, start by looking at a list of available occupations and jotting down any that you find exciting or interesting. Where do you find this information? There are a number of Web sites that list Canadian occupations and a brief description of each.

✔ **Human Resources Development Canada (HRDC)** (www.hrdc.gc.ca/common/home.shtml): For a comprehensive list including descriptions of Canadian occupations, this site is one you must visit. That's not all there is here either: HRDC is a virtual treasure chest of information, including, but not limited to, résumé writing, career development and assessment, job and industry profiles, and even job listings.

✔ **HRDC Occupational Profiles site** (http://jobfutures.ca/jobfutures/alphabetical_index): This site includes over 25,000 occupations and is

broken down into categories and subcategories so it is reasonably easy to navigate. I suggest you go through the alphabetical listing and see if any occupation catches your attention. Then read the description and, if it sounds interesting, jot it down. Make a list of these occupations or, better yet, print them out!

✔ **National Occupation Classification system** (http://cnp2001noc.worklogic.com): This popular site has a comprehensive up-to-date overview of occupations. The classification recently was updated from the 1992 version to reflect current conditions in the Canadian workplace.

✔ **College Grad** (www.collegegrad.com/careers): This is an American site but it has lots of valuable information on different types of jobs.

Another valuable resource is *The Cool Careers Yellow Pages* found in *Cool Careers For Dummies,* by Marty Nemko and Paul and Sarah Edwards, published by John Wiley & Sons, Ltd. The careers listed are U.S.-based, as are the Web sites. However, it provides a good starting point and thorough job descriptions. The authors also give good reasons for why they think the careers on the list are "cool."

Human Resources Development Canada (HRDC) has a great Web site (www.hrdc-drhc.gc.ca/sector/english/industryprofiles), with information on virtually every industry in Canada. Another great resource is the Occupational Outlook Handbook (www.bls.gov.oco).

✔ **Think about the types of people you want to work with.** You can pin down potential jobs by deciding which type of people you want to work with and seeing if it suggests anything to you. You may want to work with young children. Depending on what kind of children you want to work with (disabled children, gifted children, underprivileged children), potential jobs may reveal themselves.

✔ **Explore a not-so-popular industry.** If your job requirements are really generic, and you're not so concerned about which industry you work in or with whom, think about entering a not-so-popular industry. There is generally less competition for jobs and more opportunity for advancement. For example, if you want to be a human resources manager, think about looking for a job in a lesser-known industry, like solid waste management. They still need human resources managers, don't they?

✔ **Ask your family and friends to brainstorm with you.** Show them your list of job requirements and see if they can add to your list of potential jobs.

Chapter 3

Getting Set to Pound the Pavement

*T*ime and again, qualified applicants are frustrated because they don't get that job they had their hearts on — the one they knew they were qualified, if not overqualified, for. Unfortunately, the reality is that the best jobs don't necessarily go to the most qualified applicants, but to the most organized ones. Don't get mad if you don't get the job, get organized! This chapter helps you put together your job-hunting headquarters — the place from which you'll conduct your job hunt — and gives you some ideas (and opinions!) on which job-hunting tools you need to assemble there (and which ones you can do without).

Set Up Your Mission Control Centre

Mission Control will be your centre of operations — a place where you strategize, make contacts, and prepare your job-search tools. It can be as fancy as a well-lit home office or as basic as your dining room table — just make sure it is a comfortable place to work. If you have an office in a dark room in your cold subterranean basement, with a desk and chair and a single light bulb, it is unlikely you will even want to venture down there to work on your job hunt, let alone maintain a positive attitude once you are there! In this section, I tell you about some things you should consider when setting up your job-hunting Mission Control centre.

Keep interruptions to a minimum

Your Mission Control centre should be a place where you can go without fear of interruptions (it's embarrassing when you have to tell your kids to be quiet when you're talking to a prospective employer on the phone). However, sometimes you have to balance what you want with what you've got. For example, if you have toddlers at home, there are very few places you can go to get away from them (not to mention the safety aspect of leaving them alone for even a minute!). You are better off waiting until they are napping or engrossed in their favourite TV show to make that phone call.

Here are a few places you don't want to set up your Mission Control:

- **Your back patio:** While this seems like a great idea on a nice summer day, you won't think so when your papers get scattered by the wind.

- **Your garage:** Far too cold and dirty!

- **Your kitchen:** Your family will just expect you to cook for them instead of working on your own stuff! You will also have to pack up your stuff several times per day (making it much less convenient to get back at it).

- **Your unfinished basement:** Concrete floors, cobwebs, and light bulbs on pull-strings. Yuk!

- **Your walk-in closet:** Some people will go to any extreme to get a little privacy. But in return, you get bad lighting and potentially claustrophobia! I don't have to mention the spare bathroom, do I?

You may already have a home office or space with a computer and desk. If you don't, take a look at this list and see if any of the room "conversions" I suggest will work in your home:

- **Set up your spare bedroom as an office:** Try to make it as inviting and well lit as possible. If you have to keep the bed in the room, make sure you have enough space to be comfortable — and don't succumb to the temptation to take a nap during the day!

- **Take over your dining room table:** If you are like many people and you don't use the dining room, this could be a great place for you to set up headquarters. This is an ideal central location if you have kids and need to keep an eye on them.

- **Transform your loft or den:** A rarely used space like a loft or den would be an ideal place to set up your Mission Control. These rooms are often well lit and cozy.

If you don't have any spare or unused rooms in your home, you can even set up your Mission Control in any room that has extra space. Just place your desk and computer in part of a larger room. You may find, however, that this option sacrifices some of your privacy and peace and quiet.

Let there be light

Remember what I said about the single light bulb in the dark basement office —
I wasn't kidding. You'd be surprised at the number of people who try to be
productive in that kind of environment. Make sure your headquarters has lots
of light (preferably natural lighting). If you don't have access to natural light,
try one of these options:

- **Hang a few mirrors on your walls:** Mirrors make a room look both
  bigger and brighter.

- **Install a fluorescent light in your ceiling:** This is an inexpensive way to
  improve the lighting in your office.

- **Make the most of your lamps:** Buy a good desk lamp and place a few area
  lamps around the room.

- **Paint your walls white:** This will make the room brighter. Dark walls
  make a room look and feel smaller, no matter how much light — natural
  or artificial — you may have.

- **Use a higher watt light bulb:** And make it a 100-watter, not a mere
  40-watter. I know this seems obvious, but you might be surprised when
  you look at what kind of light bulb you are using. And use one that's clear,
  not frosted.

Make sure you can be productive

Your workspace needs to be a place where you can actually be productive.
Have all your job-hunting tools within easy reach. That includes your computer,
phone, fax machine, and any other equipment or tools you will use. I tell you
about these later in this chapter.

You should also attempt to set up your work area in a space in your house
that isn't too high-traffic — you know, kids tromping in from the park, dog
padding in from a walk. A large, flat work surface on which to spread your
papers is a necessity, but, if at all possible, you don't want to have to clear off
your work surface every time you fold up your job-hunting efforts for the day.
Find a place where you can spread out — where nobody will spill coffee on a
copy of your résumé, if you just happen to leave it out. This is why I strongly
discourage you from setting up in the kitchen. However, this could be an
ideal use for that dining room table that never gets used!

If there is no unused space in your house, invest in a large plastic tote into
which you can pack up your papers each day. This helps keep piles to a
minimum, your papers safe from spills, and, best of all, you always know where
your stuff is.

Make the space inviting

Set up your headquarters in an inviting space — a place where you like to spend time. If you don't like your workspace, you will probably find yourself making up excuses not to get down to the task — simply because it is not a pleasant place to be.

Try out some of these ideas to make your workspace more inviting:

- **Add a plant or two:** Plants always make a space more appealing. You can add a silk plant for that basement office, where natural light may be limited.

- **Get a heat source:** For any space, really, but especially if you have a basement office, a space heater is a must. It's hard to work on a computer if your fingers are stiff and cold.

- **Hang some photos or artwork:** You can put up photos of your partner, your kids, or fun times with friends. Kids' artwork always looks good on your walls, too.

- **Play some music:** Whether it be a radio or a CD player, music breaks the monotony and can put you in the right frame of mind.

- **Set up a relaxation corner:** Put a soft, oversize chair in a corner with a lamp beside it for a break from sitting at your desk.

Pay attention to ergonomics

When I talk about *ergonomics*, I am referring to the way the space and furniture of your office work together and how they affect you physically. For example, a chair that is too low can cause problems in your shoulders when you work on a computer for an extended amount of time.

Other than taking frequent coffee breaks to give your body a break, which would, unfortunately cut into your productivity, here are some ideas to make your workspace as ergonomically correct as possible:

- **Get rid of the glare on your computer screen:** While natural lighting is great for your attitude, it can cause glare on your computer screen. Have no fear, however; you can just get a glare screen to cut back on the sunlight reflecting into your eyes. Or the cheaper alternative is to move the computer to a place where there is no glare.

- **Look after your neck and shoulders when you talk on the phone:** Consider investing in a headset for your phone. Trying to write and talk on the phone at the same time can be a pain in the neck — literally!

✔ **Make sure you have an adjustable, comfortable desk chair:** Your chair needs to have good back support and also be adjustable to allow you to work at the proper position in front of your computer. If you are still using the wooden chair from the kitchen, consider buying yourself a new office chair — your back (and your butt) will thank you. Make sure your chair directly faces your desk and computer screen.

✔ **Position your computer screen at the right angle:** Your computer screen should be at a height where you can look straight at it without looking up or down, with the keyboard directly in front. This will help reduce neck strain.

✔ **Take care of your arms and wrists while you type:** Make sure your arms and wrists don't become fatigued from the position they are in when you use your computer. If you are experiencing wrist and arm pain, there are braces you can buy to help you avoid developing carpal tunnel syndrome.

Basic Tools for Your Job Hunt

Now that you know what kind of space you require for your headquarters, it's time to get down to the nitty-gritty and decide which electronic and computer-oriented tools you need. In this section, I give you some options that won't break you financially.

Computers, the Internet, and e-mail

I suppose you could say that it was easier, in some ways, to find out about and apply for a job before we had computers. Back in the dim dark ages (pre-1990), you combed through the classified section in your local newspaper, heard about job openings through word of mouth, even screwed up your courage to make a few *cold calls* here and there (where you call an employer out of the blue to ask about a job). When it came time to apply, you mailed, faxed, or dropped off your résumé in person. Computers definitely have their challenges. (You spilled tea in your keyboard *again?* Your Internet service provider just went down in flames and you can't browse the Web or check your e-mail for a few days? Believe me, you have my sincerest sympathies.) But I think these challenges are far outweighed by the new opportunities. In the case of you, the job hunter, computers, the Internet, and e-mail give you an infinite number of ways to crank up your job hunt — and get results.

You need to go online
I'm about to give you a bunch of good reasons to use a computer and the Internet in your job hunt:

✔ **You can create and store different versions of your résumé and cover letter.** The beauty of a word processing program, like Microsoft Word or WordPerfect, is that you can make changes with little more than a few keystrokes, then save the updated versions to your hard drive, or, if the computer isn't yours, to a floppy disk. Today, employers *expect* you to tailor your résumé (see Chapters 6 and 7) and cover letter (see Chapter 8) to each position you apply for — immediately bringing their attention to the skills you have that are applicable to the job. To do this, you *need* the word processing and storage capabilities of a computer.

✔ **You can organize your job hunt using *online* or *off-line databases.*** Many online job banks, like HotJobs.ca (`www.hotjobs.ca`), Monster.ca (`www.monster.ca`), or Workopolis (`www.workopolis.com`) provide free online database tools that, again, let you store multiple versions of your résumé and cover letter and keep track of the jobs you have applied for through that site. (See Chapters 12 and 13.) Off-line databases, like Microsoft Access, let you set up a file system to keep track of what jobs you applied for, when you need to follow up, whom you contacted — basically all aspects of your job hunt.

✔ **You can apply for jobs electronically.** Do this by submitting your résumé and cover letter to an employer by e-mail. Many online job banks also let you post your résumé online for prospective employers to see. (See Chapter 13.)

✔ **You can find *more* jobs in the first place.** With so many job hunters surfing the Web and applying for positions electronically, many companies now post jobs online, often before they use more traditional advertising methods, such as print newspapers. Not using the Internet in your job hunt will limit the number and variety of jobs you learn about.

✔ **You can learn more about a company you're interested in, and use additional resources to help you with your job hunt.** Check out company Web sites (see Chapter 13) and take advantage of e-mail to network with other industry contacts, prospective employers, and fellow job hunters (see Chapter 14).

So, we've established that you need to use a computer and the Internet during your job hunt, but do you need to drop what you're doing, jump in the car, and head to a computer store to buy one — right now? Frankly, no, as long as you have regular access to one. Most public libraries provide free Internet access to the public, as do many government offices, such as Human Resources Development Canada, and community, career, or business development centres. If there's a university or community college near you, the institutions will probably let you use their computers for a small fee or even free of charge. Hey, you can even hit up your friends and family. They know it's for a good cause.

If you live in a larger urban centre, stop by an *Internet café,* a place that houses a number of computers with Internet access, where you can surf and slurp to your heart's content. Well, that's not quite true. They do charge you and there is a time limit. But you can always buy more time when you get your second cup of joe. Many Internet cafés have other equipment, like scanners and fax machines, and some of them even have trained staff to help you out of a cyber-bind. This is an inexpensive way to access the Internet, work on a computer, and get some technical help to boot! Consider whether you would rather spend $6 per hour drinking coffee in an Internet café or $1,000 to have access to a computer in your own home — especially if you are thinking about purchasing that computer only to help you with your job hunt. Depending on your financial situation, your money may be better spent elsewhere.

You have to weigh the cost of the computer and the amount of time that you'll use it with the convenience of having your own system at home. Can you afford the $1,000+ for a new computer — or even the several hundred for a used one — and then add the cost of Internet access? If you're currently unemployed, this might cause you undue hardship. If you don't have a use for a computer now, will you have a use for it after you find a job? You probably don't want to spend $1,000 on a computer just to help you land a job, and then not use it again. On the other hand, computer skills are a prerequisite for most jobs today, so adding a computer to your set of job-hunting tools and becoming proficient in its use will probably benefit you in the long run.

One other option is to lease or borrow a computer. However, leasing ends up being more expensive in the long run.

A few words about e-mail

E-mail is a great tool for certain tasks:

- Applying for jobs, by submitting your résumé and cover letter electronically
- Following up on your applications
- Making "electronic" cold calls to employers (instead of using the phone)
- Networking

The introduction of e-mail has made it much easier for recruiters to contact potential employees, as well, either to obtain more information or to set up an interview.

Most job hunters list a Web-based e-mail address on their résumés. A *Web-based e-mail address* stores your messages on the Web site with which you register, not on your own computer. And because it's Web-based, you can check your e-mail from any computer, anywhere. A Web-based address is private and convenient. Popular Web-based e-mail providers are canada.com (www.canada.com), shown in Figure 3-1, Yahoo! Canada (www.yahoo.ca), and Hotmail (www.hotmail.com). A bonus: setting up an e-mail account is free, and so is accessing it. I have more to say about applying for jobs online in Chapter 13.

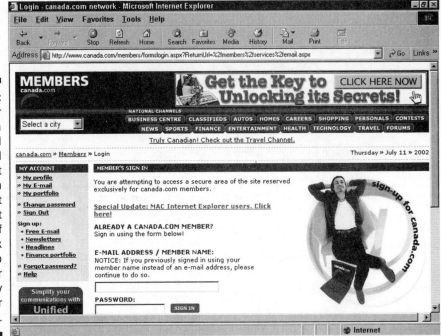

Figure 3-1:
Register
for a
Web-based
e-mail
account at
canada.com
and use that
account
instead of
your work
account to
protect your
privacy
during your
job hunt.

If you use a Web-based e-mail account to apply for jobs, remember to check your account regularly (as in every day, not every week). Nothing is more frustrating for a recruiter, like me, than trying to contact someone I really want to interview, only to be met with no response. So make a note to check your account frequently. Otherwise, you could turn off a potentially interested employer.

When you register for your Web-based e-mail account, be careful when you pick your *user name,* the part of an e-mail address that comes before the "@" symbol. I once saw someone applying for jobs online using hotstud@… as a user name. Who could take someone like that seriously? Try to use your own name in your e-mail address. Recruiters are also more likely to remember you, when you send a follow-up e-mail or call them. The more they see your name, the more likely it is that your name will stick in their minds.

If, when registering for your account, you find that you apparently have an evil twin somewhere in the world that's already got an account on the system with your name, try adding an underscore or some numbers to personalize it. For example, Brenn_anybody66@canada.com.

Telephone choices

Even though e-mail is a well-established form of communication for most of us, when it comes to contacting potential employees most recruiters still use that time-honoured tool, the telephone, because — assuming the candidate's there at the other end of the line — it's a sure-fire way to speak to them, while e-mail often takes longer.

But what if you're not there? What if, like pretty much everyone these days, you lead a busy and productive life outside of the fact that you're also looking for a job?

You have a couple of choices in the never-ending quest to make yourself more accessible to employers:

✔ Get a cellphone.

✔ Rely on an answering machine, voice mail, or an electronic answering service, such as that offered by Bell Canada or Telus.

If you have a telephone-based Internet connection that ties up your line, you may also need to consider either a second line (I know, more money!), changing to a new Internet system, or subscribing to a system where your phone takes messages while you are online. Your phone company can provide you with information on your options.

Should I get a cellphone?

If you have an answering machine or an answer service at home, and you respond to these messages regularly, there is no need for you to make the investment in a cellphone for the sole purpose of your job hunt.

Cellphones (and cordless phones, for that matter) don't always have the best reception — you know, you cut in, you cut out, it's sometimes difficult for the person on the other end to hear what you're saying. It can be kind of tough to put your best foot forward. If you're driving, it's worse: your attempts to impress the recruiter will be accompanied by a symphony of horns, engine sounds, and human voices. Don't even think about speaking to a prospective employer if you've got your kids in the car.

If you already own a cellphone, and use it regularly, great. However, only list your cell number on your résumé if you either have it on regularly, or if you have voice mail on it that you check regularly.

Answering machines and answer services: Keep it clean

Most of us either own an answering machine or subscribe to an electronic voice mail answering service as part of our phone package. As long as you check your messages regularly (daily), this is an effective way for a recruiter to get in touch with you.

But keep your outgoing message clean and professional, guys. A real-life example of an answering machine greeting: "Hi, this machine is attached to a cute little kitty. If you don't leave a message, you will fry the kitty — you decide!" Use a generic, professional greeting, at least until you find the job you want.

Fax machines

If you have a computer and you are able to submit your résumés by e-mail, a fax machine may not be a necessary purchase. On the other hand, if you are asked to submit copies of your school transcripts, degrees, or diplomas, faxing is a good way to get these to a prospective employer quickly. A fax machine also has the capability to make quick-and-dirty copies of documents — which beats having to rush out to the convenience store. Having access to a fax machine allows you to respond quickly to job ads, if the employer doesn't list an e-mail address, and send out additional information, such as copies of your transcripts — thus enhancing your professional image.

While a fax machine may come in handy (once in a while), I don't believe it's a vital piece of equipment for an effective job hunt. Most employers who don't accept e-mail attachments don't assume you have a fax machine, and will make allowances for the time it takes you to find a fax service or mail your résumé and cover letter.

If you own a computer, it may have a built-in fax modem. This allows you to send documents directly from your computer to a fax machine. The downside is that your computer needs to be on in order to receive faxes, and the documents usually have to originate on your computer, or be scanned in. You can always have your subsidiary documents scanned by a friend and saved to disk, then send these off as requested from your computer fax. This would apply to transcripts, diplomas, and other appendices you would normally attach to your résumé.

Hand-held computer organizers

You can spend hundreds of dollars on a hand-held computer, like a Palm Pilot, which allows you to plan your schedule and store tonnes of information, like phone and fax numbers and e-mail addresses. Some of the more expensive models have a *downlink* that allows you to copy the information to your personal computer. You can also pay a lot less for a more compact unit, with less memory but similar features. These are handy little gadgets — I tend to use mine (the cheaper unit) on a daily basis — but, if money is tight, you really can do the same thing with a good old-fashioned notebook or daytimer.

A few more items you need

Okay, it may seem obvious, but, as the Boy Scouts say, "Be Prepared!" Here are a few more tools that will come in useful for your job hunt:

- Calendar
- Highlighters (to highlight those keywords in job ads)
- Hole punch
- Notepad
- Paper clips
- Paper for printer
- Pens (that work!)
- Stapler
- Tape and glue (to paste job ads into pages)
- Telephone book

TIP

Keep a journal

Keep a journal of your job hunt — perhaps a large binder so you can organize it alphabetically, with the job ads that you respond to, a record of your correspondence (including a copy of the résumé you send), any research you do, and notes regarding follow-up). Much of this information can also be kept electronically, but it's important to be able to access it double-quick if a recruiter phones you, either to ask for more information or to set up an inter-view. Talk about being on the spot! You will also be adapting your résumé to each job you apply for (see Chapters 6 and 7), so it's really important to know which version you sent! If you learn anything about the companies themselves, have a contact name, or even get a business card, add these to your binder. Record whether you have received any follow-up from the company, and if not, the date you will follow up with them.

Chapter 4

Landing a Job (Without Losing Your Mind)

In This Chapter
▶ Sticking to your schedule
▶ Adopting the right mindset
▶ Staying sane along the way

Many job hunters are so enthused about looking for a new job that they just plunge right in without a plan or direction. That's kind of like getting into a car without knowing your route. Sooner or later, you're likely to get lost, run out of gas, or wonder why you're driving in circles! When you begin your job hunt, knowing where you are going and how you are going to get there helps keep you on track and increases your chances of being hired.

But don't get me wrong! Enthusiasm is great — in fact, it's an absolute necessity if you want to get an edge over other job hunters. The right mindset shifts your job hunt into high gear and helps you achieve your goals faster and with a great deal less stress than if you have a negative, self-defeating attitude. In this chapter, I show you how you can acquire the right mindset, or attitude, to help you land the job of your dreams. I also give you some tips to help you stay sane and reduce the stress of looking for a job, including prioritizing your time, taking breaks, and rewarding yourself.

First, a Schedule

Looking for a job can seem daunting at first, but if you tackle it one step at a time and set up a schedule for yourself, you'll find that it's actually not that tough. Check out Ian Richard's job-hunting schedule in this section. Ian is a recent engineering grad with several co-op work terms under his belt. He just finished a summer position and is now looking for a full-time job. Ian is approaching his job hunt as if it's a job in itself, so he's scheduling his day around job-hunting tasks. He has set up his Mission Control centre, and he has a computer with Internet access (see Chapter 3). Ian is ready to start pounding the pavement — virtually and otherwise.

If you work full-time, the schedule I outline below might not work for you. Try dividing up the tasks and doing something each evening. You'll need to find some time during the day to phone prospective employers, but most of the work can be done on evenings and weekends. Make sure to take some time for yourself, though!

Day 1: Monday

In the morning, Ian researches 10 "choice" employers. He lists 10 employers he really wants to work for, then tries to dig up everything he can about them. They may or may not have any job vacancies posted but, hey, many job openings are never advertised, so it's worth a shot! He uses his networks, his past work experiences, the Internet, the phone book, and goes to the library to research trade magazines and newspapers.

Ian's list includes the following information about his top 10 employers:

- ✔ Contact information
- ✔ Names of the recruiter, supervisor, and manager
- ✔ What the company does
- ✔ The company's Web site address
- ✔ Anything interesting about the company

He files this information in his organizer, be it in a file on his computer or on sheets of paper in a binder, for future follow-up.

At lunchtime, he goes to work out at the gym.

In the afternoon, he makes a list of his networking contacts. Chapter 14 discusses using and enhancing your networks in your job hunt. Ian has kept in contact with his co-op employers, fellow students, professors, and other acquaintances on a fairly regular basis. These names form the beginning of a networking list. He's collected their phone numbers and e-mail addresses and put them in his handy-dandy organizer, as well. Ian will add to this list as he makes more contacts.

Following up with a contact, his civil engineering professor, he makes a lunch date for Tuesday.

He reviews the Careers section from the Saturday edition of his local newspaper. Ian keeps a copy of Saturday's careers section, as that's the day most jobs are advertised, and puts it aside until he has a chance to look at it. He clips interesting ads and pastes them into the Job Ads section of his organizer for follow-up later in the week.

Day 2: Tuesday

Day 1 was pretty well a research kind of day, but Ian is chomping at the bit to actually get down and apply for some jobs. Whoa, there! As I discuss in Chapter 11, you may only have one shot at a job, so you need to make sure you do it right the first time. A little research and time spent laying the foundation can really help you in your quest for employment.

In the morning, Ian gets busy on the phone. He contacts five employers from the "choice" employers list he made yesterday. During the telephone conversation, he tells them that he's looking for a position and lets them know what he finds interesting about the company. He asks if they have any vacancies, or if they anticipate anything coming open in the near future. He tries to talk to the supervisor or manager of the department he's interested in, rather than the human resources department. He asks if it's okay to forward a résumé, and determines whether it can be e-mailed and whether it has to be scannable (see Chapter 9). He double-checks whom he should send it to and verifies this person's mailing address and e-mail address. When he ends the call, he makes a note to send out his *application package* (his résumé and cover letter) the next day.

Once he's completed those five phone calls, he e-mails a thank-you note to each employer he spoke with. In the brief note, he thanks them for taking the time to talk to him and tells them that he appreciates being considered for any openings the company might have in the future. He doesn't attach his résumé and cover letter to the thank-you notes. He sends it the next day, instead, once he's had a chance to customize it for each company. See Chapters 6 and 7 for more on customizing your application package and other ways to make yourself stand out.

Ian meets his civil engineering professor for lunch. He brings along copies of his résumé.

Having been busy on the phone in the morning, Ian turns to his e-mail account in the afternoon. He sends an e-mail to everyone in his network, letting them know what he's been up to of late, and what he's accomplished — that he's completed several work terms and has now graduated from university. He lets them know that he's in the job market, specifies the type of job he's looking for, and asks for any referrals to companies that might be hiring. For those colleagues in his network who do not have e-mail access (yes, there are still people who don't use the Internet!), and also for more promising contacts, Ian makes telephone calls to connect on a more personal level. Chapter 14 has great tips for how to make networking contacts via telephone or e-mail.

Ian retrieves the job ads he clipped yesterday from Saturday's paper, and researches the companies. Before he blindly shoots off copies of his résumé, he knows that he needs to get a better sense of what the companies are all about, so he can tailor his application package accordingly. He goes online and visits their company Web sites, recording the contact information and something he finds interesting about each company. He'll use this to customize his résumé and cover letter.

He also sets up a lunch date for Thursday, with a supervisor from his last co-op job.

Day 3: Wednesday

Today's the day. Ian actually applies for jobs. However, he can't stop doing what he's been doing on Monday and Tuesday:

- ✔ Researching
- ✔ Generating leads
- ✔ Networking

In the morning, Ian customizes his résumé and cover letters to send to the "choice" employers he spoke with on Tuesday. He knows that the chances of getting a job are directly related to the amount of effort he puts into it. So he takes the time to personalize *each* cover letter and résumé based on his research from Monday and the added information and insight he acquired on Tuesday while talking to the employers. Each cover letter (Chapter 8) mentions the phone conversation, mentions what he finds interesting about the employer, and describes what he can bring to the company. The résumé is customized to each company depending on what they said they might need in the future. Then he puts the applications in the mail. See Chapters 6 and 7 for more on customizing your résumé, and Chapter 8 for tailoring your cover letter.

For résumés he e-mails as attachments, he types a quick accompanying e-mail cover note. Check out Chapter 9 for information on electronic résumés and e-cover notes.

For lunch today, Ian heads back to the gym, and this time works out with a friend from university — a good networking opportunity.

That afternoon, Ian contacts employers from selected job ads he clipped from Saturday's paper for additional information. Ian's initial contact with these employers, who are actively recruiting, is a quick phone call to find out whom he should be talking to and to get a little more information about the position. If he can't talk to them directly, he leaves a voice mail message asking for a return phone call. In the message he leaves, he tells them what interested him about the company and asks how they prefer to receive applications (via post or e-mail) and in what format (formatted, scannable, or plain text). (By asking a question like this, Ian increases his chances of receiving a call back.) Also, while he's trying to make sure he sends his résumé the right way and in the right format, he's also attempting to lodge his name and voice in the recruiter's memory. This increases the chances that the recruiter will flag his résumé rather than overlook it.

He rules out any employers whom he does not feel will fit with his objectives.

Ian then customizes his résumé and cover letters for those selected job ad vacancies. He takes the time to revise his Objective, beef up the Skills and Accomplishments section, and tailor his cover letter to show the recruiter what he can do for the company. In his cover letters, he thanks the recruiter for taking the time to talk to him, in the hopes that they'll remember the conversation. He keeps a copy of all the ads he's responded to and the corresponding cover letters and résumés he has sent. He identifies dates for following up on these applications and notes them in his organizer.

For those jobs to which he's applying electronically, Ian includes a shorter e-cover note and attaches the longer cover letter and résumé in a single file.

Day 4: Thursday

At this point, Ian has some application packages in the pipeline and has put out some feelers in his network. He will continue to research his choice employers, apply to job ads, and follow up with his network to keep generating new leads. But now it's time to follow up on the application packages he has already sent.

In the morning, Ian sends hard copies of résumés and cover letters to the employers to whom he sent electronic versions on Wednesday. He uses good quality paper and double-checks his formatting, spelling, and grammar.

Start planning your career before you finish university or college

In high school:

✔ **Work part-time.** Baby-sitting, delivering newspapers, and mowing neighbours' lawns shows you are willing to work, and these can lead to a better paying part-time position.

✔ **Get involved in extracurricular activities and clubs.** You will acquire transferable skills like a strong work ethic, a positive attitude, and the ability to work in a team environment.

✔ **Volunteer for school, church, or community organizations.** Helping with Sunday School at church is a fulfilling way to acquire some planning and teaching skills and the ability to work with young children.

✔ **Consider participating in programs that expose you to different occupations.** Some examples are job shadowing, career fairs, work experience classes, take your kid to work days, and junior achievement programs.

✔ **Get out there and see the world.** Don't underestimate the value of travel as an educational tool and one that helps you acquire a multitude of skills. Student exchanges and programs such as Katimavik (www.katimavik.com) are worth exploring. In Katimavik, sponsored by the government of Canada, you participate in community life in three provinces, where you acquire a variety of useful experiences working as a volunteer on local projects.

In university or college:

✔ **Get the best grades you can.** While some students consider the final result (a diploma or degree) most important, if you are concerned with getting the best job possible, good grades are one way of standing out.

✔ **Ask your professors to recommend related associations or networking groups you** can join as a student member. Many of these associations and groups offer special activities where students can learn and mingle directly with professionals in your chosen field. Membership has its benefits! You can then have access to their job bank for a reduced price (student memberships are much cheaper than professional memberships).

✔ **Pay a visit to the campus job placement office.** Get to know the staff, or offer to volunteer in the office — you may be first in line to hear about a new job!

✔ **Join clubs and campus volunteer organizations.** These look great on your résumé and show that you are willing to work and are able to work in team environments.

✔ **Find a part-time or volunteer job in your occupation of interest during the school year or full-time during summer break.** Even if you have the opportunity to take a higher paying job outside your field, consider that even one summer of experience in your chosen field will give you the competitive advantage over another graduate with no experience.

✔ **Join the student association for your faculty or department.** Network with professors and department heads in your area of specialization. Also, network with recent graduates to find out what professors and classes they found most beneficial.

✔ **Don't wait until the last semester of your final year to start looking for a job.** Throughout your last year, and earlier, start using the network of professors and students you've established. Ask for job leads and advice on landing a job in your chosen field, finalize your résumé, and start searching.

Time to follow up with some of the networking leads. Ian takes the rest of the morning to make networking phone calls and write e-mails to help him generate new leads. He records all leads in his organizer, along with referral information so he can follow up later. He e-mails thank-you notes to those contacts who give him a hand.

Then he makes tracks for his lunch meeting with his former co-op supervisor, armed, as always, with extra copies of his résumé.

That afternoon, Ian jumps back online. He registers with a couple of popular online job banks, like HotJobs.ca (www.hotjobs.ca), Workopolis (www.workopolis.com), and Monster.ca (www.monster.ca). He can do several job-related tasks at these sites, all without leaving his chair. After selecting his privacy settings, he posts his basic résumé and cover letter online. He does some initial category research to identify more jobs that interest him. He follows company links to learn more about the organizations. He records all this information in his organizer. If he chooses, he can also save links and jobs he applies for in a personal online account. On HotJobs.ca, this feature is called MyHotJobs. See Chapter 9 for more about protecting your privacy online.

Day 5: Friday

This is the last workday of the week and the last chance before the weekend to contact anyone in person. So Ian decides to focus for the morning on follow-up phone calls, initial telephone contacts, and cold calls. He spends the afternoon tying up loose ends from his job-hunting activities during the week so he can relax on Saturday and Sunday.

On Friday morning, Ian telephones 10 employers he found while online yesterday. He makes initial contact and finds out more information about the job. He then makes follow-up calls to the employers to whom he sent application packages earlier in the week, to confirm that they received his material and determine whether they need any more information from him.

When the clock strikes noon, our tireless job hunter heads once more to the gym for an invigorating (and de-stressing) workout. He deserves it, don't you think?

In the afternoon, he customizes his electronic résumé and e-cover note to apply to online jobs directly. In each cover note, Ian makes sure to mention that he has reviewed the company's Web site and to point out something that interests him about each job. He makes a note in his organizer to follow up next week and see if his application was received.

Days 6 and 7: Saturday and Sunday

While he plans to have weekends off, Ian does take some time to review the Careers section of the local newspaper and to check out the new jobs on Career Click (www.careerclick.com), the online version of newspaper career ads across Canada. He clips or prints any of interest and files them in his organizer for follow-up on Monday.

That Winning Attitude

Having the right mindset is very important when embarking on your job hunt. The attributes and mindset that make you a good employee — dedicated, hardworking, industrious, and positive — will also make your job hunt a success. Treat your job hunt as a job in itself and you'll be well on your way.

You have to be prepared to work at finding a job. Some people find a job immediately — for one reason or another. Perhaps they are well known in their field or community, or perhaps they're just lucky. In any case, this is rarely the way things happen when you are looking for a job. You need to have staying power — the ability to stay focused.

Job hunters need to have a strong sense of what they want to do and how they are going to go about getting it. You need to know your end goal — keep your mind on the finish line! On top of that, you need to have a positive attitude. This comes through in every part of your job hunt — from the way you write your cover letters to how you follow up after a cold call. You need to stay positive, focused, and not take rejection or lack of acknowledgement personally.

Your success depends on the way you look at things — just as it does with every experience in life. You can either see the glass as half empty, or as half full. Each task in a job hunt can either drain your energy or enhance it — depending on your attitude. Some experiences, I grant you, such as a killer rejection (you know, the "Are you kidding, what makes you think I'd hire you?" kind) are a real drain, but you can and should rise above these.

Another reason to keep an upbeat attitude is that you avoid one of the worst traps a job hunter can fall into — desperation. Recruiters are interested in the person with self-confidence and a positive outlook — not the applicant who conveys that "I need a job so bad, I don't know what I will do if you don't give me one" or "If you don't hire me, I will lose my house!"

Staying positive is something you have to work at! In this section, I outline some suggestions to help you find a balance and keep an optimistic attitude.

Be yourself

This may seem obvious, but you might be tempted to pretend you are something you are not in order to land that job — thinking you can always correct the "misrepresentation" later, right? Not! First, your actions are dishonest, and second, when you try to be someone or something you are not, you will always be nervous and second-guess yourself. If, however, you convey your real self, you will be more relaxed, less on guard, and more likely to land a job. If you get the job, you will be more likely to succeed. So it really pays to be yourself. Show recruiters the real you.

Having said that, and remembering to show the real you, there's nothing wrong with showing the *best* of you! Think of an hour in your recent past when you were most confident, most together, and, throughout your job hunt, project that version of yourself.

Celebrate small successes

If you get a call from a recruiter asking for more information, that's great. At least your résumé got noticed! A call for an interview is an incredible achievement — especially considering the large number of applications generally received by a recruiter for a given job. You are at the head of the pack! You may not have clinched the job just yet, but you're well on your way. Take pride in these accomplishments and your attitude will stay healthy.

Cultivate a sense of exploration and fun

Think of your job hunt as a mission — exploring new frontiers. You don't know what's out there, who the employers of choice are, and perhaps don't even know exactly what you want. (Check out the self-assessment exercises in Chapter 2 to help steer yourself in the right direction.)

Try to learn from and take pleasure in the job hunt itself. It helps to think of your job hunt as a game — sometimes you will advance a few squares and sometimes you won't. Consider leads that go somewhere as advancing in the game and try to capitalize on what you learn from each advancement. Think of your job search as a Snakes and Ladders game — a rejection is a snake and a success is a ladder. You may go back a few steps but it doesn't take long to get ahead again. While luck is a factor, the more you play the job search game, the more skilled you become and the more you increase your odds of coming in first. Keep a playful demeanour throughout your job hunt. It will help you maintain a positive frame of mind.

You can do fun things to help you deal with rejection. I had one client who set up a dartboard and made targets for each rejection or "no response" she received. She even assigned points to each and had a great time playing with the darts to see who she could hit! It really improved her dart game, too! Another client fed her rejection letters to the noisy dog next door. (I kind of like that idea!)

Set goals that you can achieve

Make sure the goals you set for yourself on a daily basis are achievable. When you draw up your weekly schedule, the way Ian did earlier in this chapter (see the section "First, a Schedule"), don't overestimate what you can do in that time. Pat yourself on the back when you cross items off your list.

Stay focused on your goal

Remember that finding and landing a job takes time. While you need to work continuously toward your goal, you also need to be patient. Keep plugging away, move ahead with the process, follow the advice in this book, and eventually, success will be yours. It's a bit like that children's story of *The Little Engine That Could.* The little engine had the mindset "I think I can . . . I think I can. . . ." Try to internalize this kind of positive reinforcement throughout your job hunt to stay focused and avoid becoming discouraged. And no, you don't have to quote *The Little Engine That Could* — at least not out loud.

Take some time for yourself

Job hunting is a lot of work, and, like any job, you need to take some time away from it (all work and no play is not good for your attitude, and besides, it makes you dull, too, right?). Finding a job is a job in itself. You can't do it constantly without taking breaks and making some time for yourself — just as you would if you had a full-time position.

Walk the talk

Make sure that your positive attitude and enthusiasm come through in all parts of your job hunt: in your preliminary phone conversations with recruiters, in your cover letters, during your interviews, and even when you're negotiating a job offer. Enthusiasm is catching. If you're consistently upbeat during your job hunt, you'll infect all the right people.

Watch your stress level

Get some exercise. Spend some quality time with your family. Keep a balance in your life and don't become obsessed with your job hunt.

Part II
The Right Stuff: Résumés and Cover Letters

The 5th Wave   By Rich Tennant

"ACCORDING TO THIS RESUME YOU'VE DONE A LOT OF JOB-HOPPING."

In this part . . .

You arm yourself with the tools to put together an outstanding application package. After deciding which résumé format is best for you, you need to get down to brass tacks and write that résumé. Don't forget about tailoring it for each job you apply to, either. Once you're pleased with your résumé, you need to turn your attention to its able-bodied counterpart: your cover letter. Think of Batman and Robin, or Superman and Lois Lane. But your cover letter is much more than trusty sidekick to your résumé — these tools go hand in hand to form your application package, and you do need to put in some time crafting your cover letter, too. This part also shows you how to adapt your résumé and cover letter for a journey through cyberspace.

And you're not done once you mail, fax, or e-mail that application package. You need to gently nudge the recruiter closer to offering you an interview through persuasive — but not pushy — follow-up techniques.

Chapter 5

Résumé Formats: Finding Your Match

*Y*our résumé is an important job-hunting tool, helping you get your foot in the proverbial door and keep it there (without losing your toes), eventually landing a job. A well-organized résumé, with relevant information tailored to the company and job you are applying for, goes a lot further than a glossy sales presentation–style résumé (that often requires professional assistance to prepare and is difficult to adapt to different jobs).

You need to pick the résumé format that best suits you and the position you are applying for, and ensure that the information the employer seeks is easy to find. In this chapter, I take you on a tour of three common *résumé formats,* or *styles*. These are simply ways of organizing the information in your résumé so that you present yourself in a way that shows you in the best light, given your employment goals and history. I also give you the skinny on each format, because one may be terrific for someone with one type of employment background looking for a certain kind of job, but spell disaster for somebody else with a different job market history heading in a different direction. It's all about fit, and when it comes to résumés, one size definitely does not fit all. Once you choose the résumé format that suits you best, the next step is to fill in the details (see Chapters 6 and 7).

What's in a Résumé?

Your résumé is an introduction to you. Note my use of the word "introduction" in that last sentence. Your résumé is not your life story — but a snapshot of who you are. It should be a general overview of you, professionally speaking, giving the person who reads it a quick idea of what makes you tick and what you can do. Focus on what's important and leave out the extra detail. You can fill that in when you place your follow-up call (see Chapter 10), or during the interview itself (see Chapter 17).

Regardless of the résumé format you choose, there are certain pieces of information you need to include. Here are the typical components of a résumé, though the order in which they occur differs depending on the style you're using and the requirements of the job:

✔ Personal Information

✔ Objective

✔ Summary of Qualifications

✔ Skills and Accomplishments (used in some formats, not others)

✔ Employment History (also used in some formats, not others)

✔ Education

✔ Other Information

It's important to make sure your résumé is well written, well organized, and has no spelling or grammatical errors. This sounds like a given, I know. But you'd be surprised at the number of résumés that cross my desk riddled with typos. Unless there is a truly exceptional mitigating circumstance (for example, if the candidate has recently orbited Mars), I don't give these résumés a second glance.

Three Dependable Résumé Formats

While there are some variations, there are three commonly used résumé formats:

✔ **Chronological:** The chronological résumé places emphasis on your employment history. Each entry in that section includes your job title, the name of the organization for which you worked, and your dates of employment there, from most to least recent position. It includes your job duties and accomplishments, described in a fair bit of detail. You also list your education and other necessary components, but it's the history of you and the working world that takes centre stage. This résumé style is sometimes called *reverse chronological,* because the most recent information appears first.

✔ **Functional:** The functional résumé focuses on your skills, abilities, and accomplishments, rather than on your employment history or education. This format also allows you to highlight your transferable, or soft, skills, not necessarily related to any one job. Actual jobs, employers, and dates of employment get second billing and may not be listed at all.

✔ **Combination:** The combination résumé combines the best of the chronological and functional formats — on the assumption that an employer wants to know where you acquired the skills you claim to have, as well as what those skills are. While the layout varies, this format usually begins with a functional section that highlights your skills and accomplishments, followed by a chronological listing of your employment history and education. The Employment History section includes a brief overview of your duties and accomplishments in each position.

By the way, if you're doing an online version of your résumé, any of these three résumé formats are acceptable, with some technical adjustments to help it glide through cyberspace without a glitch. Chapter 9 discusses how to make your résumé Web-friendly.

What's the difference between a curriculum vitae and a résumé?

A *curriculum vitae* — also known as a *CV* or *Vita* — is a detailed, structured, and lengthy listing of your education, publications, projects, awards, and work experience. It can be as long as 20 pages! It works best for job hunters with extensive academic and professional credentials who are applying for positions in education or research. As a recruiter, I cringe when I receive a CV from someone who's applying for a regular job. Far from impressing me, it befuddles me — and heads straight for the paper shredder. Unless you are a rocket scientist or an academic looking for work in your field, steer clear of a CV. Don't call your résumé a CV thinking to impress a recruiter — it won't work!

The Chronological Résumé

The chronological résumé, shown in Figure 5-1, is by far the most common format in use today, and the one with which employers are most familiar. It lists your education and employment history first, beginning with your most recent and working backward. Employers are comfortable with this résumé style because they perceive it to be fact-based, as well as easy to read and understand.

Pros

A chronological résumé gives an employer a reasonably detailed overview of your work experience. It emphasizes the job you are doing currently, because that's what you list first, but he can easily scan down to get an idea of your previous positions.

A chronological résumé works best in these situations:

✔ If you have solid experience in the field in which you are applying

✔ If you meet the educational requirements of the job in question

✔ If your employment history follows a logical chronological path showing growth and development

✔ If the strongest aspect of your work experience as it relates to this position is your most recent job

✔ If the name of a previous employer could carry some weight in the decision-making process. Perhaps they are a competitor, supplier, or a prestigious employer in your field.

Cons

The chronological format makes it difficult to draw attention to any job other than the one you held most recently. But what if the job you want to highlight was one you held many years ago? The rigid structure of the chronological résumé dictates that you list it somewhere in the midst of your other jobs — or perhaps even near the end. Conversely, if your most recent job is the one you'd rather an employer not focus on, having it sitting there, front and centre, can be just as bad.

A chronological résumé may not be what you need in these situations:

✔ If you have changed jobs frequently

✔ If you are changing your career goals or focus

Mitchell Graeme
116 Boulton Avenue
Edmonton, Alberta T6E 1JO
(780) 498-1100
mitchell_graeme@shaw.ca

OBJECTIVE
To apply extensive skills in forestry and environmental planning to a senior position in the environmental consulting sector. My positive attitude and strong work ethic combined with research, public liaison, and project management skills would make a positive, immediate, and effective contribution to your team.

SUMMARY OF QUALIFICATIONS
- Registered Professional Forester with 10 years of experience in the forest industry
- 12 years' experience in environmental planning in the resource sector
- Coordinated resources to meet provincial regulations including environmental impact assessments, mine licences, forestry and environmental approvals
- Extensive experience in project management, working with regulatory bodies, and coordinating public involvement.

EDUCATION
1981 **Bachelor of Science in Forestry** University of Alberta Edmonton, Alberta

EMPLOYMENT HISTORY

1989 to Present
Senior Environmental Planner, Burns Lake Mine, Eldersly, Alberta
Oversee environmental and reclamation programs for surface coal mine operation. Ensure appropriate permits and licences to operate mine are obtained in a timely manner. Maintain compliance with operating approvals and appropriate legislation. Accomplishments include:
- Acting as the internal project manager to develop the EIA for a major mine expansion. The project came in on time and well under budget and met all regulatory requirements on the first submission.
- Member of the provincial Coal Task Force responsible for the development of guidelines and codes of practice with involvement from government and stakeholders (Water Quality Standards Committee, Lake Development Guidelines, Selenium Committee, Coal Exploration Code of Practice)
- Through development of a public involvement and government liaison program, improved relations between the company and the local community.

1981 to 1989
Forest Officer II Alberta Forest Service, Fort McMurray, Alberta and Edson, Alberta
Timber harvesting, planning, supervision, and inspection, land use activities including oil sands exploration and conventional oil and gas development, forest fire suppression, recreation, public awareness programs. Accomplishments include:
- Participated in the development of the Northeast Region Geophysical Guidelines

OTHER INFORMATION
Member of the Canadian Land Reclamation Association
Industry advisor to Lakeland College Land Reclamation Program
Alberta and Saskatchewan Environmental and Reclamation Committee (ASERC), Coal Association

Figure 5-1:
Your employment history takes centre stage in a chronological résumé.

- ✔ If you are trying to land your first job
- ✔ If you were fired from your last job
- ✔ If you want to emphasize areas of your work experience other than your most recent job
- ✔ If you want to change industries, but your experience to date isn't in the industry you're trying to transfer into
- ✔ If you have large time gaps in your résumé, and it's not clear whether you've been on an extended vacation, on a training stint, or unemployed
- ✔ If you are an older job hunter with a number of jobs dating back many years and you do not want to emphasize your age

What to include in your chronological résumé

Here's what you should include in your chronological résumé:

1. **Personal Information:** Include your name, address, phone number, fax number (if applicable), and e-mail address. Be sure prospective employers can reach you at the address, and particularly at the phone number, you provide.

2. **Objective:** Tailor it to the job you are applying for. (See Chapter 6 for more details on how to write this.)

3. **Summary of Qualifications:** This is like an executive summary of your life as it applies to the job. It is what you have done that qualifies you for this position. This section should be brief and to the point — specifically highlighting your most important qualifications for the job in question.

4. **Education:** List your education in reverse chronological order (most recent first), complete with details on what you majored in, plus degrees, diplomas, and certificates you earned.

5. **Employment History:** List your work experience by job title, starting with your current or most recent job. Give the dates for each job (months and/or years are fine). List the name and location (address and province) of the organization for which you worked. Briefly describe your main duties in each job.

Your Employment History section can actually come before your Education section on your chronological résumé — there are no hard-and-fast rules about this. It depends on which aspect you want to emphasize — whichever you think will carry more weight with the employer. My advice: Put your education first if the job description requires a specific degree or accreditation. Only do this, of course, if you *have* that degree or accreditation! Otherwise, tuck it in after Employment History.

What not to put in your résumé

- **Birthdate:** You don't have to give an employer any information about your age.

- **Citizenship:** If you are legally entitled to work in Canada, you don't need to give any more information.

- **Marital or family status:** Whether you are married or not, or have a family or not, isn't relevant to whether you are qualified for a given job.

- **Social Insurance Number (SIN):** Some people still put this on their résumé. In fact, you don't have to give this until you are actually employed.

- **Weight and height:** This isn't relevant to your qualifications (unless there is a specific physical requirement, but that can be determined at a pre-employment medical).

6. **Other Information:** Personal information such as languages and interests are the last section in this résumé. Here is where you list relevant personal information about yourself. It is your chance to show there is more to you than just work — that you are a well-rounded individual.

The Functional Résumé

A functional résumé highlights your skills, experiences, and accomplishments, rather than your education and employment history. The skills and experience you list is general — not tied to a particular academic course you've taken or job you've held. The orientation of a functional format is what you can do for the employer, rather than your employment history. This is based on the belief that those things you have accomplished generally and the skills you have acquired are more important than what you've done or haven't done in any particular job. See Figure 5-2 for a sample functional résumé.

A *true* functional résumé omits the section on work experience altogether. In practice, though, most job hunters who use the functional style do address their work experience to some degree.

Pros

A functional résumé is useful when you lack recent work experience that's directly related to the position for which you're applying. Because it's less structured than the chronological style, you can direct the reader's eye toward

Marissa Matthew
11939–45 Ave. SE
Toronto, Ontario S1T 1X6
(406) 434-3333
matthewm@hotmail.com

OBJECTIVE
An executive assistant role in the public service that requires strong organizational, administrative, and people skills and where there is an opportunity to make a positive contribution to the department.

SUMMARY OF QUALIFICATIONS
Over 12 years of progressively more responsible work experience in a growth-oriented, fast-moving, demanding industry. Well-developed communication, organizational, and customer service skills. The ability and desire to proactively understand and meet the needs of all clients.

SKILLS AND ACCOMPLISHMENTS

Administrative:
15 years of experience in administration of a large corporate office. Possess excellent organizational skills. Have a proven ability to prioritize and meet business deadlines in a fast-paced, demanding environment. Strong computer skills and an ability to learn new programs quickly. General office administration skills: maintaining files, scheduling meetings and conferences, receptionist duties, faxing, photocopying, correspondence, ordering office supplies, preparing and distributing mail. All work done with accuracy and attention to detail. Self-motivated with the ability to work with minimal supervision. Accounting, budget preparation and administration, bookkeeping skills. Strategic planning, policy analysis, and marketing skills.

Communication:
Possess clear and concise writing skills. Exceptional research skills. Possess good communication, interpersonal, and problem-solving skills. Have well-developed word processing skills and have worked extensively with Windows, the Internet, and e-mail. I am able to learn new computer skills quickly. Able to communicate in a professional and courteous manner with clients and co-workers in face-to-face, written, and telephone environments.

Customer Service:
Possess the ability to successfully adapt to changing business and client needs and I am able to see these changes through to a successful completion for both my clients and employer. Have a proven ability to work well with clients and co-workers in both one-on-one and team situations. Have demonstrated an ability to anticipate and address client needs and individual requirements. Public relations skills, event planning, fund raising for volunteer organizations.

EDUCATION
1988–1989 **Travel and Tourism Honours Diploma,** Career College, Edmonton, AB

OTHER INFORMATION
Current member of the executive committee, Evergreen Toastmasters Club
Planning committee member, Women's Conference
Interests include gardening, camping, travel

Figure 5-2:
You highlight general skills, experiences, and accomplishments in a functional résumé that aren't tied to a specific job.

what you want noticed. The functional format lets you use unpaid and non-work experience to your best advantage. It also allows you to either eliminate or downplay unrelated work experience that does not support your current objective.

A functional résumé works best if the following hold true:

- You are an entry-level job hunter and have minimal work-related experience.
- You are a new graduate.
- You are a seasoned pro with a great deal of experience in your field. In your case, listing all your previous jobs would be redundant.
- You are applying for a job in a field in which you have no experience.
- You have special issues or circumstances that you do not wish to draw attention to prior to an interview. These could include a disability, an involuntary termination, an illness resulting in an absence from work, or taking time off to raise a family.
- You are re-entering the workforce after a lengthy absence with little experience directly related to the job for which you are applying.
- You want to emphasize skills that you have but have not used in any of your previous jobs.
- You have had several jobs, but no increase in responsibility or growth.
- You are applying for a job where your qualifications, if presented in chronological form, would not portray you as a strong candidate. This might happen if any of the following apply:

  - You have had a number of jobs and not stayed at any for an appreciable length of time. In a chronological format, your job-hopping tendency would be all too apparent to the employer, since you have to detail your dates of employment.

  - Your most recent work experience doesn't support your objective. A chronological résumé might highlight weak and unrelated experience. Say, for example, that you worked as a social worker for 20 years, and then ran your own bed-and-breakfast for 10 years. Let's also say that you're trying to get back into social work. In a chronological style, your 10-year fling with the B&B shows up first, drawing attention to the fact that you haven't actually worked in the field of social work for a long time. In a functional résumé, you list your skills and accomplishments related to social work first, as these are the most applicable to your objective.

  - You have had a variety of jobs that aren't related to each other and that don't match your current objective. In a chronological format, you list all your jobs. If you have held a variety of unrelated jobs, this suggests that you don't really know what you want to be when you grow up. In a functional résumé, you can pull out the skills you acquired in these unrelated jobs and present them in a more cohesive way.

- You have worked for a number of different companies, but always in the same position. If you apply for a different position, the chronological format would actually be redundant, because it shows the same position and duties for all the jobs you list. You could highlight different skills in a functional résumé.

The primary benefit of a functional résumé is that you can accentuate those skills and accomplishments that your *target employer* (an employer you have researched and targeted as the company you want to work for) is likely to find most interesting. Part III delves into researching jobs.

Cons

You've heard the expression "That's only one side of the story." Well, that sort of describes the relationship between the functional and the chronological résumé formats. Your skills and accomplishments, as highlighted in the functional résumé, commendable as they may be, do not tell the whole story about you. Your employment history (from the chronological résumé) tells something, too. My recruiter colleagues say that when they receive a functional résumé, their immediate reaction is often suspicion — that the applicant has something to hide. The less information you offer about your previous jobs and the dates you were employed in those jobs, the more raised eyebrows you invite.

Employers want to see some sort of continuity in your work experience. They want to be able to link the skills you claim to have to the jobs you have held. The more recent these jobs are, the better — but this isn't obvious on a purely functional résumé.

Stay away from a functional résumé if the following apply

- You want to emphasize a pattern of growth or increased responsibility in your work history.

- Your past or most recent work experience is strongly related to your job objective.

- Your most recent employer is highly regarded in the field, and you expect this to improve your chance of getting in the door.

What to include in your functional résumé

Here's what you should include in your functional résumé:

1. **Personal Information:** Include your name, address, phone number, fax number (if applicable), and e-mail address. Be sure prospective employers can reach you at the address, and particularly at the phone number, you provide.

2. **Objective:** Tailor it to the job you are applying for. (See Chapter 6.)

3. **Summary of Qualifications:** This is like an executive summary of your life as it applies to the job. It is what you have done that qualifies you for this position. This section should be brief and to the point — specifically highlighting your qualifications for this job.

4. **Skills and Accomplishments:** This is the meat in a functional résumé. It is where you list your skills (usually transferable, or soft, skills) and competencies that relate to your objective. In Chapter 6, I tell you how you can identify your skills and how to write these down so they sound impressive. You should first list those skills that relate most closely to the job you're applying for, or are the most impressive. If you are applying for a job as a controller, you will probably put budget and cash-flow management skills first. Give details such as the amount of the budget you managed, and the number of employees in the company. Include any related professional accomplishments in this area, too.

5. **Employment History:** Surprised to see this here? In a true functional résumé, you eliminate this section altogether and focus on the transferable skills you've acquired through your work experience, usually folding it into the Skills and Accomplishments section. So, you do end up discussing your work experience a bit, but without listing specific positions.

6. **Education:** List your education and professional training. This section might be brief, as you will probably include the skills acquired as part of your education in your Skills and Accomplishments section.

7. **Other Information:** Employers like to hire well-rounded people. Carefully selected personal information, such as whether you speak a second language, or any special interests you have, make up the last section in this résumé. It's your chance to show the employer that there is more to you than just work — you like to play, too! Chapter 6 gives you more ideas on how to write this section.

Don't confuse accomplishments with responsibilities

A common error that people make on their résumés is confusing their responsibilities, or duties, in a particular job with their accomplishments in that job. A *responsibility* is a task you perform as part of your daily job requirements — it's expected of you to earn your paycheque. An *accomplishment,* on the other hand, is something you achieve that is beyond the scope of your job duties — something you'll likely get a healthy pat on the back for from your boss. A prospective employer is naturally interested in the responsibilities you had in your previous jobs, but it is your accomplishments that catch their eye. Your accomplishments are what make you exceptional — what make you stand out from the crowd of other applicants.

A lot of job hunters mistakenly list only their responsibilities on their résumés. To help you identify your accomplishments in a given job, use the three-step PAR Formula (Problem, Action, Results). Think of a problem you had to solve. Then, describe the action you took to solve it. Finally, define the positive result of your action. I've applied the formula here to a situation Cassandra faced as a human resources coordinator. Her job responsibilities included maintenance and organization of employee personnel records:

1. **Problem:** Employee records were being mis-filed and were therefore not easily accessible or usable.

2. **Action:** She researched databases, did a cost-benefit analysis, presented a proposal to management, and received approval to implement a new computer-based human resources information system. She then purchased the database software, adapted it to the company's needs, and ensured that all employee records were entered into the system.

3. **Results:** The new system became an integral part of the overall site information system and made it easy to retrieve human resources–related data. Managers and supervisors had access to the records they needed to manage employees on a timely basis.

Try to write out several accomplishments for each job position using the PAR formula, then summarize these into one- or two-sentence statements to put in your résumé. In the above example, I would summarize the accomplishment in this way: "Researched, adapted, and implemented a human resources information system that led to an increase in efficiency of information management and retrieval."

The Combination Résumé (The Best of Both Worlds)

This is the résumé that delivers both sides of your story. The combination résumé is a mix of the chronological and functional formats. It's attractive to a lot of job hunters because it allows you to showcase your most marketable skills *and* provide an overview of your work experience that ties in with those skills. What could be better? The section that highlights skills and accomplishments related to your target job is backed up by a relatively detailed chronological listing of your employment history and education. Employers like it too because it shows what you can do but then backs this up by showing where you acquired (and honed) these skills. See Figure 5-3.

Pros

A combination résumé is most effective when you want to emphasize both your skills and work experience.

Because you include an overview of your work experience in a combination résumé, any nagging suspicions on the part of the employer, which could crop up when information is omitted, hopefully won't (I knew you were the honest type all along). This format can also be easily revised when you apply to different positions.

A combination résumé works best in the following situations:

- You want to highlight skills and accomplishments specific to your target job and show where you acquired them — be it through another job or in an educational program.
- You have had no luck getting past the initial screening process with a chronological résumé.
- Your work experience taken on its own does not form an obvious link to your target job.
- Your education is an important part of your overall skills presentation.
- You have three or more years' experience in a similar position and want to emphasize specific skills and accomplishments you have acquired.

Cons

Unfortunately, the combination résumé can become lengthier than the chronological or functional résumé, and this turns off some employers. Other than this, I think a combination résumé should be your résumé of choice, as it is fast becoming an accepted and often preferred résumé format among employers. Nonetheless, it's not for everyone.

A combination résumé might not be best for you if the following apply

- You have a clear trajectory in your employment history that shows you are suitable for the job. In this case, a chronological résumé would be fine.
- You are a new graduate and have no work experience. You will want to list your skills and accomplishments from your courses at university and from earlier life experiences. A functional résumé is your best bet.

Erika Sky
George Johnson Boulevard
Vancouver, BC VOE AS0
(250) 514-1100
esky@telus.net

OBJECTIVE
Primary objective is to work as a team leader for a non-profit global organization in a position which involves travel and temporary relocation around the world. To apply communication and technical skills, professional experience, and language abilities in a leadership role on special projects.

SUMMARY OF QUALIFICATIONS
- Environmental scientist with extensive experience in public relations.
- Speak and write English, French, and Spanish fluently.
- Research and writing skills well developed.
- Supervised project teams in field setting.
- Public participation and government liaison skills well honed.

SKILLS AND ACCOMPLISHMENTS

Communications:
Planning, coordination, and organizational skills. Design and set-up of program displays. Copy-writing of brochures, posters, banners, annual reports, application forms. Research, develop, write, create props, deliver, and promote an assortment of interpretive programs. Technical research and report writing. Compose regulatory applications and correspondence. Research, write, and edit feature articles for newsletters and magazines.

Technical:
Assessed disturbances and land use on private and public lands. Worked with and gathered data from the Guatemala Audubon Society, the Ministry of Natural Resources, and the United Nations Development Program. Planned and coordinated logistics for focus groups and environmental awareness workshops. Provided regional environmental operations support. Organized, designed, and presented environmental education workshops for local communities.

Administration and Leadership:
Developed relationships with governing bodies. Good project facilitation, planning, and coordination skills. Organized, designed, and presented environmental education workshops for local communities. Coordinated focus groups in Mayan, Spanish, and English languages. Supervised six project interns. Developed strategic plans for multiple programs.

EMPLOYMENT HISTORY

Communications Coordinator, Interpreter **Brook Research Station,** Vancouver May 2000 to present
Research, plan, coordinate, and organize conferences, workshops, interpretive programs, and tours. Planned, researched, wrote, and edited feature promotional articles. Responsible for liaison between the public, the government, and the Research Station.

(continued)

Figure 5-3:
A combination résumé allows you to highlight your best qualities.

Special Supplement Coordinator   **Globalworks,** Prince George, BC   **Volunteer**
April 1999 to April 2000
Planned, researched, wrote, and edited feature promotional articles. Negotiated with publisher for supplement details and pricing.

Environmental Assistant   **BioAnalytic Labs,** Fort McMurray, Alberta   October 1998 to January 1999

Assisted in data collection and analysis of oil sands projects.

Research Assistant   **Earth Angels/Penn State University,** Guatemala, Central America
February 1998 to May 1998

Worked with local residents to ensure their interests were considered and represented in industrial and environmental projects.

EDUCATION
2001 **Public Relations Diploma Program**   Grant MacEwan Community College, Edmonton, Alberta
1997 **B.Sc. Environmental and Conservation Science**   University of Alberta, Edmonton, Alberta

OTHER INFORMATION
Interests   Volunteer work, mountain biking, cross-country skiing, reading.

Languages   Fluent in English, French, and Spanish.

What to include in your combination résumé

Here's what you should include in your combination résumé:

1. **Personal Information:** Include your name, address, phone number, fax number (if applicable), and e-mail address. Be sure prospective employers can reach you at the address, and particularly at the phone number, you provide.

2. **Objective:** This is similar to the Objective statement you'd use in a functional résumé. Tailor it to the job you are applying for. It should be one or two sentences highlighting what you can bring to this position or to the company. (See Chapter 6 for more details on how to write this.)

3. **Summary of Qualifications:** Summarize your qualifications under a separate heading — adapt this to your target job.

4. **Skills and Accomplishments:** List first those skills that relate most closely to the job you're applying for, or that are the most impressive. You can include any related professional achievements in this area, too. Refer to Chapter 6 for tips on writing this section.

   Keep the Skills and Accomplishments section reasonably brief. You don't need to include as much detail as you would in a functional résumé.

5. **Employment History:** List your work experience in this section. Organize it by date, starting with your current or most recent job. Give the dates for each job (months and/or years). List the name and location (town and province) of the organization for which you worked. For each job, include a capsule summary of no more than two or three sentences that outlines your responsibilities and major accomplishments.

6. **Education:** If the job description in the posting requires a degree, and you have it, put this section before Employment History. For example, if the job description asks for a bachelor of science degree, and you have a two-year college diploma but lots of experience, opt to put your Education section after your Employment History section, so you have a chance to let all that great experience shine.

7. **Other Information:** You need to exercise some caution with what you list here. Some employers might consider that salsa class you take twice a week kind of frivolous, and it might reflect on you as a candidate. I can just hear them thinking to themselves, "So what time does she need to leave work to become this dancing queen?" Listing a second language, or the fact that you somehow managed to practice your way through 10 years of piano lessons to win professional accreditation, is fine — it's a strategic move, even. Remember, employers want to hire well-rounded people. Just keep that weekend garage heavy-metal band thing to yourself.

Chapter 6

Developing Your Résumé

● ●

In This Chapter

▶ Defining your competitive advantage

▶ Examining each section in a résumé

▶ Appreciating how each section relates to the résumé as a whole

▶ Writing your résumé

● ●

*Y*our résumé is a pretty important tool in your job hunt. It's a best-foot-forward overview of who you are and what you can do for a company. This and the next chapter are about crafting your résumé to show yourself in the best possible light to employers. There's a fair amount you need to know about writing your résumé — so much, in fact, that I split it up into two chapters. This chapter looks at the different sections in a résumé and shows you how to put yours together. Chapter 7 deals with issues and potential pitfalls you might encounter as you write your résumé.

Your résumé is many things. Here are a few things it is not: It is *not* a one-size-fits-all document, nor is it your one-way ticket to a new set of business cards. Your résumé is only one of several tools you will use to land a job. So don't focus all your time, effort, and money preparing an elaborate résumé. A *professionally developed* résumé (prepared by a company that specializes in developing résumés for a fee) may stand out somewhat from the crowd, but, on its own, it's unlikely to get you any closer to landing a job. The bells and whistles that professional résumé writers provide are really just that — fluffy extras that don't really impress employers, but end up costing you money. And unless you plan on spending more money getting the same writer to do each cover letter you send out, it quickly becomes obvious to the employer that you didn't do your own résumé anyway.

On its own, a nice-looking, well-written résumé won't land you a job, either. But I guarantee that a poorly written résumé full of spelling mistakes won't even get you an interview. Somebody once sent me a résumé that read, "I do not wish to cause you any incontinence but. . . ." This person later sent a revised copy with the word "inconvenience" replacing "incontinence." Needless to say, that one went straight to the recycle pile.

It *is* important to make sure that your résumé is well written, well organized, and has no spelling or grammatical errors. You also need to research the job you're applying for (and the employer you're applying to) (see Chapters 11, 12, and 13) and ensure that you present your relevant skills in a way that makes the employer sit up and take notice.

What Makes You Competitive?

Today's job market is a competitive place, and you need to figure out how you're going to compete in it. This is called *defining your competitive advantage*. You need to understand what it is about you — your skills and accomplishments, your employment history, and your education, all of it — that makes you the best candidate for a job. I suggest you do this before beginning to write your résumé. In this section, I show you how.

Nowadays, a job may not go to the most qualified candidate, but to the person who markets themself the best. The company recruiter who receives 200+ résumés for a single job is not concerned, initially, with selecting the best candidate, but with eliminating résumés to make a *short list* (a smaller number of résumés to go through in more detail and hopefully find some promising candidates). If nothing makes your résumé stand out, there's a good chance it won't make this first cut.

What is it about you that makes you the best candidate for this job? Aside from your skills and accomplishments, employment history, and education, as they appear on your résumé, you could gain a competitive advantage for any of these reasons:

- ✔ The neat, professional appearance of your cover letter and résumé.

- ✔ Your positive attitude and enthusiasm for the job, which also comes through in your cover letter and résumé.

- ✔ The extra effort you put into learning everything you can about the company before you apply — which will be apparent in your cover letter and résumé, trust me.

- ✔ The good word put in for you by someone you know who has a contact at the company.

- ✔ The brownie points you'll score by calling the recruiter yourself, or stopping by for a visit.

Remember, at this stage you are just trying to get out of the starting gate and make it to the front of the pack. If you manage this, you are likely to get an interview and the opportunity to market yourself in person.

Does a cover letter give you a competitive advantage?

What makes you competitive in the job race? What can you do to ensure your résumé makes it past the starting gate and into the race? You can tell employers what your competitive advantage is in a cover letter, but there is no guarantee it will get noticed. A résumé and cover letter tailored directly to the job are important but do not necessarily give you a competitive advan-tage, because there are many applicants who take the time to do this. (On the other hand, if you don't do it, chances are you *won't* make it to the short list.) You need to write a good cover letter bringing out your skills package, then follow up to make sure your cover letter gets noticed! Chapter 10, "Following Up: The Art of Gentle Persuasion," gives you additional tips.

Know thyself

During your job hunt, how you present and differentiate yourself from the competition is a key factor to your success. You want to come across as a winner and a professional! To get yourself on the right mental track to pre-sent this image, start by reviewing your past experiences, work performance, and successes. Identify your strengths, values, personal style, and, especially, your weaknesses. Know what makes you unique!

Use your unique qualities to help you in your job hunt. Perhaps one of your strengths is persistence — you keep working at a problem until you find a solution. You can use this in your job search — tell employers this is one of your strengths and use this quality to find a way in the door! Maybe you have a strong work ethic, with a direct, hands-on approach to problem solving. Identify your unique qualities in your cover letter to prospective employers, and in your cold calls, as part of your overall *skills package*. Your skills package describes what makes you unique — what skills you have to offer an employer.

 Identifying your unique characteristics, strengths, shortcomings, and values is not only important in positioning yourself ahead of the pack in your job search, but also in assessing yourself to decide if there is a fit between you and the organization you are applying to.

If the shoe fits . . .

If you know that you and a particular company are a good fit, this becomes a part of your competitive advantage. So, how do you figure this out?

Most people pursue job opportunities by trying to prove that they are the best candidate for the job — that they are the best fit for that company. But what about switching this around? What about whether the job and company are the best fit for you? Job hunters often lose sight of this, but believe me, if you do figure it out, then it'll stand out in your résumé and cover letter, greatly contributing to your competitive advantage. How? Well, it will be obvious to the recruiter that you took the time to research the company, because you point out, in your cover letter, specific reasons why you think this is a good fit.

Determining fit

To determine if there is a fit between you, an employer, and a job, you need to take another close look at yourself. You started this in Chapter 2 as part of your self-assessment. Now, take a more detailed look at your past experiences with the aim of learning more about your needs, goals, and values, in order to determine fit.

Ask yourself these questions:

- **Do you have any specific skills you want to use or develop?** For example, you may want to develop your project management skills rather than perform specific tasks. So, companies looking for *multi-functional employees* (those who can perform multiple functions for the employer) will interest you.

- **What values and interests do you want to express through your work?** You might believe very strongly in helping people. You could choose to pursue a job that involved this. (You could also pursue it in your volunteer life outside of work.) Are you a creative person? Do you want to be able to be creative in your job, or can you satisfy this part of you in another area of your life?

- **What sort of environment do you want to work in?** This is very important when determining the fit between you and an organization. In my own recruitment practice, I had a client who was an academic — with a PhD in forestry — accustomed to a university environment where research and sharing knowledge was the focus. He moved to a software development company in private industry where deadlines were vital and getting a lot of work done in a short period of time was part of the organizational culture. After a few months, both he and the company realized there was no fit between them, which in turn led to his looking for another job. Someone else, however, might thrive in a fast-paced action-packed environment.

- **What type of career path do you want to pursue?** Are you seeking advancement possibilities, the opportunity to develop new skills, or do you want to become an expert in your field? Perhaps you want recognition for your achievements, or maybe you want to be the person behind the scenes.

Quality counts more than quantity!

Where have you heard this before? It is certainly true when you are job hunting. You don't gain a competitive advantage by sending out hundreds of résumés in response to online job ads or newspaper ads without putting in additional effort to make your application job-specific or do any follow-up. Most of the time, mass mail-outs include a generic cover letter (if they even include a cover letter) and are obviously part of a fishing expedition — to see if any employers bite. There is nothing about these résumés that makes them stand out, and rarely do the senders follow up on the status of their applications. The mail-outs usually end up in the recycle file under the desk!

Many job seekers delude themselves into believing they are accomplishing something by sending out hundreds of résumés — thinking that at least one of them has to result in a job offer. Spend your valuable time locating jobs and employers that fit with your values and goals. Then take the time to ensure your résumé and cover letter respond to the skill sets the employers are seeking.

The answers to these questions should give you some insight into what you need from a company to have it fit with your values and goals. To find out if a company matches your needs, you need to look beyond its company Web site (although this is a good starting point from which to learn about the products of the company and contact information). Check out Chapters 11, 12, and 13 for some valuable tips on how and where to find this type of information.

Putting Your Résumé Together

So, do you have to spend a lot of time, and possibly money, putting together a résumé? Or does there come a point where the extra effort you might put into your résumé would be time better spent actually looking for a job? While your résumé is very important because it is a snapshot of what you can offer a company, remember that a fancy résumé alone will not land you a job.

In this section, I take you through 10 steps that help you to develop a résumé that is not too long, not too short, and, as Goldilocks says, "just right." A well-written résumé geared toward your *target job*, the specific job you're applying for — combined with a killer cover letter, artful follow-up, and fearless networking — will stand you in much better stead than spending all your time creating a fancy résumé with a lot of bells and whistles.

For some great online help with developing some of the sections below, try out a few of these sites:

- ✔ **Monster.ca (www.monster.ca):** The Canadian version of this online job bank has a section on résumé writing that includes a helpful list of do's and don'ts.

- ✔ **Ontario Ministry of Education (www.edu.gov.on.ca/eng/career/.html):** This Web site provides great résumé writing tips, and includes a list of common résumé mistakes.

- ✔ **Resumania (www.resumania.com):** Although it's an American-run site, it's got great advice about what *not* to write on your résumé. It's pretty funny, too.

- ✔ **Résumé Tutor (www1.umn.edu/ohr/ecep//):** This site is set up like a workbook, and helps you develop individual sections of your résumé.

For a review of the different sections in a résumé, flip back to Chapter 5.

Step 1: Tell us about yourself

The first section of your résumé contains your personal and contact information: your name, home address (including city, province, and postal code), and your home phone number.

In addition, think about including some of these types of contact information:

- ✔ Cellular phone number
- ✔ E-mail address
- ✔ Fax number
- ✔ Pager number
- ✔ Web site address

Help wanted

In addition to paid consulting firms, you can access professional assistance in writing your résumé through employment counseling agencies, Human Resources Development Canada (HRDC) offices, and career placement offices at colleges and universities. If you don't know where to start, or want to run your résumé by someone for feedback, these can be great (and often free) resources. Consult the Landing a Job For Canadians For Dummies Directory of Job Resources for a list of HRDC offices across Canada.

If you're employed while looking for a job, you may be tempted to list your office phone number or office e-mail address, so that you're immediately available to speak to an employer or respond to an e-mail. Be cautious, however, about what you do on company time. A recruiter should be able to determine if you are working and contact you when you are off or send you an e-mail asking you to contact her. A prospective employer may be justifiably concerned about your honesty if you blatantly conduct your job hunt on your current employer's time.

Register for a Web-based e-mail address, such as Canada.com (www.canada.com) (which forwards e-mail to your home address — a nice feature because you don't have to log on to the site to check your e-mail, although you can if you want); Yahoo! Canada (www.yahoo.ca); or Hotmail (www.hotmail.com). Using a Web-based e-mail address has several advantages. It allows you to keep all your contacts in a single location, lets you check your e-mail from a remote location, and protects your privacy if you post your résumé online (see Chapter 9).

Keep in mind that if you provide an e-mail address or fax number, the recruiter may actually contact you using either of those methods, despite what everyone says about the popularity of the telephone. If you list an e-mail address, make sure you check your account on a regular basis.

Those of you in the arts often have a Web site where you display samples of your work. While it is okay to include your personal Web site address along with the rest of your personal information, make sure you still list your relevant skills, education, and work experience on your résumé. Don't assume the recruiter will take a 10-minute break from reviewing résumés just to log on to your Web site. He probably doesn't have time when he is developing the first short list. Let your résumé catch his attention first.

Step 2: Clarify your objective

Your objective comes after your personal information. An effective *objective statement* tells a recruiter directly and succinctly why you are a good fit for the job you're applying for. Frankly, it also convinces him to keep reading your résumé. It's your first, best — sometimes only — chance to make a great impression. Some employers have been known to throw résumés whose job objective doesn't grab them right into the filing pile. Hey, they're busy, and they might have dozens, if not hundreds, of résumés come in for a single position.

Here are three example objective statements that work:

> ✔ "To apply my skills and experience in the care of elderly people to a leadership position in the health care field. I have a strong work ethic, a positive attitude, and I sincerely believe I can make a difference in the quality of life for seniors."

✔ "Hard-working enthusiastic project manager who wishes to combine related experience and information technology skills in the role of client services manager. A company that values innovation and multitasking abilities will find my communication, management, and computer skills an asset."

✔ "Highly motivated biologist with 10 years' field experience and 5 years' proven managerial experience. Would like to apply strong organizational, leadership, and technical skills toward making a positive and immediate contribution to your team."

If you are uncertain about what position you are seeking, omit this section rather than use vague language. The objective "To apply my skills and experience to a challenging growth-oriented position" really says nothing about you. If you are going to include an objective, make it convey useful information about you and show that you know what the employer needs. Specify what you can do for the company, what specific job you are aiming for, and what you can bring to the job. Use descriptive words such as "Motivated BComm with demonstrated experience in . . . Strong interest in development and application of. . . ."

Tailor your objective to each position you apply for. This is your chance to give the employer a quick overview of your goals and show him how you see yourself contributing to the company. Craft your objective in terms of how your experience can answer a company's need — what you can do for them, not the other way around.

Your objective should include the type of job you are applying for (if relevant) or the title of the position (if you are applying for a specific job), the industry you are applying to, and the skills you bring to it. Briefly describe how you feel you could contribute to the company.

Step 3: Choose a format

In Chapter 5, I discuss the pros and cons of the three most common résumé formats: chronological, functional, and combination. Choose the style that fits you and your situation best. I prefer the combination résumé, because it includes a functional Skills and Accomplishments section along with a chronological listing of your employment history. It not only tells the employer *what* you can do, but also shows them that you have actually *done it*. Sometimes, we recruiters like to have things spelled out for us, so we don't have to spend time searching for information. You know, "*Where* did she get experience in data management," or "*What* type of skills did he acquire as a welder's assistant?" As I note in Chapter 5, however, there are lots of circumstances in which one of the other two styles is a better choice.

Step 4: Find an example and use it!

Why reinvent the wheel? There are many online résumé resources that are both easily accessible and free (a real bonus). My suggestion is that you research sample résumés that target a similar job and where the applicant has a similar background to yours. Be sure the example you choose uses the format you have chosen for your résumé. Don't get me wrong! Don't copy the résumé — just use it as a guideline for example words and phrases to describe objectives and to help you define your soft and technical skills. For more résumé-oriented as well as other types of job-hunting resources, check out the Landing a Job For Canadians For Dummies Directory of Job Resources, printed on yellow paper so you can't miss it.

These Web sites have examples of résumés that you can look through:

- ✔ **Quintessential Careers** (www.quintcareers.com/_samples.html): This site has examples of Web-based résumés that also function well off-line. You need Adobe Acrobat Reader to view these résumés, which you can download for free at www.adobe.com.

- ✔ **Rebecca Smith's eResumes and Resources** (www.es.com): This popular Web site is a well-known resource for online résumé tips, but it also has a great collection of résumé examples you can look through. Click on the Gallery link.

Step 5: Present your skills and accomplishments

If you looked at the sample résumés in Chapter 5, you likely expect me to talk about the Summary of Qualifications section here because that is what comes next on your résumé. Don't worry — I haven't forgotten. I suggest you save that section 'til last for writing purposes, because it's often easier to write once you've completed the other sections. You write it last, but put it up front so it catches the recruiter's eye. Watch for instructions toward the end of this section.

Let's skip to skills and accomplishments. We all have them — sometimes it's just hard to verbalize or even remember all of them. To top it off, it feels like you are tooting your own horn! But you know what? There's nothing wrong with that — especially on a résumé. If you don't tell the employer what you can do and what you have accomplished that is out of the ordinary, who will? So, go for it! Toot away! Tell them what you can do and, more specifically, what you can do *for them*.

In this section, I help you identify your skills and accomplishments *and* show you how to relate them to the job for which you are applying. I break these down by résumé type because the level of detail you put in differs depending on the résumé style you choose. You don't include a Skills and Accomplishments section at all in a purely chronological résumé, but you go into great detail about this area in a purely functional one. In a combination résumé, you present your skills and accomplishments in point form, but the process of identifying them is the same.

In a functional résumé

If you're using the functional résumé format, you may not have a lot of actual work experience behind you. Relax! The Skills and Accomplishments section in a functional résumé allows you to highlight your general abilities and achievements, which, while they may not be *directly* related to a job you've had, are still relevant to the job you're applying for. You can also include skills you have acquired through school and other non-related work you have done. That's the beauty of the functional style.

Follow these steps to get this part of your résumé in shape:

1. **Define your *key aptitudes*.** A *key aptitude* is an area you excel in that directly relates to the job for which you're applying. Let's say you've got your eye on a sales and marketing representative job for a soft drink manufacturer. First review the job posting and highlight the key requirements. For example, the ad says they are looking for well-developed oral and written presentation skills, an ability to set and reach targeted sales goals, and well-honed marketing skills. They'd also like you to be a self-starter and a fast learner, with a desire to succeed. Here's how you could identify the key aptitudes required for the job:

   • Oral and written presentation = Communications

   • Targeted sales goals = Sales

   • Well-honed marketing skills = Marketing

   • Self-starter, fast learner, desire to succeed = Attitude

Based on what they're looking for, go through your own work, volunteer, life experience, and education, and make a list of what you have done or can do that applies to the position in each of these key aptitude areas. (If you are applying for a non-advertised job, you may be able to identify the aptitudes required through an information interview or a written occupational profile (see Chapter 11)).

If you can come up with *several* skills or accomplishments that relate to those required for the job, you possess a *key aptitude*! You often have specific skills and accomplishments in each key aptitude area. Let's say that you are a new graduate with a business degree in marketing, and you have some part-time retail experience, where you excelled in sales.

Also, you did several marketing projects at school on actual companies; you received high grades and passed the final projects on to the companies. So, looks like marketing is one of your key aptitudes.

Try to limit your list to four key aptitudes directly related to the job you are applying for. For example, you may also have an artistic aptitude — but will including it on your résumé help you land a sales and marketing job for a soft drink manufacturer? You can always adapt the aptitudes you include to different jobs. Yes, you may be talented at many different things, but no recruiter has the time to slog through 25 examples of that talent.

2. **List your skills and abilities related to each aptitude.** Under each key aptitude, list your skills that relate directly to it. If your key aptitude is sales, some of your skills might include excellent people skills, strong client follow-up skills, and a belief in being proactive with respect to determining client needs. Identify your skills by doing an inventory of your experience and education and listing what you have done or learned that applies to your job goal, under the appropriate heading.

Remember to look at both your technical skills and your soft skills when making this list. *Technical skills* are skills that are required to perform the job, whereas *soft skills* are skills that make you a better employee: a positive attitude, a strong work ethic, loyalty, organizational ability, the ability to learn quickly, and commitment. The best thing about soft skills is that they are eminently *transferable* — you can generally take them with you from one job to another. Whether you want to be an event planner or an accountant, soft skills such as a positive attitude and good organizational skills apply to both.

3. **List your accomplishments related to each aptitude.** Identify your top three accomplishments in each of your jobs, volunteer work, or other experience. Try to answer questions like these: What did you do? What did you direct others to do? What did you manage, create, approve, or instigate? What was the outcome of your actions? If you have many accomplishments, narrow them down based on which ones will have the greatest applicability to the job you're applying for. What have you done that most applies to your *target job?*

People often list their *responsibilities* in a job instead of their *accomplishments.* To help define your accomplishments, use the PAR formula (Problem, Action, Results), which I discuss in the sidebar "Don't confuse accomplishments with responsibilities" in Chapter 5.

Use results-focused verbs rather than functional verbs when writing your accomplishments. Instead of writing "*Supervised* five sales staff," write "*Increased* client base by 25% by introducing new tracking system to five-person sales staff." The verb "supervised" only describes a responsibility, whereas "increased" describes an actual achievement that had a positive effect on the business.

Keep in mind that the skills and accomplishments you include in this section of your résumé need to be relevant to your target job. Honesty is important, but you can be strategic at the same time. Research the company you're applying to. Find out what they're looking for in an ideal candidate. Then, tailor your résumé accordingly, to highlight those abilities that most closely match what the company is after. You'll stand out, and your résumé will stay well away from the dreaded shredder.

In a combination résumé

The Skills and Accomplishments section tends to be shorter in a combination résumé, usually because your Employment History section is longer — you have more actual work experience. You can format your skills and accomplishments as a short bulleted list of those that are most relevant to your target job.

Follow the same steps I outline above to identify your skills and accomplishments for a combination résumé. Then, do a round of edits, and include only your top skills in each key aptitude. Format them in point form, with less explanation.

Step 6: Describe your educational background

Your degrees, diplomas, and certificates not only illustrate your academic achievements but also show a recruiter that you are industrious and want to improve yourself. In this section of your résumé, you show them that you've got the right stuff education-wise to do the job, and that you continue to learn and improve yourself, staying up-to-date in your field.

Include all your post-secondary degrees in this section, including college and technical school diplomas and certificates. You can also include academic awards or scholarships, and relevant professional development courses.

List the highest level of education you attained first. For each entry, include the type of degree, diploma, or certificate you earned, your major, the name of your college or university, and the year it was awarded. If you do not have a degree or diploma, list on-the-job training courses or other courses or programs you have taken in this section.

If this is one of the first jobs you are applying for out of school, include your grade point average or your rank in your class, if it's above the class average.

The order in which you place your Employment History and Education sections isn't written in stone. I like to see Education first because it is a shorter section, but there are situations that warrant a quick reversal. For example, if you are high on work experience and low on education, put your Employment History section first. However, if you recently graduated from university or college and have little or no related work experience, put your Education first. If a specific degree or accreditation is one of the top criteria in the job ad — for example, CMA (Chartered Management Accountant) or P.Eng (Professional Engineer), put Education first again (assuming you are either a CMA or a P.Eng).

Step 7: Recount your employment history or experience

The amount of detail you put in this section depends on the résumé format you choose — which in turn depends on your individual circumstances and goals. In a *purely* functional résumé, you may decide to leave this section out altogether. At the very minimum, though, it's a good idea to list the dates of employment, job title, employer, and location. Order your jobs from most to least recent.

TIP

Should you list all your jobs on your résumé?

This is a long-standing debate, for sure. I mean, how many recruiters really, truly, want to read about your summer job as a camp counselor when you were 18, made next to no money, and generally looked at the job as a paid summer vacation? More to the point, how many recruiters would you *want* to know about your summer jobs or your part-time job as a pump jockey at the local gas station 30 years ago? This can be an issue for older workers who have held many jobs, or for someone who hasn't stayed in a single job or industry for a significant length of time.

Your most recent jobs are usually the most relevant to an employer. If the waitressing job you held 20 years ago has little in common with the position of office manager that you are currently applying for, leave it off your résumé. If you've held numerous jobs or have industry-hopped, and listing your jobs in a strictly chronological fashion would look more like a grocery list than

the stellar work experience that it is, use the functional résumé format and group your jobs under broad headings such as Health Administration, Training, or Sales and Marketing. List the relevant jobs under each heading. You can even omit dates of employment if you've held a great number of jobs.

My advice: Go ahead and leave a job off your résumé if it was just a "filler" job or if it is not relevant to the position. Always be prepared to explain why this job was not included on your résumé, if you are questioned at an interview. In order to not make a blatant exclusion on your résumé, you can use years to indicate the dates you worked at your jobs — for example, use 1999–2001 instead of the actual dates of employment. The other option is to put length of time instead of dates — 4½ years at Job A, 3 years at Job B.

Go into more detail about your employment history if you're using the chronological or combination style. After listing the who, what, when, and where of a particular job, go on to (briefly) describe your primary duties. Try to show that you've moved up the line, whether in the form of a promotion (the best way to demonstrate this) or increased responsibility (still a good way). This is especially important if you've been with the same employer for some time.

If you are short on work experience, label this section of your résumé Experience instead of Employment History, and list your school projects and volunteer work.

Step 8: Tell us more about yourself

Label this section Other Information and divide it into as many of the following headings that apply to you:

- ✔ Awards and Recognition
- ✔ Interests
- ✔ Languages
- ✔ Professional Affiliations
- ✔ Publications
- ✔ Volunteer/Community Involvement

You can give details, but remember to focus on telling the employer information about yourself that either impresses them or further demonstrates your suitability for the job. Make sure you present a consistent picture of yourself. If you're applying for a job at Greenpeace, for example, don't list hunting as an interest.

Step 9: Summarize your qualifications

Told you I'd get to this. Isn't it much easier to summarize your résumé once you have figured out what you are going to say? The Summary of Qualifications section is generally the most challenging part of your résumé to write, which is why, even though it's one of the first sections that gets read, it should be the section you turn your attention to last, when you've finished the rest of your résumé and have a clearer impression of the snapshot it creates.

This can be a very powerful section, functioning as the one-two punch that gets recruiters to sit up and take notice. It allows you to capture your experience and draw attention to skills that apply directly to your targeted job, which may not be obvious from the position titles in your Employment History section.

It can be in bullet form (no more than six points) or in paragraph form (no more than six sentences). Before you write this section, carefully review the details of your Skills and Accomplishments section and your Employment History section.

Here is an example Summary of Qualifications section for an accountant applying for a position as controller with a software development company. Note how the skills identified are directly related to the job and the company:

- ✔ "Certified Management Accountant with 10 years of experience for a large corporation and 12 years' experience as a managing partner in a private consulting firm."

- ✔ "Basic computer programming skills (Visual Basic and Pascal) and extensive database experience (Microsoft Access)."

- ✔ "Working knowledge of the software development industry and the market your company operates in."

- ✔ "Solid understanding of how accounting systems in large organizations similar to your clients' operate, and willing to bring this knowledge to your operation."

Even if you don't have a lot of related experience in the field you're applying for, you can still identify and list skills that cross over between occupations. For example, if you are currently a loans officer applying for a sales position, your summary of qualifications might read like this:

- ✔ "Increased loans portfolio and client base by 35 percent."

- ✔ "Demonstrated ability to cold-call and develop long-term relationships with large corporate clients."

- ✔ "Received company award for providing outstanding customer service (nominated by clients)."

The skills you choose to highlight in your Summary of Qualifications section should be the ones you believe most pertain to the job for which you are applying. This is the section the recruiter will likely read first, so you really need to sell yourself here (in a good way!). In the sales example in the previous list, the applicant uses action words and discusses results. He takes the skills he acquired as a loans officer and applies them to the skills required for a sales representative.

This section may be deleted in a purely chronological résumé. However, highlighting your key skill areas applicable to the job you are applying for is so important, I recommend you always include it regardless of the résumé style you choose. In a combination résumé, some people combine the Summary of Qualifications and the Skills and Accomplishments sections, if the résumé starts to get too long. How long is too long? A two-page résumé is ideal — a three-pager is acceptable. Anything longer starts to read like an autobiography.

One page is rarely long enough. I don't recommend it, as the recruiter's first impression is likely to be "Hmm . . . hasn't done too much, has she?" However, while it is rare, if an employer specifically requests a one-page résumé, find a way to condense it to a single page. The ability to follow directions is one way employers create a short list.

Step 10: Get feedback

Bet you knew this was coming! Asking for feedback is an important part of developing your résumé. Show it to several friends or colleagues and ask for a critical evaluation. Ask them to pay special attention to your Skills and Accomplishments section — they will probably come up with an ability or achievement that wasn't obvious to you, or that you may have overlooked. After all the time and thought that goes into putting your résumé together, you're so close to it that it is easy to lose your objectivity. This is the time when another pair of eyes can really help you to improve your résumé.

Ask your reviewers to note the following:

✔ Typos and missed or misused words

✔ What they like and what impresses them about your résumé

✔ What they don't like or find confusing

✔ Whether they would hire you based on your current résumé

✔ If they wouldn't hire you, what changes you need to make to sway their opinion

INSIDE SCOOP

Should you include references in your résumé?

Your references are your secret weapon in your job hunt, and you need to manage them carefully — a good reference can clinch the job or encourage an employer to consider bringing you back for a second interview. Many job seekers include references on their résumés in the belief that it's part of a complete résumé package, or that it's expected, or that it's just plain polite. However, that can backfire — if you list a bunch of people on your résumé that you want to say nice things about you and then hand your résumé over to a prospective employer, you could really get caught if that employer decides to call any of those people before you've had a chance to alert them. Looks like your secret weapon suddenly isn't so secret anymore.

The bottom line? Don't include references on your résumé. Some recruiters and employers have been known to call the references before contacting the applicant for an interview. Instead, type out your references' names, positions, and contact information on a separate piece of paper and bring it with you to interviews. If the employer asks you for your references, go ahead and hand over that list then . . . but not before.

Keep these points in mind to help you manage your references:

- Make a list of the people you'd like to use as references before you send out any résumés, then call them and explain you are looking for a job and ask if you can use their name as a reference.

- Provide three references from directly related jobs, if possible. If you have not had any work experience, it is okay to provide character references, but try to use people in authority positions with whom you have done some volunteer work.

- Once you have landed an interview and passed on your list of references to the employer, call your references and give them a few details about the job you've applied for. That way they can tailor the reference to the actual job. They'll appreciate the heads-up from you, and will be more likely to deliver that golden reference you hope for.

- Send your references a thank-you note — even if you don't get the job. That way, the next time they get called, they'll remember you in a favourable light.

Chapter 7

Refining Your Résumé

• •

In This Chapter

▶ Polishing, tweaking, and otherwise perfecting your résumé

▶ Customizing your résumé

▶ Avoiding common résumé mistakes

▶ Handling sensitive information on your résumé

• •

You discovered your perfect match in Chapter 5: You know whether you are going to use a chronological, functional, or combination résumé format. Chapter 6 showed you how to develop the nuts and bolts of your résumé — how to actually put it together. In this chapter, I give you some tips on how to polish your résumé and get it to the stage where you can actually send it out to prospective employers. I also tell you how to steer clear of easily made résumé mistakes and how to present sensitive information.

Taking Your Résumé to the Next Level

You should feel good about your résumé and be comfortable giving it to prospective employers. Your résumé should make both a positive and personal statement about who you are. Formulating your résumé and getting it down on paper is one thing — and, yeah, it's probably the most challenging and time-consuming part. But would you believe it's often the details of a particular résumé, the finishing touches, that determine its fate — whether it goes to the discard pile or the interview pile? Have you thought about what kind of paper you're going to use? What about font and type size? This section shows you how to refine your résumé in a way that gives you that extra bit of confidence when sending it out there. You want to put your best foot forward, don't you?

Reality check! Volume of applications overwhelming for employers

The sheer volume of résumés submitted today for any given job can overwhelm employers. With the increased number of *online job banks* (Internet job sites where employers post jobs), which increase both the exposure for the job (anyone who has access to the Internet can see it) as well as how easy it is to apply (you just cut-and-paste your résumé), it is not unheard of for a company to have hundreds of international and national responses for a job that once would have attracted only 20 applicants. Even companies that don't advertise on the Internet directly will often have their jobs posted as an additional service when they place a newspaper ad.

To be successful in your job hunt, find a way to make an employer notice your résumé. Don't think in terms of "I have all the skills for the job," but rather, "What can I do to make them notice and shortlist my résumé?" Think of yourself as a "product" — you need to make sure the customer (employer) needs or wants you (and what you have to offer). You also need to differentiate yourself from other similar "products" being offered to the employer.

Form

Ideally, your résumé should be no longer than two typed pages. While one page is rarely long enough to include all your relevant information, résumés longer than two pages may be loaded with, well, *irrelevant* information, and therefore don't hold the recruiter's interest. Having said that, if you have 30 years of experience, three degrees, and tonnes of expertise, you've earned yourself a little leeway in the length department, but keep it to under three pages.

Presentation is very important! How professional your résumé looks is key to getting your foot in the door. Or to put it another way, a poorly presented résumé could well keep that door firmly shut — no matter how qualified you are. Why? Because the recruiter takes in the overall appearance of your résumé before actually beginning to read.

Having said that presentation is important, I don't mean that you have to get fancy and include logos, tables, and multiple fonts. There is such a thing as overkill. Making sure your résumé looks neat and professional is very important, but ensuring the relevant information is included and is easily found will go further to help you land that job than elaborate packaging. Fancy formatting and logos can also backfire when you send a résumé via e-mail. As I discuss in Chapter 9, it may get reformatted on the trip through cyberspace and will not look so pretty at the receiving end.

Your résumé's presentation is your chance to make a great first impression. And we all know how difficult it is to change first impressions — good or bad.

Here are some things to keep in mind about the form, or shape, your résumé takes:

- ✔ **Use a consistent font and type size throughout.** Use a *sans-serif font* (a font without the little swirls and flags on it), like Arial or Helvetica, so that your résumé can be scanned, if the employer has that technology (see Chapter 9). Adjust your font size and margins to keep your résumé to two pages, if possible, but don't go below a font size of 10 if you want to make sure people can read the fine print.

- ✔ **Highlight relevant information so that it's easy for the recruiter to spot.** Use bulleted lists instead of paragraphs, particularly in your Skills and Accomplishments section.

- ✔ **Avoid typing errors, or *typos*.** When an employer is trying to narrow down a large pile of applications, this is one criterion she *will* use. Be sure to have someone (or maybe several people) proofread your résumé for you.

- ✔ **Watch out for grammatical errors, too.** Ask someone you know with a strong command of the English language to "edit" your résumé before you send it out. (An English teacher would be good!)

- ✔ **Print your résumé on high-quality bond paper in white or off-white.** *Rag* (textured) paper is particularly good to use. Steer clear of brightly coloured paper.

- ✔ **Use a good-quality photocopier if you are photocopying your résumé.** Don't make the employer squint and scratch her head as she tries to read your name.

  If you own a bubble-jet printer, while your résumé may look good right after it is printed, any drop of liquid will cause it to smear. It is best to photocopy your bubble-jet printed résumé on high-quality paper to make sure it stays in the best shape possible.

- ✔ **Mail your résumé and cover letter in an 8¾" x 11½" or 9" x 12" envelope.** It is much easier to read than a résumé folded like an accordion.

Content

Content is king! Your résumé may only be a snapshot of you, but it should present the best picture you can take. I discuss writing your résumé in more detail in Chapter 6, but here are a few tips worth repeating:

✔ **Customize your résumé for each job you apply to, by highlighting skills and accomplishments that are relevant to the job in question.** Research the organization you're applying to *and* the industry it's part of. Use some of the key words and ideas that you come across in your objective statement and your summary of qualifications. (Chapters 11, 12, and 13 give you great tips on how to research online and off-line.)

✔ **State your job or career goal clearly in your objective statement and make sure that the body of your résumé supports it.** You want your résumé to have continuity.

✔ **Omit the Employment History section if you are short on work experience.** List your school projects and volunteer experience under the heading Experience, instead.

✔ **Use action verbs to highlight your skills and accomplishments in past jobs.** For example, "*Upgraded* computer system" instead of "Responsible for upgrading . . ." and "*Increased* sales by 45%" instead of "Sales went up by 45% during my employment."

✔ **Leave off your references.** But be prepared to provide their names and phone numbers on request. Call your references in advance to let them know that you have a job interview and that they might be contacted. You do this to reconnect with them, so that you are fresh in their minds, and also as a courtesy, so that they have some time to think about what they'll say should they get a call.

Tailor-made: Why you need to customize your résumé

Back in the days when résumés were typed on a typewriter (oh, come on, it wasn't *that* long ago), it was incredibly time-intensive to create new résumés for each position you applied for, because you had to retype the entire résumé. Nowadays, thanks to Bill Gates et al., it's relatively easy to customize your résumé on a computer, showing how your credentials match the needs of a particular employer. Today, most employers *expect* you to take the time to tailor your résumé to the position you're applying for.

When I say *customizing* your résumé for different jobs, I don't mean that you have to recreate it from scratch. Think of customizing not as giving your poor résumé a major overhaul every time you apply to a new organization, but as tweaking it here and there as necessary. Your *base résumé,* which consists of your skills and accom-

plishments, your education, and your employment history, remains the same. What changes is *how* you present this information to different employers — highlighting a specific skill for one, maybe downplaying the same skill for another. It's like a car that gets a new paint job every now and then. Customizing your résumé could mean reordering the sections or emphasizing certain aspects of your work experience that apply to the position you're going for, or the industry in general. It may mean revising your Summary of Qualifications section to highlight different abilities, reworking the wording of your skills and accomplishments or replacing them with others more closely related to the job. Most importantly, remember to customize your objective statement so that it's clearly related to each new job you apply for. (See Chapter 6.)

✔ **Have two or three trusted people in mind for your references.** They can be people you've worked with professionally, who would be able (and willing) to give glowing reports about you and your capabilities. Or they can be people in a position of authority who can comment on your character and who will tell your prospective boss what an all-around star you are.

Résumé Blunders

A single mistake on your résumé can result in immediate banishment to the rejection pile. Remember that a recruiter tries to narrow the list of applicants to a manageable number as quickly as possible, and she uses this form of pre-screening frequently. There are numerous common résumé *faux pas,* but you can easily sidestep them with a little advance warning.

Your résumé doesn't match your objective

Most job hunters know the refrain very well (because books like this drum it into you): Adapt your objective statement to each job. But that's only half the equation. Go ahead and adapt that objective, but remember that the employer is going to want to see a correlation between what you say your objective is and the skills and accomplishments, education, and employment history that follow. Take the time to revise your résumé to highlight those skills and accomplishments that are directly related to the job you're applying for.

Your résumé leaves out your accomplishments

Interestingly enough, job hunters often neglect (or forget) to include their work- or life-related accomplishments on their résumés. Why? They either don't take the time to identify them or they mistakenly list work-related responsibilities in their place. Your accomplishments show what you have actually achieved in your past jobs, and therefore reflect well on you. They also provide concrete examples that support the skills you list. Your responsibilities only show what was *expected* of you in a job. It's like listing your job description, and that won't do you much good. Be sure to list accomplishments that are related to your target job. (See Chapter 5 for more information on how to differentiate between responsibilities and accomplishments.)

Your résumé is too long and too wordy

There are likely some things you've written that even your favourite high school teacher — or your own mom, for that matter — won't read. A résumé that's unnecessarily long and filled with extraneous information tops this list. Try to keep your résumé to two pages or less. You don't need to go into as much detail about a job you held 15 years ago as you do, say, about your current or recent positions. Keep descriptions brief, factual, and to the point. Instead of rhyming off every minor duty you've ever had, focus on the skills and accomplishments that relate to the job you're applying for. Remember, your résumé is just the first step toward getting an interview — don't try to conduct the interview on paper!

Your résumé is riddled with typos

This is a guaranteed "do-not-pass-go" sentence and I can't repeat it enough. Do not rely on your computer to spell-check your résumé. If you use a word incorrectly but spell it right, spell-check on many word processor packages lets it pass. Ask someone who knows their way around the English language to proofread your résumé before you send it out.

You may be tempted to pay someone to write your résumé for you. Now, a professionally developed résumé looks great, is usually well written, and, very importantly, has no typos or grammatical errors. You've got it locked up, or so you think. You write up your cover letter — diligently tailoring it to the particular job you're applying for — and send the package off. You could find yourself out of luck, however, if your cover letter has spelling mistakes or grammatical errors — errors, of course, that your professionally developed résumé *doesn't* have, because it was professionally developed. This is a red flag to any recruiter. The typos in your cover letter will send your entire résumé to the recycle pile.

Don't take this chance. Write your résumé and cover letter yourself (refer to this book for help whenever you need to). You'll likely do just as good a job as any professional service — if not better — plus, you'll save money. Make sure that your cover letter is error free, and carefully review any changes you make to tailor your résumé to a specific job. See Chapter 8 for advice on writing your cover letter.

Dealing with the Touchy Issues

Putting your résumé together is not just a fill-in-the-blanks kind of exercise — which is why I don't recommend relying on those résumé-building sites you can find online, though they can be a good *starting* point and fun to explore. Each and every one of us has a different background. Many of us have special situations — some that may be a little tough to explain and that require careful handling on a résumé, and in an interview (see Chapter 17).

Here are a few tips on how to handle touchy issues concerning your résumé:

✔ **Leave out personal information unless you think it will increase your chances of landing the job.** This includes your height, your weight, and your medical, marital, and family status (the number of kids you have). For example, if a recruiter is looking for someone who needs to travel extensively in a job, it might be to your advantage to state that you are single and ready and willing to travel. If a job requires you to relocate to a smaller or remote community, having a family and being willing to move them will be to your advantage, so you might want to include this information. On the other hand, if you have a family and a job requires a lot of travel, telling the recruiter that on your résumé would likely take you out of the running. Of course, you may not really want a job like that, anyway.

✔ **Be upfront about long time gaps between jobs.** Explain them in terms of what you did, and, if possible, how it benefited you in your career. Obvious gaps in a résumé may raise suspicion and could result in an employer choosing not to interview you. Don't be afraid to represent gaps truthfully, whether you were laid off, went traveling, tried another type of work, worked at numerous temporary jobs, had to care for a sick family member, or took time off to be a full-time parent.

If you've had many jobs in a short period of time, explain them in a brief note under the job heading, don't hide them. Maybe you needed to pay your bills while you searched for a job in your field of interest. Maybe you were paying your way through college or working part-time while earning a degree.

Taking time off to parent your children is not a bad thing! Try something like this when it comes time to put this on your résumé: "Full-time parent: Involved in logistics of planning, organizing, budgeting, and managing household of five. Includes community work, organization of extracurricular activities, volunteer boards, and committees." See how impressive that sounds? Phew, talk about hard work!

If you have short time gaps in your employment, you can just list years rather than months-and-years to show your employment history.

WORLD WIDE WEB

Résumé help online

There's a multitude of résumé-building sites online. These vary from large online job banks, like Monster.ca (`www.monster.ca`), which have a section that contains résumé templates, to smaller Web sites that specialize in résumés. You can get some good tips on writing your résumé from these sites. However, most of the templates can't be customized for individual situations and don't go into enough detail to draw out more personalized parts of a résumé, such as your job-related accomplishments. Still, visiting a few of these Web sites can be a good starting point.

These are some of the more popular résumé-building Web sites:

✔ **Campus Access.com** (`www.campusaccess.com/campus_web/career/c3job_res.htm`): This Web site gives you tips on résumé content, vocabulary, and format. It also includes a list of good "résumé words" such as the action-oriented words you should use to describe your skills and accomplishments.

✔ **Job Hunter's Bible.com** (`www.jobhuntersbible.com/résumés/résumés.shtml`):

This site is actually a collection of links to other Web sites about résumé writing. You can use this site as a starting point to find out more about how to write a résumé and what to include.

✔ **Next Steps** (`www.nextsteps.org/net/résumé/résumés.htm`): This Web site is quite user-friendly, with advice on what to include in your résumé, what to omit, different résumé formats, and quick tips on writing your résumé.

✔ **Ontario Ministry of Education** (`www.edu.gov.on.ca/eng/career/résumé.html`): A great site on résumé writing tips, run by Ontario's provincial government. I especially like the list of common résumé mistakes.

✔ **Résumé Tutor** (`www1.umn.edu/ohr/ecep/résumé`): This U.S.-based Web site is run by the University of Minnesota, and provides a pretty good résumé template.

✔ **The Riley Guide** (`www.rileyguide.com/letters.html`): Includes tips on résumé writing, as well as an extensive collection of FAQs. A good all-around job-hunting site.

✔ **Tell the truth.** Some studies estimate that as many as one-third of all job hunters provide false or exaggerated information on their résumés, ranging from innocent omissions to blatant lies. Not sure what I mean? Check out this list, and stay away from the following:

- Beefing up your past salaries
- Embellishing your job responsibilities, as well as your skills and accomplishments
- Enhancing your past job titles
- Inventing past employers
- Stretching dates to cover gaps in your employment.

Chapter 8

A Killer Cover Letter

*Y*our cover letter is your opportunity to personalize your job application and immediately highlight your key skills and accomplishments that apply to the job. It's the employer's introduction to you, a sales pitch, *and* a proposal for further action, all in one. Your cover letter is a way of attracting an employer's interest, and getting them to take the next step and look at your résumé in greater detail. Attitude and personality come through in a cover letter. You can show industriousness and enthusiasm just by the way you word it.

How much effort do you need to put into your cover letter? After all, you've just shed all that blood, sweat, and tears over your résumé, and now I'm suggesting you do it again — in the form of an actual letter, no less! Well, there are two schools of thought: One of them suggests that you cobble together a few sentences and print them off on a sheet that goes on top of your résumé — you know, just in case the recruiter looks at it. The other suggests that you put as much time into crafting your cover letter as you do your résumé. My own philosophy falls somewhere in the middle. You have already developed your résumé (see Chapters 5, 6, and 7) and done a pile of research about the company to which you are applying (you have, haven't you?), so your background work is already done. (If you're unsure where to begin your research, take a look at Chapters 11 and 13.) You need to take the time to highlight a couple of key points to catch the employer's interest. What better place to do it than in a cover letter? Don't spend hours crafting a masterpiece — a simple bestseller will do!

In this chapter, I tell you how to put together a killer cover letter. I provide you with a template you can use to organize your cover letter, so all you have to do is fill in the blanks. Well, I'm exaggerating a bit here, because you need to fill in the blanks with company- and job-specific information. The good news is that you should have done most of this research already to adapt your résumé to individual job targets. And — you knew I was going to get to this — what about electronic cover letters? This chapter shows you how to get your cover letter cyber-ready, too.

Getting Ready to Write

Nowadays, formal letters are no longer one of our regular channels of communication. Some of us applaud this — all together now . . . "We love e-mail!" Some of us passionately dislike it. But that's a discussion for another book. The point is, we seem to have lost a lot of our basic letter-writing skills, which makes it all the more difficult to sit down in front of a computer screen and compose a brilliant cover letter — particularly one that makes a request involving employment. Fact is, though, a potential employer expects you to write a *cover letter,* a letter that accompanies your résumé and introduces you to them.

So you've found a job you think you'd like to apply for. Your résumé's primed, and you've tailored it to the job. Now get ready to write a cover letter that grabs the employer's attention and makes it immediately clear why you're a great fit. Here are a few steps you can take to gather the information you need for your cover letter. Get out a pen and piece of paper, and write it down. These lists will form the basis of your letter when you get down to actually writing it.

1. **Make a list of what the employer is looking for.** Go over the job ad and list the skills and qualifications they're after. What skills, education, and work experience do they want?

2. **Match your skills and experience to the job.** Write down a couple of directly related accomplishments that you are especially proud of. What are the top two or three qualities that you would bring to the job? List these in terms of how they will benefit the employer.

You'll probably be able to do this fairly easily because you've already targeted the job and adapted your résumé. Hint: If you get stumped here and can't easily figure out why you and the job belong together, take another look at the job; you and it may not be such a great match, after all.

3. **Look for links between you and the employer.** Go online and research the company. Check out the Web site, if they have one. A company's Web site is a great place to get more information regarding their products, their culture, and, of course, the actual job. Problems finding their Web site? Go to Dogpile (www.dogpile.com) and do a search on the company name. Dogpile is a *metasearch engine,* a cool tool that searches other *search engines* (Web sites that help you find information on the Internet),

Why waste the time? Isn't all the important stuff in my résumé?

I've heard my fair share of recruiters say that they don't read cover letters and go straight to the résumé to get the detail they need. But, for every recruiter who says the cover letter isn't important, you'll find another who says it is! The prevailing mindset among recruiters who do read them is that those job hunters who don't bother to include one are either hunting casually or are just too lazy to write one. Yikes! You don't want to be tarred with that brush. Don't make the assumption that the person who reads your résumé doesn't care about cover letters. Cover all your bases, so to speak, and include one.

so you are likely to find the company Web site, if they have one. See Chapter 12 for more on metasearch engines and other Internet search tools. See Chapter 13 for how to research companies, industries, and jobs online.

Look for something about the employer that appeals to you and that you think you're especially suited for. You will use this in the body of your letter. You can also look up the company's annual report (check out the directory of annual reports on Sedar (www.sedar.com), which is sometimes a more honest window onto a company, since it can't rely on glitzy Web effects and smooth-talking copy to attract you.

4. **Figure out what about this particular organization makes you want to work for them.** What do you find appealing? Is it the job itself, or their products or services, vision, organizational culture, or goals? Hey, it could even be the location or the salary! This is also fodder for a great cover letter (just don't mention that it's the salary that attracted you!).

Anatomy of a Cover Letter

With the exception of *e-mail cover notes*, a shorter form of cover letter that you send along with an electronic version of your résumé, all cover letters contain the same type of information in the text. (I get to e-mail cover notes later in the chapter.) You just need to fill in the details specific to your target job. Figure 8-1 is a template you can use to develop your cover letter. Figure 8-2, on the opposite page, is an example of an actual cover letter that closely follows the template. In this section, I explain the different parts of the cover letter, as shown in Figures 8-1 and 8-2.

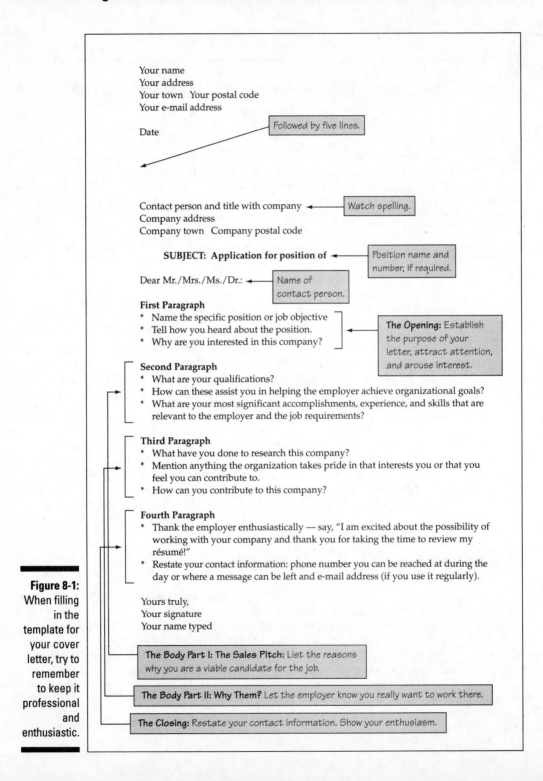

Your name
Your address
Your town   Your postal code
Your e-mail address

Date

> Followed by five lines.

Contact person and title with company ← Watch spelling.
Company address
Company town   Company postal code

SUBJECT: Application for position of ← Position name and number, if required.

Dear Mr./Mrs./Ms./Dr.: ← Name of contact person.

First Paragraph
* Name the specific position or job objective
* Tell how you heard about the position.
* Why are you interested in this company?

> **The Opening:** Establish the purpose of your letter, attract attention, and arouse interest.

Second Paragraph
* What are your qualifications?
* How can these assist you in helping the employer achieve organizational goals?
* What are your most significant accomplishments, experience, and skills that are relevant to the employer and the job requirements?

Third Paragraph
* What have you done to research this company?
* Mention anything the organization takes pride in that interests you or that you feel you can contribute to.
* How can you contribute to this company?

Fourth Paragraph
* Thank the employer enthusiastically — say, "I am excited about the possibility of working with your company and thank you for taking the time to review my résumé!"
* Restate your contact information: phone number you can be reached at during the day or where a message can be left and e-mail address (if you use it regularly).

Yours truly,
Your signature
Your name typed

> **The Body Part I: The Sales Pitch:** List the reasons why you are a viable candidate for the job.

> **The Body Part II: Why Them?** Let the employer know you really want to work there.

> **The Closing:** Restate your contact information. Show your enthusiasm.

Figure 8-1:
When filling in the template for your cover letter, try to remember to keep it professional and enthusiastic.

Jake Austin
65 Johnson Springs Road
Scarborough, ON M1V 1X3
E-mail: jakeaustin21@hotmail.com

June 24, 2002

Ms. Mariah Ryan, Human Resources Coordinator
ABC Software Management Inc.
Box 6191 Stn. Main
Winnipeg, MB   R1N 1B4

SUBJECT: Application for position of Help Desk Support Agent

Dear Ms. Ryan:

I was very interested to see your advertisement on HotJobs.ca for the position of Help Desk Support Agent. My personal career goal is to work for a progressive growing company such as yours, providing software support and network administration. When I reviewed your Web site, I was intrigued by your focus on creating software products for the forest industry. Having worked in the pulp mill in my hometown for three summers, I am enthusiastic about software systems that can improve the efficiency of forestry operations and would like to apply my computer programming background in this industry.

Throughout my career, I have demonstrated an ability to meet organizational objectives and demands. I work well with other individuals, and as such have been promoted to supervisory positions and given greater responsibilities. My education and work experience have exposed me to many aspects of the computing industry, including networks, technical support, Web page design, and programming. I am currently working toward my CCNA and A+ certifications, as I feel it is important to keep my industry knowledge up-to-date.

As I researched your company, I became very excited about the possibility of working for ABC Software Management Inc. and providing support for your programs. In addition to my strong technical skills and my forestry experience, I can bring excellent communication, analytical, and problem-solving skills to this position.

I have attached my current résumé for your consideration. I would be happy to have a preliminary discussion with you to see if we can establish a mutual interest. If my skills match your anticipated needs and you would like to schedule an interview, please call me at (416) 488-0833. I will be available at your convenience.

Yours truly,

Jake Austin

Jake Austin

Figure 8-2:
Your cover letter is your first introduction to who you are. Make sure you take the time to write one.

Before you start writing

Follow standard business letter format when you write your cover letter. Don't get fancy. From start to finish, here's a quick breakdown of the sections your letter should include. These sections are indicated in Figure 8-1. Refer to this list as you write.

- **Heading or Return Address:** Include your name, complete mailing address, and your e-mail address, if you like.

- **Date**

- **Inside Address:** Include the name and title of the person you are sending your application package to — likely the recruiter or the person who would be your supervisor, the full name of the company, and the complete mailing address. Make sure you spell the addressee's name correctly. Unsure? Phone the company and ask. We all like to see our name in print, but it isn't the same if it is misspelled — and they will see you didn't take the time to check. Remember, attention to detail is a transferable skill!

- **Subject Line:** Specify the position you're applying for, as well as the *position number* (this is the number the employer uses to track the position relative to others it has open. It's for their own records. The job ad, whether in a newspaper or on a Web site, will list this number.

- **Salutation:** Dear Mr./Mrs./Ms., Dear Sir or Dear Madame (with an "e"!). Dear Sir/Madame is also acceptable. Using a first name (Dear Ed), unless you know the addressee personally, isn't such a good idea. Again, make sure you spell the name right!

- **Opening:** This section is usually a single paragraph.

- **Body:** This one can be one or two paragraphs, usually two.

- **Closing:** This section is also usually one paragraph.

- **Signature:** Don't forget to give them your autograph.

First paragraph: The opening

In your opening paragraph, you want to establish the purpose of your letter, attract attention, and arouse interest.

Here are a few ways to open your letter:

- **State why you are writing by naming the specific position:** "I am excited about the possibility of being considered for the position of Heavy Duty Mechanic with ABC Company."

✔ **If you are not responding to a job ad but just fishing to see if anything is available, list your job objective here:** "I am very interested in becoming part of the Total Work Solutions team. If you are seeking a well-rounded Marketing Representative with experience in numerous sectors, my résumé may be of interest to you. I can bring to your company 15 years of experience in marketing and sales, including several years at a management level."

✔ **Tell the recruiter how you heard about the position:** "Your recent ad for a Database Administrator posted on HotJobs.ca caught my eye." Recruiters really appreciate this because it tells them where their ad is getting results.

✔ **Cash in on referrals, if you have them:** "I recently met a colleague of yours at the Alberta Congressboard annual conference in Jasper. He recommended your firm as one of the leading architectural shops in the Edmonton area and suggested you might have an opening for an up-and-coming architect with lots of enthusiasm, innovative ideas, and a great work ethic."

✔ **Insert a brief sentence that ties your interests in to what the company does:** "I referred to your Web site and was intrigued by the match between the software applications your company develops and my own extensive experience with database development."

Second paragraph: The sales pitch

The objective of this section is to list the reasons why you are a great candidate for this job. Remember that list you made earlier in the chapter? This is where you get to use that information. Focus on what the recruiter is looking for and use some of the words from the advertisement if possible.

In the second paragraph of your cover letter, you need to do the following:

✔ **Provide an overview of your qualifications:** "I believe my M.B.A., combined with my background in computer programming and management, would enable me to quickly understand and resolve client-related issues as Client Services Manager with your firm."

Suggest how your qualifications would allow you to help the company achieve its organizational goals. Be sure to focus on how you can help the employer rather than why you want the job.

✔ **Talk about what you *can do* for *this company* rather than what you *have done* for other companies:** "My strong sales skills and client base in your industry will help you to significantly increase your sales."

Or

"I can bring to the position of Quality Assurance Coordinator a strong ability to troubleshoot software problems."

✔ **Highlight your most significant skills and accomplishments, education, and employment history that are relevant to the employer and the job requirements:** "My combined knowledge of management and information technology would allow me to relate to your clients and would enhance my ability to understand their problems. I am intrigued by the mission statement on your Web site and especially your combined focus on growth while maintaining client service. I believe I have the experience and the skills to help you achieve this goal."

If you can pick out one or two things about the job that appeal to you and link your experience and interests to these, you have the beginnings of a great cover letter.

Third paragraph: Why them?

This is the part a recruiter really likes to see. It is where you show that you have actually done some research and really want to work for him. Not the guy down the road, but him! And then you get to tell him why. Here are a few ways to let an employer know you really want to work for him, and aren't just sending out résumés at random:

✔ **Explain *what* you have done to research this company:** "In checking out your Web site . . ."

✔ **Mention anything the organization takes pride in that interests you or that you feel you can contribute to:** "I was especially intrigued by the recent award your company received for Excellence in Customer Service. I would very much welcome the opportunity to apply my strong public relations skills to enhance your service focus."

✔ **How can you contribute to this company? What do you have to offer them?** "I am a published writer with 10 years of copywriting experience. I can bring to your company a fresh perspective plus the experience of writing for many different media."

Fourth paragraph: The closing

Make it easy for the employer to contact you by restating your contact information here. Try to find a way to show your enthusiasm without going overboard. This is your final chance to make an impression.

Here are a few closing statements to end your cover letter with style:

✔ **Hoping to hear from you:** These closings aren't aggressive, but do leave the impression that you'd really like to talk to them further.

"I am excited about the possibility of working with your company and appreciate you taking the time to review my résumé! Until we meet, thank you for taking a closer look at my qualifications."

"My résumé will give you a better indication of the skills that I can bring to this position. Please give me a call to discuss this further."

"Thank you for your time. I look forward to hearing from you."

"Thank you for taking the time to look at my résumé. I would appreciate the opportunity to speak with you personally."

✔ **A little push:** These closings go a step further than those above. By providing contact information, you gently pressure the reader to contact you.

"I will be in Edmonton [or wherever the job is] on [list a date]. Is there any chance we can meet to discuss how I can be of benefit to your company? I can be contacted at [phone number/e-mail address]."

"Your consideration of my qualifications is much appreciated. You can reach me at my home phone [list] or by e-mail [list] if you wish to discuss this further."

"Do you need more information than I have included on my résumé? I would be pleased to answer any of your questions. You can call me at [list phone number] or e-mail me at [list]."

✔ **Pushing harder:** Telling the employer how and when you will get back to her is a common approach used by sales teams and more aggressive job hunters. Experts are split on whether this tactic works. For those of you who prefer this approach, here are a few ideas for closings:

"I look forward to speaking with you personally to discuss your specific needs and my ability to meet them. I will call you next week to see if there is any additional information you require."

"I welcome a personal interview to discuss how my qualifications can enhance your company. I will e-mail you next week to see if we can meet."

"I will be in touch within a few days to confirm your receipt of my résumé and to answer any questions. I realize your time is valuable and I appreciate your consideration."

One thing to keep in mind if you are applying for a sales job is that your sales ability and the effort you put into closing the "sale" could be what sets you apart from the rest. You need to consider the company and industry to which you are applying before deciding what type of closing to use.

A few more tips

If you are asked to include your salary expectations in your cover letter, you have a couple of options:

- ✔ **Ignore the request and do not include it.** Most companies won't hold this against you because they realize it is to their advantage, not yours, to declare this up front.

- ✔ **Suggest a range.** You can research salary ranges for this type of job and say where you think you would fall based on your experience. "I believe the salary range for this position is $27,000 to $35,000. With my seven years' experience in a similar position, I think I would be in the higher end of the range." Check out Chapter 18 for more on researching salaries.

- ✔ **Tell them what you want.** I don't recommend this because it takes away your negotiating power later and could potentially put you out of the running if your expectations are too high. Once you have had a chance to sell yourself as the best candidate, you have more negotiating power.

- ✔ **Rely on their sense of fairness.** Tell them you believe they will pay within fair market value for the position. I recommend this approach because, while you do address salary, you still have room to maneuver. Try this on: "Regarding my salary expectations, I trust that your company pays fair market value for this position. I am prepared to discuss actual salary when we get further along in the recruitment process."

Balance professionalism with friendliness in the tone of your cover letter. Keep it professional, but not uptight! On the other hand, there is such a thing as being too friendly.

Out of these three examples, strive for the balanced approach:

- ✔ **Totally uptight:** "I am interested in a position with your company because I believe my credentials precisely match your needs. I am available at your convenience to discuss a possible mutually beneficial employment relationship."

- ✔ **Too friendly:** "Hey, I know you don't know me from Adam, but if you give me half a chance, I'll show you what I am made of (ha, ha). Just kidding, but I am worth a shot. Believe me!"

- ✔ **Tactfully balanced:** "After looking at this position and your company in more detail, I am intrigued by the opportunity you have available. I hope you don't mind if I call you next week to discuss this a little further."

Online inspiration

You can also refer to these Web sites if you need a little more help with your cover letter:

✔ **About.com** (`jobsearchtech.about.com`): This Web site provides cover letter tips and links to other cover letter sites.

✔ **Career Toolbox** (`www.myfuture.com`): This site, while geared in many respects to new graduates, gives great information on

how to write a cover letter, complete with tips on do's and don'ts and sample letters.

✔ **The Riley Guide** (`www.rileyguide.com/letters.html`): The Riley Guide is a comprehensive job-hunting Web site. Not surprisingly, it has a section devoted to cover letter writing.

Here are a few more things to remember when putting together your cover letter:

✔ **Proofread your letter.** It's a reflection of your communication abilities. Typing errors and spelling mistakes won't wash — the recruiter _will_ notice!

✔ **If you are sending your résumé by snail mail, print your cover letter on the same quality white or off-white paper as your résumé.** Use the same font as you did in your résumé for continuity's sake. You want to present a visually appealing package.

✔ **Send your letter and résumé in a full-sized envelope.** Don't fold it. Include a return address and make sure you use enough postage.

Keep a record of each application package that you send out, for follow-up purposes.

The Electronic Cover Letter

An _electronic cover letter,_ often called an _electronic cover note_ or an _e-cover note,_ is an e-mail form of a cover letter. You have several options with respect to cover letters when applying for jobs online:

✔ You can have a _brief_ e-cover note and then attach your full cover letter and résumé as an attachment to the e-mail.

✔ You can have an electronic cover letter with the main elements of a cover letter and attach your résumé only.

- You can have an electronic cover letter and cut and paste your résumé into the body of the e-mail. See Chapter 9 for information on how to create plain-text documents.

- You can do the cut and paste thing and then follow up with a full-fledged cover letter and résumé attached to the e-mail.

My own preference is to adapt the cover letter to a shorter e-cover note and cut and paste the résumé into the e-mail. Include a statement like: "In case it works better for you, I am also forwarding my résumé and cover letter as an attachment." Follow this with another e-mail with the formatted cover letter/ résumé attached. Here's why I think it's worth the extra effort:

- It is reasonably easy to write your electronic version of a cover letter once you have a longer version to work from.

- You don't want your e-cover note to get separated from your résumé. File storage is much simpler when you are dealing with just an e-mail or a word processing file — not both.

- This gives you the opportunity to send a formatted résumé as well as the plain-Jane version.

- If something goes wrong in the first e-mail transfer and your plain-text cover note and résumé appear as anything but plain to the recruiter when she opens your e-mail, you have a second chance to get it right when you send the formatted versions of your cover letter and résumé in a separate e-mail.

- Your name is likely to stick in the recruiter's mind (having seen it twice already!).

Some of the other job-hunting books out there tell you to send your résumé and cover letter in separate attachments, but I like to step outside the box. Some recruiters, including myself, prefer to have both the cover letter and résumé in the same document. It's more convenient. Sending them as separate attachments is like sending two envelopes — one for your résumé and another for your cover letter.

Whichever option you choose, you will still need to introduce yourself and your résumé in an e-mail. Electronic cover letters are much shorter than the full meal deal because the rules of communication change when it comes to e-mail messages — people, including recruiters, don't like to read long e-mail. It's a bit more of a challenge to condense the information in your cover letter into a few short paragraphs and still capture the interest of the recruiter. But it can be done! Check out the sample e-cover note in Figure 8-3. It's an electronic version of the cover letter in Figure 8-2.

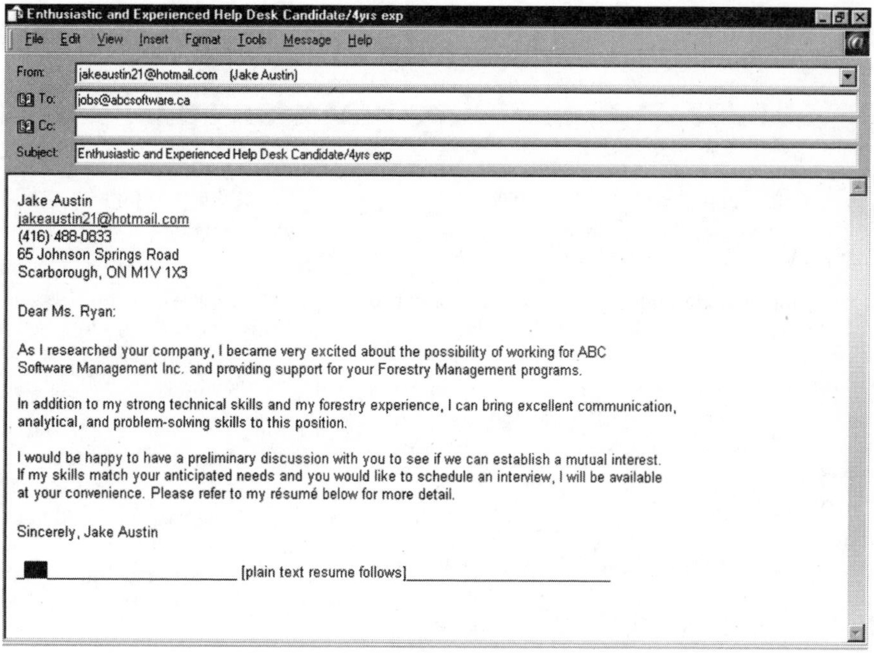

Figure 8-3:
Your e-cover
note should
entice the
recruiter to
read further.

```
Enthusiastic and Experienced Help Desk Candidate/4yrs exp
File   Edit   View   Insert   Format   Tools   Message   Help

From:     jakeaustin21@hotmail.com   (Jake Austin)
To:       jobs@abcsoftware.ca
Cc:
Subject:  Enthusiastic and Experienced Help Desk Candidate/4yrs exp

Jake Austin
jakeaustin21@hotmail.com
(416) 488-0833
65 Johnson Springs Road
Scarborough, ON M1V 1X3

Dear Ms. Ryan:

As I researched your company, I became very excited about the possibility of working for ABC
Software Management Inc. and providing support for your Forestry Management programs.

In addition to my strong technical skills and my forestry experience, I can bring excellent communication,
analytical, and problem-solving skills to this position.

I would be happy to have a preliminary discussion with you to see if we can establish a mutual interest.
If my skills match your anticipated needs and you would like to schedule an interview, I will be available
at your convenience. Please refer to my résumé below for more detail.

Sincerely, Jake Austin

_____ [plain text resume follows]_____
```

Keep it short, and content is king

The first thing to remember about an e-cover note is to keep it short. People
don't read lengthy e-mails! So get to the meat right away! The next thing to
remember is that content is king: What your e-cover note says is far more
important than how it looks. So spend your time on getting the content right
rather than trying out fancy e-mail formatting techniques. Chances are the
fancy formatting will get lost or transformed in cyberspace, anyway.

Please, don't hit Delete!

You're going after the same goal with your e-cover note as with a regular-length
cover letter: grabbing the recruiter's attention and enticing her to actually
open the e-mail message (rather than hit the Delete key), which, lo and
behold, just happens to contain your résumé. Every e-mail has a subject line.
What you put in that line can either entice the recruiter to read further or to
move on to her next e-mail. Your subject line should be catchy but not goofy.

Cover letter mistakes that aren't easily erased

Other than what I consider the cardinal sin of job hunting — not even sending a cover letter — here are a few things to be aware of that could cost you an interview:

- **A lack of coherence between your résumé and cover letter:** Make sure that the objective in your cover letter matches the objective in your résumé. I once received an application package with a cover letter that indicated the applicant was applying for the position of Intermediate Help Desk Agent. That seemed fine, since that was the position I was recruiting for. Then I looked at the accompanying résumé, which indicated that the same applicant's objective was apparently to work for a premier Web design company creating groovy Internet sites. Uh, excuse me?

- **A lack of relevance:** Only highlight the skills, education, and work experience that relate directly to the job you're applying for.

- **Being sloppy:** Cover letters with typing or grammatical errors are not acceptable. Your cover letter doesn't have to be fancy, but it should be neat and professional looking. Keep to a standard business format. Proofread your cover letter, and then have someone else proofread it for you. Pay attention to detail. Nobody's impressed when you misspell their name, and this holds especially true for prospective employers.

- **Focusing on your faults:** Confessing your shortcomings can eliminate you from the running, right off the bat. Try to emphasize your strengths, rather than draw attention to your weaknesses. Instead of writing something like, "While I have no experience in this area, I am a fast learner," try this: "I can bring to your company a great attitude, a willingness to learn, and exceptional organi-

zational and communication skills combined with a solid technical base." Wow, this applicant sounds great!

- **Hitting an off-colour tone:** Being overly assertive can be mistaken as being pushy, and that will turn potential employers off. Don't be goofy in your cover letter, either. Try to show enthusiasm without seeming silly.

- **Making demands:** Stay away from statements that make demands on the employer. For example, something like, "I am interested in a growth-oriented position where I will be adequately challenged and compensated," puts the onus on the employer to challenge you and pay you well. Instead, word your letter in terms of what you can do for the employer: "I would like the opportunity to apply my strong organizational and sales skills to help your company expand and thrive."

- **Sounding arrogant:** Don't write something along these lines: "I already have an attractive offer but would like to explore this opportunity with you," unless you are, frankly, an incredible catch. The subtext here says, "If you don't grab me now, you'll lose me!" The recruiter won't like the connotation. Most recruiters will be less than heartbroken to lose someone with an attitude like that.

- **Sounding desperate:** "I have been out of work for six months and desperately need this job to pay my rent!" is not what the recruiter wants to hear. She may feel sorry for you, but she's unlikely to consider your application for this reason alone. She wants to know what you can do for the company, not the other way around. This will be one of the first applications to hit the dreaded paper shredder.

Here are a few examples of subject lines that work:

- ✔ Enthusiastic geologist looking for work
- ✔ Very interested in position of . . .
- ✔ My skills match your needs

Make your e-content count

The body of your e-cover note is organized somewhat differently from your non-virtual cover letter, because you need to keep it short. Information that's essential in a regular cover letter, such as the date and the employer's address, don't need to be included. Here is a quick overview to help you build your e-cover letter:

- ✔ **Salutation:** Use the name of the person in the job ad or "Dear Sir/Madame."

- ✔ **Body:** Keep it to one or two paragraphs. Focus on showing them that you have researched the job and how you can benefit the company. Bring in helpful information, like a referral.

- ✔ **Closing:** Tell them that you will contact them in the near future, or how they can get in touch with you, and refer them to your résumé for more information.

If you paste your e-cover note and résumé directly into the body of a single e-mail, put your contact information at the top of the message field instead of at the top of your résumé, which will begin farther down, after your e-cover note. Most résumé data systems read from the top of the e-mail down, so it makes sense to have your vital statistics come first.

Chapter 9

Cyber-Résumés

In This Chapter

▶ Preparing your résumé for a journey through cyberspace

▶ Knowing when to use a formatted, scannable, or plain text résumé

▶ Protecting your privacy online

So if it wasn't enough trying to put together a well-organized, neatly formatted résumé, now you have to think about developing an electronic résumé as well? Why can't you just cut and paste your résumé into the body of an e-mail or send it as an attachment? For that matter, why do you have to apply electronically for jobs at all? Whatever happened to good old snail mail, bond paper, and the telephone?

Today, because the Internet is so accessible, a single online job ad can draw hundreds of applications. Many employers are using the Internet as a tool to find qualified employees; some are using online recruiting exclusively. Becoming e-savvy with your résumé can increase your chances of being hired. That's why you need to take the résumé that you so painstakingly developed and do even more work on it! Sorry folks — but it will be worth it in the long run.

There are three commonly used electronic résumé formats:

✔ Formatted

✔ Scannable

✔ Plain text

In this chapter, I tell you all you need to know about these formats, how to modify your résumé to fit each of them, and when to use them. I also discuss online privacy concerns that you should consider when you take the leap into cyberspace job hunting.

A (Brief!) Introduction to Online Job Hunting

Whether we like it or not (and some of us do!), technology has entered our lives and we either have to go with the flow or be swept aside by the wave. With quick and easy access to the World Wide Web, many Canadians are incorporating online resources into their job-hunting game plan. At the same time, Canadian (and other) employers are using the Internet to recruit job hunters like you, because it is accessible, inexpensive, reasonably easy to use, and expands the scope of the search to attract candidates from across Canada and — if required — beyond.

You don't have to look far to find jobs online. Though I dive into this in more detail in Part III, it's worth telling you about some of the types of Web sites you'll likely be logging on to, searching through, and maybe posting your résumé to. There are online job banks, such as HotJobs.ca (www.hotjobs.ca), which have job postings and career-management features. Industry-specific Web sites, also known as niche sites, carry job postings within a particular occupation or industry. An example of this type of site is CanadaIT.com (www.canadait.com). There are also location-specific Web sites, which carry job postings within a particular geographic location, such as a region, province, or city. Company Web sites are another great place to look for jobs, as well as to find out a little about the company's products and corporate culture. You can also check out e-mail lists and online newsgroups. More on all of these in Chapter 13.

Employers look for an efficient way to manage the large number of résumés they receive when they hire online. Many of them use electronic tools, such as an *applicant tracking system* — software that lets a computer sort and store résumés according to criteria the employer specifies, and a *résumé management system* — a computer program that organizes résumés. Some use *search and retrieve software* that scans a résumé and uses keyword searches to match the résumé (and the person behind it) with a job in the organization.

There are several methods of submitting your electronic résumé:

- E-mailing your résumé directly to an employer in the body of an e-mail or as an attachment.

- Posting your formatted résumé to an online job bank, where it is stored for you. When you find a job you want to apply to, you submit your résumé to the employer directly from the site. Some online job banks that offer this service include HotJobs.ca (www.hotjobs.ca), Workopolis.com (www.workopolis.com), and Monster.ca (www.monster.ca). Something you may not realize is that if you post your résumé to one of these job banks, employers who have paid to do so can check out your résumé (without you knowing it) and contact you directly if they're interested. Find out what the site's privacy policy is and make sure you are comfortable with it before you post.

✔ Filling in an online form on an employment Web site and submitting the form to an employer. In this scenario, you don't submit your actual résumé, but fill in pre-selected blanks on the form. Employers often set these forms up to make it easier for them to shortlist candidates.

✔ Posting your résumé to your personal Web site.

"Oh, no!" I hear you saying. "Does this mean I have to develop yet another résumé?" The good news is, no, you don't need another résumé, you just have to change the look of your current or *base résumé*, and add a few *keywords*. Résumé scanning programs look for keywords that are related to the job in question and shortlist résumés accordingly. See "The Scannable Résumé" in this chapter for more on putting keywords in your résumé.

Creating Your Electronic Résumé

There are a few technical things you need to do to make your base chronological, functional, or combination résumé cyber-friendly. You don't have to substantially revise the content of your base résumé to do so — except to adapt the résumé to the individual job you are applying for.

You should have your résumé available in three electronic versions:

✔ **A formatted version:** This is essentially the résumé you put together in Chapter 6 and made better in Chapter 7. It contains various fonts, bullets, italics, and other displays of formatting wizardry. You can use this résumé when a job ad asks you to submit your résumé as an e-mail attachment.

Some online job banks, such as Workopolis (www.workopolis.com), let you post a formatted résumé. In some cases, though, the job bank changes the résumé to plain text, which dumps all the fancy formatting and adds strange characters instead. If you store a résumé on an online job bank, make sure you go back in and check the format afterward.

✔ **A scannable version:** Wait, where did all that fancy formatting go? You want to be sure that your résumé will scan properly, so get rid of all the bullets, frilly fonts, and italics. In this version of your electronic résumé, in particular, use *keywords* that will be picked up by the employer's search-and-retrieve software. Use this résumé when a job ad asks you to submit a scannable résumé or when you have some reason to believe a company might be using résumé scanning software to sort and shortlist résumés. See the section on "Scannable Résumés" for tips on when to send out a scannable version of your résumé.

✔ **A plain text version:** This is the *ASCII* (American Standard Code for Information Interchange) text version that you often hear about. Your plain text résumé is the one you use to paste into the body of an e-mail or cut and paste into online application forms. The reason you use plain text (ASCII) is that not all e-mail programs read formatted text the same way. I can't count the number of times I have received résumés with tonnes of gobbledegook in them because they got warped in cyberspace. Use plain text to make sure your résumé looks the same when it arrives at its destination as when it left.

Here are some great Web sites that you can access to help you make your résumé flow smoothly through cyberspace:

✔ **Rebecca Smith's eRésumés and Resources** (www.eresumes.com): A well-known and highly recommended site to help you design an electronic résumé. You can also view many different samples of résumés on this site at www.eresumes.com/gallery_rezcat.html.

✔ **The Riley Guide** (www.rileyguide.com/eresume.html): The Riley guide includes tips on résumé writing, and electronic résumés in particular. This site also contains an excellent collection of tips on job-hunting.

The Formatted Résumé

The traditional word processor–formatted résumé, shown in Figure 9-1, still has a use today — especially if you mail, fax, or deliver it to a prospective employer. If you are asked to send your résumé as an e-mail attachment using a specific word processing program (such as a .doc attachment), great! You can keep the formatting, and your résumé will look the same when the recruiter opens the file.

A couple of points to keep in mind about sending your faithful formatted résumé electronically: Some employers don't accept résumés as e-mail attachments because of the possibility of viruses lurking in the file. In addition, there is no guarantee the recruiter uses the same word processing program as you do — in which case, the formatting may be messed up anyway. So, there is no guarantee your résumé will be received, let alone that the attachment can be opened and read. But you can always phone and follow up to find out and it's a great excuse.

When you send your résumé electronically as an e-mail attachment, try to apply the tips in this list to make it easier for the employer to read:

✔ Include a plain text résumé and plain text e-cover letter in the *text* of the e-mail message. That way, if the recruiter does not want to open an attachment, she doesn't have to do so.

✔ Include a reference to the job in the subject line of the e-mail.

Brianna Maxwell
Box 6412
Edmonton, AB
T6E 1X7
780-888-5521
E-mail: bmaxwell@hotmail.com

OBJECTIVE
To acquire a position in Office Administration where I can make a difference to the bottom line of the company by offering superior customer service and skills.

SUMMARY OF QUALIFICATIONS
I have over 15 years' experience in Office Administration. I have developed strong organizational, time management, and customer service skills working in a single-person office. My technical skills include strong computer skills, bookkeeping, telephone skills, and overall office management.

EMPLOYMENT HISTORY

1999 - Present   Canadian Tire   Edmonton, AB
Service Representative
- Customer service and follow-ups
- Supervised Service Department
- Responsible for depot returns and special orders

1992 - 1999   Black Office Systems   Edmonton, AB
Office Administrator
- Responsible for overall office administration and customer relations
- Proficient in Excel, Rbase, Simply Accounting, Word
- Filing, typing, accounts receivable, and payroll

1985 - 1992   Kings Auto Body   Edmonton, AB
Office Administrator
- Responsible for overall operation of office
- Computerized accounting
- Word processing
- Customer service and receptionist

EDUCATION
1984   Clerk Typist Course   Yellowhead Region Education Consortium
1976   Small Business Accounting   Lakeland College

Other courses: Computer training, Customer service, Employment standards, Credit operations and collections, WCB workshop, Bookkeeping/payroll for small business

INTERESTS
Camping, fishing, travel, reading

Figure 9-1:
A formatted résumé can use highlights, fonts, tabs, and bullets to make it more visually appealing.

✔ Send your résumé and cover letter as one file. A lot of job-hunting books tell you to send them as separate files, but that's like sending two envelopes! (Most recruiters just cut and paste them into one file, anyway, so you might as well lighten their load from the start.)

✔ Save your résumé using the **Save As** function to an earlier version of your word processing program. You may be using Microsoft Word 2002, but there is no guarantee that the person opening your document has that updated version of the software — they may still be working on Word 5. An earlier version of a software program often cannot open a document created by a newer version unless the sender has saved the document as an earlier version.

Read the job ad carefully and follow the instructions; recruiters provide them for a reason. They may specify that you send a plain text résumé included with your formatted résumé, in the text of your message, or ask you to submit your résumé as a TXT (plain text) or DOC (formatted résumé) attachment or a scannable résumé instead of a formatted one. Looking for a job isn't one of those enterprises where you're easily granted a second chance. If you send the wrong format by accident, it'll end up in the discard pile.

The Scannable Résumé

A *scannable résumé* is a semi-plain print résumé that a recruiter scans into a computer database using optical scanners. The résumé scanning program reads the résumé and records the applicant's relevant skills and accomplishments, education, and employment history in the form of predefined, industry- and job-specific *keywords*. Résumé scanning software speeds up the shortlisting process by only retrieving résumés in which specified keywords appear.

Résumé scanning software may be part of an electronic applicant tracking system used by companies to manage and shortlist the résumés they receive.

If you think your résumé will be scanned, you need to make it scanner-friendly. How will you know? One way is to ask — call the recruiter or send an e-mail. The larger the company, the more likely that it uses some sort of résumé scanning software, along with an applicant tracking system. To be on the safe side, you could assume your résumé will be scanned, and send out your scannable version as a matter of course.

You can mail, fax, or e-mail your scannable résumé to a recruiter. It's all the same to the scanning program.

Creating your scannable résumé

Your scannable résumé needs to be simply formatted to ensure that the scanner accurately converts it to *searchable pure text* (text that can be read by the computer). Some people advise that you omit bullets, italics, bold, and tabs, but I don't think you need to go quite that far. Those formatting elements can remain in your scannable résumé, as long as you also keep a few points in mind. Use your formatted résumé as a base. (See Chapter 6.) Make sure you adapt the résumé to your specific job goal and add keywords related to your target job throughout the text of the résumé.

The key to a super-scannable résumé is to use a *sans serif* font, such as Helvetica or Geneva, without decorative flourishes at the ends of the letters. Scanning programs have difficulty interpreting serif fonts like Times New Roman. Choose a type size between 10 and 14 points. Arial is a good font to use. Your scannable résumé should look clean and simple but not stark, like the example in Figure 9-2.

Here are a few more points to remember when you prepare your scannable résumé:

- ✔ Two-column pages can be misinterpreted — translated into machine language using each line as a résumé line and not taking columns into account — as the résumé scanning software usually scans from left to right.

- ✔ Leave out the pretty pictures and graphics. They usually cannot be interpreted.

- ✔ Add a space before and after slashes (/) so the letters do not touch.

- ✔ Use solid bullets instead of open ones, which can be interpreted as the letter "O."

- ✔ Omit ampersands, percentage signs, and foreign characters, as they may not scan properly.

- ✔ Use italics and bold, as long as the letters don't end up touching as a result of the formatting. ***This usually doesn't happen with a sans serif font.***

- ✔ Make sure you have keywords throughout the résumé that apply to your target job. This increases the likelihood that the company's scanning software will shortlist your résumé. However, don't add keywords that don't accurately and truthfully describe you and the skills and experience you have.

- ✔ If you're mailing your résumé via post instead of e-mailing it, use plain white paper, and don't staple the pages. Use a full-size envelope to avoid creases in the résumé that might ruin the scan.

Brianna Maxwell
780-888-5521
Box 6412
Edmonton, AB
T6E 1X7
E-mail: bmaxwell@hotmail.com

OBJECTIVE
To acquire a position in Office Administration where I can make a difference to the bottom line of the company by offering superior customer service and skills.

SUMMARY OF QUALIFICATIONS
- I have over 15 years' experience in Office Administration.
- I have developed strong organizational, time management, and customer service skills working in a single-person office.
- My technical skills include computer skills, bookkeeping, telephone skills, and overall office management.

EMPLOYMENT HISTORY

1999 - Present **Service Representative** Canadian Tire Edmonton, AB
Duties: Customer service and follow-ups; Supervised Service Department
Responsible for depot returns and special orders

1992 - 1999 **Office Administrator** Black Office Systems Edmonton, AB
Duties: Responsible for overall office administration and customer relations; Proficient in Excel, Rbase, Simply Accounting, Word; Filing, typing, accounts receivable, and payroll

1985 - 1992 **Office Administrator** Kings Auto Body Edmonton, AB
Duties: Responsible for overall operation of office; Computerized accounting; Word processing; Customer service and reception

EDUCATION
1984 Clerk Typist Course Yellowhead Region Education Consortium
1976 Small Business Accounting Lakeland College

Other courses: Computer training, Customer service, Employment standards, Credit operations and collections, WCB workshop, Bookkeeping/payroll for small business

INTERESTS
Camping, fishing, travel, reading

Figure 9-2:
The scannable résumé looks plain and simple but still gets your point across.

The word on keywords

A *keyword* is a descriptive word or phrase that you include in the scannable version of your résumé and that a company's applicant tracking system then uses to match your résumé to a given job. When a position becomes available, the recruiter has the task of defining a group of keywords that relate to the job and inputting these into the system. When the résumé scanning program scans and reads the résumés that have been submitted, it looks for these keywords. The more keywords you have on your résumé that apply to the job, the more likely it is that your résumé will make the short list. So, make sure your scannable résumé has a good number of keywords that relate to the job you're applying for, the skills required, and perhaps also to the industry in general.

The keywords you select will come from reviewing the job ad to see what skills, education, and work experience they're after and incorporating these into your résumé. You can (and should) also research the industry in general to see if you can locate any buzzwords there. Keywords can be job titles, skills, computer programs, degrees, languages spoken, abilities — anything you think the employer is looking for. If you are a computer programmer who specializes in Visual Basic and are looking for that kind of job, put the keywords "programmer" and "Visual Basic" in your scannable résumé. If you are looking for a job in human resources, include the keywords and phrases "negotiations," "labour relations," "employee relations," "human resources," "good people skills," "employee benefits," "recruiting," "selection," "interviewing," "reference checks," "union," "collective bargaining," or "training."

Another way to identify keywords is to contact the recruiter to get more information on what he is looking for. (This is a good tactic both to get noticed and to increase your list of keywords.) If you're replying to a job ad, look for keywords in the description of duties and the qualifications required. You can also search occupational descriptions. Coming up with the relevant keywords to use on your résumé is key to making a short list. When you are doing your industry research, you will likely come across industry-specific jargon or lingo which, some recruiters suggest, you should try to include in the text of your résumé because the words could be picked up by scanning software and increase your chances of being shortlisted. One way to make sure they stand out in your résumé is to include a section called Relevant Keywords.

It's a good practice to include keywords in any electronic style of résumé (including formatted and plain text), in case a recruiter scans all résumés and doesn't let you know, or uses a more high-tech applicant tracking system that doesn't require résumé scanning software. While not currently widespread, this type of advanced tracking system could be the norm in the future.

The Plain Text (ASCII) Résumé

The *plain text résumé* is aptly named — it's really plain Jane. It's a not-so-pretty version of your résumé that you either submit in the text of an e-mail, post to an online application form (where you fill in the blanks for spaces like address, objective, education, and experience), or post to an online job bank, like HotJobs.ca (`www.hotjobs.ca`), which allows you to cut and paste your entire résumé onto the site. Submitting your electronic résumé in plain text is the fastest way to get it to an employer, but in order for it to make its way through cyberspace and reach its destination with everything intact, you need to dump the fancy formatting and use *ASCII* (American Standard Code for Information Interchange) plain text format — a very basic computer language used so that computers around the world can communicate with each other.

If you send the regular formatted version of your résumé in the body of an e-mail, you may be doing the cyber-equivalent of putting paper through a shredder. What comes out the other end could be unintelligible. Chances are that lines will end up cut off and your résumé will be filled with all sorts of gobbledegook (like a bullet turning into *&43*-#)*, unrelated letters, and funny figures. Rather than try to decipher it, the recruiter may just toss it into the discard pile. To avoid this, you need to send a plain text résumé, with no formatting.

Many online job banks require you to fill in a form, rather than allowing you to save and submit your neatly formatted résumé. Your best bet to ensure that your résumé looks good and is readable when it's posted online is to cut and paste your plain text résumé into the boxes in the form. If you paste your formatted résumé into the boxes, it likely will be converted to plain text anyway, and you could end up with an unintelligible mess!

Creating your plain text résumé

The simplest way to convert your résumé into plain text is to use the **Save As** function in your word processing program and save your formatted résumé as a Text Only file type or a Plain Text file type. Your program will advise you that you will lose some formatting when you do this, but that's okay — it's what we've been trying to do all along! (Very considerate of your program to let you know, though.) Another way of converting and editing a plain text résumé is to copy your formatted résumé into a *plain-text editor* (such as Notepad or Wordpad) and edit out the fancy formatting there.

When you reopen your résumé in plain text résumé format, be prepared for a shock. The plain text format doesn't support any of the formatting that most of us love — it will look pretty stark (see Figure 9-3). It doesn't support tabs, centring, or special characters (&, %, #), either. But hang on, you're not done

Other types of ASCII file formats

There are three popular file formats for electronic résumés, all coded in ASCII:

✔ **Plain text format, identified by the TXT file extension:** This is the most versatile and popular format. Most word processing packages give you the option to save your résumé in this format.

✔ **Rich text format, identified by the RTF file extension:** This format allows more formatting options and is compatible with most word processing software. Use a rich text file if you are not sure what word processing package the receiver is using.

✔ **Hypertext format, identified by the HTM or HTML file extension:** Use this format to post your résumé to your own Web site. It can be a great way to display a portfolio of your work and add detail to your résumé. However, you still have to attract people to your Web site to see it.

yet. In order to make your plain text résumé sail glitch-free through cyberspace and be intelligible to the person reading it at the other end, you may need to do some cleanup.

Be sure to go through this checklist for plain text résumés:

✔ Use a *fixed-width typeface,* such as Courier, because each letter takes up a fixed amount of space. If you were to use a *proportional typeface,* such as Times New Roman, the spaces between the letters are adjusted so that they look a little better, but, because of this, you won't know when you actually have 65 characters in a line (unless you count each character). I tell why this is important later in this section.

✔ Check your e-mail settings if you are going to e-mail your plain text résumé. Keep the font standard (Courier is a safe bet) and make sure your e-mail sending format is plain text, not html. If you send the résumé in html, it includes a lot of Internet-related codes that make the document difficult to read. Test by sending your résumé to yourself, a couple of friends — hey, even your mom.

✔ Use CAPITAL LETTERS for section headers because bold, italic, and underlines will not show up.

✔ Use the space bar to indent lines; do not use Tab or Indent.

✔ Avoid columns and use spaces instead. You know how nice columns look when you format your résumé and how easy it is to find information when you have a heading in one column and the information next to it? Well, when you save a column as plain text, it doesn't recognize any of the indents, tabs, or column formatting. Your pretty columns end up all over the place!

```
Brianna Maxwell
780-888-5521
Box 6412
Edmonton, AB
T6E 1X7
E-mail:  bmaxwell@hotmail.com


OBJECTIVE
To acquire a position in Office Administration where I can make a
difference to the bottom line of the company by offering superior customer
service and skills.


SUMMARY OF QUALIFICATIONS

I have over 15 years of experience in Office Administration.
I have developed strong organizational, time management, and customer
service skills working in a single-person office.
My technical skills include computer skills, bookkeeping, telephone
skills, and overall office management.


EMPLOYMENT HISTORY

1999 - Present    Service Representative    Canadian Tire    Edmonton, AB
Duties: Customer service and follow-ups; Supervised Service Department;
Responsible for depot returns and special orders

1992 - 1999    Office Administrator    Black Office Systems    Edmonton, AB
Duties: Responsible for overall office administration and customer
relations; Proficient in Excel, Rbase, Simply Accounting, Word; Filing,
typing, accounts receivable, and payroll

1985 - 1992    Office Administrator    Kings Auto Body    Edmonton, AB
Duties: Responsible for overall operation of office; Computerized
accounting; Word processing; Customer service and reception


EDUCATION
1984    Clerk Typist Course    Yellowhead Region Education Consortium
1976    Small Business Accounting    Lakeland College

Other courses:
Computer training, Customer service, Employment standards, Credit
operations and collections, WCB workshop, Bookkeeping/payroll for small
business


INTERESTS

Camping, fishing, travel, reading
```

Figure 9-3:
The purpose of a plain text résumé is not to look pretty but to get the information to an employer in a format she can read.

- ✔ Change bullets to an asterisk (*) , hyphen (-), or plus sign (+).

- ✔ Omit special characters like em-dashes or smart quotes.

- ✔ Use lines of asterisks or hyphens to make sections stand out in the text. This is a good tool for subheadings that are bolded in the formatted résumé.

One problem with saving your résumé as plain text is that your lines may end up not being the same length (you may have three words on one line and 15 on the next). You don't have this problem with formatted word processed documents because they all have an automatic *word wrap,* which starts a new line automatically when you get to the maximum characters one line can hold. To make sure the receiving computer gets a document that doesn't have sentence fragments, keep your line width to 65 characters and hit **Enter** at the end of each line. Yes, this is a pain, but if you don't do it, you can end up with lines ending in odd places, which makes your résumé look very disjointed. Here's a tip: Put a sticky note on your monitor where the 65 characters is and just hit **Enter** each time your line gets to that point.

Another thing to be aware of when you convert to plain text format is that headers join footers at the bottom of your résumé. So, if you've formatted your name and address as a header, be sure to move it back up into the actual text. Delete any footers, such as page numbers, because they too require special codes that plain text can't read. You never know what characters you will end up with!

Most important, don't try to make your ASCII résumé fancy — no one expects a plain text résumé to have all the bells and whistles.

Sending your plain text résumé

If you have never done it, you may be concerned about how you go about putting your plain text résumé online. Have no fear! It's a piece of cake. While all online job banks do things slightly differently, it's basically a case of first registering on the Web site, then following the site's instructions to cut and paste your résumé into the right place. Make sure you go back and view your résumé to see what it looks like after you have gone through the instructions on the site. Directions may not have been entirely clear and your résumé may end up missing important pieces of information. I consistently receive résumés from one job bank specifically with missing name and contact information.

Web résumés — with all the bells and whistles

A *Web résumé* is also called an *HTML résumé*. It generally finds a home on your Web site. You can add a multimedia dimension to it by using sound, video, or film. It can be as short as a page or two, or it can be a lengthier document with links to examples of your work, complete with animation, graphics, and any sort of fancy formatting you might want to use. Check out the free Web page builder site at Homestead

Technologies (`http://professional.homestead.com`).

Who posts Web résumés? Usually architects, graphic designers, photographers, animators, writers, etc. It can be a powerful sales tool for people in creative lines of work, where making a portfolio accessible to potential employers — and clients — is *de rigueur*.

A Final Word about Online Privacy

Privacy and protection of personal information has been an important consideration in the minds of Canadians when using the World Wide Web. We are very cautious about putting information about ourselves anywhere that it could possibly be misused. This includes posting our résumés online. In this, we are unlike our U.S. counterparts, who have wholeheartedly embraced the Web, spending millions of dollars a year online, conducting banking online, and searching online for jobs.

What you need to know about privacy

Most employment Web sites and online job banks encourage you to add your résumé to an online database that employers can search when they are looking for applicants with specific skills or qualifications. For example, when you go to post a résumé on Workopolis.com (`www.workopolis.com`), you are given the option of making your résumé totally private — so only companies you apply to can see it — or public, so it is visible to all employers who have paid for résumé access.

HotJobs.ca (`www.hotjobs.ca`) has come up with a way to address Canadian job hunters' privacy concerns. You can apply directly to any given posting without having to submit your information to a database.

HotJobs.ca (`www.hotjobs.ca`) has a HotBlock feature that allows you to block up to 20 individual companies from viewing your résumé, or you can put on a Total Block, which prevents companies other than those you've applied to from viewing your résumé. HotJobs.ca also has a policy of not allowing recruitment agencies (they call them staffing firms) to review résumés on the site, unless you apply to a job the agency is recruiting for.

Some employment Web sites have an open résumé database where anyone can view the résumés. They may or may not have to sign on as an employer, but no fees are charged to view the résumés. One such site is Canjobs.com (`www.canjobs.com`). I would not advise posting your résumé on this, and other sites like it, if you are at all concerned about privacy. Your résumé becomes part of the public domain and can be accessed by anyone, with no prescreening criteria.

Here are some things to consider before posting your résumé online:

- **The potential that your boss may see your résumé online.** Research shows that numerous employers actively look for their employees' résumés online. Does that mean you should not post your résumé on the Web? No, but learn the privacy policy of sites to which you are posting your résumé so you know who will have access to it. If access is open to the general public or any employer who signs up, you might want to rethink posting on that site.

- **The likelihood that your résumé will be *reverse-spammed*.** This is technical lingo for your résumé being taken from one database and copied to another without your permission. This, of course, would negate any privacy protection you may have thought you had. If you lose control over the location of your résumé, you've also lost your ability to take it off-line or make revisions.

- **The possibility that your employer has a monitoring program in place to monitor your outgoing and incoming e-mail, as well as the Web sites you visit.** Many job hunters conduct part or all of their search from their computer terminal at work. Don't assume your communications and activities in your work environment are private!

- **The prospect that your cyber-résumé will encounter an identity thief.** These guys review open résumé databases on the Web and generally are up to no good. What are they looking for? Good job candidates whose identities and credit ratings they can scoop!

Protecting yourself

If you post your résumé online and it becomes part of a database that's accessible to anyone who pays to see it, your personal information (your name, phone number, address, e-mail address, employment history) becomes public knowledge. This can potentially lead to numerous problems, but the good news is that you can protect yourself if you are aware of this potential downside.

Reduce your exposure

You can substantially reduce your exposure and privacy risks by following some basic steps. First of all, review the privacy policy of each employment Web site before you post your résumé. Some sites, like Monster.ca (www.monster.ca) and Workopolis (www.workopolis.com), have special protection in place to prevent hackers from running programs that collect résumés from their databases and post them to other sites on the Web.

Also, choose sites that allow you to apply for jobs without first registering your information. On the HotJobs.ca Web site (www.hotjobs.ca), you can apply to any given posting without ever submitting your information to a database.

By posting on a résumé database that is open to the public or any registered employer you expose your personal information to anyone who wants to take the time or pay the fee to register. Check out the site by asking the contact person what their privacy policy is and how they protect your résumé. If their answer is not satisfactory, don't post your résumé on that site. An open résumé database has no password protection and leaves your résumé available for all to see. Again, not only does everyone have access to your résumé, but you have no idea where else your résumé might show up. This is one way that obscure or up-and-coming job banks boost the number of résumés on their site in order to attract more job hunters and larger employers with more money to spend.

Another tactic is to apply for jobs posted by employers directly rather than by an agency or staffing firm. An agency can circulate your résumé to different employers without you even knowing it.

Be sure to keep a list of where you have posted your résumé online, and delete the résumé once you get a job. This will help keep the job bank up to date and also reduce the possibility of your résumé being nabbed, without your permission, for another site.

If you have a résumé on your Web site, use password protection

Have you heard of Internet spiders? These insect-like programs crawl across the Web, pick up résumés, and database them, usually to sell to other job banks. Once this happens to yours, you may never be able to delete it from circulation. Furthermore, once your résumé is on the Internet, you have no control over revisions and updates.

Most Web site hosting services allow you to password protect your Web pages. If yours does not, you should seriously consider changing to a service that does. With password protection, only those to whom you give your password have access to your résumé.

What do you want in a résumé database?

Don't accept that access to résumés on a database is "blocked." This usually means only that you can block certain e-mail addresses or accounts from looking at your résumé. Unfortunately, it doesn't take much for someone to get around that! All anyone has to do to see your résumé is to log in from a different account.

The safest approach is to post your résumé to a password protected, confidential résumé database, where *you* decide who has access to your résumé. The leading online job banks, like HotJobs.ca (www.hotjobs.ca), have this feature. On HotJobs.ca, a "full block" on your résumé makes it "private." It will never appear in company searches.

Chapter 10

Following Up: The Art of Gentle Persuasion

In This Chapter

▶ Realizing that your work isn't over after you send in your application package

▶ Letting the employer know you're "the one"

▶ Following up without overdoing it

▶ Identifying other opportunities to follow up

I n today's job market, it isn't necessarily the best candidate who gets the job, but the candidate who markets himself the best. The recruiter who receives 200 résumés for one job isn't concerned initially with selecting the best candidate, but with whittling the résumé pile down to a manageable short list. If nothing makes your résumé stand out, it won't make this list. Assuming you aren't relying on sheer luck to get you into the interview room, you need to persuade the employer to notice your résumé, and then take the next step and interview you. This chapter focuses on following up — making yourself stand out *after* you've submitted your résumé and cover letter.

Closing the Loop: Why You Can't Afford Not To

Time and again, qualified applicants are frustrated because they don't get that job they had set their hearts on. The reality, of course, is that the best jobs don't always go to the most qualified applicants, but to those who get their résumé noticed. These savvy job hunters are experts at following up. I know, I know, the last thing you want to do after customizing your résumé for a particular position, writing a targeted cover letter, and sending the whole package off, is more work! Aren't your résumé and cover letter shining examples of why you are the number-one candidate for the position? Haven't you done enough already? Well, yes — and no.

When you consider the huge number of applications that are usually received for a single job posting, doing nothing other than sending out résumés and cover letters leaves you dependent on two not-so-dependable things: an outstanding set of credentials that match the employer's needs exactly, or sheer luck. It can't hurt to have another trick up your sleeve. Following up with a recruiter could be the crucial step necessary to lift your résumé out of the bulging pile in his in-basket and onto his desk. You can't afford not to!

Persuading an employer to interview you really is an art. Fortunately, you're reading this book, so you'll be able to turn this art into action. You have to know how to go about it, what techniques to use, and, most of all, when to stop pushing. You need to find a way to connect on a personal level with the employer — so they know who you are. You need to develop a strategy that allows you to maximize your exposure and make the most efficient and effective use of your time.

There is a fine line between getting noticed and making a pest of yourself. If you sense anything that suggests you are starting to bug the recruiter, back off. For example, if she tells you that she'll be in touch with *you* if anything changes, take that as a hint and make yourself scarce. Then follow up on another job you've applied for.

Before You Send In Your Application

Whether you're mailing, faxing, or e-mailing your job application, contact the recruiter ahead of time — preferably by phone — to give him a friendly heads-up that he'll be hearing from you. That way, when your résumé and cover letter do cross his desk, he'll likely remember your call. This gives you an advantage over other applicants (unless they're reading this book too!).

When you make this pre-emptive phone call, you can also ask the recruiter for the following:

- The name and title of the person to whom you should address your cover letter (it may be the recruiter himself or the person in the organization who supervises the position being recruited for).
- A little more information about the position or about the company.

A variation of this phone call is to deliver your application in person. A smart move, since the recruiter will then be able to link your résumé with a friendly face, a confident smile, and a firm handshake.

Following Up (Without Being a Pest)

Once you have sent away your cover letter and résumé, you can't just wait for the employer to notice them. You need to do some additional follow-up work to increase your chances of getting an interview. There are three widely accepted methods of following up:

- ✔ By phone
- ✔ By e-mail
- ✔ In person

In this section, I go over the pros and cons of each method. You need to decide which one's best for you and for your particular situation.

When should I follow up?

Wait one week or so after submitting your application package before you follow up. Following up by phone is reasonably easy, and, while you may not get to talk directly to the person in charge of the hiring — say hello to voice mail — she'll listen to your message and make a note that you called. You can also choose to follow up by e-mail, which is the easiest and least intrusive method. A word of caution, though: limit yourself to three follow-up e-mails if you do not receive a favourable reply. Only send more if the recruiter's given you no reason to stop asking. For example, if she replies that she is interviewing and that you are not on the short list, stop there! If she replies that no decision has been made, go ahead and follow up one more time. Of course, following up in person is the most effective method, but isn't always feasible.

If three weeks go by and you hear nothing from the recruiter, you can contact her to see if the position has been filled or if they have started interviews.

Part of your overall job-hunting plan should include pre-application phone calls or e-mails to recruiters to introduce yourself and ask for a little more information about the position. You should also include following up as part of your strategy, and try to follow up on several leads a day.

By phone

Following up by telephone is generally easier than in person. It's less intimidating, and you can have a script in front of you. (Just be careful not to _sound_ like you're reading it.) It also makes sense to follow up by phone if you are applying for a job in another location.

Bypass Human Resources!

Being a human resources professional, I hate to say this, but here goes: Don't focus your energy on the human resources department! A good HR professional works closely with each department and *assists* them with their recruitment needs. That means, they *help* to write the job ad, decide where to place it, go through current applications and staff files, and help to shortlist the résumés that come in. However, for the most part, it's the department head or supervisor for the position being recruited that ultimately decides who gets interviewed. They are part of, and often conduct, the interview.

This means the person with the actual power is the one who'll be your boss — not the recruiter.

Do your research ahead of time and find out who has the clout to hire you, or at the very least, who is picking the people to be interviewed.

Remember, though, that human resources may be able to push your résumé along if it doesn't seem to be going anywhere. Having the company recruiter as an ally never hurts. Just don't put all your eggs in his basket.

Give the recruiter a call one week or so after you submit your application package. If luck is on your side and you actually get him at his desk, tell him you wanted to make sure he received your application: "My name is Ian Richard, and I am inquiring about the position of engineering technologist. I wanted to confirm that you've received my application and find out if there is any additional information you require." If he confirms, you can ask a few other questions (see the subsection on in-person inquiries, later in this section). If he didn't receive your application, ask for his direct fax number or e-mail address and send it immediately.

If you get the recruiter's voice mail, make sure you leave your name and phone number (complete with area code) and the reason for your call: "I am calling to see if you received my application for the position of. . . ." Ask him to call you back to confirm that he received your package, adding that if you don't hear from him, you'll call back in a couple of days. If he does call you back (and believe it or not, some recruiters do!), thank him for taking the time to call you and ask if he requires any other information from you to complete your package.

If you sense that you are not a welcome caller, you may want to cut the conversation short after asking whether the recruiter received your application: "I realize you are a busy person and I want to thank you for your time." If he seems okay with talking to you, close the conversation this way: "I really appreciate your taking the time to talk to me. Do you mind if I follow up with you regarding the status of my application in two weeks?"

If the recruiter sounds a little hostile, it's best not to ask about a second follow-up call. If a month goes by, however, and you haven't heard from the recruiter one way or another, it's perfectly acceptable to call at this point to find out whether the position has been filled. If it has been, you can cross it off your list.

When you make this second follow-up call, keep it short: "This is Ian Richard. I talked to you several weeks ago regarding the position of engineering technologist. I just wanted to follow up to see if the position has been filled." If it has been, close the conversation by thanking him for his time. If it hasn't been filled, continue by asking him to tell you the status of your application.

By e-mail

Another tactic is to follow up by e-mail, giving the recruiter a gentle electronic reminder of your existence. Ask whether the position has been filled, or if he requires more information from you. Try sending a message like this: "I am just following up on my résumé submitted [insert date]. I wanted to know if there is any other information I can provide to help make your decision regarding interviews. Thank you for your time."

If you don't hear back from the recruiter after your first message, try again in about a week or so, with something that will show you are enthusiastic and industrious: "Since I last e-mailed you, I have done some additional research into your company that makes me even more excited about the prospect of applying my technical abilities and skills to this position. If you would like to discuss this further, please feel free to contact me at [insert your phone number and e-mail address]."

When you review your job-hunting log and realize that several weeks have gone by since you fired off your résumé and cover letter and followed up, you can contact the recruiter again — either by e-mail or phone — and ask what his timeline is for making a decision, and whether he'd like you to send any other information, such as more details about a particular job you've held, school transcripts, and so on.

In person

When you follow up in person, try to do so within a week of sending in your résumé. That way, your résumé and cover letter will likely still be fresh in the recruiter's mind. And if he's still accepting applications, hey, yours will come along with a face attached to it. Bring an extra copy of your résumé and cover letter with you. (While this is a great follow-up technique, it is also a good way to submit your application the first time!)

Your biggest challenge probably will be getting past the receptionist at the front desk. Try this for a get-by-the-secretary kind of opener: "I recently sent in my application for the position of . . . and I had a couple of questions I wanted to ask your recruiter. Would you mind seeing if the person responsible for hiring for this position has a couple of minutes to talk to me?" It is much more difficult for the receptionist to give you the brushoff in person than over the phone.

Once you get in the door and are face to face with either the person to whom you sent your application or the person responsible for hiring, you need to introduce yourself, tell him why you're there, and make a good (albeit quick) first impression. Here's a good opener: "Hi. My name is Fiachra Wolf. I am sorry to bother you but I was in the neighbourhood and I thought I would stop by to discuss with you my application for the technologist position. In case you don't remember my résumé, I brought an extra copy with me." Give him the copy of your résumé and cover letter.

After introducing yourself, it's your chance to get a bit of insight from the recruiter concerning the hiring process. Here are a few questions you can ask:

- ✔ "Can you tell me when you plan on conducting the interviews?"
- ✔ "Can you tell me if there is anything specific you are looking for with respect to experience?"
- ✔ "I have experience in the oil and gas sector as an engineering technologist. Do you think that experience would be considered valuable?"
- ✔ "Do you have any questions about the information provided on my résumé?"

Keep a close eye on the recruiter's body language. If he starts to look a little fidgety or seems to be losing patience, cut it short and leave. Chances are that he won't mind answering a question or two, but that will probably be the extent of it. Leave the office on a positive note by thanking him for taking the time to talk to you. If he seems open and friendly, ask for permission to follow up: "Do you mind if I call you in a couple of weeks to check on the status of my application?"

You can do your second follow-up by telephone, unless you have lots of time or are in the neighbourhood anyway. I once had a fellow show up once a week for three months to see if any jobs had become available. He came armed with new résumés each time and was always polite. Guess what? We got to know him and interviewed him. He was eventually offered a position and he turned out to be a star employee.

Showing up on someone's doorstep and asking to speak to the person in charge of hiring can be an effective way to get noticed. Be sure to dress in something more professional than jeans or your Friday evening party clothes, however. This first impression could make or break your chances at an interview — you want to increase your odds in any way you can.

This might not sit well with you if you're into free expression and believe that part of your right to express yourself is to pierce, dye, or paint parts of your body. But these might be offensive to, or considered unprofessional by, a potential employer. If you are serious about persuading an employer to interview you, lose the earrings, colour over the hair dye, and take some nailpolish remover to that new mango shade you tried out. On the other hand, if these things are very important to you, you will want to seek out an employer who is like-minded.

So-called "innovative" tactics guaranteed to tarnish your interview chances

Sometimes, in the quest to stand out from the crowd, job hunters go a little overboard. Each and every one of these tactics was really tried out on me or someone close to me. Good thing I kept notes, because now I can share them with you.

✔ **Dressing for a barbecue instead of an interview when you drop off your application package.** My stepsister, Jane, is a manager at a bank, and is responsible for the hiring. When a résumé is dropped off, she usually gets to see the person delivering it. She was recently more than a bit put off when a young woman applying for a teller position dropped off her résumé dressed in a red, skintight skirt and cropped top. Based on appearance alone, Jane didn't exactly rush to book an interview.

✔ **Letting your mother do your job hunting for you.** Unfortunately, sometimes mothers do this of their own volition, without asking your permission! Particularly zealous moms have hit me up in restaurants or even called me at home asking me to give their kids a job (small town living at its best!).

✔ **Phoning a recruiter long distance without checking the time zones.** Calling at 5 p.m. on a Friday afternoon is not a good idea, even though it might only be 2 p.m. in your time zone. Be considerate about when you call.

✔ **Sending a holiday greeting card to a recruiter.** Christmas cards are for people you know and with whom you want to keep in touch. Sending a Christmas card to a recruiter is just a touch too familiar (maybe even tacky?) for my taste.

✔ **Sending a gift to a recruiter.** It's unethical.

✔ **Sending a singing telegram to a recruiter to explain to him why you should get the job.** Isn't that what your résumé's supposed to do?

✔ **Sending an e-card to a recruiter.** Again, these are inappropriate if you're just sending it to get noticed. It's okay if you're thanking someone for taking the time to talk to you or for giving you a referral. If you do send an e-card, send it from a well-known company. Many people remain wary about opening unrecognizable attachments or following a link to an unfamiliar Web site. Better yet, skip the e-card phenomenon altogether and send a good old-fashioned handwritten note by post. Just make sure that you have a valid reason for sending it.

When a colleague of mine interviewed a young woman for a summer position at a coal mine, he was so enthralled by the stud in her tongue that he stared at it the entire time. Finally, he lost his composure altogether and asked her, "Doesn't that thing in your tongue hurt?" In the end, he didn't offer her the position, and, interestingly enough, he couldn't pinpoint what was or wasn't on her résumé that led him to his decision. Well, I can pinpoint it, no problem. It had less to do with her résumé than with that tongue stud.

Other Opportunities to Follow Up

Following up isn't just something you do after you send out a job application. There are other times during your job hunt when following up by e-mail or phone call can increase your chances of landing a job:

✔ **After an interview:** Follow up with a thank-you note after an interview.

✔ **After an information interview:** Send a thank-you note or call to thank your contact personally.

✔ **When someone mails job- or industry-related information to you at your request:** Send a thank-you note or call to thank them and to acknowledge that you received the package.

✔ **When you've made a contact worth keeping:** You never know when this person might be able to help you out down the road, or when you might be able to return the favour! This is an integral part of building and maintaining your network. (More on the value of networking in Chapter 14.)

Part III
Where the Jobs Are

The 5th Wave   By Rich Tennant

"Frankly? I'd stay away from using 'plucky' as a keyword unless you're looking for a job at a chicken processing plant."

In this part . . .

Y ou become a super-sleuth, boldly going to little-known
places to uncover hidden job leads. This part covers
online and off-line researching techniques and gives you
the inside track on where to find jobs.

Once you read this part, you'll no longer consider
"networking" a dirty word. I tell you about the how's and
why's of effective networking, and how this important
activity can make all the difference in your job hunt.

Chapter 11

Researching Jobs

· ·

· ·

*T*his chapter discusses the most important, and most often overlooked, component of a successful job hunt: research. What kind of research do you need to do? Well, it primarily involves sussing out information about different industries, fields, occupations, and employers, in order to hit upon the right job for you. But you might also want to learn more about résumés and cover letters, for example, or any other aspect of your job hunt.

The information you need to get your hands on can come from many different places — newspapers, networking, online sources, employers themselves, or career services, to mention a few. The key to finding a job that matches your abilities, passions, and values is to find the information you need and then use that information to your advantage.

Why Research Pays Off

I haven't met too many people who knew exactly what they wanted to do when they finished high school or university — in part due to lack of knowledge about what jobs are available. Most of you will probably admit that you don't exactly have a crystal-clear picture of what jobs are out there at this stage in your life. Even if you have been in the workforce for a while, you might still consider your options limited, even though you know there have to be cool jobs out there somewhere. But where?

How can you find out more? By researching! There's no trick or magic to research — it's a process of investigating different sources until you find what you're looking for. If you don't do your research, you could end up floundering — you may end up in a job you don't like, taking courses in one area when all along your heart is elsewhere, or working for a company that doesn't match your values. In this section, I shed some light on the benefits of researching jobs, as well as the consequences of *not* doing your research (not to scare you off or anything).

Oh yes, one other important reason research pays off — have you ever been asked what your salary expectations are? Most people don't know how to answer this question without actually researching companies and salary ranges in their field.

Benefits of researching

What can you gain from doing your research? It kind of depends on what stage you're at in your job hunt.

If you are just trying to figure out what you want to do with your life, research will open more doors for you — doors you may not have even known existed! Research puts you in touch with people — it opens doors to networking (see Chapter 14) and may even help you access the *hidden job market* (jobs that are never advertised).

It's also much easier to make an informed decision about your job or career path if you know the possibilities. You figure this out through research, whether it's by reading books, visiting career fairs, cruising around different employment-related Web sites, or conducting information interviews where you talk to people who are currently working in a job you think you might be interested in. I discuss information interviews later in this chapter, in "The Art of the Information Interview." As for researching jobs on the Net, that's covered in Chapters 12 and 13.

If you are at the stage where you have decided on a job and are ready to start looking, research again opens doors for you. Don't groan when you read this — your research doesn't stop once you've found a couple of jobs that interest you. Your chances of landing an interview improve if you've done your research and are able to relate your experiences and skills directly to the company and the job. In Chapters 6 and 7, I tell you how to adapt your résumé to each job you apply for. I do the same for cover letters in Chapter 8.

Are you sold on research yet? If you still aren't convinced, here are some of the additional benefits of researching jobs:

> ✔ **Learning more about yourself and what you want out of a job and, eventually, a career:** Self-assessment helps you learn more about what you are good at, what you like, and what you want out of a job. Check out Chapter 2 for a handy list of questions to ask yourself.

✓ **Learning about different occupations and industries to decide which you would like to work in:** When it comes to jobs, you aren't limited to that list you had to make in that careers class you took in high school, or to that other list of so-called "acceptable" jobs your parents just love to remind you about. There's a world of possibilities — and jobs! — out there. You just have to go find it.

✓ **Finding out more information about specific companies:** Research helps you determine whether you want to apply for a job, and perhaps even pursue a career, with a given company. Landing a job you like is important, but it's just as important to work at a company that fits with your own goals and values.

✓ **Learning how to market your most important asset — you:** The best jobs don't necessarily go to the smartest or the most qualified people out there, but to the job hunters who know how to market themselves the best. Part II is full of tips on crafting your résumé and cover letter to make sure you come out on top. Following up after you've applied is another great way to differentiate yourself from your fellow job hunters. I cover that in Chapter 10.

✓ **Discovering where the jobs are:** There are more jobs out there than meet the eye. The traditional medium of newspaper ads is not the only place to look. Effective research helps you uncover jobs in unconventional places.

Consequences of not researching

Many people, in their enthusiasm to jump into their job hunt, don't bother to do research. Not taking this time can set your job hunt back in several ways:

✓ **It can confuse you:** I talk about the importance of a job search strategy in Chapter 4. But even a well thought-out strategy can founder if you do not have a destination in mind. Where are you going? Knowing *how and when* you are going to conduct your job search can be ineffective if you don't have a clear idea of *where* you want to go and what you are searching for. You could find yourself going down roads and applying for jobs that are not really what you want to do.

✓ **It can overwhelm you:** Looking for a job is far less daunting if you have done your research and have a clear plan in mind. Research can help you develop your plan and establish your goals. When you have a destination and a road map to follow, you are far less likely to get lost on the way and become frustrated.

✓ **It can cause you to waste that precious job-hunting time:** If you don't do your research, you could find yourself wandering aimlessly through the maze of available job-related resources, applying for jobs you don't even want and making very inefficient use of your valuable time.

✔ **It can be the reason why you don't find a job:** The worst-case scenario is that you don't find a job. By not researching, you may miss a large number of possible job leads, may not market yourself to your fullest potential, or may spend your time on unproductive tasks.

So, as you can see, research is a very important part of your job hunt — you can increase your odds of landing a job that will make you happy!

Getting the Goods: Where to Find Jobs

Where you get the goods depends on what you're shopping for, right? If you're looking for information about a specific company, you're most likely to find it on the company's Web site (see Chapter 13), in its annual report, or even from people who work there. Don't turn to that same annual report if you're looking for the goods on a particular industry, however. You'll have to look somewhere else for that kind of background — for example, from online industry profiles, or maybe by setting up an information interview with someone working in the industry.

The kind of information you need, and where you go to access it, changes depending on what stage you're at in your job hunt. I've identified four stages leading up to the interview, and the sort of research each requires:

1. **Identifying your job/career goals:** In this first stage, you are looking for different options and self-assessment tools. You are trying to find out what your likes, talents, and values are, and to work from there toward a job or career path that lets you best express them. You also need to research the different jobs and careers available to try to match your own goals to a job. You can check out Chapter 2 for help with this stage of your job search.

2. **Researching industries, occupations, and specific companies:** Making informed employment-related decisions requires gathering information not only about jobs, but also about companies, industries, and the job market in general. You may need to do this type of research as part of your goal of identifying your dream job, or once you have made a career choice and want to look into specific industries or companies.

3. **Assembling the right tools for your job hunt:** Before you can actually launch your job hunt, you need to make sure you have the right tools — namely, a knockout résumé and a killer cover letter. A good place to research this stage of your job hunt is in Part II of this book!

4. **Locating jobs to apply for:** You've made the decision about what you want to do and now you have to start looking for a job. This stage of your job hunt is exciting, so exciting that it's the stage where most job hunters want to start — forgetting that they first need a job goal and the right

tools for the hunt. While there's still a lot of research to be done once you get to this stage of your job hunt, luckily for you, there are lots of places to do it.

In order to be creative and find the job of your dreams, you first have to know where to look. Ninety percent of job hunters look in the newspaper job listings (and studies show that only 10 percent of jobs are advertised). That means you will be competing with 90 percent of job seekers for 10 percent of the available jobs. Now is the time to buck tradition and go where other job hunters fear to tread. While you can't afford to overlook newspaper ads, take another step and look for jobs where the other 90 percent of jobs can be found and only 10 percent of the job hunters are looking.

You have many research tools at your disposal. I list a variety of these in the remainder of this section and tell you when each would be most useful.

Newspapers

Newspaper ads are an obvious and easily accessible source of job leads, career tips, and company and industry information. Daily newspapers are indexed and archived in libraries in most large urban centres.

Virtually every community in Canada has some form of newspaper where local or regional jobs are advertised, many of which are available online. Communitynews.ca (www.communitynews.ca) has an online database of more than 670 newspapers across Canada. Some of their listings do not have Web sites detailed, but if you find the name of the newspaper, you can use Google.ca (www.google.ca) to search for the Web site address. You can also source Sun Media–owned weekly and daily community newspapers and magazines on CANOE (Canadian Online Explorer) (www.canoe.ca), shown in Figure 11-1, and CanWest-owned newspapers on www.canwestglobal.com. Many of the daily and weekly newspapers in Canada are owned by these two companies.

A comprehensive list of daily and weekly community newspapers in Canada is available on the Canadian Community Newspapers Association (CCNA) Web site (www.ccna.ca).

While they are not geared toward job postings, online news sites are a good source for other types of information. These Web sites usually archive their articles and offer search capabilities. If you are looking for information on a specific occupation or industry, try searching one of these news sites:

- ✔ canada.com (www.canada.com)
- ✔ CBC News (www.cbc.ca)
- ✔ *The Globe and Mail* (www.theglobeandmail.com)

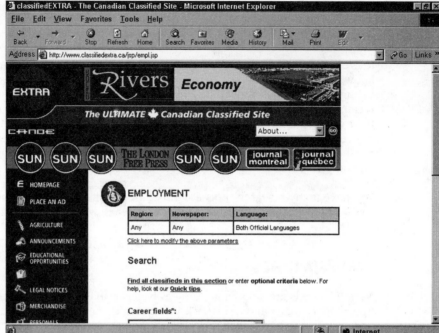

> ✔ *National Post* (www.nationalpost.com)
>
> ✔ *The Toronto Star* (www.thestar.com)
>
> ✔ Yahoo! Canada News (ca.dailynews.yahoo.com)

If you are looking for a professional position and you are willing to relocate if necessary, don't overlook our national newspapers — the *Globe and Mail* (www.globeandmail.com) or the *National Post* (www.nationalpost.com). The online copies of these newspapers don't have their actual job listings (the *Globe* links to an online job bank), but you can review their Careers sections in copies of these newspapers at libraries in major centres.

Magazines

Often articles on specific issues and companies in Canada can be found in Canadian magazines. Many of these now have an online component and archive past issues. Here are a few worth checking out when you want industry- or company-specific information:

> ✔ *Canadian Business* (www.canbus.com)
>
> ✔ *Maclean's* (www.macleans.ca)

> ✔ *Money Sense* (www.moneysense.ca)
>
> ✔ *Profit Magazine* (www.profitguide.com)

For an up-to-date and comprehensive list of Canadian magazines, including many regional magazines, check out Canadian-based Publications Online (www-2.cs.cmu.edu/Unofficial/Canadiana/CA-zines.html#Magazines). You can also link directly to the most up-to-date editions of magazines.

Industry-specific publications

Virtually every industry has trade-related magazines or newsletters and many issues include job-related information and information on specific companies or the industry itself. You can find out the up-and-coming companies in the industry and the latest in industrial research and development activities. Some magazines may be archived online, while others will provide related articles in response to your phone call or e-mail request.

Trade industry publications will often post job openings that may not be found in newspapers because the employer is specifically trying to target a particular audience. Researching trade journals and applying to advertised positions is likely to give you a better hit rate than just applying to newspaper and online ads.

You can also find trade-specific magazines by using search engines (see Chapter 12) and searching for specifics such as the name of the industry and magazines. For example, go to Google.ca (www.google.ca) and type in **"human resources magazines"** or **"accounting publications."** Be sure to specify "pages from Canada" in your search (there is a box you check off).

Company annual reports

Though they can at first be a bit intimidating, company annual reports provide very valuable information about the products, current state, and future direction of a company. You can generally get a copy of an annual report by contacting a stock brokerage firm, by contacting the company directly, or, again, by going online.

You can access company annual reports through these Web sites:

> ✔ **Reports at CNW** (reports.cnw.ca): Using this site, you can actually subscribe to have annual reports sent directly to you.
>
> ✔ **Sedar** (www.sedar.com): Sedar stands for the System for Electronic Document Analysis and Retrieval. It is a site set up to make documents on companies easily available to the public.

✔ **UBC Library** (www.library.ubc.ca/home/catalogue): Actually a great source for any kind of company-specific information, including annual reports. This site also tells you how to read annual reports.

Online subscription-based databases

Collecting and archiving information online is becoming big business. Companies specialize in collecting data and making it available to the public for a fee — but you may be able to subscribe on a trial basis for free. Databases may be geared toward one sector or topic or may be general, covering many topics. For example, Electric Library Canada (www.elibrary.ca) is a subscription-based online research tool specializing in newspapers, TV and radio interviews, and magazines. To find databases related to your topic, check out iTools (www.itools.com). Look under their Research Tools section for hundreds of newspapers and magazines in the eLibrary.

Chambers of Commerce

If you are looking for information about a company or about job prospects in a specific location, the local Chamber of Commerce can be a great source of information. The Chamber of Commerce is your business connection to a community and should be able to give you the information you are looking for or direct you to someone in the community who can. Check out the Canadian Chamber of Commerce Web site (www.chamber.ca/newpages/site.html) to find links to Chamber publications and offices in every province.

Career fairs

Career or job fairs can both put you in contact with recruiters for numerous companies *and* expose you to a large number of different job possibilities — all under one roof. Remember to bring copies of your résumé (see Chapters 5, 6, and 7 for help with your résumé), a list of potential questions for recruiters (see the section "The Art of the Information Interview," later in this chapter), and have a 15-second overview of your job objective prepared.

Your 15-second objective could sound something like this. "Hi! My name is Tara Philips. I am interested in a position as an account executive. Ideally I would like to work for a smaller firm that has opportunities for international travel."

You can then get more information about the company by asking the recruiter or company representative some of the questions you would ask in an information interview. This is, in fact, your opportunity to conduct an informal information interview. If you come prepared to the career fair, you may even make some contacts that could eventually lead to a job. Be sure to ask for each recruiter's business card so you can follow up afterward (see Chapters 10 and 14).

Career fairs are usually advertised in your local newspaper and at colleges and universities. Some are annual events, so you might be able to do an online search (see Chapter 12) to get more information. Type in **"career fairs"** in the search engine's search field to see what's coming up.

Online career fairs are becoming more popular, as well. These are often staged by first-tier online job banks (see Chapter 13).

Industry-specific trade shows

Trade shows and conferences bring large numbers of people from a single industry together in one place and are a great way of finding out about the nature of work and job possibilities in a particular industry. Lectures, courses, and seminars offered on specific subjects are also good places to meet industry representatives. These are awesome networking opportunities and places to get leads on job openings or information about specific companies or industries.

Remember to collect business cards from everyone you meet and follow up with a quick note after the event. I usually write something about the other person on the back of each card so I remember who they are. See Chapter 14 for ideas on how to network at trade shows and conferences. To find out where and when trade shows and conferences are in your area and industry — you guessed it! — do an online search on your favourite search engine using the keywords **"[name of industry] trade shows Canada"** or **"[name of industry] conferences Canada."**

University or college career centres

Whether you're an alumnus or alumna, or a student, the campus placement office is definitely somewhere worth registering with and checking back with frequently for help during your job hunt. (You might even want to volunteer to work in the office so you get the inside edge on new job postings.) Employers looking for new grads or alumni with specific skills *do* use these services. It is often much easier to get an entry-level job this way than to apply for a job where experience is required and then trying to bluff your way in.

Campus career centres may also be able to meet some of your other research needs, such as providing occupational and industry information, résumé and cover letter tips, and even interview suggestions.

Networking

This topic is so important and vital to a successful job hunt that I devote a full chapter to the subject. (That'd be Chapter 14, if you'd like to turn there now.) Networking means making connections with people who you may or may not know that may be helpful in your job hunt. Networking really works! It is based on the principle that it's easier to get information and help from people who know you than from people who don't. Networking can be done informally at social gatherings and casual meetings, formally at regular networking meetings, or online through discussion groups and forums.

Discussions with experts in the field

It sounds obvious, but you'd be surprised how many of us hole up with our stack of references or computers and try to conduct our job search solo. Perhaps you need to fill in the gaps after you've reviewed written material or maybe you want to explore a subject or career further. In either case, another way to get the information you want is to ask someone.

Experts can be your professors from university, industry officials, media experts, previous grads from the same program, famous people in the field. Sometimes even casual acquaintances, friends, and extended family turn out to have information you can use or to know someone in the field that interests you. See the next section "The Art of the Information Interview" for more suggestions.

The Art of the Information Interview

An *information interview* is a discussion with someone for the purpose of learning more about a topic or career of interest to you. The benefits of conducting information interviews are numerous:

- It helps you determine whether the job, company, or industry is a fit with your abilities and values.

- It confirms (or refutes) knowledge you may already have and provides information not available in written form.

- It helps you organize your academic training or continuing education by identifying which courses you should take.

- It shows you the best way to gain entry to your chosen profession

- It provides you with tips and information about the job and career field that could be valuable when preparing your résumé and in job interviews.

✔ It might lead you to other potential contacts who know of openings or can refer you to more contacts. It's an opportunity to expand your network!

✔ It gives you a chance to see the organization from the inside.

Generally, an information interview takes place with someone who is already employed in the position or who has inside knowledge about what a job requires. You use information interviews when you are trying on different jobs to see if they fit or when you are trying to determine if a particular company or job fits with your abilities, passions, and values.

Never use an information interview as an opportunity to ask for a job. If you have requested an information interview, stick to just that — asking for information. Having said that, it is quite possible that an information interview could eventually lead to a job. In addition to providing you with career information, it is a great way to start developing your network.

As the purpose of an information interview is to collect information, anyone who is knowledgeable about the field that interests you should be able to help you with your research. Ask everyone you know if they have any contacts in the field you'd like to explore. You'd be surprised who people know! You can also search for articles and call the people quoted in them, do an online search for companies, and contact people in the field. Another source is the campus employment services office at your university or college, or the alumni association.

When you have compiled a list of potential contacts, you need to phone and try to set up an appointment. Start by introducing yourself and telling them you are trying to learn more about the industry to help you decide if it's a good employment choice for you. Ask them if they can spare 15 to 20 minutes, at their convenience, to talk to you *in person* about their job. Be prepared for the person on the other end to say they are too busy. Just thank them politely and ask them if there is someone they could recommend that might have more time.

Before you go for (or even phone to set up) an information interview, make sure you know something about the company *and* have a list of questions prepared. You should have done some research on your career of interest so you can ask informed, intelligent questions. Be prepared for them to want to talk to you over the phone, so don't start calling until you have done your background work.

Here are some questions you could ask in your information interview:

✔ What special knowledge, skills, training, or experience do you have (or need) for this job?

✔ What do you like most/least about your job?

✔ What is your level of freedom to solve problems and take action on the job?

✔ Tell me about your working conditions (physical, environmental, sensory, stress).

✔ How does your work contribute to the organization's overall goals or mission?

✔ Is there a career path in your field?

✔ What potential or drawbacks do you see for this field in the future?

✔ What is the salary for entry-level and more advanced positions in this field?

✔ Can you suggest specific courses I should take to prepare myself for this field?

✔ Can you give me some suggestions as to what else I can do to prepare myself for entry into this field?

Be on time for the interview and keep within the allotted time frame. Have your list of questions ready and write down the answers. Once you have finished the interview, if there is time, you could ask for a quick tour of the office. Be sure to thank the interviewee for her time. Within several days of the interview, send a handwritten thank-you card, thanking her again.

Job shadowing

When you have read about a career or a company that interests you and conducted information interviews to see if you would like to pursue it further, you might want to think about one more check — just to make sure. Job shadowing involves asking someone working in the field to let you accompany them during a typical workday. This allows you to see firsthand what is involved in the job and whether you would enjoy it. The best way to set up a job shadow appointment is similar to the way you would set up an information interview, except that you ask to be allowed to observe them in their job for a half or full day. By the time you leave, you should have a good idea about what the job entails, the work environment, the interactions with other people, and what you like or dislike about the job.

Again, be sure to follow up the next day with a thank-you note. Listing what you found helpful about the day would also be a good idea, so your contact knows his time was not wasted.

How to Research Effectively

Feeling a little overwhelmed? No wonder! I've just bombarded you with multiple resources to use, and you might feel like someone has just thrown you into the ocean and told you to sink or swim. Don't yield to the impulse to say "forget it" and just jump in headfirst. Remember what the consequences could be if you don't do your research — confusion, frustration, inefficient use of your time, and eventual failure to find a job. To help you keep your head above water, read on for some ideas on how to research effectively.

Make research part of your routine

Try to include research as a regular part of your job-hunting strategy. If you do a couple of hours a week of research, you can keep generating job leads or move the job leads you have ahead so you don't lose steam. Schedule a couple of two-hour blocks for research each week and you should be able to stay ahead of the game.

If you have a specific research project to undertake, such as learning more about a single company with which you are going to do a follow-up tomorrow, you should spend your scheduled research time doing that. If you don't have any hot leads or specific tasks, break down your research time into specific blocks. For example, spend an hour researching jobs online (see Chapters 12 and 13), half an hour going over newspaper ads, and another half an hour following up with networking calls.

Stay on track

Staying on track is sometimes easier said than done. For example, you are researching online job-related newsgroups and one catches your eye that has nothing to do with job searching. It's so easy to click Subscribe and immerse yourself in a discussion about model airplanes. When you are researching, you will come across many things that are not related to job searching, in every research medium. Is it ever tempting to wander off track! Set goals and time limits for yourself. For example, by the end of the day you want to apply to four new jobs. Or by noon tomorrow you want to get the contact information for 10 new companies you have not approached.

Don't just apply for a job to see if you have a chance or to feel like you are doing something productive. It is not productive use of your time to apply for jobs you are not interested in or don't have a chance at. For example, for a new business grad to apply for the position of chief operating officer at Microsoft would be a waste of time.

Keep track of your leads

You can gather information the old-fashioned way, by taking notes, clipping articles, photocopying related information, and making lists. If you don't have your own computer, this is likely the only way you can keep track of your job search. You also have to do this when you use your library to do research because you likely won't have access to your computer (unless you are terribly sophisticated and take a laptop with you).

If you have a computer, you can use it to help you keep track of the information you gather. You can use electronic notepads to keep notes, bookmark good Web sites, and categorize information. You will probably still require a manual system, such as a binder, for newspaper clippings and photocopied information.

Use the Internet, by all means, but use off-line resources, too

The Internet has made information readily available and easily accessible. Never before has so much information about so many topics been at your fingertips. Online you can find job ads, company data, and tools to assist you in all stages of your job search. In fact, there is now overlap between off-line or traditional media and online media. Many of your traditional sources of information, such as newspapers and periodicals, also have an online component. Even annual reports, career fairs, networking opportunities, college career centres, and job boards are found online.

While the Internet will be one of your most important career resources, it should not be the only resource. Never underestimate the value of books, newspapers, and other traditional forms of media to learn more about a specific topic. Schedule some of your research time as online time, but try to keep at least an hour or two a week for off-line research.

Remember the library?

One thing I remember vividly from the olden days (when you *had* to do your research at the library as there was no Internet), is how much the librarians knew. They always seemed to know where to look and could help me find what I wanted. When you find the copious quantities of online information hard to digest or sift through for quality, you can turn to your local librarian. Chances are he or she can help you narrow down your search and point you in the right direction. Sometimes it seems as though libraries are being forgotten in the wake of the Internet. Don't forget about this valuable resource. It's a very cost-effective place to conduct research.

There's another bonus! Libraries across Canada offer free Internet access to members, and often library staff are available to help you.

And believe it or not, you may not be able to find what you want on the Internet, either. There are many books and magazines that you cannot access online but that you should be able to find at your local library. These could help you with your job hunt (in fact, you may have taken *this* book out of your public library!). Most libraries in larger urban centres also archive newspapers from across the country, letting you expand your job hunt geographically.

Chapter 12

Casting Your Net: Job Hunting on the Internet

....

In This Chapter

▶ Understanding how the Internet can jump-start your job hunt

▶ Realizing the pitfalls of spending time online

▶ Getting to know the tools available to you

....

*I*n Chapter 11, I tell you how to research jobs effectively — and creatively — using traditional channels such as newspapers, magazines, and career fairs. But, you know, tradition can get boring after a while, can't it? While there's definitely a place for traditional research in your job search strategy — indeed, this kind of research forms the basis of a successful search — now it's time to take your job search to the next level. I'm talking, of course, about the online level.

In this chapter, I help you familiarize yourself with the online tools that allow you to navigate effectively around the Internet.

As wonderful as the Internet is, there is a downside. This downside is information glut: there's too much information and not enough time to properly evaluate it. The result? Unproductive use of your precious and hard-won job-hunting hours! After all, you're not a Web specialist or a professional researcher (your résumé probably looks impressive enough without adding "Internet expert" to it as well). So, I also pass along some online researching tips to help you cut to the cyber-chase, so to speak, and find the job-related information you require.

Come on, then. Time to buck tradition.

Net Benefits: What's Good about Going Online

The numbers are in, and they're big. Researchers estimate that close to 75 percent of Canadians are connected to the Internet, either at home or at work. With quick and easy access to the World Wide Web, many of us are checking out online job banks and other employment-related Web sites and incorporating them into a comprehensive job search. Nowadays, you can target your job search to a particular industry or geographic location, and do so from the comfort of your own home or office. At the same time, employers are using the Internet for recruitment because it's accessible, inexpensive, reasonably easy to use, and expands the scope of their search to attract candidates from across the country (even outside our borders). International Data Corp. predicts that the North American e-recruiting industry will grow eight-fold, from US$847 million in 2000 to US$6.6 billion, by 2005.

The World Wide Web has truly enhanced the information and options available to you as a job hunter. For example, you can do the following:

✔ Search for job postings on *online job banks* — Web sites that list and organize job vacancies.

✔ Log on to company Web sites to find out more about potential employers and job vacancies.

✔ Explore *industry-specific Web sites* to narrow your search to your industry or area of expertise.

✔ Cruise *location-specific Web sites* that have job listings from employers in your own geographic location, from other cities and regions in Canada, and from all over the world.

✔ Subscribe to newsgroups, discussion groups, and e-mail lists to enhance your network and help in your job search.

✔ Post your résumé to online databases for employers to review.

I show you how to make use of these cyber-tools later in the chapter. For help posting your résumé online, check out Chapter 9.

Another reward of job searching online is your ability to do a keyword search. When you perform a *keyword search,* you instantly narrow your search to postings that include only the words you specify — your keywords.

Let's say you're toying with the idea of packing up and moving to Vancouver — you've always wanted to give that West Coast lifestyle a try. Since you found out that you're not in line for your grandmother's inheritance, after all, you figure you'd better get busy and look for a job out there. Log on to a search engine like Google (www.google.ca) and type **"Vancouver jobs"** in the search field. Be sure to tick off the box for Canadian Only Web sites. Figure 12-1 shows you what Google comes up with. You can then click any of the links Google retrieved to go to a site related to jobs in Vancouver. You sure can't do this kind of fancy searching in newspaper ads! See the sidebar "Making the most of keywords," later in this chapter, for tips on coming up with effective keywords for your search.

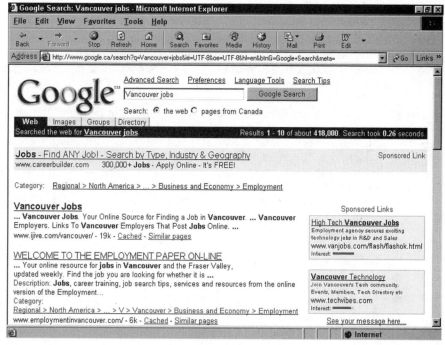

Figure 12-1:
A keyword search lets you instantly narrow your job search to postings that include only the words you specify.

So, the World Wide Web is a great place to find jobs — we've established that. But that's not all it is. It's also a great source of other kinds of employment-related information. You can find resources to help you plan and manage your job search, templates to help you write résumés and cover letters (see Chapter 9 for online résumé help, and Chapter 8 for Web sites dedicated to cover letters), and information on just about any employment-related subject you can think of. I've put together a list of these useful Web sites, as well as other resources, in the yellow-paged Landing a Job For Canadians For Dummies Directory of Job Resources in this book.

One of my favourite resource sites is that of Human Resources Development Canada (www.hrdc-drhc.gc.ca/common/work.shtml). The site provides links to many Canadian job banks, HRDC office locations, labour trends, occupational and industry profiles, and career planning assistance. Check it out!

Avoiding Online Hazards

The Web is like a box of chocolates. You never know what you're going to get until you bite into it. Nearly all employment-related Web sites provide you with information and links to help you out with your job search. Most of the time you get more information than you bargain for. You get answers (unfortunately, sometimes, too many answers), but they aren't always trustworthy answers relevant to your job search.

Not all the information on the Web is of equal value — you have to filter out the high-quality stuff from the not-so-high-quality, or even downright incorrect, stuff. Make sure you check more than one Web site when you are looking for an answer to a question or for advice. This way, you can cross-reference the information to make sure it all jives.

Another cyber-pitfall is trying to figure out when enough is enough! When do you have enough information? When have you spent enough time online? Multiple links on most sites lead you to still more information. You may find yourself clicking related links, going off on tangents, and occasionally forgetting what it was you were looking for in the first place — or wondering if you already found it and just didn't recognize it! You want to stay focused, search specifically for the data you need, and avoid getting sidetracked by interesting links. You need to be sure that you work smart: using your time efficiently and effectively should be your goal.

Here are a few tips to help you keep focused online:

✔ **Follow a link only if you need to look for something specific:** Most sites give you information or job listings and then list links (other sites) you may be interested in following. Clicking links can give you more information or just lead you on a merry chase. You may well find lots of interesting stuff, but before you know it, *poof*, your afternoon is shot.

✔ **Use the Back button on your Web browser program to return to the previous site:** Going back to your starting point like this helps keep you grounded and focused. If you click a link and it opens in another window, you can just close it to go back to your starting page.

Your *Web browser program* is the program you use to search the Internet — Internet Explorer and Netscape are the most popular.

✔ **Return to the original site if you can't find what you're looking for after three clicks on a linked site:** Chances are you'll find it somewhere else with less effort. Use the Back button on your browser.

✔ **Verify information once, but no more:** When you find a reference or a piece of information, by all means find an additional site to verify it. But then stop! Looking further is likely to give you the same information and waste your time.

I'm as strong an advocate of using the Internet in your job hunt as the next person. Just remember that overreliance on the Net takes the personal touch out of looking for and landing a job. Granted, there is something very appealing about sitting in front of your computer, searching online job banks, crafting cover letters and posting your résumé, all from the comfort of your home. But this often takes the place of personal contact in your job hunt. Bottom line: Adopt a balanced approach to your job hunt, taking advantage of all the Web has to offer (and it's a lot), but temper it with off-line tactics, such as face-to-face networking.

How are employers using the World Wide Web?

The answer to the question is, *more than ever.* According to a 2002 report from iLogos Research, the percentage of Global 500 companies conducting recruiting online jumped from 29 percent in 1998 to 91 percent in 2002. Of the Global 500 located in North America, 95 percent were recruiting online in 2002. Employment-related Web sites have made it easy and inexpensive for recruiters to use the Internet to manage and organize their recruitment efforts. They can post job openings, browse through résumés to pre-screen applicants, and use pre-screening checklists and questionnaires to help narrow down the list of potentials. They can post links to their own company Web sites and correspond via e-mail with potential hires to create a short list of qualified candidates — all in less time than it would take with traditional recruitment methods. Most employers either use the Web directly, by advertising on online job banks and corporate Web sites, or indirectly, by advertising online through employment agencies and newspapers. Employers can also pay a sub-

stantially higher fee to subscribe to résumé databases run by many of the online job banks. Job hunters post their résumés to these databases and potentially can be contacted directly by an employer.

There remains a large number of potential employees, however, who are not connected to the World Wide Web and who don't use the Internet during their job hunt. Or perhaps they're using different Internet search criteria from the recruiter. Employers want to reach these candidates, too. So while the benefits of using the Internet are evident, the majority of employers who do use it in their recruitment efforts do not rely on it entirely.

Best-in-class employers use a balanced, or integrated, approach to recruiting — combining online and off-line, or traditional, recruitment methods (see Chapter 11). The savvy job hunter should also balance her job hunt across different sources in order to maximize the chance of landing a job with her employer of choice.

Tools at Your Fingertips

The World Wide Web is a collection of resources and Web sites that essentially has no form of organization. Sounds comforting, doesn't it? Those analyst types who love to publish estimates say that there are more than 3 billion documents on the Web — it's a "web," all right, but a tangled one that's forever expanding with no rhyme or reason to its structure. So how on earth do you locate the job-related information you need? Good question! There are two ways to explain how to get information off the Web: in techie terms and in understandable terms. I don't know about you, but my vote is for less technical lingo and more straightforward explanations. What matters is that you know where and how to find the information you need, right? There are three types of search tools you can use to find information online:

- Search engines
- Directories
- Metasearch engines

Search engines and directories

A *search engine* is a program that searches or "crawls" the Internet looking for sites that are related to keywords you enter in the search field. A *keyword* is a word or group of words that represents the type of information you are looking for. Very few search engines use computer-based "crawl" technology exclusively anymore — most have also partnered with at least one directory or have even created their own directory of select Web sites.

Directories are listings of Web sites. These listings are selected by editors and categorized into different groups. A directory is kind of like your list of book-marks or favourite Web sites, but much larger in scope. Directories are "human powered," meaning they depend on human editors to provide their listings. In directories, as in search engines, you use keywords to find information, but they do not scan the entire Web — just the Web sites within the directory.

There is good news for cyber-dummies! In the olden days (you know . . . a couple of years ago, in cyberspace terms!), search engines usually returned only crawler-based results, while directories returned only human-powered listings. Today, many search engines have the means to search a directory as well as crawl the Web looking for your keywords. One such search engine is AltaVista Canada (www.ca.altavista.com). Some directories have also incorporated search engine results. Yahoo! Canada (www.yahoo.ca) is both a directory and a search engine. It searches within its own directory first, but if it can't find what you have asked for, it searches the Web.

To cover all your bases, or in case you can't find a specific Web site or piece of information, use two or three search engines or directories, or use a _metasearch engine_ (a search engine that searches other search engines). More about metasearch engines in a little while. Why? Well, no two search engines search the Web the same way, just as no two directories have the same collection of Web sites in their listings. Some perform pretty superficial searches, while others are in-depth. It all depends on what you're looking for. Imagine you want to look online for jobs in Edmonton. You type in **"Edmonton jobs"** in the search field, and click Search. Some search engines and/or directories will just look for combinations of those two words in the name of the Web site, while others will actually look through the sites themselves to see if they include the words "Edmonton" and "jobs."

Search engines

Here is a list of some of the more popular search engines on the Web:

- **AllTheWeb.com** (`www.alltheweb.com`): This search engine is also known as FAST Search. It isn't a Canadian-specific site, but it does search Canadian sites. You have to be specific in your keywords and include the word **Canadian** to narrow it down to Canadian sites. It also allows you to search in the language of your choice. It does an in-depth search of both sites and directories. For fun, try doing a search on your own name.

Making the most of keywords

When you're hunched over your computer combing the online classifieds, you want the search engine or directory you're using to do the search for you, not to create more work for you! That's why it's essential to use targeted keywords, which, when entered into the search engine or directory, are specific enough to return to you only those job postings you may be interested in. Think of keywords as Internet filters. The more specific you can make them, the better they'll be at keeping unwanted stuff out.

Here are a few keyword categories related to job hunting, followed by some examples of keywords you can use:

- **The occupation you seek:** Trade jobs, accounting jobs, senior executive jobs, teacher jobs, and so on.

- **The location you seek:** Edmonton jobs, Montreal jobs, Toronto jobs, Halifax jobs, Northwest Territories jobs, and so on.

- **Job-related information:** Résumé writing, cover letter templates, job interviews, and so on.

- **General information:** Canadian jobs, jobs in Canada, job search assistance in Canada, careers in Canada, employment in Canada, and so on.

If you want to search for a specific phrase and don't want the search engine to look for individual occurrences of the words, use quotation marks around your keywords. For example, type **"Canadian jobs"**.

✔ **AltaVista Canada** (www.ca.altavista.com): AltaVista Canada is a powerful search tool that lets you comb through Canadian sites only, or expand your search to international sources. AltaVista began life as an e-mail search index, and grew into one of the first search engines on the Web. It continues to expand, and has recently added a directory (powered by LookSmart) to its list of features.

✔ **Excite** (www.excite.com): Once exclusively a searcher of Web sites using "crawl" technology, Excite has also jumped on the computer-based-and-human-guided search bandwagon and now gives you the option of searching directories in addition to Web sites. As with many search engines these days, the search component is a minor part of the site itself. Excite has up-to-date news, shopping, and other features.

✔ **Google** (www.google.ca): Shown in Figure 12-2, Google is one of my favourite search engines. It does in-depth searches of Web sites, as well as some directories, and has won high marks for returning relevant search results. Google may return more sites than you bargain for — that's how detailed its searches are. Google also allows you to narrow your search to Canadian Web sites only.

✔ **Northern Light** (www.northernlight.com): Northern Light is well known as a site for academic research. You can do specific searches using the Business Search or Power Search features. Northern Light now has a directory that it searches, as well. This is a great site for researching companies and articles related to specific industries.

✔ **Sympatico-Lycos** (www.sympatico.ca): This Canadian-based company offers both directory and search engine services in addition to many other features, including free Web page publishing and national and global news. You can search in French or English and also have the option of searching Canadian sites only.

Directories are databases of human-selected Web sites organized into specific categories. They are a way of trying to organize the World Wide Web and weed out the sites that are lower in quality. Directory editors review sites for possible inclusion in the directory, and the public is encouraged to suggest sites that should be included — and even submit their own. When you search a directory, it only looks for matches within the directory itself, not on the entire Web. The advantage of a directory, in theory, is that because the sites are reviewed, only higher quality sites are listed. Of course, the disadvantage is that if you are looking for a specific Web site — perhaps the Web site of a particular business — it may not be listed in the directory simply because no one has ever submitted it for review.

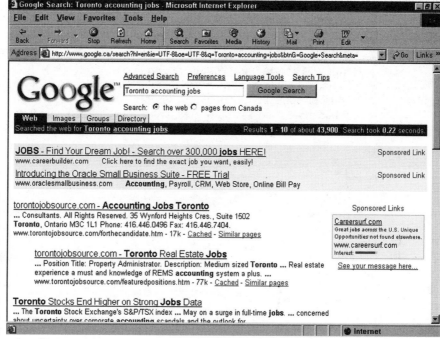

Figure 12-2:
Use very specific keywords on Google to narrow your search results.

Some of the more popular directories include the following:

- **Ask Jeeves** (www.askjeeves.com): Another of my favourite sites, Ask Jeeves is a directory whose search function is set up in a question-and-answer format — a neat concept. It's fun to try this site out just to see how accurate it is in interpreting your question and directing you to the appropriate site.

- **LookSmart** (www.looksmart.com): LookSmart has more than 2.5 million sites included in its directory, and more than 250,000 categories. Its paid editorial staff choose sites on a pay-for-inclusion basis rather than based on the quality or relevance of the site. This means that the top sites that your search returns aren't necessarily the ones of the highest quality or relevance, but simply the ones who forked over the dough to be at the top of the heap. Some search engines (such as AltaVista) have added directory services to their sites by tying into the LookSmart directory.

- **Lycos** (www.lycos.com): Lycos started out as a search engine, then shifted to a directory in 1999. It takes its Web-based listings from AllTheWeb.com and its directory-based listings from the Open Directory Project.

- **Open Directory Project** (www.dmoz.com): The Open Directory Project is the largest directory on the Web. It relies on more than 17,500 volunteer editors to select and screen the Web sites to be included in its directory.

More and more search engines are coupling with the Open Directory Project to supplement their search capabilities, because access is free. The directory includes a very large comprehensive listing of sites that is growing daily.

✔ **Yahoo! Canada (**`www.yahoo.ca`**):** Shown in Figure 12-3, this is the Canadian offshoot of the very popular American directory. Yahoo! is still the Web's most popular search service — with about 150 editors on staff. It has more than 1 million sites listed, and supplements its own search results with those of the search engine Google (`www.google.com`).

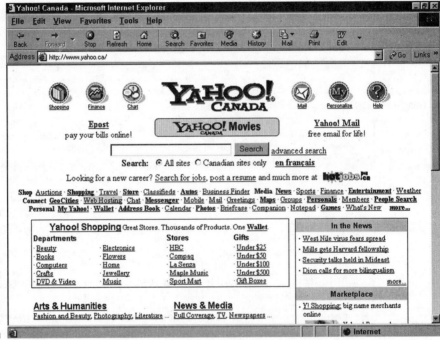

Figure 12-3:
Yahoo! remains the Web's most popular search service.

Metasearch engines

Every search engine has its own method for scouring the Net. This is why you get different results depending on the search engine you use. If you type **"Cover letters"** into each of the search engines I describe in the previous section, each one will come back to you with different results, or if they happen to return the same results, they display them in a different order. One result may show up 2nd on Google (`www.google.ca`) and 175th on AltaVista (`www.ca.altavista.com`). Be honest — when you do a search for information, do you go through every listing a search engine returns? Or do you, like most of us, only look at the first page of listings (usually about 10 sites)? Enter the metasearch engine. A *metasearch engine* uses other search engines and directories to do the searching for it — it simply organizes the results. Because it uses so many search engines and directories, a metasearch engine does a more thorough search, and you are more likely to find what you are looking for.

Metasearch engines make searching the Web easier. A metasearch engine enters your keywords into each search engine or directory it accesses (usually between 10 and 20). These individual search engines then crawl the Web and return a list of sites that the metasearch engine organizes and presents to you in some form. Some metasearch engines display the top results from all search engines in a single list, while others break down the results by search engine.

While metasearch engines can give you quick results, most only search the search engines and directories that pay to be included in them. This means sites that do not pay for inclusion (including Google (www.google.ca) and Northern Light (www.northernlight.com) — both very good search engines) will not be searched. I suggest you use both a regular search engine, such as Google, plus a metasearch engine if you want to cover all the bases.

Give these popular metasearch engines a try:

- ✔ **Dogpile** (www.dogpile.com): Dogpile is a fun-to-use site with a name that is easy to remember. It searches 13 major search engines and directories and returns the top 10 sites each search engine finds. It includes its own directory as one of the search results. (See Figure 12-4.)

- ✔ **Ixquick** (http://ixquick.com): This popular site is one of the newest metasearch engines on the Web. It has some innovative technical features that make it quite fast and easy to use. Ixquick tells you how many and which search engines return each Web site by using a star rating system. Each site is only returned once, with an indicator of how many times it appeared and on which search engines.

- ✔ **MetaCrawler** (www.metacrawler.com): Metacrawler searches several search engines and directories and organizes the results into a single list. It lists the sites it returns in order of relevance to your inquiry. This means it tells you if the site is 100-percent related to what you are looking for (perhaps it found the keywords listed in the title and the text) or, say, 85 percent related to what you are looking for. It will list the 100-percent relevant site first, then the others in order of relevance.

- ✔ **Search** (www.search.com): Formerly known as Savvy Search, this site combines the results from search engines, directories, and paid listings sites. You can also search 800 specialized search engines around the world. For example, you can search the employment search engine directly for a specific job, and it scans numerous job banks — all over the world — returning a list of postings that match your search. It also has some fun features, like a listing of the top 100 searches made that week. Cool tool!

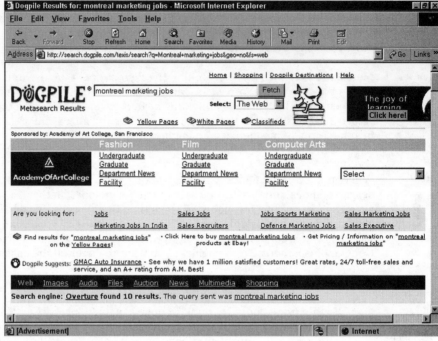

Figure 12-4:
Dogpile is a
popular
metasearch
engine that
shows you
the top 10
results for
each engine
it searches.

Chapter 13

Finding Jobs Online

• •

In This Chapter
▶ Examining online job banks
▶ Using industry- and location-specific Web sites
▶ Exploring company Web sites
▶ Subscribing to newsgroups and e-mail lists

• •

*I*f you already know your way around the Net, you've come to the right chapter. If, on the other hand, you think of yourself as "getting acquainted" with that weird world inside your computer, take a look at Chapter 12, where I explain several of the wonderful tools available to you on the Web. In this chapter, I take it one step further and tell you where on the Internet to find jobs.

The Internet is an incredible resource for job hunters, but it can sometimes be too much of a good thing. There is so much information available that you may not know where to start, or which sites to visit to make the most effective use of your time. I help you make some sense of the job-related information available online — showing you how to weave your way through the Web to a job.

Online Job Banks

Once you have your résumé and cover letter ready (see Chapters 5, 6, and 7 for résumé help; see Chapter 8 for help with cover letters), you are ready to start applying for jobs. But you have to find them first. Finding jobs online is what this chapter is all about. In Chapter 12, I tell you about different online search tools and networking tools available to you. In this chapter, I help you find your way around the seeming maze of *online job banks* (Web sites that list and organize job vacancies). When you first log on, it can be pretty intimidating. In addition to the job banks I single out in this chapter, you can also flip to the bright yellow Landing a Job For Canadians For Dummies Directory of Job Resources for more great options.

There are two kinds of online job banks you need to know about:

- ✔ **Higher-tier, or first-tier, job banks,** which have an abundance of job postings and career-management features
- ✔ **Lower-tier, or second-tier, job banks,** which have fewer jobs and some career-management tools, but are more basic, without a lot of "extras."

There are two other kinds of Web sites of particular use to job hunters, though the primary function of these sites is not job posting:

- ✔ **Industry-specific Web sites, also known as niche sites,** which carry job postings within a particular occupation or industry
- ✔ **Location-specific Web sites,** which carry job postings within a particular geographic location, such as a region, province, or city. I discuss industry-specific and location-specific sites later in the chapter.

First-tier job banks

What elevates a job bank to the first-tier level? According to my own (highly scientific) rating criteria, a first-tier job bank has to offer more than just basic job search and résumé-posting options. It needs to be useful to you, the job hunter, in other ways, too. Career management tools, enhanced privacy options, articles of interest, and job-hunting advice are a few of the important extras I look for. And, of course, lots and lots of job postings!

Here are some of my favourite Canadian-focused first-tier job banks:

- ✔ **HotJobs.ca (**www.hotjobs.ca**):** Shown in Figure 13-1, HotJobs.ca, the Canadian affiliate of the U.S.-based HotJobs.com (www.hotjobs.com), is one of the most popular job boards in Canada, boasting thousands of current jobs from hundreds of companies. HotJobs.ca's user-friendly interface allows you to navigate through listings quickly and easily. You can search by keyword, company, city, and more. On HotJobs.ca, you can create your own personalized MyHotJobs account to help organize your job hunt. With a MyHotJobs account, you get a password-protected home page, résumé editing tools, access to job-seeker statistics, an online shopping cart of positions, and a complete history of sent cover letters and résumés. In case you are concerned about your privacy, HotJobs.ca's enhanced privacy feature, HotBlock, allows you to control who sees your résumé and who doesn't. You can block specific employers from viewing your résumé, which is great for people who worry about their current employers finding out that they are looking for a new position elsewhere.

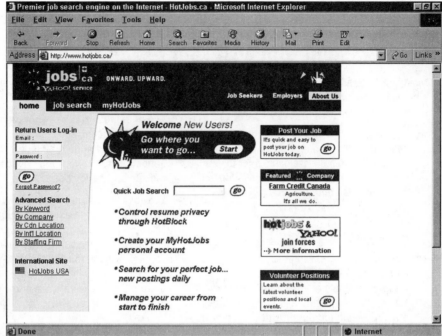

Figure 13-1:
The MyHotJobs feature on HotJobs.ca lets you store your résumé and manage your job search.

✔ **Ijive Careers/Flipdog.com** (`http://ijive.careers.flipdog.com`): This fun and well-used international job bank has a large Canadian component. You can find more than 16,000 Canadian jobs on this site. It has an easy-to-use search engine that lets you search by keyword. You can get expert career advice on this site and read up on additional job search tips. You can also research employers from this site through a feature that allows you to type in a company name, which prompts the job bank to search a directory by company. This puppy posts jobs from literally every populated country on the planet — to varying degrees. So, if you're looking for a job in South Korea — look here.

✔ **Monster.ca** (`www.monster.ca`): This well-used job bank is the Canadian affiliate of the U.S.-based Monster.com (`www.monster.com`). You can track your online applications, and even register to receive an e-mail notification when a job matching your criteria is posted. The site has an easy-to-use search engine that allows searches by job-specific keywords, occupational categories, or location. You can create your own My Monster account to store multiple versions of your résumé and cover letters, which lets you apply online to jobs directly from the Monster.ca site. You also have access to career-related information and articles, as well as links to other job-hunting resources.

Should you post your résumé online?

Most first-tier and many second-tier job banks allow you to post your résumé online. There are several reasons why you might want to do this:

✔ **It's easy:** Posting your résumé online sure beats turning the house upside down looking for a stamp . . . or tromping over to your local convenience store to use their fax machine, assuming they have one. And if you save your résumé on the site's database, you can apply for multiple jobs, all with a simple point and click.

✔ **It's potentially great exposure:** Lots of job banks grant employers access to their résumé databases — for a fee, of course. Your vital stats could wind up on the desk of your dream employer. But remember: Choose sites that allow you to control the privacy of your résumé.

✔ **It's where recruiters go:** The Internet has become a tried and true channel for recruiters. It's easy and inexpensive — a powerful tool to help employers manage their recruitment efforts.

So those are the pros of posting online. Here are the cons:

✔ **You could lose track of your résumé:** Your online résumé may be copied into other job banks without your knowledge. If this is a concern to you, check the privacy policy of the site before you post.

✔ **You need to do so much more in an effective job hunt, and it's easy to get complacent after posting your résumé online:** Posting a résumé is only a small (very small) part of your job search. You don't need to post your résumé on every job bank you visit. Choose a couple of the well-used sites (I recommend HotJobs.ca (www.hotjobs.ca), Workopolis (www.workopolis.com), and Monster.ca (www.monster.ca)) and post it there.

Focus your efforts on sending your résumé to individual employers and following up, to complement posting your résumé online. You'll greatly improve your chances of landing that plum job by broadening your reach like this.

✔ **Workopolis (**www.workopolis.com**):** Workopolis has a multitude of resources for job hunters, including career-related links and information, and, of course, jobs — lots of them! Very similar in features to Monster.ca, this site also has a user-friendly search engine that lets you search by job-specific keywords, occupational categories, or locations. Its My Workopolis feature allows you to create numerous versions of your résumé and track your own searches. It also has a Fast Track feature that takes you directly to industry-specific Web sites for additional information and direct access to jobs in that industry.

When using first-tier job banks such as HotJobs.ca (www.hotjobs.ca), Monster.ca (www.monster.ca), or Workopolis (www.workopolis.com), be sure to expand your search beyond broad occupational or industry categories. Take advantage of the advanced job search and keyword provisions on these sites. Be specific when you run your keyword search — if you're looking for a human resources job in Winnipeg, type **"Human resources professional Winnipeg"** in the search field. Take advantage of the tools on these sites that let you plan and manage your job hunt (MyHotJobs, My Monster, My Workopolis). These great features allow you to store multiple versions of your résumé online, save your job searches, and generally keep yourself organized. Some job banks even let you enter specific criteria about the job you are looking for, and then notify you by e-mail when jobs matching your criteria are posted.

Second-tier job banks

While these smaller job banks do cover a broad range of employment interests, they're just not in the same league as the first-tier sites I discuss in the previous section, with respect to the following:

- ✔ The number of jobs posted on the site
- ✔ The number of visitors to the site
- ✔ The number of extras

But sometimes, bigger isn't necessarily better. If you want to be smart and cover all the bases, check out a couple of second-tier sites to supplement your trolling on the big ones.

These second-tier Canadian job banks are worth a second look:

- ✔ **ActiJob** (www.actijob.com): Easy to use (not to mention great-looking), this Canadian site offers résumé posting services and links to other job-related sites. It enjoys the distinction of being one of two sites recommended on Human Resources Development Canada's (HRDC's) online placement and recruitment services page (http://jb-ge.hrdc-drhc.gc.ca). See Figure 13-2.

    The search engine on ActiJob sometimes returns a lot of irrelevant job postings that don't match your search criteria, so be prepared to pick through these to find the gems.

- ✔ **Actual Jobs** (www.actualjobs.com): This job bank is relatively easy to use, and has more than 11,000 job postings from clear across Canada at any given time. Why? Because it browses other recruitment sites and picks up postings from them. The site's sorting feature lets you search according to province. It has a good search engine and a few other features, including a résumé management service that's a little more flexible than many other sites. On Actual Jobs, you can create your résumé from scratch, post it anonymously, store as many versions as you want, edit them anytime, even print them out in a well-designed layout.

Figure 13-2:
Check out
the great-
looking
graphics on
this site that
guide you to
jobs and
job-related
information.

✔ **CanJobs** (www.canjobs.com): Headhunters and recruiters love this job bank because it is cheap and easy for them to place an ad, and it automatically posts to provincial and major city job banks that it also owns. As a job hunter, you search for jobs by location first, then by occupation. There are a number of extras on the site to help you manage your job hunt, such as a résumé databank, online application abilities, and a job-search agent (a newsletter that advises you about new postings).

✔ **Jobs.ca** (www.jobs.ca): Well worth visiting, this job bank does have some nifty bells and whistles. Try out its trademarked "Job Basket™" technology to view job postings, submit your résumé online, update your résumé, learn of any changes to job ads that you have already applied for, and even find out who has read your résumé. It's a popular place for both job hunters and employers.

I discuss other second-tier job banks in this book's yellow-paged Landing a Job For Canadians For Dummies Directory of Job Resources.

Industry-specific Web Sites

Sometimes called *niche sites,* these Web sites are dedicated to a specific industry or occupation. They are usually general information sources on different aspects of the particular industry — with a job bank or job posting section included on the site. One niche site may specialize in jobs in the high-tech sector, while another may be all about accounting jobs. Your job-hunting strategy (which I discuss in Chapter 4) should include regular visits to these sites, assuming you know what type of job you're looking for, or in what industry. These sites don't always have a huge number of jobs posted (sometimes as few as a dozen; other times, up to several hundred) and many don't have any real form of organization, either (other than, perhaps, the date the job was posted). You may have to do a little more work to find a job on an industry-specific site, but the benefit is that the jobs you *do* find will be in your field of interest. Here are a few examples of industry-specific Canadian sites:

- ✔ **Canadian Forests** (`www.canadian-forests.com`): Dedicated to all aspects of the Canadian forest industry, this site also posts forestry-related jobs all over Canada.

- ✔ **Canadian RN** (`www.canadianrn.com`): This site is devoted to the nursing industry in Canada. It provides a listing of nursing jobs across the country, sorted by province. Other features include articles of interest, up-to-date news, and a directory of nursing-related resources.

- ✔ **Education Canada Network** (`www.educationcanada.com`): Visit this site if you want to delight and inspire, er, teach. In addition to job listings, you'll find information related to the teaching profession, a discussion board, and listings of events related to employment, such as upcoming job fairs.

- ✔ **JobCafe** (`www.jobcafe.ca`): Shown in Figure 13-3, JobCafe will get you prepped if you want to work in the Information Technology industry. Here you can find job postings, up-to-date industry news, and career development information.

Locate industry-specific sites by doing a targeted keyword search. If you're gunning after a job in sales, type in **"Sales jobs"**. Your search should return numerous niche sites devoted to jobs in sales. You can also check out the yellow directory in this book.

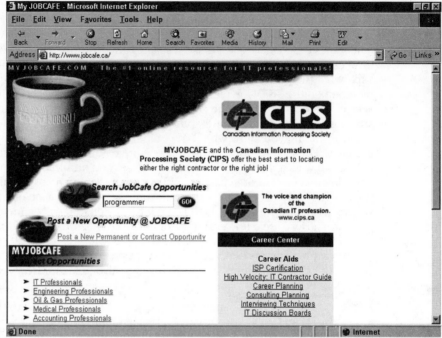

Figure 13-3:
Log on to
JobCafe if
you're
looking for
work in the
high-tech
industry.

Location-specific Web Sites

Location-specific sites focus on job postings in a specific province, region, or
city. Maybe you're tired of Toronto, sick of Saskatoon, or feeling marooned in
Dawson Creek. Part of your job-hunting strategy may be to relocate to another
part of the country, or to another country altogether (see Chapter 22). In a
case like this, when your first job-hunting criteria may be location and the job
itself secondary, you need to change your strategy somewhat. The first thing
you should do is buy a newspaper — one from the community in which you
are planning to relocate. In the olden days, this was easier said than done if
you lived in Vancouver and wanted to find a job in Fort McMurray, but now
most newspapers are available online, and most also have online databases
where they post the job ads that appear in the print edition. You can find print
editions of newspapers that serve cities and larger communities in libraries
and bookstores like Chapters and Indigo. After you've combed through the
dailies, log on to a location-specific site, like one of these:

✔ **CareerClick** (www.careerclick.com): Shown in Figure 13-4, this geographically based job bank gets its postings from the pages of its affiliate
newspapers, from large employers and recruiting firms, and from individual
online postings. To search for positions in areas not included in the list
of locations, try adding your preferred location to your keyword search.

For example, search for **"Hinton, Alberta"**, leaving the Location feature defaulted to Any Location and Category defaulted to Any Job Category. CareerClick also allows you to post your résumé online and save multiple copies of your résumé.

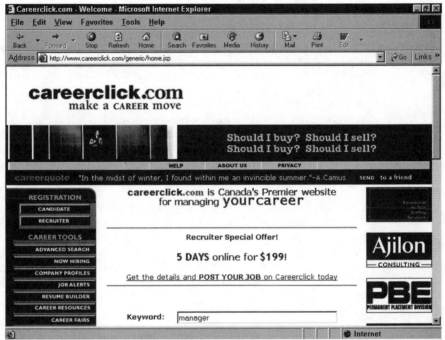

Figure 13-4: CareerClick offers a Job Alert newsletter that lets you know when a job related to your interests is posted on the site.

- ✔ **Fort McMurray Jobs** (`www.ftmcmurray.net/jobs.htm`)**:** So you heard that Fort McMurray, Alberta, is the place to go for a high-paying job. Check out this site that lists jobs in this city and provides links to major employers' Web sites. It even gives you contact information for employment agencies in Fort McMurray. This site is a must if you are thinking of going west.

- ✔ **Sask Jobs** (`www.sasknetwork.gov.sk.ca/pages/joblinks/html`)**:** This is a great site sponsored by the Saskatchewan government, with links to jobs in both the private and public sector in Saskatchewan.

How do you find location-specific job banks? First take a look at the Landing a Job For Canadians For Dummies Directory of Job Resources, then hit the search engines for a little help. Do a keyword search with the job and location in quotes to narrow your search even further. Type **"Accounting jobs AND Montreal"** into the search field, if you're looking for an accounting position in Montreal. Not sure about the job, but settled on the place? Go to a metasearch engine, such as Dogpile.com (www.dogpile.com), and type in **"Jobs in [name of city]"**. For example, **"Jobs in Toronto"** will get you a good cross-section of job banks and employment-related sites in Toronto.

Company Web Sites

Company Web sites are more than just a virtual business card these days. They give businesses the opportunity to showcase their products, advertise their services, and list job vacancies. A company's Web site can also tell you something about that company's values and corporate culture.

Many company Web sites have a page dedicated to job vacancies. These may or may not be posted elsewhere on the Internet. You can usually send an e-mail, complete with résumé and cover letter, directly to the e-mail address listed on the Web site (it's generally a jobs@company.com type of address). For information on making your résumé cyber-ready, see Chapter 9.

Most employers that use e-recruitment post job vacancies simultaneously on their corporate Web sites and on online job banks. Those with Web sites that don't have corporate career content rely exclusively on online job banks like HotJobs.ca (www.hotjobs.ca), Monster.ca (www.monster.ca), and Workopolis (www.workopolis.com). Some employers use a few other sites as part of their recruitment strategy, depending on their budget, the job, and the target audience.

Join the association

Many occupations are affiliated with professional associations, and these, in turn, often have Web sites. Association Web sites are similar to industry-specific, or niche, sites, in that they focus on a specific occupation or industry. However, the primary focus of an association Web site is to provide information and services to its membership — not to advertise jobs. You may have to become a member of the association in order to access the job advertisements on the Web site. From a time perspective, unless you are already a member of a professional asso-ciation, you might be wasting your time trying to access job postings on these sites. On the other hand, if you qualify for membership in an association, they can be great sources of career-related information and networking opportunities. Think about joining up!

The Associations Canada Web site (www.associationscanada.com) has a list of professional associations related to various occupations and industries in Canada.

When a company advertises job openings elsewhere than on its own Web site — either in online job banks or in traditional sources, such as newspapers — the company's Web site address will usually be easy to locate in the ad.

Before you apply for a job advertised online, make a point of checking out the employer. Part of this sleuth work includes visiting the company's Web site. Make a point, in your cover letter, of letting the employer know that you've done this legwork. For example, you can write, "After a review of your corporate Web site, I am excited about the idea of working for your firm!" or "The work you are doing in [list an area in which the company is involved] intrigues me and I would like to talk to you more about a possible position."

Using Online Networking Tools: Newsgroups and E-Mail Lists

Newsgroups and *e-mail lists* are types of online communities, usually dedicated to a specific topic. Some sample topics (I swear these are all true): Calgary jobs, model airplanes, VB computer programmers, Bichon Frise dogs. Joining a newsgroup or e-mail list can be like jumping off a giant springboard and soaring high into an untold number of cyber communities. These groups are terrific networking tools.

Without getting too technical, newsgroups and e-mail lists work like a bulletin board. You post a message to the newsgroup or list, and everyone in the group or on the list has an opportunity to read that message — and possibly respond. The main difference between the two is this: With an e-mail list, your posting is sent to all members of the list, directly into their e-mail inbox; with a newsgroup, members have to sign on to the newsgroup (it's like another folder in your e-mail program) and click your posting to read it. Either tool is a great way to get the word out that you are looking for a job, or to search for jobs posted on the newsgroup or list.

Recruiters often search e-mail lists and newsgroups that are related to the position for which they are recruiting, and post job vacancies there. What great targeted advertising!

Here are a few newsgroups dedicated to job postings:

- ✔ `can.jobs`: Postings of any kind of job anywhere in Canada
- ✔ `calgary.jobs`: Postings of any kind of job in Calgary
- ✔ `misc.jobs`: Postings of any kind of job anywhere
- ✔ `tor.jobs`: Postings of any kind of job in Toronto

You can use search engines to find discussion boards, job search forums, e-mail lists, or newsgroups that discuss topics of importance to professionals in your area. If you belong to a professional association, you can visit its Web site to find forums or mailing lists to which members subscribe.

To sign on to a newsgroup or e-mail list or to search for topics of interest, you can look in one of these popular directories:

- **Yahoo! Groups** (www.groupsyahoo.com) **(Newsgroup directory):** Using this site as a jumping off point, you can start your own group or search for groups that are already part of the Yahoo! Groups network.

- **eScribe.com** (www.escribe.com) **(E-mail list directory):** eScribe.com is a service for e-mail list owners who want to make their lists available to others. They provide *public* access (to anyone who is interested in joining) and *private* access (for group members only — you have to have a moderator give you permission to join). You don't need any special software to join; you just register your e-mail address and some personal information and then you start receiving messages that are posted to the list.

Users tend to have strict rules about how and what to post. It's a good idea to learn the etiquette of the particular newsgroup or e-mail list you want to subscribe to, *before* you begin posting messages. Lurk before you post — review previous postings to the group and read the frequently asked questions. If in doubt whether it is kosher to post your résumé or to ask about a job, just send out a posting and ask.

It's also easy to over-subscribe to newsgroups and e-mail lists in your eagerness to find a job, or because some topics just sound, well, interesting. The number of postings you receive can grow exponentially. My advice is to stick with one or two that are directly related to your job hunt and then unsubscribe when you have found a job. You can always subscribe later to other lists that interest you.

Chapter 14

Networking: It's Not a Four-Letter Word

*T*here is nothing magic about networking, really. It is simply an exchange of information, ideas, and contacts between people. Networking is about making connections and developing mutually beneficial relationships with others. It's a you-scratch-my-back, I'll-scratch-yours scenario. You have to be willing to do something in return for receiving help, though, or your networks will quickly become ineffective.

Many job hunters don't see the value of networking, can't find the time for it, or are afraid to do it. If you recognize yourself in any of those descriptions, you've come to the right chapter. In this chapter, I walk you through the art of networking. It is a skill you can develop, and, once you actually start using it, you soon come to rely on networks for many things, not just help with a job hunt. Networking is a key tool in your job hunt and it can open many doors for you. It can help you do everything from researching leads (an early part of the job-hunting process) to landing an interview (closer to the end of the process!). There are many ways to network, both formal and informal. In this chapter, I tell you how to develop your networks and use them effectively to land a job.

Networking Isn't Just a Funky Trend

Some of us cringe at the word "networking," hoping it's just a trend that's here today and gone tomorrow — kind of like baggy pants, purple hair, and pierced body parts. Networking may intimidate those of you who think of it as trying to "sell yourself," especially if you don't think of yourself as a super-star salesperson. (Hey, some of you might not even want to be a superstar salesperson!)

Fortunately, the reality of networking is totally different. It's not about marketing or selling yourself, but rather about making connections with people. The concept is easier to grasp if you actually take *you* out of the equation altogether and focus on others, on reaching out.

If you think about it, you'll realize that you network all the time, probably without knowing it. Think about that time at work when you needed a supplier or someone with different expertise. You knew that a friend of yours fit the bill, so you called him up, discussed the project, and ended up giving him the contract. In return, you're confident he'll keep you in mind for situations that may require your expertise. Networking occurs on a personal level, too, between friends, parents — even between family members. These people can be valuable sources of information, assistance, and advice.

Networking can be a big help when you're looking for a job. For job hunters, *networking* means asking your professional or personal contacts for job-related information and referrals. You then contact people specifically to ask them for help — either to make further connections or for specific information about a job or company.

Remember that you have to be prepared to *give* as well as *receive* from your network. Don't network just for the purpose of advancing your own job hunt, or you'll be sorely disappointed. Focus on what you can do in return for the person you're networking with. How can you help her out? Focus also on building an ongoing relationship where you'll hopefully have the chance to help each other out again and again. That's the right networking attitude.

So, How Important Is Networking?

Well, that's a good question. I mulled this one over with several recruiters I know. The consensus among those who think networking is the best way to find a job is that between 70 and 80 percent of all jobs are filled through networking (some of you know it as word of mouth). To make the best use of this tool, this group of my colleagues argues, you must follow an elaborate network-building process; you focus the bulk of your time on making contacts, asking for help to make more contacts, following up on these contacts, and so on, and so on. . . .

Dave and Diane's networking success stories

My friend Dave has used networking to help him land several jobs. In one case, he attended a conference with a colleague from another company who mentioned they had a position open. Dave had missed the newspaper ad because he was not job hunting at the time. This networking contact gave him the opportunity to submit an application, and he got the job. Another bonus was that because of the working relationship with his referrer, he applied with a favourable recommendation.

Diane, an employment agency manager, found that networks she developed while attending college in her forties helped her land her dream job. She took the time to meet and build friendships with people in their first and second years of the program. One of those people went on to establish her own recruiting business and contacted Diane about "filling in" on a temporary position in a government office during vacation time. That "temp" position went on for over a year, and she further enhanced her networks during that time. Someone in her network actually forwarded her name to a contractor, who hired her as an area manager with an employment agency — her dream job!

My view is that networking should be an important part of your job hunt, but don't spend all your time on this and ignore other important parts of the process — sending out résumés and cover letters, making cold calls, and following up.

If you are self-employed or thinking of starting your own business, there is absolutely no substitute for networking. It is still the most effective way to build your clientele. The best way to develop your business network is to join groups and organizations and develop ongoing relationships with people who can use your product or service or who can refer you to others who do. Chapter 21 discusses the ins and outs of starting your own business in Canada.

Formal Networking

Formal networking is when you get together specifically for that purpose — to connect. It is networking by design. Everyone who attends the meetings or gatherings knows the score. It is an accepted fact that you are there not just to get something out of the meeting in the way of leads or information, but also to help others if you can. This differs from informal networking — chance meetings or daily interactions with people, during which you exchange information or assistance.

Some of the arenas ripe for networking include conferences and workshops, information interviews, and professional associations.

At conferences, trade shows, and workshops

Workshops, conferences, tradeshows, and seminars are places where you learn something, right? Yes, but don't overlook that these are great places to meet other people in your field. What incredible networking opportunities! And yes, I would classify these as formal networking because, let's face it, part of the reason you attend conferences is to make contacts and network. Meeting someone across a table during a workshop or conference often leads to an exchange of information and business cards, and, *voilà* — the person becomes part of your network and you become part of theirs.

Keep in touch with the people you meet, to make sure they stay part of your network (even if it is just an e-mail note or a holiday greeting card once a year).

Networking at conferences may also lead to dinner, drinks, and a night out with other conference attendees. If drinking tends to loosen your tongue and lessen your inhibitions, be careful not to do or say anything you might regret — like bad-mouth your current employer or say anything that might not show you at your best. This could be your only chance to impress this person, and it is really easy to blow it! You could be the talk of the town — or at least the conference — the next day.

At information interviews

An *information interview* is a discussion with someone for the purpose of learning more about a job or career path of interest to you. While the purpose of an information interview is to collect information, these are also great networking opportunities. You are setting up a formal meeting — with someone who potentially could help you with your job hunt.

Networking for introverts

Let's face it, not everyone is comfortable being in the spotlight. If this sounds like you, don't be so hard on yourself. Anybody can network — some people are just more reluctant than others.

Begin by figuring out the worst-case scenario. The person you approach won't have time to talk to you or to help you. So big deal. You move on to your next contact. Once you start this process, however, you'll be pleasantly surprised at just how many people *are* willing to help you out. But remember that networking is a two-way street: Always be on the lookout for ways to repay your contact for their help. Also, keep in mind that listening and asking questions is an important part of networking. People will warm up to you if you show genuine interest in them and in what they do.

Think about networking this way: The worst they can say is no, but if you don't ask, they'll never have a chance to say yes.

How do you figure out whom you should ask for an information interview? Ask everyone you know if they have any contacts in the field you'd like to explore. Generally an information interview takes place with someone who is already employed in the position or who has insider knowledge about what is required in the position. You'd be surprised whom people know! You can also search for articles and call the people quoted in them, do an online search for companies, and contact people in the field. Another source is the campus employment services office or alumni association at your local college or university. I discuss information interviews in more detail in Chapter 11.

Through professional associations

If there is a trade or professional association connected to your field of interest, become a member. Go further than that, if you can afford the time, and volunteer for the association — whether it be as part of the conference planning committee or as editor of the newsletter. It's a great way to meet influential people in your field and you may even get your membership for free.

There's no time like school-time to join an association in the field you think you might be interested in career-wise. If you're still keen once you graduate, do some volunteer work for them. You'll make all sorts of contacts — one of which could turn into a job offer. Another bonus: a student membership is usually a fraction of the cost of a professional membership.

Log on to the Associations Canada Web site (www.associationscanada.com), where you can access a comprehensive list of Canadian trade and professional associations.

Informal Networking

You're probably looking at this and groaning — first you have to make an effort to network by design (formal networking) and then I tell you that everything you do could be a networking opportunity and you need to be poised to take advantage of these potential contacts. So when do you get to take a break from networking? You may start to feel like a salesperson! They are great at networking because it is a skill they develop in order to be good at their jobs.

No, you don't have to go through life thinking "what can I do for you and what can you do for me?" every time you meet someone. It is reasonably easy to recognize when something is said in a conversation that relates to you or that you know something about. You do that in everyday life anyway, right? This section gives you some examples of informal networking (even if you don't know it) and how to make the most of it (without making it your life).

Through extracurricular activities

You've heard the cliché about being a "joiner," but it really *can* pay off from a networking perspective. Get involved in activities outside of your work. You don't have to be out every night of the week, just enough so that you can see your circle expanding. A teacher, a Realtor, an entrepreneur, a retail supervisor, or an aerobics instructor may all be valuable contacts — and they may all be members of that book club or art class you're thinking of joining.

Joining a service group such as the Kinsmen, the Lions Club, or the Rotary Club can pave the way to great networking opportunities. I know several people who have used their contacts from these groups to either refer a person for a job or to find a job themselves. While any volunteer community organization is a good place to network, service groups or clubs are a cut above because their membership can be quite diverse, spanning the entire community. Many of these groups have international arms, as well, providing the opportunity to exchange information or attend functions far outside your normal sphere.

At church

If you are a member of a church or religious group, you likely see the same people weekly and often get to know them at church functions. This is a great place to network — you will find that people in your church will often go out of their way to help you.

In school

Don't wait until you're looking for your next job to start building your network. Start building it in high school and university. Join your school council and volunteer for committees, or join clubs or associations. Set up networking opportunities with students ahead of you in the program. They may be students today, but they could be key players in their respective fields tomorrow. So, they're a valuable part of your future network. Network with professors and department heads in your area of specialization. Add people you have done information interviews with to your list of contacts (see Chapter 11).

At social events

Parties or activities to which you take your kids are full of informal networking opportunities. I often see the same people at my son's hockey games year after year. Striking up a conversation and establishing a relationship is pretty easy, since we have something in common — we're hockey parents. From there, we work what we do into the conversation, and usually end up exchanging business cards or contact information. Just because it doesn't feel like networking doesn't mean it isn't! You've got that person's business card (or at least their name and number) in your wallet now, and that's a start.

When you see the same people repeatedly (like at the hockey arena or soccer field), you can afford to take the time to get to know them first, then ease into your networking and asking for, or providing, help.

Online Networking

While face-to-face networking is indispensable, the additional contacts you make on the Internet can increase the size and diversity of your network astronomically. Once you realize the importance of networking, the next logical step is to use technology to enhance your networks. Once you start Net-working, look out! It can be a lot of fun — you may get hooked!

The Internet is a popular place to network for two reasons:

- ✔ **It is a "safe" place for you to express your views without fear of verbal reprisal.** The Web lets you formulate and write your thoughts before presenting them.

- ✔ **It allows you to network on your own time.** We don't always have the time (or do not take the time) to network face-to-face. You can sit down in front of your computer any old time you please. You set the schedule.

Newsgroups, e-mail lists, chat rooms, and discussion forums are online communities — usually centred around a specific topic (such as Java computer programmers, Bichon Frise dogs, working from home, Calgary jobs). They are networking tools, and people interested in the specific topic often can just sign on and participate in the discussion. There may be a moderator that has to verify that you meet any membership criteria they may have — for example, being a published writer in order to join a writer's list. For the most part, however, it is reasonably easy to be accepted into an online networking group. I discuss these tools as they relate to researching jobs online in Chapter 13.

When networking online, remember that you don't have any way of verifying the identity or credentials of the person you are talking to. Be very careful about giving out personal information and arranging meetings. If you use your common sense, you should be okay — meet in daylight, in public places, and during busy hours. Also make sure a friend or colleague knows what you are doing, or, better yet, bring someone with you.

Check out these online tools to take your networking to a whole new level:

✔ **Chat rooms:** A chat room is a great way to network with people. You actually "talk" online (via your keyboard) to people in *real time*. This means you type in your comments and immediately can see what other people currently "in" the chat room reply. You can find chat rooms for just about any topic, but you do have to log on to the Web site that is hosting the chat room! There are numerous online directories to help you find chat rooms that interest you. Yahoo! Chat (chat.yahoo.com) has compiled a directory of chat rooms that you can search and easily access to find a group that applies to you. Remember to be careful about divulging personal information about yourself.

✔ **Discussion groups and online forums:** Discussion groups and online forums are places where you can post comments or questions about a specific topic. Like chat rooms, you have to log on to the Web site where the discussion group is hosted, and may have to register to become a member of the group.

✔ **E-mail lists:** An e-mail list is created when a whole bunch of people all sign up to receive e-mails about a specific topic. When you or anyone else on the list sends an e-mail to the main list address, everyone gets the e-mail. E-mail lists appeal to people who like getting the postings immediately and having them come as regular e-mail, rather than having to sign on to a site to check postings. If having a lot of incoming e-mails drives you crazy, you can always subscribe to the digest form of the list and get a batch of e-mails once or twice a day, bundled together in one message.

There are hundreds of thousands of e-mail groups in cyberspace. You can check out a large cross-section of them at eScribe.com (www.escribe.com). eScribe is a service provided to list owners who want to make their lists available and accessible to those who want to sign on. They provide public and *private access* (where you have to have a moderator give you permission to join). You don't need any special software to join; you just give your e-mail address and start receiving messages that are posted to the list.

✔ **Newsgroups:** A newsgroup is kind of like an online bulletin board. You post a message to the newsgroup and everyone on the list has the opportunity to read it. They just have to click on the message. There are legions of newsgroups online, so it can be a challenge finding one that is of interest to you . Thank goodness there is help out there — some sites have tried to organize and make sense out of newsgroups. Try visiting Yahoo! Groups (www.groupsyahoo.com). Using this site as a starting point, you can start your own group, or search for groups that are already part of the Yahoo! Groups. Yahoo! Groups is actually the product of a merger among several other newsgroup directories. The main difference between a newsgroup and an e-mail list is that with the former, your posting is sent to the e-mail address of ALL members of the e-mail list, whereas with a newsgroup, members have to go to the newsgroup folder in their e-mail program and click on your posting to read it. It is like the difference between going out for dinner (newsgroup) or ordering in (e-mail list).

Networking Your Way to a Job

Knowing how to develop your network is great, but how do you go about using it to find a job? This is when it becomes your turn to ask for help from your network. You may have maintained and enhanced your network over time, in which case asking for help in a job hunt should be reasonably easy. Even if you haven't established your network, the tips below will help you develop contacts to find job leads, obtain more information, and hopefully get a referral for a job.

When you need to start using your network for job-hunting purposes, the first thing to do is make a list of contacts you think will be able to help.

Even if you haven't formally networked up until now, make up your list, anyway. You'll be surprised at how many people you know who may be of help during your job hunt.

Networking rules

- ✔ **Introduce yourself.** Explain how you got this person's name (this may not apply if this is a chance opportunity and you were not referred).

- ✔ **Establish a rapport.** This can be done by mentioning something you have in common, such as kids in hockey together or being interested in the same career. If in person, it is best to show interest in the other person by asking questions about them and *listening* to their answers.

- ✔ **Offer them something.** It can be a referral, a related magazine article, information, anything of value to them. This shows you want to help them, too.

- ✔ **Tell them what you are looking for.** Be upfront and specific. Tell them how they can help, if they so desire.

- ✔ **Don't be offended if they do not have time to help.** But you will be surprised how many people want to.

Here is a suggested order for your list of contacts, arranged in descending order based on who is likely to be of most assistance:

Professional contacts (your primary list)

- ✔ People who work in your target industry or occupation *and* have the ability to hire you

- ✔ People who work in your target industry or occupation

- ✔ People who deal with or know someone in your target industry or occupation (customers, suppliers, instructors, colleagues, family, friends)

- ✔ People who work for the company you are targeting

- ✔ Anyone in the professional association for your field

- ✔ Well-connected people who like you (such as the mayor of your town or your financial advisor)

- ✔ Co-workers or supervisors in your current or previous jobs (of course, if your current employer doesn't know you are looking, don't use your current supervisor as a contact)

Personal contacts (your secondary list)

- ✔ Family (not just your siblings and parents; check out your extended family — second and third cousins, step-aunts and uncles)

- ✔ Alumni from your university or college currently working in your target industry or occupation. Online groups such as Classmates.com (www.classmates.com) can put you in touch with alumni from your school.

- ✔ Friends

- ✔ Instructors or professors who taught you at university or college

- ✔ People you deal with daily but who are not connected to your work, such as your hairdresser, landlord, fitness trainer, accountant, lawyer, doctor, or Realtor

Four steps to an inspired interview

Once you've made your list of contacts, follow these steps to make the most out of your networking interview.

1. **Get in touch with your contact:** Request an in-person or telephone meeting via letter, e-mail, or phone call.

   You may be trying to set up a face-to-face meeting, but your contact may have other ideas. She may not have time to meet with you, but may be more than willing to chat for a few minutes on the phone. So, as the Girl Guides say, be prepared! Write down your introduction and rehearse it before you call. It should say who you are, who referred you, and what you are looking for. Have your questions ready just in case! While an in-person meeting is preferable, you can accomplish a lot with a well-orchestrated phone conversation. Follow the template below to get the most out of your interview: Call or e-mail them with a 15-second explanation of what you are looking for and why. Fill in the blanks:

"Hi, this is [_____] calling. You may remember me from [_____] . I am just reconnecting with people to let them know I am in the job market again. I am looking for job leads in the [_____] field or names of people who might be able to help me."

Ask for an in-person meeting or schedule a further phone conversation to follow up once they have had time to think about it.

"I wondered if I could schedule a meeting to talk to you a little more about any ideas you might have." If they hesitate, try: "I can always call you back and discuss it over the phone once you have had some time to think about it."

Repeat what you are looking for, confirm your future meeting date and what you are looking for.

"I will see you [or call you] on [_____]. Just to reiterate, I am looking for job leads and possible referrals and I believe you might be the person who can help me in that area. Thank you for your time and I look forward to talking to you then."

2. **Meet with your contact:** At the actual meeting, introduce yourself, tell your contact why you have chosen to speak to her (if it was a referral, say who referred you), and what it is that you would like from her. Remember, impressions count. Treat this meeting as if it were a job interview (see Chapter 16 for information on how to prepare for an interview). Dress professionally, be on time, stay on topic, and, above all, respect *their* time.

Make sure you have a specific purpose in mind for the meeting. If you want a referral for a specific company, tell your contact. If you are looking for a job lead, ask for that specifically. If you are looking only for further contacts, ask them to refer you to individuals in your target industry or occupation. Going into a meeting without a specific purpose in mind will not only result in nothing for you to move forward with, but might also tick off the person you are talking to. Not a good idea! Keep your interview short and to the point, and be prepared.

3. **Thank your contact:** Send a note or e-mail to each person who took the time to meet with you face-to-face. Think of it as network maintenance. When my sister-in-law had the windshield on her family's van replaced, less than a week later she received a thank-you card from the owner of the garage. Not surprisingly, his is the first garage she steers others toward. That small act "networked" his business to others, without his even making face-to-face contact.

4. **Follow up on referrals:** Many contacts will provide you with referrals. Follow up and try to get a meeting — remember to let them know who referred you to them. These can only benefit you, expanding your network and increasing your chances of finding a job.

Remember to always be on your best behaviour — whether it be in an e-mail, over the phone, and certainly in face-to-face meetings with contacts. A bad first impression can follow your name much longer than even the best first impression. If you blunder, apologize — most people understand that mistakes can be made.

Networking tips

Keep these handy tips in mind to help you network more effectively:

- **Start networking early:** Don't wait until you need help to start building your network. It takes time to get networks into place and working. You should start networking when you are in college or even high school and continue throughout your career and personal life.

- **Adopt a winning approach:** To break the ice when you meet a new contact, ask them about themselves and their business first before plunging forward about yourself. As they're jawing about themselves, try to think of someone in your already-existing network who would benefit from or be of help to your new contact. Then share the name and offer to make an introduction. You'll find that it's then much easier to ask for help or a referral.

- **Be open-minded about whom you network with:** Your network does not have to include only people in your line of work. You will find different people bring different skills and opportunities to your network. My own personal network includes other parents, writers, plumbers, bankers, real estate agents, travel agents, foresters, accountants, computer programmers, businesspeople, and so on — all of whom I can draw on for their different areas of expertise. When I want the answer to a question about the benefits of rewriting a mortgage, I e-mail my banker contact. If I can't figure out how to write a formula in Excel, I contact a fellow college instructor.

- **Carry business cards — always:** Have a few business cards handy, even if you are not working. You can make up cards on any printer and can buy preprinted business card paper. Give out cards to everyone you know. Have information that identifies you on the card. For example, if you are looking for a job in a particular occupation — graphic design — put Graphic Designer under your name.

✔ **Follow up:** Keep in touch with people you have had the opportunity to meet and exchange business cards with — it is an effective way to begin networking. Collect their cards and write where you met them and something interesting they may have told you on the back. Then, send an e-mail or a written note saying it was nice to have met them and ask for a little more information about what they do. If you can pass their name on to possible contacts, by all means do so. They have been added to your network and, when you need to ask for help, they will know who you are. E-mail is an ideal way to follow up on this kind of contact as it is fast and easy to reply.

✔ **Keep your network informed about you:** Remember to keep your network informed about new developments in your life. Something as simple as a holiday newsletter (either personal or professional) can help keep your contacts posted. Remember that networking is an ongoing process. I'm not saying you have to call up your economics professor once a week and go for lunch, but you'll appreciate having kept in contact when the time comes that you need help from that person.

✔ **Make networking a habit:** Try to include making a few networking contacts in your daily action plan. See Chapter 4 for a sample job-hunting schedule.

Organizing Your Network

You don't need an elaborate database to organize your networking contacts. You do, however, need some sort of system to keep yourself organized. A computerized database, such as Excel, can really help out with sorting and cross-referencing. For example, Joe B. gave you the name of someone who worked at a specific company and you want to find that name later because there is a job open there. If you have it on the computer, you can do a search and find the information right away.

Include the following sections in a networking chart:

✔ Name
✔ Title
✔ Company
✔ Business address
✔ Home address (if a personal contact)
✔ Phone number
✔ Fax number

- ✔ E-mail address
- ✔ Nature of connection (how did you connect with this person?)
- ✔ Referrals (other companies)
- ✔ Referrals (other contacts)
- ✔ Priority (A, B, or C)
- ✔ Comments
- ✔ Other (personal info you'll use to break the ice next time you speak)

Part IV
In the Thick of It: Interviews and Negotiations

The 5th Wave
By Rich Tennant

"Very good answer! Now, let me ask you another question..."

In this part . . .

You find out about different interview formats and styles of questioning. I give you some tried-and-true advice on how to prepare for your interview and how to go in there on the big day and knock 'em dead. This part also covers negotiating job offers and employment contracts, and fills you in on some must-know facts about Canadian employment law that may affect you during the interview process, as well as later, when you're actually on the job.

Chapter 15

Interview Formats and Styles

. . . .

In This Chapter

▶ Exploring different types of interviews

▶ Adapting to various interview techniques

▶ Answering behavioural interview questions

▶ Getting the scoop on pre-employment tests that you may have to take

. . . .

Congratulations! If you are reading this chapter, you have likely succeeded in landing an interview. Stop for a minute and celebrate your accomplishment. You have managed to make your way to the head of the pack — you are one of the finalists! That, in itself, is cause for celebration.

Consider what you have actually accomplished to land this interview. You have emerged as a primary candidate from what might have been hundreds of candidates. The recruiter believes your skills fit with the position available, and now you have the opportunity to *show* them what you are made of.

In this chapter, I tell you about the different interview formats you might be faced with, including in-person interviews, panel interviews, telephone interviews, and long distance interviews using technology. I touch on the different interview styles you may come up against, including traditional, behavioural, and situational, and provide you with an overview of pre-employment tests you might encounter at some point along the way.

Interview Formats

Interviews can be conducted in four formats: one-on-one, by a panel, by telephone, or even online with the assistance of various types of technology. Most employers will eventually want to meet the interviewee face-to-face, but they may use a telephone interview as a first interview to help shortlist the applicants. Sometimes, employers use a dual interview format. First, the recruiter interviews the applicant either on the phone or one-on-one. If you pass muster in this interview, you are quite likely to face a panel for a second, and possibly more formal, interview. The group of people eyeing you on the other side of the table can include your prospective supervisor, maybe his supervisor, and sometimes a representative from the human resources department.

The one-on-one interview

A *one-on-one interview* is a face-to-face interview where you either meet with one person in the company and are sent on your way, or meet with several people in the company, each on an individual basis — a series of one-on-one interviews, if you will. One-on-one interviews tend to be less structured and less formal, even if they are part of a series.

Most of the time, an in-person one-on-one interview will be part one of a two-part process. The purpose is to pre-screen candidates and further shortlist the more qualified applicants to determine whom they will bring in for the full-meal deal — the panel interview. The second interview will probably be a panel interview with peers and managers and will have preset questions, making it a more formal process.

If you have a series of one-on-one interviews, they may be conducted by any of these people:

✔ The recruiter

✔ A prospective co-worker

✔ The position's supervisor

✔ The supervisor's boss

If, on the other hand, your interview is not the first of two interviews, but rather the only interview, the decision to move you ahead in the hiring process (conducting reference checks and potentially offering you the job) is made based on this one meeting. This type of one-on-one interview generally occurs in a smaller organization and tends to be less formal than a panel interview. You will likely meet with the supervisor or manager to whom the position reports.

You may be asked to complete some pre-employment tests at the first interview as well. Tests? Don't panic! These aren't the type of tests you can study for. I talk about pre-employment tests later in this chapter.

Your one-on-one interview can vary in length from 20 minutes to a few hours, depending on how many people you see, and whether or not you complete any pre-employment tests.

Managing the interview

One advantage of a one-on-one interview is that the interviewee often feels more comfortable (and so does the interviewer). You can end up having more of a conversation or a less structured discussion, and may be able to establish a rapport with your interviewer.

Remember, this is an interview and the purpose is to try to determine both your fit and your skill level. It is good to establish a rapport, but don't try to become too familiar with the interviewer. Always be professional. (See Chapter 17 for more interview tips.)

Potential pitfalls

If you don't hit it off with the interviewer, the one-on-one approach may not work to your advantage.

If you happen to end up with an inexperienced interviewer, he may end up not getting a handle on your skills at all.

The panel interview

Walking into a room and seeing anywhere from three to eight people sitting at one end of a long table can be very intimidating. Ah yes, welcome to the panel interview. My sister-in-law described her first ever interview when she was a shy 17-year-old as the scariest experience in her life. She was being interviewed for a municipal summer programs leader position and was appalled to see eight people sitting at one end of a conference room table (a very *long* table) waiting to interview her. She sat at the other end of the table feeling very intimidated. This type of panel interview is not rare (although being interviewed by a panel of eight is a bit much). Unless you ask at the time the interview is being set up, you may not know you are to be interviewed by a panel until you actually arrive.

Allyson had a similar experience. She was 20 years old and being interviewed for a hostess position with a major hotel chain that conducted "group" interviews all over Canada. They herded about 15 candidates into a room, where they sat across the table from several interviewers with their résumés in front of them. The interviewers would wander down the line, glancing at résumés and asking questions at random. After about 20 minutes, they placed contracts in front of the people they had decided to hire, and asked the rest to leave the room! She describes the interview as a horrible experience — and she was one of the ones to get a job!

The idea behind the panel interview is that the more people there are involved in the hiring decision, the better the chances of hiring the best candidate. Applicants meet the entire group at once. Afterward, the interview team members assemble to compare notes.

Your aura tells me you're perfect for this job

Allyson was once interviewed for the position of store detective for a large pharmacy chain. In addition to being interviewed in a hotel room, the three-person panel included a well-known psychic who sometimes helped out the police force. His role was to conduct a psychic evaluation of the candidates! She was offered the job but refused it, thinking the whole process was a little too strange for her taste.

Panel interviews are effective when they are structured and the interviewing teams use a common *assessment guide* (set of guidelines outlining critical skills and abilities required for the position) to rate each applicant. Otherwise, the interview ends up being a conversation and the final decision is a "gut instinct" one.

If you have had a telephone interview or an in-person interview with a recruiter and are called back in for second interview, chances are you will meet with a panel. Governments and larger companies usually conduct panel interviews. Smaller companies without a human resources department usually conduct one-on-one interviews.

In a panel interview, you are likely to meet the same people you would have met in a series of one-on-one interviews — only they'll all be in the room with you at the same time.

The team in a panel interview could include the following:

- The recruiter
- One or two prospective co-workers
- The position's supervisor
- The department head or manager
- The department head from a different department

In a panel interview, expect a fairly formal interview where questions are developed ahead of time and assigned to different interviewers. Usually few panel members will be trained in interviewing and the interview starts out feeling fairly "rigid." As the interview moves along, it will usually lighten up somewhat as panel members get used to their roles and questions and you all relax a little.

Managing the interview

How can you start the interview off on the right foot? My advice is to shake hands with *every* panel member before the interview begins. Even if this is awkward, it helps you to connect with them on a personal level — something that can be important if they are at one end of a table and you are at the other.

Make every effort to remember each person's name and position. One technique is to repeat the person's name after they say it. For example, when you are introduced to Bob Parker, shake his hand and say, "Pleased to meet you, Mr. Parker." Unless you are given an indication that it is okay to use first names, address the panel members as "Mr." or "Ms." Try to use their names at least once when you answer their questions in the interview. If you think you will get the names wrong, write them down. Bring a notepad and pen with you to the interview so you can write notes. A colleague of mine writes down the names in the order they are sitting so she can quickly glance down and refer to them when answering a question. She even asks for spelling clarification.

Location, location, location

In-person interviews can be on the job site, at a central location used just for recruiting purposes such as a university or college boardroom, or even in a hotel room or restaurant. It can be a little tricky meeting someone in a public place like a restaurant — especially if you don't know who you are looking for. If you are meeting him in a restaurant, ask him to advise the hostess that he is waiting for you so you don't have to search for him. If you are meeting him some other place, such as a hotel lobby or an airport (I once was interviewed in an airport when the CEO was between planes), ask him how you will identify him. Give him some way to identify you, as well (just in case). A cell phone is always a good backup in case you are totally lost — ask for his number and give him yours if you have one.

I have conducted interviews in hotel rooms when I have had no other choice, although I must admit it is not the optimal location — from either the recruiter or the interviewee's perspective. If meeting in a hotel room is beyond your comfort zone, you can do one of the following:

✔ Phone the hotel front desk ahead of time to confirm that interviews are in fact being conducted from the hotel room. A recruiter will often use the front desk to help manage the flow of interviewees.

✔ Ask the recruiter if you can meet in the hotel lobby or restaurant instead. You can say that you are sorry and don't mean to offend anyone, but that you are not comfortable meeting in a hotel room, stressing, however, that you would really like to meet with him.

✔ You can ask who will be involved in the interview. If it is a panel, you may feel more comfortable. If it is just a single interviewer, you may want to ask him to meet you elsewhere.

If the interviewer is offended that you are not comfortable in a hotel room alone with him, that is unfortunate. However, if you think about it, perhaps if they have a problem understanding your concern, they might not be the organization you want to work for!

Try to make eye contact with individual panel members throughout the interview. People may have a tendency to gravitate toward the person they feel most comfortable with or whom they perceive has the power to hire them.

It may surprise you that interviewers can be nervous too, but that's often the case! In panel interviews, you are likely to find at least one panel member that is as nervous as you are. If you include all panel members in your responses by either looking at them, answering them directly, or saying their name as part of your response, they are more likely to relax. When answering, direct your comment to the person asking the question, but also try to briefly make eye contact with other panel members. This will make the interview flow more smoothly for all of you and will also make them feel comfortable with you as a candidate.

Potential pitfalls

Generally the interview will be very structured because panel members are assigned specific questions that they will ask. This, unfortunately, can take away from the conversational aspect of the interview.

Often panel interviews do not flow as well as one-on-one interviews because most or all of the questions are set and the interviewers may not be comfortable with impromptu questions. If you don't feel that a panel interview went well, it may be due to the nature of the interview rather than your performance.

The telephone interview

Telephone interviews are conducted for various reasons:

- **As a pre-screening interview prior to an in-person interview.** Sometimes telephone interviews are used as the first interview of a two-interview process. If you pass muster, you get invited to a second, and possibly a panel interview. In some cases there may be a few more qualified applicants than the recruiter wants to interview in person. Here, a telephone interview is used to get additional information to narrow down the list of candidates for in-person interviews.

- **When the organization hires seasonal employees.** This happens frequently in the hospitality industry. Jasper Park Lodge, in Jasper, Alberta, hires a large number of employees for its busiest seasons. These employees are usually only temporary or seasonal, and the expense of bringing individuals all the way to Jasper from across Canada would be prohibitive. So the hotel conducts a large number of these interviews by telephone.

✔ **To give candidates advance notice of a job's unique or unusual nature.** This could apply to jobs that require heavy physical labour, or labour that is inherently risky, such as a job repairing telephone wires or fighting forest fires. It could also apply to jobs that require a great deal of travel. An employer will often call an applicant and give her the scoop on the job before bringing her in for an interview.

✔ **When the job is in a remote location.** If an employer is trying to attract skilled personnel to a remote location (say, Iqaluit, Nunavut or Fort Nelson, British Columbia), she will often use a telephone interview to narrow down the list of potential applicants to one or two. The phone interview in a case like this is usually two-sided — the parties evaluate each other, the job, and the location. The interview may actually result in a job offer once references are checked, if the employer feels confident about the applicant. This can occur without their ever having met face-to-face.

Telephone interviews have recently become more popular because Canadians are more mobile and are willing to relocate in their quest for a great job. Phone interviews allow companies to pre-screen potential employees before transporting them to their offices for an in-person interview. Online job banks, like HotJobs.ca (www.hotjobs.ca), Monster.ca (www.monster.ca), and Workopolis (www.workopolis.com), let job hunters seek employment farther away from home because they post ads for positions across the country (and even around the world).

From the recruiter's perspective, when reviewing applications from all over the country and from around the world the cost of conducting in-person interviews for every promising candidate could be very high. Telephone interviews are often used as a first interview to make sure the person fits with the organization, has the technical skills required for the job, and really wants to relocate.

A telephone interview that is a pre-screening interview or that is for a seasonal hospitality industry job will often be conducted by a recruiter. Other telephone interviews such as the kind you have when you apply for a job in Inuvik are likely to be conducted by the position's supervisor.

To know what to expect, you need to know what employers are actually looking for in a telephone interview:

✔ **To determine if a person actually has the technical skills needed.** This is especially important in positions where your technical skills are key to your job performance. Expect to be asked questions regarding the technical aspects of the job.

✔ **To get a handle on a person's transferable or soft skills**. This is especially important in jobs where soft skills such as good communication or problem solving are required. Expect to be asked questions that probe your soft skills, too, such as your motivation, organizational skills, and attitude. See Chapter 24 for more about soft skills.

> ✔ **To determine fit between the potential employee and the company.**
> Both the employer and the employee should be concerned about whether
> they would fit well together. Some things to be considered are the
> company culture and location. Expect to be asked questions about why
> you want to work for this company and what your goals are.

Managing the interview

Telephone interviews are an interesting twist on the traditional face-to-face
interview. Often, you are not given any warning that you are about to be
interviewed over the phone. Your phone will ring and there will be a recruiter
on the other end of the line. You expect they are calling to get more information
or to set up an in-person interview and they may say, "Do you have time to
answer a few questions right now?" Your *brain* says, "No! Don't do it! Delay!!!
You need to get ready! Review your notes! What job is this? What company is
this?" but most times your *mouth* will say, "Sure, no problem," not wanting to
offend the recruiter or lose your chance at this job. Of course, not all recruiters
do this; some are considerate and e-mail or phone you to set up a time for an
interview. However, don't be surprised if you don't get this heads-up.

It's perfectly all right to ask the recruiter if you can make it another time. It's
not unprofessional, and shouldn't hurt your chances at the job. Better to
start off on the right foot than to be so flustered that you lose your footing
completely. Any good recruiter should not have a problem rescheduling the
call. If she does, well, would you want to work for a company that obviously
puts that kind of pressure on its employees? Didn't think so.

You can also ask them to call back in a short while, to give you a chance to
finish what you are doing. My friend Dave had his children in the bath when
he received a call at 7:30 p.m. about a job. He told the recruiter that he was
bathing his kids and asked her to call back in a half hour. He finished with the
kids, found the job in his files, and pulled up the company's Web site so he
was ready when the recruiter called back.

Before they call back, or before you call them if that's the way you arranged
it, go back and review the job ad, do a little more research into the company,
and write down a few questions about the job, the organization itself, or the
industry in general. (See Chapter 17 for more information on questions you
can ask during an interview.)

Remember to eliminate potential distractions such as TV and radio, and
ensure that your kids are occupied with something with strict instructions
not to bother you until you are off the phone. In one of my job hunts, I had
set my kids up to play in another room with our new puppy, thinking I had at
least half an hour to talk to the potential employer. About 15 minutes into it,
my youngest child came running into the room yelling (loudly and clearly),
"Mommy, Buddy pooped on the floor!" I had to explain to the interviewer that
Buddy was actually the dog, not one of my children.

What kind of questions can you expect over the telephone? It really depends on the reason for the interview. When the recruiter calls, you should ask him about the purpose of the interview at the same time as you schedule it. You could say something like "Is this interview to help develop a short list for in-person interviews?" The interviewer will likely elaborate on what he wants to know. If he wants to test your problem-solving abilities or probe your technical skills, you can brush up on these before the actual interview. For general information-gathering interviews, you can expect similar questions to those in an actual in-person interview.

Potential pitfalls

During a phone interview, you don't have to pay attention to eye contact and body posture, but you do have to pay attention to your voice and how you come across. Don't pause for too long, try not to say "um," and watch the Valley Girl slang ("like, you know . . .").

Remote interviews using technology

Here we go again — talking about how technology is changing everything! Well, thank goodness computers have not yet replaced face-to-face interviews, but the potential exists.

In the future, look for more of the following types of interviews:

- **Chat room interviews:** In this format, the interviewer types questions and you type answers. Though you can't see each other, the interview is conducted in real time as if you were in a room at the same time — virtually speaking.

- **Face-to-face online interviews:** Thanks to the advent of online cameras, nifty little Net toys that sit on top of your computer, you can see and speak to your interviewer in real time. At some point, these may be built into the screens themselves. You can actually be interviewed from your own home providing both you and the recruiter have the same technology. You would actually have to own the camera yourself to participate in this type of interview.

- **Fill-in-the-form interviews:** In this format, you answer questions in an online form. You might log on to a designated Web site to access the questions, or e-mail your answers to the recruiter.

- **Videoconferencing interviews:** In this format, you and the interviewer connect over a distance via a high-speed modem, video cameras on either end, and television screens. This is not the same as over the Internet even though modems are involved. You are actually set up in a room just for videoconferencing, as the equipment is quite specialized. Many colleges are using videoconferencing to allow students outside urban centres to take classes with the larger groups and feel that they are part of the class.

Playing the name game

Sometimes, it is tough enough remembering your own name in an interview without trying to keep in mind all the panel members' names and positions! However, it is very important that you try to address panel members by name and, taking this one step further, knowing their positions will help you direct your questions (and answers) to the correct person.

My favourite name retention technique is one with which you can have a lot of fun and will help you relax a little at the same time. The key is to associate the person's name with a descriptive word that starts with the same letter or is related to the name. You can do the same with their job title. I like to make the description as goofy as I can to help me remember better.

Here are a couple of examples. You might remember Gary Fowler, Plant Manager, by associating his name with Galloping Gary, Furry Fowler, or Plant Man. Cassandra Jones, Payroll Administrator could be Candy Cassandra Jones, Pretty Payroll Person. Remember, you don't have to let anyone know how you remember their name! (I wouldn't advise it, either.)

Some companies are already using these methods to interview but few are basing their hiring decisions solely on these methods. For the most part, such technology is used to establish short lists and an in-person interview is used to make the final decision. However, I foresee a time when everyone has a computer in their home and face-to-face interviews either will no longer be the norm or may be used to *meet* rather than to *select* the final candidate for a specific job. With the move toward increased reliance on technology, however, I fear this may take the human factor out of the hiring process and is not likely to lead to better hiring decisions.

Interview Styles

Employers are constantly looking for more "objective" ways (rather than subjective ways — relying on gut feelings) to learn about prospective employees, beyond whether they actually have the skills for the job. How you will handle different situations, what you have done in similar situations in the past, and how well you will fit with the organization's culture — all are important considerations.

While interviewers are all seeking the same information, the way they ask the questions differs. You can no longer expect a *traditional interview* — where you give a straightforward answer to a straightforward question (for example, "What did you do in your last job that applies to this job?"). While most interviewers will include some traditional questions, many will combine interview styles in the hope of finding out more about the candidate.

The styles most commonly used today are traditional interviews, *situational interviews* (hypothetical questions, such as, "What would you do if . . ."), and *behavioural interviews* ("Tell us about a time when you . . ."). Traditional questions are great at measuring a candidate's hard skills, while behavioural and situational questions are great at probing soft skills (see Chapter 24). A combination of all types of questions gives a recruiter a well-rounded perspective on the candidate (but may leave you, the interviewee, wondering what just hit you!). In this next section, I tell you about each type of interviewing style and how to ace the questions thrown at you.

The traditional interview

A traditional interview is the kind most job hunters expect when they are called in for an interview — one in which they are asked straightforward questions about their work experience and goals and how these fit into the job. While such questions may not always be easy to answer, the questions themselves are easy to understand.

Here are some examples of traditional interview questions:

- What have you done that applies to this job?
- What are your long-term goals?
- Why did you leave your last job?
- What are your strengths? Weaknesses?
- What did you major in at university?

Traditional interview questions are usually pretty basic. Occasionally, there is a tendency for interviewees to try to guess what the interviewer wants to hear and give him that answer instead. For example, in response to the question "Why did you leave your last job?" an interviewee responds, "I had advanced as far as I could go and was looking for new challenges." This may or may not be true, but it sounds good and is likely what the interviewer wants to hear. When answering traditional questions try to apply what you have done in the past to the job you are being interviewed for. In answer to the question, "What skills do you have that apply to this job?" you could answer, "I have done accounting, budgeting, and spreadsheet development in an organization which is a similar size to yours."

Interviewers asking traditional questions have no way of knowing whether or not you're telling the truth. But they can check your "facts" during reference check, so don't be tempted to exaggerate. Hiring decisions based on traditional interviews are often made based on "gut feelings," as a result of how well you come across, how relaxed and confident you appear, what kind of a rapport you established with the interviewer, and if you said what they wanted to hear.

Unfortunately, if you are shy or less outgoing, your job-related characteristics and soft skills may not be adequately evaluated — the job may go to the applicant who comes across as the most polished, regardless of whether they actually *can* or *will* do the job.

In an attempt to address these drawbacks and help companies make more informed and objective decisions, other interview styles have evolved: situational interviews (based on what you say you would do in a hypothetical situation) and behavioural descriptive interviews (asking for examples of past behaviours). Both these styles are discussed later in this chapter. Chances are, however, that you will still be faced with a few traditional interview questions as part of the overall interview process.

The situational interview: A twist on traditional

Once lumped together with traditional interviews, situational interviews have emerged as a distinct interview style. As an applicant, you are asked how you would handle job-related situations. Questions used in situational interviews are derived from specific activities of the job the applicant is applying for ("What would you do if you had to repair a broken powerline?"). Most often, traditional and situational interview questions will be asked in the same interview.

The major drawback to this type of question is that it assesses the way the applicant would *theoretically* perform in this situation. This interviewing technique seems to favour applicants who can quickly assess what an interviewer wants to hear and offer this response, when in reality the applicant might take a different course of action.

Here are some sample situational questions:

- ✔ "You are given an assignment to do but not given any instructions. How would you go about completing your assignment?"

- ✔ "If you had to make a decision and your supervisor was unavailable to consult, what would you do?"

- ✔ "You have several projects on the go, all of which you have been told are a priority. Your supervisor gives you another project and tells you it needs to be done by 5 p.m. How do you deal with this?"

- ✔ "A co-worker spends a lot of time at your desk complaining about management. Your supervisor has started to notice. How would you handle this situation?"

To do well in a situational interview, answer the question in terms of a similar real-life situation that relates to the question or clearly describes what you have accomplished in the past. Respond by saying "I have actually been involved in a similar situation in a previous job. This is how I handled it. . . ."

Many interviewers using situational interviews have refined this technique by asking for a specific example to help them assess what the applicant actually has done in a similar situation, not what he or she "would" do. This leads us into the realm of behavioural interviews.

The behavioural interview

Picture this: You go into the interview all primed with the "best" answers memorized to the top 100 different questions. The interview begins like any other — with a little chitchat to build a rapport. Then, *boom!* The interviewer starts asking questions like "Tell me about a time when you made a mistake that cost the company money" and "Give me an example of a time when you had to make a major decision and your supervisor was unavailable to consult." Uh-oh! You draw a blank.

This interview technique is called *behavioural descriptive* or *competency-based* interviewing. The questions that are asked in a behavioural interview are directly linked to the *competencies* (important tasks, essential functions, or work-related behaviours) required for you to be effective in the position. The basic premise is that your recent, relevant past performance is the best predictor of future performance. Interviewers ask for examples of specific events to try to figure out how you would perform in a similar situation.

An example of a traditional question may be "How would you deal with an angry customer?" It isn't difficult to figure out what the interviewer probably wants to hear, so you end up saying something like "I would politely ask them to tell me the problem, then I would offer my assistance in solving the problem." That doesn't sound too bad. The problem is that your answer is theoretical and doesn't represent what you would actually do or what you have done in that situation. An interviewer using behavioural techniques would ask the same question somewhat differently: "Tell me about a time when you had to deal with an angry customer. What was the problem and what was the outcome?" You would be expected to come up with a real story about an angry customer and describe how you dealt with it.

The interviewer determines the knowledge, skills, and behaviours that are essential for success in a position. Depending on the actual job, examples of competencies an interviewer might probe include these:

- ✔ **Communication skills:** They want to know how effective your written and verbal communication skills are.
- ✔ **Conflict resolution skills:** Looking for how you deal with and resolve conflict.
- ✔ **Decision-making ability:** How do you make decisions?
- ✔ **Interpersonal skills:** How well do you get along with others?
- ✔ **Leadership ability:** Do you have the ability to control, plan, and lead others toward a common goal?
- ✔ **Management skills:** Can you manage people, data, and tasks?
- ✔ **Motivational skills:** Are you a self-starter?
- ✔ **Organizational skills:** Do you have the ability to organize yourself and others?
- ✔ **Problem-solving ability:** Can you identify and resolve problems?
- ✔ **Teamwork skills:** How well do you work with others?
- ✔ **Technical skills:** Do you have the technical skills to do the job?

Each job requires different skills and competencies in different areas. The interviewer has to determine which of these are most important and should be probed at the interview. Each question in the interview will be designed to determine to what extent the candidate has performed successfully in previous positions or situations similar to this position.

You can determine which competencies and behaviours will be the most critical in a job by looking closely at the job ad, by reviewing an occupational profile (if the job has not been advertised), by asking someone doing a similar job, or even by talking to someone in the company itself. Compare your findings with the above list and identify specific examples for each of the competencies. For example, your research may suggest that a job requires good leadership, interpersonal skills, and problem-solving abilities. Think of a time when you used these skills successfully. Then think of a time when you may not have been successful and what you learned from the experience.

Behavioural interviews are becoming more popular because they have proven to be much more effective in predicting how a candidate will perform in various situations. You actually have to give an answer based on what you have done in the past, and this is usually a good indication of how you would behave in the future in a comparable situation. You don't always have to give work-related examples if you can't think of one. You may have experienced similar circumstances in other aspects of your life, such as volunteering, dealing with parents, handling conflict when shopping, or even coping in a traffic incident. Interviewers are trained to probe your answer to ensure that this is, in fact, a true example. They even go so far sometimes as to ask for the name of a person who can verify your story (really!).

Acing behavioural questions

When answering behaviour-based interview questions, you need to identify the following:

- ✔ **Task:** Describe the challenge you faced. What was the task?
- ✔ **Action:** Describe the steps you took to fix the situation.
- ✔ **Outcome:** Describe how it all turned out (you saved the day, of course).

Take some time, after the question is asked, to identify a good example. It is a great idea just to jot the words *Task, Action, Outcome* on the notepad you are taking to the interview, to jog your memory as to how to respond to a behavioural question.

You know it is a behavioural question when the question starts with one of the following:

- ✔ **Describe a time when . . .** For example, "Describe a time when you had to make a decision based on incomplete information."

- ✔ **Describe your experience with . . .** For example, "Describe your experience with difficult customers."

- ✔ **Give me a specific example of a time when you . . .** For example, "Give me a specific example of a time when you were required to lead a group to successful completion of a project."

- ✔ **Tell me about . . .** For example, "Tell me about a time when you disagreed with your supervisor on the best way to complete a project."

Interviewers asking behavioural interview questions also target *negative outcomes* — situations where you messed up on the job — to find out if you learn from your mistakes. ("Tell me about a time when you made a mistake that cost the company time and money.") When preparing for your interview, identify an unsuccessful example for each competency, just in case the interviewer asks. One positive way to end an answer to a negative probe is to tell them what you have done to prevent it from happening again — what you learned from the mistake. You could say something like "The mistake caused a delay in the project, but to ensure it would not happen again, I developed a new project tracking system."

Preparing stories for a behavioural interview

Behavioural interview questions ask you to give specific examples of past experience on the job. It can be difficult to think up related real-life stories quickly in an interview situation when you are nervous. Look at the competencies you have identified for the job and try to come up with stories that reflect your ability in those areas. Also come up with examples where you may not have handled a situation well but as a result enhanced your competency in an area.

For example, the job you are being interviewed for is training and development officer in a municipal government setting. You will first look at what competencies might be required in this job. Communication, organizational, management, and problem-solving skills might be some of the areas. (Remember, if you don't know what you need to be competent at, check the job ad, consult an occupational profile, or call someone in a similar position and ask!) You need to think of the competencies in terms of what actual tasks you have done that illustrate your proficiency in each of these areas. Also think of examples of times when you may not have been as competent as you would have liked in each area and how you worked your way through it. Frame your stories in terms of task, action, and outcome.

Practise telling your stories until they are brief and concise, one to three minutes long. Here's an example:

✔ **Set the stage (Task):** "I was asked to review the current training program, which was essentially nonexistent, for a previous employer."

✔ **Demonstrate the appropriate skill in action (Action):** "My first task was to analyze what kind of training we provided and what was needed. I then did a survey of employees to find out their thoughts. I developed a system to request, track, and follow up on individual training. I also established a series of workshops to train employees on the new computer system."

✔ **Have a positive outcome (Outcome):** "My supervisor implemented my suggestions and employees have commented that the company seems to be more concerned about them than before."

Or

✔ **If the outcome was not so positive, have an outcome that created a learning experience for you:** "I learned that while you need to include employees in developing a program such as this, it is important to have management buy in, as well. If I were to do this again, I would have a management meeting ahead of time to determine what their goals were, too."

A good example shows how you solved a problem or overcame an obstacle.

Some sample behavioural questions

Here are some sample behavioural questions that may be asked during an interview to probe your competency in certain areas. Remember to answer using the three-part Task-Action-Outcome model.

Communication skills

- "Can you tell me about a time when you effectively and efficiently communicated a complex matter to another person?"

- "Describe a time when you had to present your argument or case to a doubtful superior."

- "Tell us about a written or oral presentation you have made that you are especially proud of."

Conflict resolution skills

- "Conflict is part of our everyday life. Describe a time you had a conflict with a co-worker."

- "On occasion people get angry with us. Can you give us an example of a time someone 'blew up' at you and what you did?"

- "Tell me about a time when you disagreed with your supervisor on the best way to complete a project."

Decision-making ability

- "Tell us about a time when you came across an unexpected situation and you had to make a decision."

- "Give me an example of a time when you had to make a decision and your supervisor was unavailable to consult."

- "Describe a time when you had to make a decision based on incomplete information."

Interpersonal skills

- "Sometimes when a project is completed we receive feedback that is not what we expected. Describe a situation where this has happened to you."

- "Describe a situation that demonstrates you have the ability to work with other people."

- "Tell us about an experience you had with a difficult customer."

Leadership ability

- "On occasion we find ourselves in situations where leadership skills are required. Can you tell me about a time where you effectively led a group to achieve a goal?"

✔ "Give us an example of a time when a project under your leadership did not go as planned."

✔ "Describe a situation when your leadership skills were required to resolve a problem."

Management skills

✔ "Describe your experience managing a diverse group of people."

✔ "Give us a specific example of a management problem you have been faced with and how you dealt with it."

✔ "Tell us about a time when your management skills were the reason for successful completion of a project."

Motivational skills

✔ "Give an example from your work or volunteer experience that demonstrates you are a self-starter."

✔ "Describe a time when your self-motivation resulted in a project being completed on time and within budget."

✔ "Tell me about a time when you failed to accomplish a goal you set for yourself and how you handled the situation."

Organizational skills

✔ "Tell me about a time when you had to reorganize something to achieve a work-related or personal goal."

✔ "Give an example of a project you had to organize that required multiple priorities."

✔ "Describe an event or project you were responsible for organizing."

Problem-solving skills

✔ "Describe a time when you had to resolve a problem and there was no set precedent."

✔ "Give an example of a problem you were unable to resolve."

✔ "Tell me about a problem you resolved where you were especially proud of the final outcome."

Teamwork skills

✔ "Can you tell me about a time that you, as a team member, worked cooperatively with a group to obtain a goal?"

✔ "Describe a project you are most proud of that involved a team achievement."

✔ "Tell us about a time when a team project did not go as well as expected."

Technical skills

- ✔ "Tell me about a time that you were pleased with your coolness and your ability to effectively use your training during a tense situation."

- ✔ "Describe a time when you had a difficult task to learn and how you went about learning it."

- ✔ "Describe the duties or responsibilities during your work or academic experience that demonstrate your ability to do this job."

A Word about Pre-Employment Testing

To assist them in making better hiring decisions, many employers are adding pre-employment testing to their interview processes. *Pre-employment tests* are usually designed by psychologists and other experts for the purpose of evaluating certain characteristics and skills. Often you will be asked to complete a *battery* (more than one type) of tests or a single test designed to measure several characteristics.

Here are some of the different types of pre-employment tests and what they attempt to measure:

- ✔ **Ability tests:** These tests generally measure your technical or hard skills required for a job. A classic example of an ability test is a typing test for an office assistant position or a driving test for a truck driver. These tests measure what you can do currently.

- ✔ **Aptitude tests:** While ability tests measure your current capabilities, aptitude tests look at your potential to acquire certain job-related skills, with training, and eventually perform the job. An aptitude test could measure anything from mechanical aptitude to mathematical, problem-solving, and reasoning aptitudes. It all depends on the job.

- ✔ **Personality tests:** These tests, which attempt to define personality traits, are very common in pre-employment testing. Each question is designed to probe whether you possess a certain personality trait (good ones and bad ones alike), such as whether you're a generous or selfish person. The test results are supposed to give the employer a good idea as to what type of person you are, what your attitude is, and what kind of employee you will be.

Some people claim that you can manipulate your answers on a personality or aptitude test to skew the results and make you look like a better candidate. Test designers say, no way! They claim there are too many counterchecks (additional questions that ask the same thing in a different way). Lying on the test will show up as inconsistencies and you will not appear in a favourable light.

Ability, aptitude, and personality tests are the most common pre-employment tests, but you might also be required to complete one of these "not so technical" tests, too, depending on the job you're applying for:

- **Drug tests:** Some employers may ask you to take a drug test as a condition of a job offer. Yes, this is legal in most provinces as long as an employer can justify that taking drugs impairs a person's ability to do the job. (See Chapter 18 for more on negotiating a job offer.)

- **Handwriting tests:** A handwriting test may be used for two reasons — one practical and one a little off the wall. The practical application of a handwriting test is to see how neat a person's handwriting is. This could be necessary for jobs when you actually have to do a lot of writing — perhaps filling in forms, collecting and recording data, or manually recording information. (I wonder if they make doctors take a handwriting test?) The slightly offbeat application is when an employer actually takes the handwriting sample and has it analyzed to determine personality characteristics of the writer. This kind of test has been proven to be a very unreliable indicator of performance on the job.

- **Medical tests:** If certain physical or medical attributes are required for a job (such as visual abilities for a truck driver or physical fitness for a firefighter), an employer may require that you pass a job-related medical as a condition of a job offer.

- **Polygraph tests:** Otherwise known as a lie detector test, this one is generally used only in hiring for positions such as bodyguard or where there is a possibility of industrial espionage.

- **Pre-employment checks:** Other checks the employer might request that you provide could include the following: a *driver's abstract* (a record showing your history of traffic violations), a police security check, a *social services check* (to make sure you have no child or family complaints against you), or a credit check. These vary depending on the nature of the position and the requirements of the job.

Ask about the interview procedure when you are setting up the meeting time so you know whether there will be a pre-employment test. Employers are not obligated to tell you ahead of time unless you specifically ask.

Chapter 16

Preparing for the Interview

. . . .

In This Chapter

▶ Scheduling the interview

▶ Learning the six "big picture" questions of highly effective interviews

▶ Getting ready for the interview

. . . .

*Y*ou are about to be interviewed for a *great* job (at least, you hope it's a great job!). You start looking for those books that tell you what to expect and give you hundreds of questions you can practise. Whoa! Look no further — everything you need to do to prepare for your interview is in this book. You don't need to go through a hundred interview questions to be prepared! There are just a few (well, six) "big picture" questions you need to be prepared to answer, and some basic preparation work to complete. In this chapter, I take you from the actual scheduling of your interview . . . to the night before. I tell you what the interviewer will be looking for from you and how you can prepare (without giving you a bad case of information overload) for almost any question she will throw at you.

Booking You In

Generally, an interviewer will contact you directly at the phone number listed on your résumé or cover letter to request an interview. Some interviews are set up by e-mail, so be sure to check your e-mail regularly. Try to hold off yelling "Eeeyha!" until you get off the phone!

Setting the date and time

The interviewer will give you several options for interview dates and times. She'll be flexible to a certain extent, but maybe not as flexible as you would like or need. Asking if you can put off the interview for two weeks because you will be on vacation isn't a smart move. If you can't make any of the times she suggests, offer an alternative — ask if you can do the interview before you go, for example. Offer to come in after hours or even to do a telephone interview.

Remember, the interviewer has likely gone through an extensive screening process to shortlist you, and, while she's not likely to reject you simply because you cannot make an interview at a certain time and place, she will have to do some juggling. Be considerate of her time and priorities.

Determining the interview format

It is perfectly all right to ask about the interview format ahead of time. In fact, I highly recommend it! It shows that you are detail oriented and want to be prepared. So, once the interview time and date are established, ask the recruiter what the interview format will be or what you can expect at the interview. There may be a pre-employment test or you may be interviewed by several members of the team. Knowing this ahead of time can help you better prepare for the interview. For more on different interview formats and pre-employment testing, see Chapter 15.

Six Things the Interviewer Wants to Find Out About You

Most job hunters want to know specific questions that an interviewer will ask them. That way they can be prepared with predetermined responses. But what happens if you practise the answers to those questions and she doesn't ask them, or she asks something different, or, worse yet, she asks the same question in a different way! My advice is that you try to understand what the interviewer is going to look for and know what you have to offer in each area. That way, no matter how the question is phrased, you will know what information you want to give them. In this section, I tell you the six things an interviewer will try to learn about you, and how knowing these will help you prepare for almost any question.

Getting inside the mind of the interviewer can provide you with an edge over the other candidates. While the questions asked will vary, there are really just six big picture things an interviewer wants to find out. How he asks for this information may vary, but if you think out your responses to the big questions ahead of time, you should be able to answer almost any interview question. I say *almost* because an interviewer may throw some trick questions in just to see how you react. I deal with answering tricky questions in Chapter 17.

1. She wants to find out why you want to work there in the first place

What is it that attracts you to this employer rather than another one? Have you thought this out? Can you put this into words for the interviewer?

Typical questions exploring this subject area are the following:

- **Tell me what you know about our company.** Describe their main area of business. Tell them what interests you about them.

- **What attracts you to this job?** Describe what interests you about this company and this job.

- **Why do you want to work for us?** Describe what it is about this company that appeals to you. Why do you want to work for them?

- **What do you know about this industry?** You have done your research. Tell her what you know. If research is a totally foreign concept to you, you need to read through the chapters in Part III.

2. She wants to find out what skills you can bring to the table

The interviewer has established that, yes, you have researched the company and you have made a conscious decision that you would like to work for them. The next thing she wants to determine is what you can *do* for them. What are your hard and soft (transferable) skills and how can they benefit the company?

While this is by no means an all-inclusive list, here are some typical interview questions that explore this topic:

- **Walk me through your résumé and tell me what you have done that applies to this job.** Here is where having a copy of your résumé with you at the interview is a good idea. Refer to your résumé and point out relevant jobs you have held or related things that you have done.

- **Tell me what you think you can bring to this company.** You should describe a particular skill set and relate it to the company's overall vision and to the job for which you're applying (which forms part of that vision). Describe your soft skills (see Chapter 24) and how they will help you perform this job.

- **Why should we hire you?** Never respond to this by saying, "Because I need a job!" Again, try to link your soft and technical skills to the job. Show the interviewer that you fit the requirements. Let her know you want to work for this company.

✔ **How has your previous work experience and education prepared you for this job?** Refer to relevant information on your résumé. Try to answer in terms of how your experience can benefit them.

3. She wants to find out what kind of person you are and whether you'll fit the company culture

Every organization has its own *culture* (the values and beliefs of the organization) and it is very important that new employees fit into this culture. Is it fast-paced and change-oriented? Does it emphasize teamwork? Whatever the peculiarities and quirks, the interviewer wants to find out what kind of personality and work ethic you have so she can determine whether there's a fit.

Here are some typical questions that explore the whole "what kind of person are you?" scenario:

✔ **Tell me a little about yourself.** Ideally, you should have a short (one minute) infomercial memorized about yourself. Include your education, positions you have held, specific skills related to the job, job training, when you expect to graduate (if applicable), major achievements, and your goals.

✔ **Describe your ideal job.** You should have researched the job and the company. Link your skills and experience to the position.

✔ **How do you spend your spare time?** Let her in on a few personal tidbits about you — maybe you take yoga classes, play the piano, or are a voracious reader. It's okay to include any interests that are a little off the beaten path. I say *a little,* though; some things are better left unsaid during a job interview. Total personal disclosure is *not* required if the subject is not job-related!

✔ **How do you see this job in relation to your long-term objectives?** The interviewer is asking this question to see if you will fit in and how long you will stay at the company. List any long-term objectives that this position will help you attain. Be sure you don't give her an answer that suggests you want to learn a new job and then go somewhere else to use the skills. Ideally, you want to leave her with the impression that this job is part of your career path.

✔ **What appeals to you most about this job?** Here is where your research comes in. Discuss an aspect of the job or the company that appeals to you.

✔ **How would you define success?** Tell the interviewer what you consider success to be. Try to sound enthusiastic in your answer. Employers really like to hear you associate success with doing a job to the best of your ability and enjoying what you are doing, to boot.

✔ **Tell me your greatest strength.** Think about what your strengths are and how you could use them to advantage in this job. Your research will have given you a sense of the culture of the organization, so tailor your answers. Tell the interviewer what she wants to hear.

✔ **What is your greatest weakness?** This is one of the toughest questions for an interviewee to answer. It is intended to probe whether you, in fact, know what your weaknesses are (we all have them) and what you do to overcome these. What is there about you that others find annoying? How do you try to compensate? For example, perhaps you used to be chronically late but realized that if you don't try to cram that extra task in, or if you try to be ready 15 minutes early, you can actually be on time! Your answer to this question should state your weakness (one will do) and what you are doing to overcome it.

4. She wants to find out whether you will do the job

Do you have the right attitude? The interviewer is interested not only in whether you have the ability and skills to do the job but whether you actually *want* to do the job. If hired, can you be counted on to put 100 percent into the job?

Here are some questions:

✔ **Where do you see yourself five years from now?** Tell the interviewer about your long-term goals, but try to couch them in terms of how this company fits in to your goals. She wants to know that you are planning to be around in five years.

Lose the low-fat latte

Should you bring your travel mug full of coffee to an interview? Bringing your own coffee to an interview can suggest one of two things to the interviewer. Either that you are a conscientious person who believes in the three *R*'s: reduce, reuse, and recycle, or that you are addicted to caffeine and require coffee to get through a stressful situation! I wouldn't recommend taking the chance. Leave your coffee cup in the car.

Should you accept a coffee at the interview? I always accept; I find it gives me something to do with my hands. However, some colleagues say no way — they don't want to make the interviewer go out of their way to get the coffee, and besides, they might shake and spill it, or leave lipstick on the rim. If there is a jug of water in front of you, you might want to pour yourself a glass or accept it if it is offered.

✔ **Tell me about a time when you felt your motivation was not as high as usual.** Describe any past situation where you felt you were not putting out as much effort as usual. Give the circumstances around it and tell the recruiter what you did to get back on track. When asked questions that prompt you to give a negative real-life example, the most important thing is to explain how you changed or fixed the problem.

✔ **Describe the achievement you are most proud of.** Try to describe something you are very enthusiastic about that applies to the job. For example, perhaps you are most proud of a committee you set up that improved relations between different community groups. When you tell the interviewer about this, let your enthusiasm show!

✔ **Is there something in your life that, looking back, you wish you could have done differently?** A question such as this can be very revealing, so be careful how you answer. Be sure to think about this before your interview. When you answer, don't spend a great deal of time describing the situation in your past. Instead, focus on what you are doing differently today, and how this is improving your life and, of course, your ability to do this job. A suggestion: "I believe mistakes are a part of learning so I try very hard not to make the same mistake twice. I don't dwell on what I could have done differently."

5. She wants to find out what's special about you

You are most likely one of many candidates. The interviewer wants to find out why she should hire you over all of them. You need to make it obvious.

Here are some potential questions:

✔ **If you could give me one reason why you are the person for this job, what would it be?** Let your enthusiasm show. Tell her why you want to work for them — what you can offer them.

✔ **We have interviewed five people for this position. What do you think makes you the best candidate for the job?** Again, you need to let her know you have thought out this decision and really want to work for this company. If there's a short list of five people, all with the same level of skill, the person with the best attitude and who's most enthusiastic about working for the company will likely get the job.

✔ **What is the most important quality you can bring to this job?** Again, you want to work for them. You are enthusiastic! You have a great attitude! It is the soft skills that you bring to the job that will make you a great employee.

6. She wants to find out how much money they're going to have to drop to get you

TIP

What do you expect for a salary? What about benefits? The interviewer wants to hire the best person for the job, but it has to be within her budget. Interviewers will usually wait until the offer stage to raise the issue of salary, but she may ask a few questions toward the end of the interview to get a sense of whether they can afford you. Always try to deflect these questions until (and if) you get to the offer stage so that you don't undersell yourself. I discuss salary negotiations in more detail in Chapter 18.

Here are some probing salary questions she might ask you, followed by ways to answer gracefully without revealing how much you expect:

- **What are your salary expectations?** You would like to deflect this question until you have been offered a job. You could tell her you are flexible and willing to discuss the matter further.

- **Can you tell me what you would be expecting for a salary so I can see if you are in our range?** You could ask her what her range actually is (hey, she brought it up, right?). You can then tell her whether your expectations are in the range.

- **I'm concerned that someone with your experience might be priced out of our range. Can you tell me what you are looking for in a compensation package?** As with the other questions asking about salary, you really want to deflect this question. You might ask if she could defer the salary discussion until and if they decide that you are the right person for the job.

Turn your weaknesses into strengths

When you are asked a question about your weaknesses, you can pick something that others may not consider a weakness. For example, you could say, "I am an overachiever. I tend to try to accomplish too much in a day and end up having to work longer hours to complete what I have taken on." Another possibility is to say, "I am a perfectionist. Sometimes I pay too much attention to detail. I have had to learn that not everyone is the same way and there is a limited amount of time I can spend focusing on details."

Or, "I don't know when to say no. I see something that needs doing or that would be interesting and I agree to take it on. Sometimes I find I have too much on my plate and may have to delegate some of it."

See what I mean? One person's "weakness" may be viewed by someone else as a strength. The recruiter is thinking, "Right on, we are looking for someone who doesn't mind going the extra mile or who is detail-oriented."

Know before you go into the interview what the salary range is for the position. Web sites that can help you figure this out include SalaryExpert.com (www.salaryexpert.com) and Salary.com (www.salary.com).

These six things are the only ones you need to be clear on before the interview. You need to know what it is about the company that appeals to you. If you have done your research (and you should have by now), you will know the answers to these questions. You should also know enough about yourself to answer the tricky questions like "What is your greatest weakness?" You need to know what it is about you that makes you right for, and able to do, this job. You have to be aware of what your own competitive advantage is — what sets you ahead of the rest. Your salary and benefit expectations should be clear in your mind before you go, but do not divulge these during the interview, if you can avoid it.

Getting Ready for the Big Day

Once you have set up a time and place that is mutually agreeable, you will want to start preparing for the interview. First, think about how well you have done just getting to this point. Take a minute and celebrate this accomplishment! You have managed to get an employer to notice you and realize that you have the potential to make a great employee. Okay, now let's get down to work.

Days before

In Chapter 10, I discuss some strategies to increase the odds of your landing an interview. In this chapter, we've talked about what you might *expect* in an interview. Now, let's work on increasing the odds of your actually coming in first in the race and landing the job.

Research the company and the job (and let them know you've done so)

Make sure you let the recruiter know that you have researched both the company and the position. If you have managed to land this interview without researching the company, *now* is the time to do it! Chapter 11 gives you some tips on how and where to research. This is not a step you can afford to miss if you really are serious about this job. Many interviewers will ask you what you know about the company, but, if they do not, you can ask them specific and knowledgeable questions that will show them how industrious you have been. So, step one is this: Research or review what you have learned about the company so you can be prepared.

Practice makes perfect

Another time-consuming but very worthwhile way to improve your odds is to practise the interview. Enlist the help of some of your friends, give them a list of questions, buy a case of beer or a bottle of wine (for after!), and practise. Do the interview more than once and use different questions for each round. You will be surprised at how much more confident you will feel after running through this several times.

If you own a video camera, taping your practice interview is a very good idea. Watch your interview and practise it again. You will pick up on things you did not even realize you were doing. For example, some people click their pens, others say "um" a lot, or their body language does not suggest effective listening and enthusiasm. Videotaping is a great way to prepare for an interview.

Career counselors, coaches, or recruitment consultants (all professionals whose job it is to help you find a job — see Chapter 2 for more) can also help you prepare for interviews. They can walk you through different interview techniques and practice questions. This is actually an investment that I think is worthwhile. I have held and videotaped interview sessions with people who were preparing for interviews, and it is amazing how much they improve after just a couple of practice sessions.

While it is great to be prepared for an interview, it is also possible to over-prepare. For example, preparing answers to a hundred possible interview questions might not be the best idea. The unfortunate result often is that you end up tripping over your own tongue trying to remember the "right" answer to the question and therefore don't come across as sincere. It is much better to learn about the company, know the answers to the six big-picture questions (see the section "Six Things the Interviewer Wants to Find Out About You"), understand how to field different types of questions (like behavioural and situational — see Chapter 15), and practise!

Coach your references

Make sure you have contacted all your references and coached them as to what the job is all about and the qualifications required — and do this before you go for the interview. Send them the job ad if you have a chance. I talk about managing your references in Chapter 6. If the interviewer is sufficiently impressed with you, he may ask you for your references at the interview and phone them before you have a chance to call and let them know.

I mention in Chapter 6 that you should bring a list of references to your interview with you. This is so important that it warrants mentioning here, as well. You should take a typed list of references — including name, title, company (to show how they are associated with you), and telephone number — with you to the interview. Even if you are not asked for it, give the references to the interviewer to show you have made the effort and are really interested in their following up on you.

Prepare a short infomercial

Prepare and memorize a short (one minute) infomercial that highlights your best selling points and how you can use these to the benefit of the company. If you get a chance to summarize why you are the person for the job, you can use this. Make notes to take with you to the interview.

The night before

Okay, here is where I tell you to put away this book (Hold it! Not yet!). Stop cramming and practising. Take a walk, go to a movie, have a bath, and go to bed early. In short, quit obsessing about the interview. You want to go in there relaxed and well rested so you can think quickly on your feet. Sound familiar? This is the way your teachers told you to approach exams (of course, there are always people like me who just run out of time!). It makes sense, though. At this point, you have done all you can to prepare for the interview — it is really too late to do anything else.

Just make sure you are well prepared for the next day. Have your clothes laid out and ironed (for those of you who are ironophobics, just this once, *please!*), and your clipboard ready to go, complete with everything I tell you to bring in Chapter 17. There is nothing worse than running around the day of the interview looking for your shoes and generally getting yourself in a fluster because you are running behind. Know where you are going and how long it will take to get there, in order to give yourself enough time. Then put thoughts of the interview aside for the rest of the evening.

If you don't get the job, don't beat yourself up. You can use interviews as a learning experience — the more practice you get, the better you will do next time around. It is possible you did not get a job offer because someone else was better qualified than you, had more directly related experience, or perhaps came across better in an interview. But you've come out on top once — you can do it again!

To help you in the future, you can even phone the interviewer to ask for some tips on how to improve your odds next time. Don't ask why you didn't get the job — that just puts them on the spot. Ask what you can do differently next time.

Chapter 17

Acing the Interview

- -

In This Chapter

▶ Attending to last-minute details the day of your interview

▶ Conducting yourself like a pro in the interview

▶ Strutting your stuff without going overboard

▶ Answering difficult questions with confidence

▶ Turning the tables: questions you can ask the interviewer

▶ Finishing the interview on a high note

▶ Following up after the interview

- -

You are almost there! You have prepared for this interview. You know the six things an employer wants to know. (Did you miss those six things? Flip back to Chapter 16 to refresh your memory.) You have responses ready when the interviewer asks why you'd be the best person for the job. The moment of truth has almost arrived; you're down to the last-minute details — like what do you wear and how do you put your best foot forward.

This chapter discusses interview basics: the etiquette of an interview, body language, questions you can ask, and how to deal with tricky or inappropriate questions. I also discuss how to follow up after your interview to improve your chances of landing the job.

The Morning Of

First impressions do count! Especially when you are being considered for a job and only have 30 minutes (plus or minus) to make enough of an impression to move forward in the hiring process. You have to come across as professional in *every* aspect of your interview, including your appearance, your body language, and your responses.

Dress the part

My first job interview after finishing my MBA was for a human resources position at a coal mine in a small town. I followed the "expert's" advice and purchased the prerequisite MBA-ish navy-blue suit (with a skirt, no less) and drove out to the mine. As I wandered through the muddy parking lot to the modular office, I wondered if perhaps I had misjudged my attire — especially when I noticed that jeans seemed to be the clothing of choice. Three hours later, after a tour of the mine (complete with hard hat, safety glasses, and steel-toed rubber boots) and a visit to the nurse for a pre-employment medical test, plagued by a desperate need to find a washroom and some food, I thought for sure I had blown the interview. I think my sense of humour about the men's size 10 boots and the fact that they did not go too well with my mud-caked skirt actually carried me through. I got the job and packed away the suit.

Before you go to your interview, do some sleuthing and find out what the people actually doing the job wear — scout it out or make some inquiries. Then, dress one step higher. If they wear suits to work, wear a newer one (as opposed to one you pull out of the very back of your closet), on the conservative side (no loud colours — navy or black will do). If they wear jeans, wear business casual (cotton pants and a sweater for men, dress pants or a skirt for women).

One common question for women is whether it is best to wear a trouser suit or a skirt suit to an interview. My own thoughts are that a nice trouser suit can be just as professional and can, in fact, be more practical. If you wear a skirt, you will always be conscious about how your legs are sitting and how much of your legs are showing.

Speaking of jeans, well, let's not speak of jeans. *Never* wear them to a job interview. This is the time to make a good impression, and it is easier to be more professional if you dress the part. Make sure your clothes are clean and ironed (for those of you who don't own an iron, call your mom!). Take your clothes to the cleaner ahead of time. In interviews, clothes do make the man or woman. Dirty or wrinkled garments don't go over well.

Be on time

The most important thing to remember in an interview is this: Be on time. That means you need to give yourself plenty of time for last-minute problems and checks. Be sure you know exactly where you are going or, if you do not, give yourself extra time in case you cannot find the address or a parking spot.

A good rule of thumb is to be at the interview at least 10 minutes early. I mean in the actual office — not driving up into the parking lot. This will allow you time to take your coat off, check out company literature, and go over your résumé and notes. Go ahead and introduce yourself to the person at reception. Be confident and friendly. The interviewer might ask them what their impression was and what you did while you were waiting.

Unfortunately, interviewers don't always follow the same rules of being on time that you do. It is always possible that you will have to wait beyond the time scheduled for your interview. I agree this is not professional on his part, but unfortunately, in a busy organization, this often happens. My advice is that you bite your tongue and accept his apologies gracefully. Don't complain to the receptionist, pace, make calls on your cell phone, or chastise the interviewer — you might as well just kiss your chances goodbye! When he comes to get you, shake his hand, greet him confidently, and go ace the interview!

Remember to eat

You can never be sure just how long your interview will last — 30 minutes or a couple of hours — so if it's scheduled just before lunchtime, make sure you have something to eat before you go. A grumbling stomach can be really embarrassing and can throw you off as well. Don't grab something on your way out the door and try to eat in the car. You're asking for a big spill — literally!

Visit the bathroom one last time

Make a last-minute bathroom visit. Other than the obvious reason, you will also want to take care of a few items:

- ✔ Check your hair and clothing to make sure you are "all together"
- ✔ Make sure your slip is not showing (guys, make sure you're not wearing a slip)
- ✔ Check for runs in your nylons, if you're wearing a skirt
- ✔ Do a last-minute "Static Guard" check (bring the Static Guard with you!)
- ✔ Ensure that your face is squeaky clean
- ✔ Practise smiling in the mirror — see any leftovers from lunch?

Making sure that your general appearance is tidy — basically that you are all together — will make the interview go more smoothly for you and the interviewer. You need to have as few distractions as possible to ensure the interviewer focuses on you — and not what you ate for lunch.

I was once involved in a panel interview, and the interviewee realized halfway through the interview that there was a huge sales tag hanging from the sleeve of his sport coat. He became so obsessed with hiding it from the panel (we had already all seen it) that he blew the rest of his interview. What should he have done? I recommend just pulling the tag out, ripping it off, and making a comment such as, "I guess you can all see how budget-conscious I am."

Problems with your personal appearance can throw off the interviewer, as well. A colleague of mine once interviewed a woman whose false eyelash had slipped and was hanging from her eyelid. The recruiter became so focused on trying *not* to look at this eyelash that she didn't hear a word the woman said. See how important that last-minute bathroom check is? An experienced interviewer will stop the interview, alert the candidate, and give her a chance to fix whatever's wrong. But some won't and some don't. So it's best not to take the chance in the first place. Besides, it can be so awkward!

There's something in the air . . .

You may be a smoker, but there is a strong chance that your interviewer is not. Don't smoke anytime before your interview — the smell will cling to you and can be quite overpowering to a nonsmoker. Sorry to say this, smokers, but if you smoke in your home, your clothes probably also smell like smoke. Think about getting them professionally cleaned, or, at the very least, hang them outside for an hour before your interview.

It is also distracting for an interviewer when the candidate wears a lot of perfume or aftershave. I knew one recruiter who was allergic to perfume and couldn't stop sneezing if a candidate was wearing it. If you don't feel dressed up without perfume or cologne, be very light with the scent you choose and with the amount you put on.

Don't leave home without these

You are without a doubt the star of the "show" at the interview — front and centre. But every star needs a strong supporting cast and props to make the show run smoothly.

Bring the following with you to the interview:

> ✓ **A clipboard with pen and paper:** It's okay to take notes during the interview. In fact, I encourage you to do so. Most interviewers won't be turned off by this or think you have a short-term memory problem. Quite the contrary — they'll be impressed and see it as a sign of your

professionalism. For quick reference, you can write down interviewers' names, you can jot down the TAO formula (Task, Action, Outcome), which I refer to throughout the book (but see Chapter 15 for a detailed explanation), or make a note of something you'd like to ask the interviewer later.

✔ **A list of your references:** If the interview goes well, the interviewer may ask you for a list of references. Since they won't appear on your résumé (you need to manage the interviewer's access to your references), type them up on a separate sheet of paper and bring the list with you. For more on the importance of managing your references, see Chapter 6.

✔ **Five extra copies of your résumé:** Why five? Because I like that number. No, seriously, you'll want these extra copies if you're being interviewed by a panel (see Chapter 15). You might think this is an unlikely scenario. After all, they chose to interview you, right? Shouldn't they have their own copies already? Well, yes, but we don't live in a perfect world. If we did, we'd all be permanently employed and would never have to look for a job. And you wouldn't be reading this book. Panel interviews aren't always well organized. One, or two, or three people are bound to forget your résumé in their office. So make it easy for them. After the initial "How are you and how was the drive?" discussion and before the actual questions begin, open your folder and tell them that you brought extra copies. Put them in the middle of the table, and remember to keep one for yourself.

Oh yes, be sure to bring extra copies to a one-on-one interview, too.

✔ **Samples of company literature:** You might want to come armed with a printout of their Web site, their annual report, or a recent article about them. Not only can you refer to this material when answering questions, but for those of you who aren't above a little er-um… well, brown-nosing, having these subtly visible during the interview is a great way to impress the interviewer.

✔ **Samples of your work, if applicable:** If you are being interviewed for any job that requires creative talent, you will want to bring a portfolio of your work. This could include writing samples, drafting work, architectural designs, graphics, or Web pages. These examples will show the employer what you have done or can do that directly applies to the job — and also show that you are well prepared for the interview.

Interview Etiquette

Interview etiquette is an art. You have to be on your best behaviour and make sure you do everything the proper way. Remember, you only have one chance to make a great first impression. Luckily, you're reading this book, so just relax, and read on.

Shaking hands

Make sure you shake hands with the interviewer when he comes to greet you. If he doesn't offer his hand first, offer yours. Always shake hands firmly. A limp handshake implies lack of assertiveness and confidence. Unfortunately, many women do not shake hands, or, when they do, they don't use a firm grip. That said, don't get too energetic. I have had many an interviewee grip my hand so hard it hurt, or pump my arm until I thought my shoulder would be dislocated! Another reason to make sure that a handshake is firm but not tight can be health reasons — arthritis, tendonitis, or carpal tunnel syndrome can make an over-the-top handshake positively painful.

Shaking hands accomplishes a couple of key things:

✔ It implies confidence and professionalism, and shows good manners.

✔ It is a way of making personal contact with the interviewer or panel members.

In a panel interview, make a point of shaking all the interviewers' hands. Handshaking is an important part of establishing rapport with the interviewers and helping to break the ice. The first few minutes of an interview can be awkward because both you and the interviewer are likely to be nervous. You have a lot riding on this interview and, especially in the case of panel interviews, there is a good chance you are facing at least some inexperienced interviewers.

If you are going to be sitting at the opposite end of the table, this personal contact is especially important. Even if it is awkward and they don't offer to shake your hand first, it is important for you to stand up and shake each hand as you are introduced. (Make sure you strategically dry off your sweaty palms first!) Look each person directly in the eye and repeat his or her name as you are introduced. Try to remember each person's name and position (use the name retention suggestions in Chapter 15) or take a second and write the names down.

Getting under way

Your interview will likely begin with some general comments about the weather, your trip (if you had to travel to get to the interview), or something neutral and not job-specific. Try to relax and answer the questions naturally — the interviewer is just trying to make you relax a little and set the stage.

Listening effectively

Do you ever get the feeling that someone isn't really listening to you or that they don't really care about what you are saying? They might be looking at you but something about their body language tells you they don't hear you! A person's body language is worth a thousand words, and especially so in an interview situation. Adopting the wrong body language can be doubly devastating: first, it can put off the interviewer; second, it can distract you, which means that you can't listen or answer questions effectively.

Ironically, because most of us can't help it, nervousness is probably the number one culprit causing bad body language and ineffective listening. Don't try to hide the fact that you are nervous by appearing nonchalant and laid back. It is okay to be nervous — in fact, it is expected! However, do not allow yourself to give in to nervous tendencies such as clicking a pen, tapping your thumbs, saying "um" a lot (a couple of times is okay), or otherwise making distracting noises. Control your nervousness by taking long deep breaths and focusing on what the interviewer is saying. Think about what you want to say before answering. Remember, you are not alone — the interviewer might be nervous, too!

In an interview, you want your body language to show that you are interested in what the interviewer is saying and that you are attentive and enthusiastic. Dr. Lyle Benson, an organizational behaviour consultant, has developed a technique to help you improve your listening skills — it is called BERPing (Body posture, Eye contact, Respond, Purpose).

Here's how BERPing works:

1. **B is for Body posture:** Put yourself in a position that lets the interviewer know you are alert and attentive. Don't lean back — sit straight up in your chair. Lean forward and rest your hands on the table. If there's no table, just lean forward. This body language shows that you are interested in what the other person has to say.

2. **E is for Eye contact:** Make appropriate eye contact. Maintain eye contact with the person speaking. If you're in a panel interview, try to look at each panel member in turn when you're answering a question, so they all feel included. Nod your head to show that you are listening when the interviewer is explaining something.

3. **R is for Respond:** Ask questions and clarify points. Take notes, and when you are given the opportunity, ask for more information. Show that you are listening to what the interviewer is saying by asking informed questions.

4. **P is for Purpose:** Remember *why* you are listening. You are listening to find out what the interviewer wants to know about you and your ability to perform the job.

Write *BERP* on the pad of paper you bring in to the interview with you to help you remember and listen effectively.

Answering effectively

If you have prepared and done your background work for the interview (see Chapter 16), you will already know what to expect and have a good handle on your own skills and abilities as they apply to this job. The key then becomes how you present this information to the interviewer in response to his specific questions.

Here are a few tips on how to answer interview questions:

- **Think about your answers.** You do not have to answer immediately. It is okay to take some time to think about your answer before responding. Take a sip of water before answering — it gives you a little extra time to collect your thoughts.

- **Ask for clarification if you don't understand.** Interviewers aren't perfect, and we've been known to ask the odd vague, strangely worded, and otherwise unintelligible question. It's okay to ask for more direction.

- **Don't make something up if you don't know the answer.** The interviewer will probably know you're fudging if you go this route. After all, he's an expert in the field. Just like it's perfectly acceptable to ask him to clarify what he's asking, it's completely okay to admit that you don't know the answer. It's like your mom always said: if you lie, you'll be found out.

  You'll get more respect from the interviewer by admitting you don't know the answer; however, you can put a positive spin on it by telling him either that you know where to get the answer (if this is the case) or that you'll try to find out. That way, you finish on a positive note.

When the interviewer is inexperienced

Have you ever experienced an interview that you actually had to take charge of and guide? Or perhaps you noticed the interviewer didn't really ask any questions that would give him an indication of whether you could actually do the job. Unfortunately, sometimes people doing the interview are not skilled interviewers. This type of interview may end up being more of a conversation, instead of the structured question-and-answer period it should be. It could also end up with you fielding a lot of inappropriate questions (like "Are you married?" or "Are you planning on having kids?"). Chapter 19 tells you what questions an employer is *not allowed* to ask and provides you with ideas on how to deal with these types of questions. When the person interviewing you has his own agenda and doesn't follow general interview principles, try to look for opportunities yourself to fill in relevant information.

One technique is to try to direct the questions or the conversation toward the points that the interviewer needs to know. When you get a chance to ask questions or offer information, seize the opportunity to say something like "I just wanted to let you know what really interests me about your company . . ." or "This job intrigues me because . . . and I hope you will consider me a good fit with your company."

✔ **Keep your answers concise and to the point.** Concentrate on making your answers brief. Do not go off on tangents and tell unrelated stories or keep talking once you have answered the basic question.

✔ **Back up your answers with real-life examples.** If you are asked a question ("Tell me about your experience in . . ."), describe an actual case in which you have accomplished that task in the past. It makes your answer more credible and illustrates your point. (See Chapter 15 for more on the different types of interview styles.)

✔ **Confirm that you have answered the question.** If you believe you may not have answered the question or missed the point entirely, ask the interviewer if he requires more information.

✔ **Don't try to be funny.** This may seem contradictory, since I also suggest earlier that you try to relax, but, unfortunately, when you are nervous, attempts at humour often don't come across well. You don't know your interviewer, so it's best to keep humour out of the interview — he may not realize you are joking. On the other hand, if an interviewer cracks a joke, feel free to smile or laugh at it.

Selling Yourself — Without Overdoing It

Some of the main traits interviewers look for in employees are enthusiasm, honesty, self-confidence (without your being overbearing or aggressive), a positive attitude, and a willingness to learn. A face-to-face interview goes a step further than your résumé and cover letter do. It's your opportunity to show him what you've got — that you actually possess these traits. But, how do you sell yourself in the interview without coming across as a salesperson (unless, of course, you are interviewing for a sales job)? How do you impart confidence, but not arrogance; enthusiasm, but not flakiness?

My friend Don, a manager, interviewed a fellow who was highly qualified and who, on paper and in person, conveyed strong skills and knowledge that would have served the organization well. However, during a panel interview with the entire team, he was unanimously rejected because of his overconfident and condescending approach. Don thinks the problem was that the fellow considered himself an expert, but forgot that he was in a room *full* of experts. The trick is to stay positive and confident, but a little humble at the same time.

Here are a few tips on how you can let yourself shine in an interview without appearing arrogant:

- ✔ **Be enthusiastic:** You want this job. You like this employer. You are excited to be here. Let it show! Don't try to be so professional that your enthusiasm gets left behind.

- ✔ **Be honest:** Most of us are honest folks. However, there is a tendency for job hunters to not tell the entire truth on résumés and in interviews — hoping to present their best side. Remember, if you stretch the truth even a little, it can come back to haunt you. A trained interviewer might even pick up on it in the interview, but most likely, it will catch up to you when you are actually working in the job. Many times, employees lose their jobs if employers find out they were not honest about something before they were hired — even if they are good employees. Dishonesty is something companies take very seriously!

- ✔ **Listen more and talk less:** Answer the interviewer's questions, but don't use extra words or continue after you've made your point. Many people fall into the trap of talking too much because they are nervous.

- ✔ **Prepare only as much as necessary:** Now is that an oxymoron or what? I spend a great deal of this book telling you to prepare, prepare, and prepare some more! What I mean is, don't overdo it. You don't need to go through 100 interview questions and memorize set answers. You then end up giving answers to the questions (if the recruiter even asks any of them) that sound like they came from a textbook. You lose credibility and sound insincere.

These are your important tasks in preparing for the interview:

- Research the company (see Chapter 11)

- Understand the six things that the interviewer wants to know and how they apply to you (see Chapter 16)

- Identify your key competencies as they relate to the job you're applying for (see Chapter 15)

- Identify relevant questions you think the interviewer is likely to ask you, and practise those

✔ **Don't worry, be happy:** Really! What is the worst that can happen to you in an interview? It is not a life-or-death situation. The interviewer either will offer you a job or not, but you will not be any worse off than you currently are. In fact, you will have learned a lot from going through this process; you will have gained valuable interview experience that will stand in good stead for future interviews.

Answering Tricky Questions

There are two kinds of tricky questions. The first are illegal questions, which interviewers have no legal right to ask you, but often do, regardless. The second are legal questions, which, as tough and challenging — and often uncomfortable — as they are to answer, are completely legal and allowable. In this section, I tell you why interviewers ask those tricky (yet legal) questions during the interview, and offer some suggested answers that won't backfire and reduce your chance of being hired. I give you the scoop on illegal questions in Chapter 19 as part of a discussion about Canadian employment law.

I see there is a gap in your résumé. What did you do during this period?

Unexplained gaps in a résumé bother an interviewer. He wants to see a pattern of progressive growth and work experience. Long gaps between jobs disrupt this pattern. As long as you explain those gaps, you should be okay. You're in an even better position if you actually did something growth-oriented during this time, such as self-directed study or travel. If you took time off to raise a family, say so and tell the interviewer that you filled your spare time (of which you probably had little!) with classes and volunteer work to keep up your skills.

Recommended responses to this question:

✔ "I took a break from my career for a year to travel and learn more about the world and other countries. It was a great learning experience."

✔ "I decided to focus on my children for a few years and found that I actually developed an entire set of skills that I can now transfer to a full-time job. These include time-management, conflict resolution, and organizational skills."

Not recommended:

✔ "I was tired of working and needed a break."

✔ "I decided to be a bum for a while."

✔ "I found working full-time with kids too hard, so I quit."

Why are you leaving your current job?

The interviewer wants to know what it is about your present job that doesn't fit, or work, anymore. This can be a very revealing question, as interviewees often say too much without realizing it. For example, maybe you're leaving because you hate your boss, or because you find your job boring. But giving these as reasons for leaving could raise more questions in the interviewer's mind, such as, "Why did she hate her boss so much? Maybe it wasn't so much her boss but *her* who had the bad attitude." Similarly, maybe you found your previous job boring not because you weren't challenged enough, but because you weren't actively seeking out those challenges. Who knows? You need to answer this question carefully, or the interview could backfire.

Recommended responses to this question:

✔ "I feel that I have advanced as far as I can in my current position, and I am looking for new challenges."

✔ "The company is in the process of a merger (or in the process of down-sizing) and I feel that now is the time to look for new opportunities."

Not recommended:

✔ "My employer is a real jerk."

✔ "I can't get along with the other employees."

✔ "Their expectations are too high. I have to work too hard."

Have you ever been released from a job?

If you have ever been asked this question and you weren't expecting it, you know it can throw you for a loop! This is another question that interviewers ask to see if there are any red flags in your past. Unfortunately, interviewers who ask this question may not be aware that people can be released from jobs for reasons other than wrongdoing on their part. Whether you actually made a mistake and were fired or were just the victim of downsizing will determine your response to this question. If you have been released from a job, check out the answers below. One of them may apply to you. If you've never been let go from a previous position, just say no.

Recommended responses to this question:

- ✔ "I made a mistake that cost the company money. One of the things I learned from the experience was to ensure that my manager approves all large expenditures — even if I am told I have the authority to do so."

- ✔ "The company was downsized and I was one of the people with the least amount of seniority so I was let go."

- ✔ "We merged with another company and my position became redundant. I was offered a severance package and decided to look for a new opportunity."

Not recommended:

- ✔ "My boss was a jerk and had it out for me from day one."

- ✔ "I was fired for stealing tools. But I didn't do it."

- ✔ "I got into an argument with my supervisor and he fired me."

What kind of salary do you expect?

If you can, delay discussing salary until you are close to a job offer. Unfortunately, one of the things that the interviewer wants to determine is whether the company can afford you. So, she'll probably pop this question on you in your interview — usually close to the end, but not always. I discuss negotiating a job offer — including salary — in more detail in Chapter 18, but I wouldn't want to leave you hanging here, so following are a few suggested ways to deal with this issue.

Recommended responses to this question:

- ✔ "My salary requirements are open to discussion. My focus is really on what I can do for you."

 ✔ "I am a lot more interested in getting started in my career than I am in the amount I get paid to start. I am confident that once I become a productive member of your team, my salary will reflect that."

 ✔ "Money is not my only priority. I will consider any reasonable job offer."

 ✔ "If you can tell me your salary range, I can tell you where I think I fit."

 ✔ "I believe you must have a range for this position. With my experience, I think I would be somewhere in the middle of this range."

Not recommended:

 ✔ "What does the job pay?"

 ✔ "I would like to be paid . . ." (I don't recommend this answer because it sets the stage for negotiations that shouldn't begin until they make you an offer.)

 ✔ "I would like to be paid what I am currently making, which is. . . ."

Questions You Can Ask

In the majority of interviews, you will be given the opportunity to ask questions at some point. The interviewer may do this at the beginning, just to see if you have any questions before you start. You likely won't, so you can just tell the interviewer that you would like to ask questions toward the end of the interview.

I remember being interviewed for a tree-planting job when I was 17 years old. There was very little difference between the candidates being interviewed. Fifteen of us were interviewed *at the same time* by a panel of six. Five were offered jobs, including myself. The only thing we did differently from the other candidates was ask questions. Later, we were told we were hired because we showed a real interest in the job and the company. That philosophy applies in most organizations. People who ask questions appear to be interested in the job and therefore are more likely to be good employees. Asking informed questions is a way of standing out in the crowd.

In the heat of the moment and in the relief at being close to the end of the interview, many interviewees go blank when asked if they have any questions. My advice to you is to prepare and write down several questions relating to the company (and not so much to you personally, like "How much does this job pay?" or "Can I have three weeks off next month?") prior to the interview. It is okay to say, "I have several questions . . ." and refer to your notes. You show you are prepared and have done your research.

Make sure that the interviewer has not already answered the questions you have written down. I suggest that you check off your questions if they have been answered in the course of the interview, so you do not, in your nervousness, ask about something she has covered (yes, this does happen!). This is a good reason to hone your listening and BERPing skills as well (see "Interview Etiquette" earlier in the chapter for more on the BERPing model).

Here are some examples of good questions to ask:

- ✔ "What would my key responsibilities be?"
- ✔ "What would I do in a typical day in this position?"
- ✔ "How would you describe the culture of this organization?" (Formal? Informal? Energetic? Structured?)
- ✔ "What are this company's long-term goals?"
- ✔ "What would my first project be?"
- ✔ "How much travel would be required?"
- ✔ "Where would I fit into the company's organizational structure?"

Closing on a High Note

You have been asked if you have any questions and the interview is drawing to a close. You sense that this is your last chance to make a good impression. How do you close the interview in a manner that will ensure the interviewer remembers you? You want the interviewer to know you really want the job — if you don't show some enthusiasm and desire for it, you could be out of the running. But don't try to stretch the interview out with small talk or ask a question like "So, what do you think? Do I get the job?" Ouch!

How can you let them know you really, really want the job without coming across as desperate? Summarize your selling points one last time for the interviewer. You can say something like "I know you have a busy schedule and I appreciate your time. But before we close today, could I just make sure I understand what you are looking for?" You then give them a one-minute overview of what you have to offer and why it's of value to the company. Then you add, "Do you see any gaps between what you need and what I am offering?"

End the interview by asking the interviewer politely when he expects to make a final decision. Set the stage for your follow-up by asking if you can get in touch if you don't hear from him, or to get an update on his hiring timeline. You can add that after learning more about the company and the job you'd really be interested in joining their team.

Pre-interview checklist

- ✔ Know how people dress where you are interviewing. Plan to dress to at least that standard. If it is very casual, elect to dress at least one step up.

- ✔ Make sure your interview clothes are clean and ironed.

- ✔ Know where the interview site is located, where you will park, and how to get there.

- ✔ Research the position, the company, and the industry. (I cover this in Part III.)

- ✔ Contact and coach all your references.

- ✔ Memorize a short "infomercial" to highlight your best selling points.

- ✔ Rehearse everything from making small talk to answering potentially tricky questions.

- ✔ Practise your answers to anticipated questions.

- ✔ Identify the competencies required for the job (see Chapter 15) and prepare some stories/examples to show how you can do these.

- ✔ Prepare a list of questions to ask.

- ✔ Research the market salary for the position.

- ✔ Gather everything you need to bring with you to the interview (five copies of your résumé; a clipboard, paper, and pen; your list of references; samples of your work, if applicable; samples of company literature).

Following Up without Being a Pain

The interview is over and you've said goodbye, but you have one final opportunity to leave a lasting impression. When you get home, write a thank-you note to the interviewer. Is an e-mail good enough? E-mail is certainly better than nothing, but it's easy to ignore — or delete! You're much safer (and smarter) going with a handwritten thank-you note. It's something tangible (where an e-mail isn't), and the interviewer will appreciate your going the extra mile to pick out a card or writing paper, get yourself to a post office, and pay for that stamp. He will remember you, and the great impression you made in the interview. Plus, it is unlikely he will just pitch the card in the garbage, so it will be around for a while to remind him of you.

If you've just survived a panel interview and have several interviewers to thank, e-mail is a viable option. By all means, drop each of them a quick cyber-thank-you. Just make sure that you send a handwritten note to the person who will actually make the hiring decision (this will likely be your prospective supervisor), not just the human resources manager. What should you write in your thank-you note? Tell the interviewer that you enjoyed talking with him about the possibility of working with the company. You're excited about the opportunity and hope that he'll consider you further. Thank him for taking the time to talk to you. If you have forgotten to tell him something you feel is important, such as about a course you have enrolled in to upgrade your skills, you can mention this in the thank-you note as well.

The hardest part of a recruiter's job is calling someone and telling him that he didn't get the job. In some companies, it may get put off or not get done at all. However, this is not acceptable and is plain bad manners! If you have asked the interviewer when she expects to make a final decision and you don't hear from her by that time, by all means give her or the recruiter a call. You have every right to find out where you stand.

Chapter 18

Negotiating the Job Offer

. . . .

. . . .

*Y*ou've done it! You have cleared every hurdle and the company has decided that you are the person for the job! Now it's time to get down to the nitty-gritty — negotiating the job offer.

This chapter discusses what's in a job offer — what it should contain and what it should not. I offer you some help in negotiating the offer without crossing the line. It's important to know what points are negotiable, but equally important to know when to stop. I also discuss the ins and outs of employment contracts.

Eyeing the Offer of Employment

A job offer is a process, a process that kicks off when the employer phones you to make the offer and discuss the terms. After this discussion, she'll usually follow up by writing a letter outlining those terms, and, in some cases, by negotiating an employment contract with you, which you have to sign. The initial job offer is rarely written in stone. There may be a fair amount of volleying back and forth between you and the employer, and this is to be expected. We often don't get things just the way we want them the first time we try — think about baking a cake, driving a car, or writing an exam. Negotiating a job offer is no different. The important thing to remember is that you are entitled to fair and equitable terms in the relationship with your employer. So, if at first you don't succeed, try, try again.

The verbal offer

Most offers of employment are made verbally (usually by phone) and followed up in writing. The initial phone conversation is usually more or less a formality, to make sure that you're indeed interested in taking the job. You and the employer will get down to brass tacks in the offer letter. Nevertheless, the employer may discuss some details of the offer over the phone, such as your start date or your salary. So how do you handle this if you don't even have the letter in front of you?

Here are a couple of suggestions to help you effectively negotiate start date and salary over the phone:

- **If the employer wants you to start too soon:** Let her know that it's too soon right there on the phone, before she prepares the written offer of employment. Employers are usually pretty willing to bend on this point. It's understandable that you may want to give your current employer more notice or that you may need time to relocate.

- **If the employer wants to discuss your salary up front:** Tell her that you will review the written offer and get back to her about salary. This will give you time to do a little more comparative research between the salary they're offering and the industry standard. Of course, there is always the possibility that their initial salary meets or exceeds your expectations, so you can go ahead and tell her if it does.

The written offer

What's in a written offer? A typical letter of offer includes the following:

- **Title/overview/reporting structure:** Informing you what your title will be, what your overall responsibilities will be, and to whom you will report.

- **Start date:** Informing you when you will begin work at your new job.

- **Salary:** Informing you what you will be paid (usually giving an annual figure).

- **Benefits:** Informing you what your employee benefits will be, if applicable. These may include dental, medical, and life insurance, as well as relocation expenses.

The employee benefits package is usually outlined in the broadest (and vaguest) of terms in the offer letter. To get the full scoop on things like what percentage of dental your new company pays, whether you pay part of the monthly premium, and whether health coverage for your kids is included in the plan, ask the employer up front — before you accept the offer.

✔ **Probationary period:** Let's face it. Things don't always work out in a new job. It might not turn out to be what you thought it was going to be, your spouse might hate living in the new town to which you've relocated, or you may not be what the employer thought she was getting. For this reason, most provinces have a *probationary period,* specified in each province's Employment Standards legislation. A probationary period is a defined period of time right after you begin work, during which you and the employer can basically "try each other out" without worrying about any legal repercussions if you quit, or if they terminate you. Neither you nor the employer has to give notice. In Alberta, for example, the probationary period is three months after the employee begins work. The probationary period can be extended in the letter of offer or in the employment contract for a reasonable amount of time (possibly six months or a year for executive positions), but cannot be shortened.

✔ **Relocation expenses to be paid:** Some companies will actually pay to move you and your family to your new job. There may be some conditions, though, and these will be specified in the letter. For example, the employer might cap the amount they'll pay, ask that you submit all your receipts associated with moving, or even give you a specific length of time you have to work so that you don't have to pay any of the expenses back (called "forgiving" expenses). This is to protect the employer. Say you are being paid to relocate to western Canada from Toronto. Once you make the move and have been at your new job for a couple of months, however, you find a better paying job. You'll leave the employer in the hole if you quit so soon after arriving, since they likely shelled out thousands of dollars to relocate you (and perhaps your family) clear across the country. So, they may "forgive" your relocation expenses at a certain monthly rate. If your relocation expenses were $3,500 and these are forgiven at the rate of $500 per month, if you quit after only two months you owe the company $2,500.

If an employer doesn't pay your relocation expenses, chances are these are tax deductible. Anything over and above what the employer pays could also be a tax deduction, so keep all your receipts.

✔ **Instructions on what to do with the letter:** Informing you to sign the letter and fax or mail it back within a specified period of time.

✔ **Other requirements:** The employer may require you to sign:

- An *employment contract,* a legal document that outlines the terms and conditions of your employment in detail

- A *nondisclosure agreement,* by which you agree not to give away any company secrets

- A *noncompetition agreement,* by which you agree not to set up a competing company or go to work for a competing company.

Do not accept a job offer until you see it in writing! If, when the employer calls you to make the verbal offer, she doesn't indicate that she'll be sending along the offer in written form, go ahead and request one. In any case, you shouldn't give notice to your current employer until you have the new offer in writing.

From the employer's perspective, the initial job offer, at the verbal stage, is rarely ironclad. If, for some reason, it is, she'll present it to you with a "This is the best we can offer" qualifier, but you won't usually reach this point until the offer has gone back and forth a few times. Most of the time, the verbal offer is presented as a jumping-off point, with the understanding and assumption that you and the employer will negotiate at least part of it.

Getting What You Want

Many candidates make the assumption that a job offer is final and cannot be negotiated. This is a misconception. Remember, you have come out on top of a large number of candidates. By this time, the company already has invested time and money in recruiting you, and they aren't likely to brush you off just because you want to get the best terms possible. In this next section, I discuss what parts of the job offer are negotiable and suggest how you can best go about getting what you want.

Before you begin negotiating, take a step back and make sure you really want this job. I have had many a candidate lead me on a merry dance when negotiating the terms of their employment offer, only to find out they didn't really want the job anyway. They may have just been going through the exercise for the practice or testing the waters to see what was "out there." Some even used my job offer as a negotiating tool to improve conditions with their current employer! This costs would-be employers a lot of time and money and, believe me, they don't appreciate it. Keep in mind that you shouldn't burn any bridges — some industries are like small communities and you and that employer may run into one another again.

Title

A job title may or may not be important to you, but, in any case, it's a point that can be negotiated because it costs the employer nothing. If your job title is key to whether you accept this position — some people may not want to move from a senior administrator role to a lesser-sounding position like administrator — try requesting a different job title. An employer may bend on this as long as it does not affect other employees. Calling you a senior technologist when other employees are only technologists, for example, might not sit well with your co-workers. Try asking the employer whether the job title is set in stone, or whether there's flexibility.

Start date

Most employers are flexible about the start date. She'll respect that you have to give your current employer notice. In addition, the recruiting process usually takes several months, so, while she may be anxious to have you start, asking for a week or two more is not likely to affect your job offer. However, be considerate of the company's needs, as well, and try to accommodate them. You may need to come in for a training session before you start, or work a compressed workweek until you relocate. When negotiating this point, be upfront: you can tell her that you'd like to give your current employer more notice, or that your current employment contract requires that you give longer notice.

Salary

Oh yes, salary! The toughest of all negotiations and the one most candidates shy away from. Don't outright reject a job offer on the basis of the salary being offered — try first to negotiate a higher salary. When negotiating this point, tell the employer that you were hoping to fit into a higher salary range. You can also tell her that the salary she's offering is lower than what you are currently making, but that you'd be willing to settle for an amount in the middle — if you are — and see what she comes back with.

You may have reasons for requesting a higher salary other than wanting more money to line your pockets. Don't be afraid to use these in your negotiations. For example, you might need a higher salary to cover expenses of relocating, such as hooking up utilities, real estate costs, and potentially a higher cost of living.

You can also offer to trade a higher salary for an increase in benefits, such as vacation time. Another option is to accept the offered salary but request a performance and salary review in six months' time. Remember, if you do negotiate an early salary review, be sure the date is specified in your letter of offer so that, if the employer does not follow through until later, you can ask that the salary increase (if granted) be retroactive.

Before beginning to sing for your supper in these salary negotiations, make sure you know the industry average and whether there are geographical differences — does someone doing a job in Newfoundland make less than someone doing the same job in British Columbia? You should have done this research long before now, but in case you didn't or you forgot, here are a couple of Web sites to help you check out salary ranges: SalaryExpert.com (www.salaryexpert.com) and Salary.com (www.salary.com). You can ask for a little time to research this information if you are not happy with the salary offered.

A good rule of thumb is to weigh in with a salary that is slightly higher than what you realistically expect to get. That way, if the employer comes in lower, you won't be too disappointed, and if they meet that first number, hey, it's gravy, right? Remember, though, the key word here is *slightly* — meaning a couple of thousand dollars per year, not tens of thousands!

For some tips on the sensitive issue of negotiating salary, check out JobTrak's Web site (www2.jobtrak.com/help_manuals/jobmanual/salary.html) or The Career Center (www.usfca.edu/usf/career/salary.html).

Vacation time

To negotiate vacation entitlement, you need to consider how long you have been in the workforce and the number of weeks of paid vacation you currently get. I suggest that you try to negotiate your current vacation entitlement at a minimum. For example, if you have been in the workforce for 20 years and get four weeks of paid vacation, returning to only two weeks of paid vacation (which is the minimum by law in most provinces) would be stepping back for you. Most employers understand that your experience will come with a price.

If an employer can't meet your salary expectations, zero in on vacation time — it's usually something she'll be willing to bend on.

Relocating expenses

While most companies have standard medical and dental benefit plans, you can often negotiate reimbursement for some (usually not all) of your relocation expenses, if they apply to you. Again, if you and the employer just aren't seeing eye to eye on salary, this is another point you may be able to get her to give in on, along with vacation time.

Don't expect that your employer will offer to pay to move you, your partner, your four kids, and the family canary from Montreal to Moose Jaw. The days of companies footing the bill for the entire move are long gone — except occasionally in larger companies or for executive positions. At best, your new employer will likely reimburse you for the cost of a moving truck (not the movers themselves) or for your mileage.

Knowing When to Stop Pushing

Throughout the negotiating process, remember to reinforce how keen you are about the job. Always start out negotiating by saying something like, "I am very interested in this job, but I would like to discuss a couple of things in the offer." If the employer appears to hesitate or get a little anxious during the negotiations, reassure her that you are very interested in the position, but just want to discuss a couple of details further. Still, pushing too hard may cause the employer to withdraw the offer altogether. When do you know when enough is enough — when you have been offered the best deal the employer is prepared to consider?

Listen for clues

You can usually tell when someone is starting to get ticked off, right? When you're on the phone with the employer grappling over the fine points of the written offer, listen for verbal clues in her voice to tell you when to, well, shut up and move on to the next point. Listen for these verbal clues:

- The employer's tone of voice changes from helpful to irritated.
- The employer pauses for a few seconds too long before replying to one of your requests.

Negotiating no-no's

- Don't ask for the moon — be realistic about what you request.

- Don't back yourself into a corner where you imply that you will not accept the offer if they don't agree to your changes.

- Be prepared for them to say no.

- Don't try to bid one company's offer against another company. You may end up not having any job offers.

- Never make up a fictitious company and claim they have offered you better terms. You may be told to take the other job, and end up with nothing.

- Always be prepared to compromise — give and take, not just take. For example, if you ask for an increased salary, be prepared to trade off your request for more vacation time.

- Be realistic about your expectations.

- Don't phrase your negotiations in terms of demands — use "suggestions" and "concerns."

- Don't reopen a clause you have already agreed to unless it is part of an overall package. That is, if you have already agreed to three weeks' vacation, don't change your mind later and ask for more, unless you are negotiating more vacation in exchange for lowering your salary expectations.

✔ The employer replies to one of your requests, "I have to run this one by the boss." This signals that you are crossing into territory where she has no power to negotiate. Getting the boss involved may not be a good thing. But, what's done is done, so sit tight and see what happens. I suggest you stop pushing after this one.

✔ The employer replies to one of your requests, "This is our best offer" or "This is the best we can do." This is a sure-fire clue to cease and desist.

Get ready to compromise

You may have to compromise when you negotiate your offer — it's just a fact of life. For example, the title of your would-be position may be specified in the company's policies or collective agreement, so the employer may not be able to meet you halfway where that's concerned. Salary is another area where you'll likely have to compromise. If she can't offer you your ideal salary, you could accept the offer anyway, but request a performance review after six months or one year; the understanding is that your salary level will be on the table at that discussion. If, on the other hand, she tells you that the salary they're offering you is already at the top of the range, you should think seriously about whether or not you want the job. Compromising shouldn't mean that you've lost a battle or caved in. A job negotiation isn't a win–lose proposition between you and your would-be employer, with one of you coming out on top. Quite to the contrary, it's a win–win proposition. You land a job and the employer fills a vacancy with a qualified, enthusiastic person — you!

Be realistic

You have to be realistic, as well. If you have worked for a large corporate employer for a long time and are moving to a smaller company, chances are they cannot pay what you are currently making. You have to look at what else the company has to offer — possibly independence, autonomy, new challenges, and a new location.

Don't try to play two employers off against each other by asking one to meet the offer of another. At least one of them is likely to tell you to take the other job (a thinly veiled way of saying, "take a hike!"). They likely don't want to get into a bidding war with the other employer. It's even possible that both employers will retract their offers, leaving you back where you started. If you already have a valid offer of employment from Employer A, it's okay to advise Employer B of this, but be careful *when* you say it and *how* you phrase it. I suggest you be upfront from the beginning. When you begin negotiations with Employer B, tell her about Employer A's offer and that you want to know the final terms of both before making a decision.

Examining the Employment Contract

You have successfully negotiated the offer of employment — or perhaps you were even happy with the employer's first offer and accepted it right off the bat. Congratulations, but don't break out the bubbly just yet. There may be one more curve ball they throw at you. It's called the *employment contract*, a legally binding document specifying your terms of employment with the company. Employment contracts were once reserved for high-level executives, but today, middle managers and even entry-level employees are often asked to sign them. Why? In our new information-based economy, a company's most valuable asset is information and everyone in a company from the president on down has access to confidential information. Information is easily moved around due to the technology available, so as a means of protecting that information, more and more companies are turning to employment contracts.

An employment contract typically includes *confidentiality clauses,* to ensure that you, as the employee, do not pass on *proprietary information* (developed by or for the company) or confidential information to other companies. This applies to both your term of employment and after your employment ends with this company. Often a *noncompetition agreement* is also part of an employment contract. This agreement (also known as a *restrictive convenant*) specifies that you cannot work for a competitor, solicit clients, or be self-employed in this industry in a defined geographic area and for a specified time period (which will vary by contract).

An employment contract is not necessarily a bad thing. Ideally, and when executed properly, an employment contract should clarify the rights of both the employer and the employee. For example, the employer knows the employee will not give away company information to competitors and the employee knows that she has a job for a specified period of time at a specified salary. If you are considering a job in another country, an employment contract is a must! The last thing you want to do is pack up and relocate to the far reaches of the world without knowing exactly what you are getting into.

While there may be some overlap with an offer letter, for the most part, an employment contract spells out your terms and conditions of employment in more detail. These are some of the things that may be included in the employment contract:

- ✔ **Salary:** Includes your starting salary, dates for salary review, any bonuses you will get and the criteria for receiving them, and other salary arrangements such as base compensation and commissions.

- ✔ **Benefits:** States your vacation allowance, medical and dental benefits, car allowances, training allowances, pension, relocation expenses (and how these will be repaid if you don't stay with the company for a specified length of time).

- **Title and job responsibilities:** States your job title and your major responsibilities, essentially a job description.

- **Stock options or profit sharing plan:** States any performance-related incentives and how and when these will be paid out.

- **Job location:** States where you will be working, and scope of travel if required

- **Length of contract (if not indefinite) and contract renewal options:** States the term of the contract and the process of renewal.

- **Probationary period:** The employer may extend the probationary period past that required by provincial law. If you agree to this, it means extending the time frame within which either you or the employer can terminate the employment relationship without notice. No legal remedy (meaning you can't sue each other) is available to either party if you quit or are terminated within the probationary period.

- **Termination rights and obligations:** States when either party can terminate the employment relationship and under what terms, including the length of notice required and the possible severance package.

- **Ownership of work done by the employee:** Employees may negotiate the rights to own the work they do for the company. This is a sweet deal if you can swing it! For example, a computer programmer might own the program she develops for her employer. Most often, however, you end up signing over the ownership of your work to the employer.

- **Nondisclosure clause:** States that you agree not to disclose company confidential information, including trade secrets, financial statements, pricing, or customer lists.

- **Noncompetition clause:** States that during and after your employment with this particular company, you agree not to set up a competing company or go to work for a competing company.

Protecting yourself

I know you don't enter a new employment relationship expecting it not to work out, but it is important that you feel comfortable with the terms of the employment contract, just in case. Employment contracts should be designed to benefit both parties — the employer *and* the employee. If one party doesn't feel that it's of benefit to them, then the contract has failed in its purpose.

Do not sign an employment contract without understanding exactly what it means in legal terms. You can bet the employer's lawyers have gone over the agreement at their end to make sure it is in the best interests of the employer. Therefore, you should feel comfortable taking the agreement to your own lawyer for review.

While the nondisclosure clause is pretty standard in many industries where you deal with confidential or proprietary information (and pretty much non-negotiable), you do have some latitude with the noncompetition clause — and you should use it. You do not want to get locked into a contract that keeps you out of your field for a long time and over a broad geographic area.

If a noncompetition clause is included, try to have it broken down in the following manner:

- **Industry clause:** If the agreement specifies that you agree not to work in the same industry, you want it to specify that you will not work for a *direct competitor* in the same industry. This way you are not locked out of working in your field if you stop working for this employer.

- **Location clause:** If possible, you want to limit the geographic area the agreement applies to, such as your city or region.

- **Time clause:** You want a date when the agreement expires rather than having it continue for an indefinite period. Ask for it to be for a specific period (such as one year).

Sound advice for employees

If you are asked to sign an employment contract, keep the following points in mind:

- Consult with an attorney before signing the contract. It is a legally binding document and you can bet the company has had it reviewed by a lawyer to make sure their interests are covered.

- Identify any technical work or inventions that you have done previously that will not become the property of the new employer. Specifically list these.

- Try to get bonus criteria spelled out instead of vaguely worded, as in "A bonus will be paid at the end of the year."

- Understand what the nondisclosure and/or noncompetition clauses mean. The nondisclosure clause is fairly standard in large

companies with lots of proprietary information — and not really negotiable. But the noncompetition clause is a different story.

- Negotiate for severance if you are terminated without cause or if the company is taken over in a merger or sold.

- If the possibility exists that you'll be relocated after being hired, the agreement should specify relocation benefits and pay.

At the end of the day, you need to feel comfortable signing an employment agreement. If a company is working in the true spirit of co-operation, they will be open to negotiating with you. If not, you have a decision to make about whether you want to work there or if you are willing to sign the agreement as is.

You're not signing your life away

If you feel that you are under duress to sign an employment contract, or that you won't get the job unless you sign, and the employer is not willing to negotiate any of the terms of the contract, you have two choices:

- ✔ Sign the contract and accept the job, or
- ✔ Decline the job offer

If you decide to accept the job, document your efforts to negotiate the contract, including all conversations, lawyer's advice, and written documentation. File the information away in case things do not work out at some point in the future. Then concentrate on doing the best job possible.

If for some reason your employment relationship is terminated based on the terms of the employment contract, you then have the option of filing for *wrongful dismissal* (where you claim your dismissal is not legal) in civil court, claiming you were pressured into signing the employment contract and that it is therefore invalid. There's no guarantee you will win, but at least you will have documented everything that happened until that point. It is unlikely you will have a case, however, if you did not try to negotiate the contract and signed it willingly. Therefore, it is important to seek legal counsel and to make sure the employment contract is beneficial to both parties *before signing*.

A Final Word

Both a written offer of employment and an employment contract are legal documents. You have to be happy with them before you sign. Negotiations can be touchy and tricky; you need to be careful not to push too far. However, you still have the right and the obligation to look out for your own best interests. Just keep the company's interests in mind at the same time, and you and the employer should be able to negotiate successfully.

Remember to have your employment contract checked out by a lawyer. No one will look out for you except you!

Chapter 19

What You Need to Know about Canadian Employment Law

In This Chapter

▶ Getting to know the different types of employment law

▶ Understanding how human rights laws affect the job hunter

▶ Making sure your new boss meets the minimum employment standards

*W*hen do you potentially need to turn to (and therefore know a few things about) employment law in Canada? Well, there are two times, really: during the hiring process, and when you are actually employed. Because this book is about finding a job, I focus on the former.

In this chapter, I demystify Canadian employment law and outline some of its basic principles as they relate to your job hunt — without getting into a lot of boring legalese. I also show you how to file a complaint if you feel you've been discriminated against while applying for a job.

Types of Employment Law

Constitutional law is the supreme law in Canada. The Canadian Constitution is a formal written document that sets out the rights and freedoms of Canadians and the powers of the federal government and the provinces. The Constitution designates employment law as a provincial responsibility, so each province makes its own laws related to employment. The only exception to this is if you work for the federal government or a federally regulated company — no matter what province you work in — there are federal employment laws that apply to you.

For our purposes, I discuss two types of employment law:

- ✔ **Human rights laws:** As they relate to employment, these laws consist of *prohibited grounds,* topics that an employer is prohibited from asking you about, either on an application form or in an interview, as they don't relate to your ability to perform a job. For example, he cannot take your marital status into consideration, nor the fact that you may or may not have a family. Human rights laws differ somewhat between provinces, but there are similarities between the main prohibited grounds for discrimination. Even though they are against the law, some employers *do* ask prohibited questions, either because they're unaware of the laws governing their province, or because they believe no one is likely to lodge a complaint against them.

- ✔ **Employment standards laws:** These laws relate to *minimum standards of employment,* the conditions an employer is required to meet or provide while you are employed with them. These are presented and discussed at the offer stage and/or in the employment contract, if one exists. Each province has its own minimum standards of employment. Check out the Canadian Legislation Web page (www.legis.ca/en/index.html) for links to federal and all provincial government statutes.

Human Rights Laws and You

Human rights laws are the responsibility of the individual provinces. Each province has the right to define what it considers grounds for discrimination. How does this apply to employment? Well, as a job hunter, you have the right to be considered for employment based solely on your job-related abilities. A prospective employer cannot ask you about anything that does not have an impact on your ability to do a job. If he does, then he could gain information he could potentially use to discriminate against you. Grounds for discrimination vary between individual provinces, but they do concur on some basic grounds, including race, religion, age, sex, marital status, and disability. Table 19-1 identifies the prohibited grounds for employment discrimination in each province and territory.

Redirecting prohibited questions

Depending on which province you call home, there are certain things the recruiter or employer is *not allowed* to ask you in an interview or on an application form (refer to Table 19-1). Okay, I know I just said that they are prohibited to ask you questions based on the grounds in Table 19-1, but here's the ugly truth: Even though employers are legally prohibited to ask these questions, they still do. Why? Because although your answer to the question may provide no insight into your ability to perform the job, your answer may

Table 19-1 Prohibited Grounds of Employment Discrimination Across Canada

Prohibited Ground	Federal	British Columbia	Alberta	Saskatchewan	Manitoba	Ontario	Quebec	New Brunswick	PEI	Nova Scotia	Newfound-land	Northwest Territories	Yukon	Nunavut
Age	✓	✓	✓	✓	✓	✓	✓	✓	✓	✓	✓	✓	✓	✓
Ancestry or place of origin		✓	✓	✓	✓	✓		✓				✓		✓
Assignment, attachment, or seizure of pay											✓			
Based on association	✓							✓	✓	✓			✓	
Dependence on drugs or alcohol	✓	✓	✓	✓	✓	✓								
Disability	✓	✓	✓	✓	✓	✓	✓	✓	✓	✓	✓	✓	✓	✓
Family status	✓	✓	✓	✓	✓	✓	✓		✓	✓	✓	✓	✓	✓
Language							✓							
Marital status	✓	✓	✓	✓	✓	✓		✓	✓	✓	✓	✓	✓	✓
National or ethnic origin	✓		✓	✓	✓	✓	✓	✓						✓
Pardoned conviction	✓					✓	✓			✓		✓		✓
Political belief		✓			✓		✓	✓	✓	✓	✓		✓	
Race, colour, or creed	✓	✓	✓	✓	✓	✓	✓	✓	✓	✓	✓	✓	✓	✓
Record of criminal conviction		✓					✓							
Religion	✓	✓	✓	✓	✓	✓	✓	✓	✓	✓	✓	✓	✓	✓
Sex (including pregnancy or childbirth)	✓	✓	✓	✓	✓	✓	✓	✓	✓	✓	✓	✓	✓	✓
Sexual orientation	✓	✓	✓	✓	✓	✓	✓	✓	✓	✓	✓	✓	✓	✓
Social condition/origin					✓		✓			✓	✓	✓		
Source of income			✓		✓				✓					

shed some light on other things the employer wants to determine, such as whether you'd be a good fit with the company culture, or whether you're likely to stick around once he hires you or take a hike after not too long. For example, let's say a mine is looking for labourers to work shift work and you are a female in your thirties. The employer would *really* like to know whether you have children, because, if you do, you'll need to arrange child care, and you may have the odd day when you can't arrange it and might have to miss your shift. Note how this has nothing to do with your ability to perform the actual job.

The next question is, how do they get away with it? Well, first of all, many employers don't know what the prohibited grounds are, so they ask questions out of, well, ignorance. Others blatantly disregard what the law says because they don't think anyone will ever make a complaint against them. No complaint, no problem, right? The unfortunate truth is that how you answer those questions can have an impact on the outcome of your interview. Of course, you can always choose not to answer at all. But, if the answer won't have a negative impact on your status, go ahead and answer. In the following sections, I suggest some creative ways to answer discriminatory questions.

The answers I suggest tend to deflect the questions and address whatever concerns the employer has — that is, the concerns that have prompted the question. If you want to answer illegal questions directly — for example, "Do you plan on having children in the future?" — you can do so. But I only recommend you do so if your answer will not negatively affect your chances of landing the job. You wouldn't want to say, "Yes, next year I want to get pregnant." But if you already have kids of school age or older, or have no plans to have children, you might want to say so.

You can also ask the interviewer why he needs this information, then respond to that concern directly. For example, if he asks whether you are under a physician's care, and in response to your inquiry tells you it is because they have strict insurance guidelines, you can tell him that you would have no problem passing an insurance company medical (assuming you're in good health, of course).

Age

An employer might want to know how old you are if they are in an industry or occupation where age is relevant. For example, only adults are allowed to work night shift alone in many provinces. Not-so-innocent reasons to ask this question would be to find out if you are close to retirement or if you are past prime child-bearing age (employers prefer not to have to fuss around with maternity leave!). If you are asked how old you are, you could try one of these answers: "Is there an age restriction in this industry?" or "I am legally able (or unable) to work in this industry."

Assignment, attachment, or seizure of pay

Newfoundland prohibits discrimination on the basis that you have ever had your wages garnisheed or your paycheque seized. Perhaps this might be important in some jobs when you handle cash — concern over theft, perhaps? No other province seems to consider it an issue, however.

Dependence on drugs or alcohol

It's only natural that an employer would prefer not to hire someone who has a dependence on drugs or alcohol, but asking about it is prohibited in the majority of provinces and territories in Canada. If you get asked a question about this, if you can honestly say no, go ahead and do so. Or try this: "I do not anticipate having any problems meeting the attendance requirements of this job."

Disability

Disabled adults are a source of employees too often deliberately overlooked by employers, if only out of ignorance as to the amount of special accommodation they might require (it may not be a lot!). Unless there is a *bona fide* (genuine) reason why a disability would prevent (or make it exceptionally difficult to accommodate) a person from performing a job (a quadriplegic driving a haul truck at a coal mine, for example), disability cannot be considered in the employment process. A quadriplegic lawyer, for example, would have minimum problems working as a lawyer if the right tools were available to him. If you are asked about any disabilities, try this: "I have no conditions or limitations that would affect my ability to do this job."

Family status

Depending on the job, having a family might make you a more desirable employee (say, if you had to relocate and they want someone who will stay for a long time) or less desirable (if a lot of travel is required or if you are a single parent). If you are asked about pregnancy, childbearing plans, or child-care arrangements, you can answer this way: "I do not anticipate having any problems meeting the attendance requirements of this job."

Height and weight

Believe it or not, sometimes application forms actually ask for this information (don't fill it in!). Unless there are specific physical criteria you have to pass for this position, your height and weight are not at all relevant to the job. Besides, if you are applying for a job where this is an issue, such as in the fire department, the employer can find out your height and weight from a pre-employment medical test, which you are required to pass. Being denied a job because you are overweight, for example, could be classified as a discrimination based on a disability. If you are asked to fill this in on an application form, or if you are asked to provide this information for reasons of determining your physical status, try the following: "Does the job have specific height and weight requirements? . . . I have no problem fitting the requirements of the job," or "There must be a pre-employment medical required to determine a person's ability to physically perform this job. I believe I will have no problem passing that medical."

Language

Asking about your mother tongue is grounds for discrimination in Quebec and Ontario. You do have to be proficient in the language required for the job, however. If you are asked about language, respond with this: "I am proficient in the language(s) required for this job."

Marital status

An employer might be concerned about your meeting special requirements of a job such as being on call, doing shift work, or travelling, and how this would impact on your family life. In this case he might ask if you are married. On the other hand, he might ask this question because he believes an employee who is married with children would be a better employee (or vice versa), or perhaps that a single parent is not an ideal employee, for whatever reason. In any case, asking about marital status is blatantly illegal, but as I said, he still might ask you. If you are asked about your marital status, whether your spouse is subject to transfer or about your spouse's employment, try this answer: "If the concern is about transfer or travel requirements in this position, I will have no problem meeting these obligations."

Medical information

You are not required to give any medical information unless it is job-related. If you are asked for the name of your family doctor, whether you are receiving counseling or therapy, or whether you are currently under a physician's care, try the following: "Will a job offer include a requirement for a job-related medical? I believe I will have no problem passing a job-related medical."

Name

An employer might innocently ask a question about previous names for the purpose of doing reference checks or for checking your credentials. They may also ask for not-so-innocent reasons, perhaps to find out whether you are married, or even your race, religion, or country of origin. If you are asked about a name change or what your maiden name was, try this: "I can provide you with that information if we advance to the stage where you need to check my references and credentials." Or you could always just tell them.

National or ethnic origin

All provinces and territories prevent discrimination on the basis of either national or ethnic origin. Why would an employer ask about that? Well, they might want to know whether you are legally entitled to work in Canada and just ask the question the wrong way. Or they might have a more sinister reason for asking — related to personal bias. If you are asked about your birthplace, your nationality, or proof of citizenship, try answering simply this: "I am legally entitled to work in Canada." (Assuming you are, of course.)

Pardoned conviction or record of criminal conviction

In the case where an employee has access to money or to customers' valuables, employers may want to know if potential employees have ever been convicted of a crime. Some provinces prohibit the asking of this question. Even if it is not a prohibited question in your jurisdiction, I recommend you respond this way if you are asked whether you have ever been convicted of a crime, arrested, or if you have a criminal record: "I am eligible to be bonded if that is a requirement of this job." (Unless, of course, you are not eligible for *bonding*, insurance coverage provided to companies to protect them from employee theft.)

Photographs

Yes, this does happen and is one way of revealing race, colour, or creed prior to an interview. If the job ad asks for a photograph along with the application, you can either ignore it or state the following in your cover letter: "If required, a photo for a security pass or company file will be available when I am offered the job." If you are interviewed as part of a recruitment blitz (kind of like a rotating door), the employer may ask to take a photo of you to keep track of applicants — to help him put a face to a name. If you are asked to pose for a photo after an interview, I would just say go for it. They already know what you look like anyway.

Political belief or political and/or other association

Your political beliefs and associations with various organizations cannot be considered in the recruiting process in many jurisdictions, unless they are job-related. (It's possible that the Liberal Party could successfully argue that you be a member of the party in order to work for them.) In any case, in the unlikely event that an employer asks you a question about your associations or political beliefs, you can answer this way: "I guarantee my political affiliations have no impact whatsoever on my job performance."

Race, colour, or creed

While you rarely will encounter an interviewer with the nerve to ask you questions about your race or colour, some things are obvious in a face-to-face interview. Unfortunately, this is still one of the most common grounds for discrimination in hiring. Everyone knows you are not allowed to discriminate on the basis of race, colour, or creed, but unfortunately, personal bias and prejudice may enter, and as a result, you may end up being passed over for a job. Very rarely will you know if this is the reason you did not get the job, but if you have reason to suspect such discrimination because of something that was said in the interview, you have the right to make a formal complaint (see the section "Making a human rights complaint").

Religion

While asking about religion is prohibited, an "ignorant" employer might ask out of concern that you will be able to work the hours scheduled (some religions forbid working on certain days of the week). Some organizations, such as the Catholic school system, for example, may be able to successfully argue that you must be of a specific religion in order to be employed by them.

After the September 11th terrorist attacks in the United States, religion may become more of an issue for some employers, but it is still illegal for them to ask you! If you are asked about your religious affiliation, for references from clergy, or whether you will work a specific religious holiday, try answering like this: "I don't anticipate any problem with working my required shifts," or "What are the shift requirements? If a regular day of work falls on a religious holiday that I observe, I am sure we will be able to come to an agreement."

Sex

Questions related specifically to the sex of an applicant (and including pregnancy or childbirth) are not allowed. This tends to be more of an issue in written applications than in interviews, but the point here is that you cannot be discriminated against on the basis of your sex. If you are qualified for a job and the best candidate, an employer can't refuse to hire you because of your sex.

This doesn't apply if there is a good reason to hire someone of a specific sex — like a female guard in a women's prison or a female personal aide for a female disabled adult. At the same time, employers might want to know if you plan on having kids or already have kids — questions that aren't allowed! If asked about pregnancy, childbearing plans, or child-care arrangements, respond this way: "I do not anticipate having any problem meeting the attendance requirements of this job."

Sexual orientation

Many provinces prohibit discrimination in hiring on the basis of your sexual orientation. If you are asked about your sexual orientation, try this answer: "I believe I am well qualified for this position with respect to my skills and abilities." Again, if you believe the reason you did not get a job was your sexual orientation, you have the right to file a complaint with your provincial human rights commission. See the section "Making a human rights complaint" later in this chapter.

Social condition and origin

Both Newfoundland and Quebec list this as a ground for discrimination, but it is not likely an employer will ask you any questions related to your social condition. If you do feel you have been overlooked for a job for this reason, you can appeal to the provincial human rights commission. The onus is on you to prove you have been wronged, however, so be prepared to back up your complaint with facts.

Employment equity laws and the job hunter

Employment equity laws ensure that equal opportunities are available to groups who have historically been underrepresented in the workplace. The groups affected include women, members of visible minorities, Aboriginal peoples, and persons with disabilities. Employment equity laws are the responsibility of the provincial or federal jurisdiction under which you are employed, and include the following:

✔ **Affirmative action:** Under the *Employment Equity Act* (1995), the federal public service, Crown corporations, and federally regulated private sector employers with 100 or more employees must examine their workforces to determine whether any of the four groups — women, members of visible minorities, Aboriginal peoples, and persons with disabilities — are underrepresented, taking into consideration factors such as qualifications, location, and industry. In addition, employers must identify and remove barriers to employment and, where necessary, establish goals to increase the number of underrepresented groups in the workplace.

✔ **Equal pay for equal work:** These laws ensure that two people working for the same employer in the same position doing the same duties are paid the same, regardless of gender or race. While this has been law in all Canadian jurisdictions for many years, interestingly enough, this is not the law in many places, including numerous U.S. states.

✔ **Pay equity or equal pay for work of equal value:** Another federal employment equity goal is to reduce the wage gap between so-called "men's work" and "women's work." Statistics indicate that in Canada women continue to earn about 70 cents, on average, for every dollar earned by men. To address the wage gap, some provinces and the federal government have adopted *pay equity legislation* — jobs of equal value to an organization must be paid equally.

Source of income

Four provinces list source of income as a prohibited ground for employment discrimination (Alberta, Saskatchewan, Manitoba, and Nova Scotia). Essentially this means an employer is not allowed to ask you where you get your money. Frankly, I am not sure why they would want to know this, and that is probably why the other provinces have not listed this as a source of discrimination either.

Making a human rights complaint

You think you have been overlooked for a job for a discriminatory reason. Perhaps the interviewer asked you a prohibited question, which you answered, but you believe your answer was not what he wanted to hear. You were subsequently not offered the job and you believe it was because you told the employer information about yourself that, though not related to your ability to do the job, nevertheless put forth some information about you that the employer then used to make his decision not to hire you. Or maybe one of your references was asked questions that were prohibited. If you feel you have been discriminated against either in the hiring/interview process, or on the job, you can file a complaint with your provincial human rights commission (or with the federal human rights commission, if you are employed under federal jurisdiction).

The process for making a complaint is reasonably simple and informal. You fill out a form and submit it to the applicable commission. With minor variations between provinces, the general model for processing complaints is as follows:

1. **Inquiry and settlement:** The human rights commission will inquire into the complaint and, if they find it to be a valid one, try to obtain a settlement between the parties.

2. **Dismissal or referral:** If a settlement cannot be reached, the commission dismisses the complaint or refers it to a human rights tribunal or board of inquiry, which holds a public hearing.

3. **Enforceable order:** If the tribunal or board of inquiry concludes that a person has engaged in a discriminatory practice, it may make an order, which is enforceable through the court. The person who has engaged in the discriminatory practice may be ordered to stop, to take measures to reverse the effects of discrimination, such as to rehire the employee, to pay compensation, or to adopt an affirmative action program.

If you are applying for a job under federal jurisdiction or in the Northwest Territories or Nunavut, check out the Canadian Human Rights Commission Web site (www.chrc-ccdp.ca) for information regarding human rights issues, as well as how and where to make a complaint.

For other provinces, log on to their respective provincial human rights commissions sites, listed here:

- ✔ Alberta: (www.albertahumanrights.ab.ca)

- ✔ British Columbia: (www.bchrc.gov.bc.ca)

- ✔ Manitoba: (www.gov.mb.ca/hrc)

- ✔ New Brunswick: (www.gov.nb.ca/hrc-cdp/e/index.htm)

- ✔ Nova Scotia: (www.gov.ns.ca/humanrights/umanrights)/default.htmank)

- ✔ Ontario: (www.ohrc.on.ca)

- ✔ Prince Edward Island: (www.gov.pe.ca/humanrights)

- ✔ Quebec: (www.cdpdj.qc.ca/htmen/htm/1_0.htm)

- ✔ Saskatchewan: (www.gov.sk.ca/shrc)

- ✔ Yukon: (www.yhrc.yk.ca/Pages/English/english.html)

Employment Standards Laws

Provinces have the right to pass employment standards laws within their own jurisdictions. These laws specify minimum standards of employment that all employers must follow. To the job hunter, employment standards laws are important because they inform you of the minimum standards an employer must provide to you on the job. For example, if you live in British Columbia, the minimum wage in 2002 is $8 per hour. It's against the law for an employer to offer you $7 per hour. In Alberta, however, $7 per hour is above minimum standards.

These are the areas covered in the employment standards legislation of most jurisdictions:

- ✔ **Annual vacation:** This includes minimum annual vacation entitlement, when vacation is due, and vacation pay rates.

- ✔ **Hours of work:** This includes daily or weekly maximum hours, overtime rules and rates, lunch or coffee break regulations; call-in periods, split shifts, and minimum consecutive hours of work.

- ✔ **Maternity leave:** This includes your right to paid or unpaid leave for maternity reasons, timing, and return to work provisions.

- ✔ **Minimum wages:** This includes minimum wages. The wage you're entitled to may depend on your age. Younger workers (under the age of majority) may have a lower minimum wage.

- ✔ **Statutory holidays:** This includes the minimum number of statutory holidays to which you're entitled.

- ✔ **Termination:** This includes the minimum notice period to which most employees are entitled before termination. See the sidebar "Minimum notice laws work both ways."

- ✔ **Wage protection:** This includes when wages are to be paid, statement of wage requirements, deductions allowed, and assignment of wages.

- ✔ **Miscellaneous:** This includes various provisions that may vary between jurisdictions in Canada.

One other point to note is that in some provinces, employment standards legislation does not cover entire industries such as farming, fishing, and domestic employment because of the unique working conditions in each of these areas. Furthermore, the legislation will often not cover individuals who are part-timers, subcontractors, contingent workers, home workers, or those on fixed-term contracts. Even in covered industries, legislation may not apply to all employees — for example, overtime provisions may not apply to managers. The actual exemptions to each act are listed in the written statutes.

To find out more on employment standards, contact your provincial government employment standards branch or check out the links below:

- ✔ Alberta: (www.gov.ab.ca/hre)
- ✔ British Columbia: (www.wwlia.org)
- ✔ Manitoba: (www.gov.mb.ca/labour/standards)
- ✔ New Brunswick: (www.gnb.ca)
- ✔ Newfoundland: (www.gov.nf.ca/labour/labour/labstnd)
- ✔ Nova Scotia: (www.gov.ns.ca/labr)
- ✔ Ontario: (www.gov.on.ca)
- ✔ Prince Edward Island: (www.gov.pe.ca/commcul)
- ✔ Quebec: (www.cnt.gouv.qc.ca/en/normes)
- ✔ Saskatchewan: (www.labour.gov.sk.ca)

Minimum notice laws work both ways

Minimum statutory notice periods required by employers when laying off an employee may also apply to an employee quitting a job. When an employer terminates your employment after, say, three years, he has to give you two weeks' notice. This, however, works both ways — when you give notice at a job you have been at for three years, you are required to give two weeks' notice. While it rarely happens, if you do not the employer has the option of suing you and making you pay him the money in lieu of notice. Make sure that you keep this in mind when you are offered a new job and you need to give notice to your current employer. Of course, this doesn't even take into account the ethics of quitting without giving adequate notice or how not giving your old employer notice will appear to your new employer.

The Landing a Job For Canadians For Dummies Directory of Job Resources

The 5th Wave — By Rich Tennant

"I'm sure there will be a good job market when I graduate. I created a virus that will go off that year."

In this directory . . .

You have access to information that can help you at every stage of your journey toward employment. I list many online resources for job hunters, such as online job banks, industry- and location-specific employment sites, plus others that deal with everything from résumés and cover letters to self-assessments. There are off-line resources, too, that you can check out. While I provide you with as many resources as I can throughout *Landing a Job For Canadians For Dummies,* there just isn't enough room to list everything. That's where this directory comes in. If there's a source that I think will help you out in your job hunt, but there wasn't room for it elsewhere, chances are it's in here. Happy hunting.

The Landing a Job For Canadians For Dummies Directory of Job Resources

· ·

In This Directory

▶ Expanding your list of handy employment-related Web sites

▶ Picking up extra job-hunting tips — from interviews and occupational research to résumés and salary negotiations

▶ Contacting your local Human Resources Development Canada (HRDC) office for a wealth of job-hunting help

· ·

This book is designed to help you land a job by providing you with the tools to realize this goal. You might, however, want to get a little more information on a topic I cover elsewhere in the book, so I've compiled this directory to give you some starting points. Each resource I list has an accompanying explanation that draws out what's special about the resource. Inevitably, and regrettably, the links in this directory are dynamic and will change. If you find outdated links in this directory or in any part of this book, please e-mail me at e-lynx@shaw.ca and put the words "Broken Link" in the subject line. Here's a list of the topics I cover in this directory:

✔ Human Resources Development Canada (HRDC) regional Web sites

✔ Interviews

✔ Job-hunting tips and resources

✔ Newsgroups and e-mail lists

✔ Occupational research

✔ Online job banks

✔ (Other) job-hunting books

✔ Résumé and cover letter tools

✔ Salary stuff

✔ Self-assessment tools

D-4

✔ Staffing and temp agencies

✔ Working outside Canada

Mind the Micons

You'll notice that the descriptions of Web sites in this directory often have little graphics just beneath the URL. These are *micons* (miniature icons), and I include them to help you decide at a glance whether a Web site suits your needs. Here's a quick rundown of the five employment-related micons used.

This micon alerts you to a Web site that requires you either to register to use the site or to sign in whenever you visit it.

This is your tip-off to a site that has a great design, is easy to use, and is loaded with relevant information for you — the job hunter.

This micon signals a grad-friendly Web site. If you've recently graduated from university or college, you'll find employment information especially tailored to you and your stage in the game.

You may be able to post your résumé on the site, or it might have loads of résumé-related information.

This micon identifies a Web site that has international links or offers services in a language other than English.

Human Resources Development Canada: Regional Offices

Human Resources Development Canada (HDRC) is one of the best job search resources you can access. In addition to the comprehensive series of Web sites and online resources, there are HRDC offices in many communities in Canada where you can talk to employment counselors, access videos and written materials to help with your job hunt, and tap into their online job bank. In this section of the directory, I list the contact information for the central online information site, where you can find the office nearest you, as well as for the provincial HRDC offices.

HRDC Office Profiles

www.hrdc-drhc.gc.ca/menu/profile-search.shtml

Office Profiles is a national online site that provides you with all pertinent information on the HRDC location of their choice. It includes all general contact information, main telephone numbers, services offered, hours of operation, kiosk locations, resource centres, service areas, and more.

For information on any of these offices or services, call toll free: 1-800-O-Canada (1-800-622-6232).

Alberta, Northwest Territories, and Nunavut

www.ab.hrdc-drhc.gc.ca/common/home_e.shtml

Canada Place
9700 Jasper Avenue, Suite 1440
Edmonton, Alberta
T5J 4C1
Phone: (780) 495-6598

Check out www.hrdc-drhc.gc.ca/profiles/list-AB-e.shtml for a list of all HRDC offices in Alberta, the Northwest Territories, and Nunavut.

British Columbia and Yukon Territory

www.bc.hrdc-drhc.gc.ca/common/home_e.shtml

Library Square, Suite 1400
300 West Georgia Street
Vancouver, British Columbia
V6B 6G3
Phone: (604) 666-8257

Check out www.hrdc-drhc.gc.ca/profiles/list-BC-e.shtml for a list of all HRDC offices in British Columbia and the Yukon.

Manitoba

www.mb.hrdc-drhc.gc.ca/menu/home.shtml

Suite 750
266 Graham Avenue
Winnipeg, Manitoba
R3C 0K3
Phone: (204) 983-3928

Check out www.hrdc-drhc.gc.ca/profiles/list-MB-e.shtml for a list of all HRDC offices in Manitoba.

D-6 Human Resources Development Canada: Regional Offices _____

New Brunswick (Subregional Office)

www.nb.hrdc-drhc.gc.ca/common/
  home.shtml

1081 Main Street
P.O. Box 6044
Moncton, New Brunswick
E1C 9G8
Phone: (506) 851-6940

495 Prospect Street
Fredericton, New Brunswick
E3B 9M4
Phone: (506) 452-3279

Check out www.hrdc-drhc.gc.ca/
profiles/list-NB-e.shtml for a list of
all HRDC offices in New Brunswick.

Newfoundland & Labrador

www.nf.hrdc-drhc.gc.ca/menu/home.htm

689 Topsail Road
P.O. Box 12051
St. John's, Newfoundland
A1B 3Z4
Phone: (709) 772-5339

Check out www.hrdc-drhc.gc.ca/
profiles/list-NF-e.shtml for a list of
all HRDC offices in Newfoundland and
Labrador.

Nova Scotia

www.ns.hrdc-drhc.gc.ca/english/
  index.htm

Metropolitan Place
99 Wyse Road
P.O. Box 1350
Dartmouth, Nova Scotia
B2Y 4B9
Phone: (902) 426-4302

Check out www.hrdc-drhc.gc.ca/
profiles/list-NS-e.shtml for a list of
all HRDC offices in Nova Scotia.

Ontario

www.on.hrdc-drhc.gc.ca/english

4900 Yonge Street, 2nd Floor
North York, Ontario
M2N 6A8
Phone: (416) 954-7527

Check out www.hrdc-drhc.gc.ca/
profiles/list-ON-e.shtml for a list of
all HRDC offices in Ontario.

Prince Edward Island

www.pe.hrdc-drhc.gc.ca/common/
  home.shtml

85 Fitzroy Street
P.O. Box 8000
Charlottetown, Prince Edward Island
C1A 8K1
Phone: (902) 566-7658

Check out www.hrdc-drhc.gc.ca/
profiles/list-PE-e.shtml for a list of
all HRDC offices in PEI.

Quebec

www.qc.hrdc-drhc.gc.ca/html/menu_e.
  html

Guy-Favreau Complex
200 René-Lévesque Blvd. Ouest
West Tour, 5th floor
Montreal, Quebec
H2Z 1X4
Phone: (514) 982-2384

Check out www.hrdc-drhc.gc.ca/
profiles/list-QC-e.shtml for a list of
all HRDC offices in Quebec.

Saskatchewan

www.sk.hrdc-drhc.gc.ca/common/
  home.shtml

South Broad Plaza
2045 Broad Street
Regina, Saskatchewan
S4P 2N6
Phone: (306) 780-6232

Check out www.hrdc-drhc.gc.ca/
profiles/list-SK-e.shtml for a list of
all HRDC offices in Saskatchewan.

Interviews

Visit one of these Web sites to brush up on
your interview skills and etiquette before
the big day.

Ask the Interview Coach
www.asktheinterviewcoach.com

A fun, informative site: It is also written in
an easy-to-understand manner and answers
most any question you'll have about interviewing. It also offers some practical advice
on how to improve your performance in an
interview. For a fee, if you have any other
questions you can even e-mail the coach.

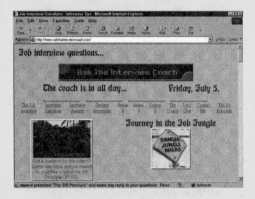

Career Consulting Corner
www.careercc.com/interv3.shtml

*Though not as extensive as other sites, this
one lets you get to the heart of the matter
quickly — there are fewer practice questions,
but the ones there are excellent:* Check out
this page for some good interviewing tips
and practice questions. You can also find
sample questions to ask the employer
here. This is a small site but it is a quick
reference if you don't want to wade through
hundreds of practice questions.

How to Interview.com
www.howtointerview.com

*Register to receive a free newsletter on how
to interview better:* This site has articles
and interview tips to help you interview
like a pro.

Job-Interview.net
www.job-interview.net

Get some interview practice on this site:
A great site to help you prepare for your
upcoming interview, Job-Interview.net
covers all the bases. This site tells you how
to prepare for the interview and identify
possible interview subjects and possible
questions. Worried about skills and abilities
questions? There are hundreds to practice
on. You also will find sample questions to
ask the interviewer and, as a bonus, sample
résumés and cover letters.

Job-Hunting Tips and Resources

Not all employment-related sites worth
visiting post job vacancies. There are some
super *gateway sites* out there — so called
because they open the door (or the gate, if
you're getting really detail-oriented) to
additional resources you can use during
your job hunt. Because it's all too easy to
get sidetracked when you're searching for
information, I'll help you out by pointing
the way to a few of the best sites.

D-8 Job-Hunting Tips and Resources

Canadian Careers.com

www.canadiancareers.com

★★
★★

This award-winning site is a virtual treasure chest of resources and information: It once offered a job bank service but discontinued it in 2001 to focus on what it's really good at — providing great information and links for job hunters. Check this site out first if you're looking for occupational profiles, industry-specific job banks, or just about any kind of career-related information. The site also provides links to other specialized Canadian job banks for specific occupations or groups. Visit www.canadiancareers.com/ces1.html for direct links to these job banks.

The Canadian Jobs Catalogue

www.kenevacorp.mb.ca

Loads of links: An extensive site with both free and pay-for-access areas. It has links to sites specializing in, among other subjects, résumé and cover letter writing, employment law, hot companies, career training, and relocating. It also has links to job banks and recruitment sites.

CanLearn Interactive

www.canlearn.ca

★★
★★

Start mapping your job route now: This government-sponsored site is a one-stop resource for the information and interactive planning tools you need to explore learning and education opportunities, research occupations, develop learning strategies, and create the financial plans to achieve your goals.

Government of Canada Human Resources Management

www.hrmanagement.ca

If you have a question relating to employment law, check here first: This site has links to all employment standards legislation for all provincial government departments.

Interbiznet

www.interbiznet.com/hunt

Subscribe to this site's daily newsletter: This site has been around since before the Internet got really popular and has evolved with it. It primarily targets e-recruiters, but is also a great general job-hunting site, with articles, links, and tips that job hunters will appreciate. You can subscribe to the daily newsletter, *1st Steps in the Hunt — Daily News For Online Job Hunters,* for fun tips and information related to your job hunt.

iTools

www.itools.com

Give your research a boost: Looking for job-related information, but don't have much time? Log on to iTools and cut your research time way down. This site isn't devoted to researching job leads — it's a generic search engine geared to all kinds of research. But for your purposes, you can certainly use it to research jobs. You can access Web sites, directories, and discussion groups, as well as research tools like encyclopedias, newspapers, and magazines — all from one site. Give it a try!

Job Hunter's Bible

www.jobhuntersbible.com

A fun and informative resource: This Web site is a supplement to Richard Nelson Bolles's bestselling book, *What Color is Your Parachute?* The site is full of job-hunting information and tips from his book, as well as links to other great job-related sites on the Internet.

Job Search Skills

www.edu.gov.on.ca/eng/career/
jsearch.html

★ ★
★ ★

Rx for your job hunt: This site, sponsored
by the government of Ontario, provides
information on all aspects of job hunting,
including résumé and cover letter writing,
interviewing, researching leads, entrepreneurial skills, and *employability skills* (the
soft, or transferable, skills that make you
employable).

Newspapers in Canada

www.altstuff.com

*A great resource if you are looking for infor-
mation on a specific community or searching
for jobs in a community.* This is a listing of
newspapers in most every community in
Canada. It includes online and off-line contact information as well as Web addresses.

Ontario Prospects 2001

www.edu.gov.on.ca/eng/general/
elemsec/job/prospect/eng/index.html

★ ★
★ ★

Geared to younger job hunters: This well-
designed site is an initiative of the Ontario
Ministry of Education. It's aimed at young
people and recent graduates looking for
their first jobs. It includes a look at some
prospective Hot Jobs in the future. Young
adults learn how to discover their strengths,
market themselves, and choose what paths
there are to follow, and the site includes a
great list of additional resources to check
out. I only hope the government updates
this soon.

Paths to Equal Opportunity

www.equalopportunity.on.ca/eng_g

For job hunters with disabilities: Sponsored
by the Government of Ontario, this site is a
great resource for people with disabilities
looking for employment, or employers
looking to hire people with disabilities. It
discusses relevant issues and provides links
and resources.

Another good site for job hunters with
disabilities is www.workink.com.

The Riley Guide

www.rileyguide.com

★ ★
★ ★

Puzzling job-hunting questions answered:
While not a Canadian-run site, the Riley
Guide is well worth visiting nonetheless
to review its excellent collection of tips
and resources. I doubt you have many
employment-related questions that the Riley
Guide can't answer. The section on how to
get the most out of the Internet during
your job hunt is particularly helpful.

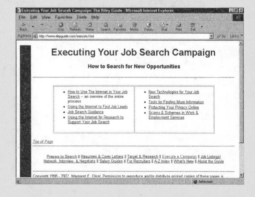

WinningTheJob.com

www.winningthejob.com

Sound job-hunting and career management advice: WinningTheJob provides useful tips and strategies for navigating today's competitive job market and workplace. The site has a series of articles and other resources to help you conduct your job hunt and land a job.

WorkInfoNET

www.workinfonet.ca

A first-class site containing practical job-hunting tools: Sponsored by the federal government, this site has links galore and a search engine that combs more than 20 different job banks. You will find occupational and labour market information, self-employment information, province-specific links, and, oh, virtually any and all information relevant to finding a job in Canada.

Newsgroups and E-mail Lists

In this section, I list directories you can search to find newsgroups and e-mail lists related to your profession or specifically for job postings.

I also list a sample of employment-related newsgroups. Usenet newsgroups can be an excellent source of job listings. Don't be surprised, however, when you find that the local groups contain many irrelevant postings. Some recruiters feel that the best way to get the word out about their positions is to post to every newsgroup that has the word "jobs" in it, without regard to the group's geographical focus.

Directories

eScribe.com

www.escribe.com

A directory of e-mail lists: eScribe is a service provided to list owners (people who have set up their own private lists on specific topics) who want to make their lists available to others to sign on to and to access. They provide public access (you just sign on) and private access (you have to have a moderator give you permission to join). You don't need any special software to join — you just give your e-mail address and immediately start receiving messages that are posted to the list.

Yahoo! Chat

http://chat.yahoo.com

Find the right group to chat with: Another great product from the king of directories. Yahoo! has compiled a directory of chat rooms that you can search and easily access to find a group that applies to you.

Yahoo! Groups

www.groups.yahoo.com

Make this directory your starting point: Start your own group or search for groups that are already part of the Yahoo! group. Yahoo! Groups is actually the product of a merger among several other newsgroup directories that now use Yahoo! technology.

Newsgroups

National

`can.jobs`: jobs all over Canada

Provincial

`ab.jobs`: Alberta
`bc.jobs`: British Columbia
`nb.jobs`: New Brunswick
`nf.jobs`: Newfoundland
`ns.jobs`: Nova Scotia
`ont.jobs`: Ontario
`qc.jobs`: Quebec
`sk.jobs`: Saskatchewan

Local

`calgary.jobs`: Calgary
`edmonton.jobs`: Edmonton
`hamilton.jobs`: Hamilton
`island.jobs`: Vancouver Island
`kingston.jobs`: Kingston
`kw.jobs`: Kitchener-Waterloo area
`mtl.jobs`: Montreal
`ott.jobs`: Ottawa
`sudbury.jobs`: Sudbury
`tor.jobs`: Toronto
`uvic.jobs`: Victoria
`van.jobs`: Vancouver

International

`alt.jobs`
`biz.jobs`
`biz.jobs.offered`
`comp.jobs`
`comp.jobs.offered`
`misc.jobs`
`misc.jobs.contract`
`misc.jobs.misc`
`misc.jobs.offered`

Occupational Research

One of the first steps toward landing the job of your dreams is to decide which occupation you're interested in. The Web sites profiled in this section are great starting points for researching industries and occupations, finding out a little more about the ones you're keen on, and taking one more step along your journey to that fulfilling job you've dreamed of.

CanLearn Interactive Student Planner Occupations Databank

**www.canlearn.ca/English/learn/
learning2.html**

Details on future earning potential: This federal-government-sponsored site contains loads of information about different occupations, including future earning potential and how to break into the occupations. This site is a must-visit!

The College Board

**http://cbweb9p.collegeboard.org/career/
bin/career.pl**

Find out what educational background you need for a given occupation: After you've figured that out, stick around and click through to the section dedicated to salary ranges to find out what you can expect to make. (The figures are in U.S. dollars, but you can do the math.)

College Grad

www.collegegrad.com/careers/all.shtml

In-depth descriptions of occupations: This U.S.-based site is a wealth of resources for recent grads. In particular, I like the descriptions of different occupations. In addition to providing descriptions of various careers, it also discusses job-hunting techniques, résumés and cover letters, salary ranges, interviews, and job offers.

Human Resources Development Canada Industry Profiles

www.hrdc-drhc.gc.ca/sector/english/
industryprofiles/prsearch2.shtml

This section of the HRDC site provides an overview of various industries: You can access information on the history of a given industry, its principal characteristics, and change and innovation within that industry.

National Occupation Classification (NOC)

www.worklogic.com:81/noc/search.html

A great resource for occupational research: This index lists more than 30,000 occupations and is updated annually. You can find out more about each occupation and what you need to do to break into it. The number of options out there will blow you away!

Occupational Outlook Handbook

http://stats.bls.gov/oco

This site has printable PDF files: Administered by the U.S. Department of Labor, the *Occupational Outlook Handbook* is a nationally recognized source of career information, designed to provide valuable assistance to individuals making decisions about their future work lives. Revised every two years, the *Handbook* describes what workers do on the job, working conditions, the training and education needed, salaries, and expected job prospects in a wide range of occupations.

Online Job Banks

The number of online job banks is increasing monthly. All offer access to job postings; the better ones include additional features to help you manage your job hunt.

First-tier Canadian sites: The first part of this section about online job banks is dedicated to Canadian-based job banks. I first profile the *higher-tier,* or *first-tier,* job banks, which have an abundance of job postings and career-management features. These sites are at the head of the pack when it comes to the services they offer, the employment-related information they make available, and the sheer number of jobs they post. Make any one of these your first stop when you set out to land that job.

Second-tier Canadian sites: Then I turn to the *lower-tier,* or *second-tier,* job banks, which have fewer jobs and some career-management tools, but are more basic, without a lot of extra features. Because the employment-related services these job banks offer are pretty cut and dried, they're just not, in my opinion, in the same league as the first-tier sites I describe in the previous section. Visit these sites to make sure you cover all your bases, but only *after* you exhaust the first-tier sites.

Industry-specific sites: I also include my favourite *industry-specific Web sites,* also known as *niche sites,* which carry job postings within a particular occupation or industry. While you shouldn't overlook first- and second-tier job banks, don't forget to check out industry-specific niche sites and online communities that may have job boards, newsgroups, or mailing lists tailored to an occupation that interests you.

Some of these sites allow you to post your résumé at no charge. However, most of them don't have search capabilities, so you can't do a keyword search for a particular posting, or anything like that. Jobs appear in the order they were posted, so you just scroll down and check them out.

Location-specific sites: Check out this list of *location-specific sites*, which carry job postings within a particular geographic location, such as a region, province, or city.

International sites: After the Canadian part of the tour, you can venture further afield if you like, and visit some of the international job banks I profile. In addition to the job banks, I list several Web sites that are not themselves job banks but provide lists of and links to job banks in specific countries or regions.

Government job banks: For those of you inclined to pursue a job in the public sector, or for those who are already civil servants, I provide Web addresses for the federal government's job bank, as well as for those of the provinces and territories.

First-tier Canadian sites

Campus Worklink (now Workopolis Campus)

http://campus.workopolis.com

Campus Worklink has joined forces with Workopolis.com: The resources and connections of Campus Worklink combined with the techno-wizardry of Workopolis.com make this a site new grads must visit. The site includes tonnes of job postings for students and new grads, a huge student résumé database, employer profiles, career

planning links, and articles and resources to help you plan your job search. This site is truly geared toward university and college grads, however. You need to first register, then phone your school to get an access code even to view job postings. You can look at the articles on the site without this code, however, and there is some great information there — specifically aimed at problems and issues new grads face.

Canada Job Bank

http://jb-ge.hrdc-drhc.gc.ca

The online version of the National Job Bank run by Human Resources Development Canada (HRDC): This is the job board you used to go visit in your local HRDC office, when the postings were mounted on a cork bulletin board and you needed a referral to get an interview. Things have certainly changed! This bilingual service is free to both job hunters and employers. In its prior, bulletin-board existence, the National Job Bank was not well used for managerial or professional positions. With the increase in online recruitment sites, it has now become a well-used site for all types of positions. The site also allows you to target the geographic location of your search. It boasts great links to government resources and information for provincial and federal programs, in addition to the National Job Board.

Electronic Labour Exchange

www.ele-spe.org

Here's an interesting twist on online job hunting that may turn up something that fits your goals to a tee: This government-sponsored site uses innovative "matching technology" to allow you to search for jobs that match with your skills, goals, and experience. No cutting and pasting of

your résumé on this site, however! Both employers and job hunters are required to fill in an extensive online form with specific criteria. Once you complete the form, you can search the site using its free "matching" service, which allows you to do a search to see if any jobs match your qualifications. Employers can also perform a search to determine whether any applicants match the criteria they fill in. You can narrow your search geographically, to within provinces or cities. While fun to use, entering all the information in the online form can be time consuming.

HotJobs.ca
www.hotjobs.ca

Log on to one of the fastest-growing and most popular job banks in Canada: HotJobs.ca, the Canadian affiliate of the U.S.-based HotJobs.com (www.hotjobs.com), boasts thousands of current jobs from hundreds of companies. HotJobs.ca's user-friendly interface allows you to navigate through listings quickly and easily. You can search by keyword, company, city, and more. On HotJobs.ca, you can create your own personalized MyHotJobs account to help organize your job hunt. With a MyHotJobs account, you get a password-protected home page, résumé editing tools, access to job seeker stats, an online shopping cart of positions, and a complete history of sent cover letters and résumés. In case you are concerned about your privacy, HotJobs.ca's enhanced privacy feature, HotBlock, allows you to control who sees your résumé and who doesn't. You can block specific employers from viewing your résumé (great for people who worry about their current employer finding out that they are looking for a new position elsewhere).

Jobshark.ca
www.jobshark.ca

A good site with some unique features: This is a great-looking site that's fun to use. In addition to being able to post your résumé, access resources, and create your own account to manage your job hunt, you can pay $10 to have your résumé moved to the front of the pack for 3 months, so it gets seen first by employers searching the database. Jobshark.ca has software that matches your profile (it takes about 15 minutes to create) with job postings and automatically advises you via e-mail when a match occurs. You can also register for the site's Video Profile feature. For an additional fee ($75 to $99, depending on length), you can have a video clip of yourself taken and added to the site for employers to view. Clips are up to 1.5 minutes in length.

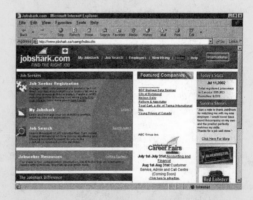

Monster.ca

www.monster.ca

A very useful selection of career management tools and fun to use, to boot: Monster.ca is the well-known Canadian version of the U.S. job bank Monster.com. The Canadian site offers both French and English and has an easy-to-use search engine that lets you search by job-specific keyword(s), occupational category, or location. Create your own My Monster account to store different versions of your résumé and cover letters, to apply online to jobs, to track your online applications, and to create automatic job-hunting agents that send you a heads-up e-mail when a job listing matches your criteria. Monster.ca is great — once you find your way around. It's a big site, though, so it can take a while.

Workopolis

www.workopolis.com

A great multi-use Web site with more than just jobs: Look here for information on just about anything related to your job hunt. This site has resources, links, information, and jobs — lots of them! Choose the English or French language option when you first sign on, then surf the numerous jobs posted on the site. There's a feature called My Workopolis, which allows you to create numerous versions of your résumé and track your own searches. You can also sign up for CareerAlert, and be notified when a new job is posted in a specific category. The only concern I have about this site is that it is so large and has so many features, it takes a while to find your way around.

Other Sites to Check Out

www.careerexchange.com
www.headhunter.net
www.jobsearch.ca
www.positionwatch.com

Second-tier Canadian sites

Actijob

www.actijob.com

Great graphics on this site, but aside from looking good, it's also user-friendly: This is a fairly basic bilingual job bank that allows you to search job postings, as well as résumé writing and posting services, plus links to related sites. While it has a smaller number of job vacancies posted, it has an impressive list of employers who post on it. It's also quite easy to navigate.

Actual Jobs

www.actualjobs.com

A large job bank that crawls the Web: This site is relatively easy to use, and has about 22,000 cross-Canada job postings at any given time. Actual Jobs browses other recruitment sites, like Monster.ca, picking up job postings and organizing them. You can post your résumé on Actual Jobs, and

D-16 Online Job Banks

the site owners claim that recruiters throughout Canada and the United States can see it. Actual Jobs also offers a résumé posting service with a dictionary of active words to help you write your résumé.

CanadaJobs.com

www.canadajobs.com

A pretty basic site, CanadaJobs.com does a good job at advertising job openings and making it easy to apply: The postings are predominantly in eastern Canada, though. And while there's no way to do a province-specific search, it's no great hardship, since there isn't a huge number of jobs posted here. The site does let you search by category and keyword, though, and has some good links to other job-hunting resources.

CanJobs

www.canjobs.com

You can access province- and city-specific sites in every province and territory from this site: CanJobs is the parent site to province-specific job banks like AlbertaJobs.com. They've even gone one level further and developed sites for individual cities in each province, like EdmontonJobs.com. All the sites use the same database, so if a recruiter posts on the Edmonton job bank, you can access it from CanJobs.com, too. This site is popular with headhunters and staffing agencies. You can search by occupation or geographic location. There are a number of extras on the site, such as a résumé databank, online application abilities, and a job-search agent (a newsletter to advise about new jobs) to help you manage your job search.

CareerOwl

www.careerowl.ca

Dedicated to helping employers find talent Canada-wide, CareerOwl is free for jobseekers, low cost for Canadian employers and open to all: Jobseekers can view postings and access site resources without registering. If you choose to register, you can store information, be contacted by employers without releasing contact information, and receive email notification of postings, based on an extensive profile. The site offers additional special features if you are highly qualified. There are more than 3,000 jobs posted at any one time, so it's worth taking a look.

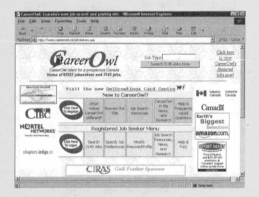

+Jobs Canada

www.canada.plusjobs.com

A good site with reasonable traffic volumes and a smaller number of jobs so it is reasonably easy to locate a specific job: +Jobs Canada offers a rather unique service in that, for an additional fee of $39, you can post your résumé to more than 200 different online job banks. Unfortunately, I wouldn't recommend using this feature, because once your résumé is out there you lose control over it. If you want to change something, or take it off line, you won't be able to! The site also has links to its affiliate sites in the United States, Australia, the United Kingdom, and Denmark, should you be interested in searching for a job in these countries.

Jobs.ca

www.jobs.ca

Jobs.ca has a feature called Job Basket that gives job hunters some control over their résumé and statistics about who views their résumé online: Jobs.ca is a user-friendly site that is popular with recruiters. You can search via keyword, location, or via industry/occupation. Its Job Basket feature allows you to view job listings, submit and update your résumé, be notified of updates regarding jobs you've applied for — even find out who's read your résumé. Unfortunately, you can only post your résumé in plain text format, so it doesn't look that hot at the receiving end. Overall, though, this is a functional site that does the job because it's well organized, easy to use, and has lots of jobs posted.

JobsCanada

www.jobscanada.com

Try this site's nifty JobMatch feature: On JobsCanada, you enter your personal information into its JobMatch Profile Manager, which is then matched with jobs entered by employers. Entering your information in the Profile Manager takes a while, but is worth the time. Checking out the results of the match is kind of fun, too. You can check out jobs without signing in, but you need to enter your information if you want to make use of the matching program. The site has a nifty resources link to industry news and other job-hunting resources. Worth a visit.

NetJobs

www.netjobs.com

Basic job-hunting and résumé posting services: Net Jobs is a combined Canadian and U.S. site, so a search could potentially return postings in both countries. It has easy search capabilities offering a keyword search and allows you to search by either job title, date of posting, or company. I'd like to have a word with the designers, though, because you only have a very small space to view jobs (about 10 centimetres), which is rather irritating to work with.

Industry-specific sites

Association of Universities and Colleges of Canada

www.aucc.ca/en/index.html

Academically inclined? This Web site offers complete, up-to-date information on Canadian universities, publications, international activities, and scholarships. It also offers a comprehensive list of on-campus jobs across Canada, in both academic and administrative capacities.

Canada Computer Work.com

http://canada.computerwork.com

If high-tech is your thing, you've made the right cyber pit stop: You can post your résumé, create your own Workstations to have jobs e-mailed directly to you, and search by skills, job titles, or location. This site has more than 500 jobs posted, so it's worth the trip!

Canada IT.com

www.canadait.com

A Canadian Information Technology site that offers more than just job postings: The site also offers company profiles and regularly updated industry news. Job postings are organized by province but can also be searched by job type, company name, job title, date posted, or by city/region. There are more than 2,000 IT-related company profiles on this site. One concern: it can be difficult to navigate because there's so much information crammed onto every page.

Canada's Information Resource Centre HOTlinks

http://circ.micromedia.on.ca/hotlinks/ associations/main.htm

This site points you in the right direction to find an association that is applicable to your occupation or field of interest: Associations Canada contains more than 19,000 listings of professional associations operating in Canada. This site is excellent if you want to narrow your job hunt to within a specific occupation. To make the best use of this site, look for an association that applies to you and see if they have job postings. Many offer job-posting services, but some are open to members only. But if the association is in your field, you may want to become a member or obtain a trial membership by asking the site administrator.

Canadian Council of Human Resources Associations

www.chrpcanada.com

Log on here if you're into HR: This association is an umbrella association of human resources associations in Canada. The site provides links to each of the provincial human resources associations — most of which offer job posting services in the human resources field.

Canadian Forests

www.canadian-forests.com

A great site listing forestry-related jobs all over Canada and the United States: The Canadian Forests site is a Web site dedicated to all aspects of the Canadian forest industry, and it has a section devoted to employment that includes a newsletter.

Canadian RN

www.canadianrn.com/index.htm

The site now posts international jobs as well as Canadian jobs: This site is devoted to the nursing industry in Canada. It provides articles of interest, up-to-date news, and the JobMart feature — a listing of Canadian nursing jobs, sorted by province. It also has a directory of nursing-related resources and some career tips.

Charity Village

www.charityvillage.com

All you want to know about the non-profit sector, including how to find a job in it: A megasite with news and information about this growing sector, the employment component of Charity Village posts both paid and volunteer jobs in non-profit organizations. You have numerous search options: by location, by keyword, by date posted, by job category, or by organization type.

Cool Jobs Canada

www.cooljobscanada.com

Check out this site if you're in the market for a job in the hospitality or tourism industry: Search jobs in Canada by region, employer, or most recently posted. You can post your résumé for 60 days. You can also access Cool Jobs Australia from this site, if you're interested in a tourism or hospitality job on the other side of the globe.

Education Canada.com
www.educationcanada.com

This site is dedicated to helping education professionals find employment: It has more than just job listings where you can search for teaching jobs by province. It provides information related to the teaching profession, an employment-related discussion board, and listings of upcoming events related to employment. You can store your résumé and cover letters online to make applying easy.

Engineering Central Canada
www.engcen.ca

Are you an engineer? Start looking here: This new site lets you post your résumé and search for jobs by category and keyword. It's experiencing some growing pains, but it's well designed and ultimately will be a good resource for engineers looking for Canadian jobs.

JobCafe.com
www.jobcafe.ca

Look here for both permanent and contract work in the IT field: JobCafe has more than just job postings. You can find current industry news and career development information in its Career Centre.

Job Universe
www.jobuniverse.com

A great resource for IT professionals looking in (and outside) Canada for a job: You'll find useful resources and career management tools, such as the MyJobUniverse function, where you can create and post your résumé, apply online to jobs, and register for e-mail updates.

Space Jobs
www.spacejobs.com

Blast off to a career in the space/aeronautical industry: Space Jobs posts national and international jobs, and also has up-to-date space industry news.

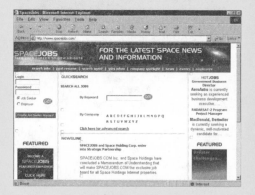

SystemsAnalyst.com
www.systemsanalyst.com

Employment opportunities for Information Technology professionals: From this site, browse industry jobs, create and post your résumé online, and use its Career Alert e-mail notification tool. The site is also linked to a number of partner sites that can help you with other components of your job hunt, such as interviews and salary information.

Location-specific sites

Alberta Learning Information Service (ALIS)

www.alis.gov.ab.ca/employment/jp/
  jobbanksab.asp

Look no further for job banks dedicated to Alberta jobs: This site is sponsored by Alberta's provincial government and has links to and descriptions of other Alberta-specific job banks.

BCjobs.NET

http://bcjobs.net

For job hunters looking for a job in British Columbia and employers looking to hire there: Unlike many of the province-specific sites, this one is independently owned and is not under the umbrella of a larger national site. You can post your résumé, apply for jobs directly, and receive job alerts when a new posting comes in.

Careerclick.com

www.careerclick.com

Job postings and career management tools: Careerclick.com gets its job postings from pages of its affiliate daily newspapers, from large employers and recruiting firms, and from individual online postings. To search for positions in areas not included in its list of locations, try including your preferred location in your keyword search. For example, search for Hinton, Alberta, leaving the newspaper choice defaulted to All Papers. Careerclick.com now allows you to post your résumé online and save multiple copies. It even offers a Job Alert newsletter that lets you know when a posting related to your interests comes up.

Find a Job Canada

www.find-a-job-canada.com

Jobs in western and northern Canada: A relative newcomer to the job bank scene, Find a Job Canada is a good resource for people looking for a job in western Canada. You can search jobs by location or by category, and can sign up for a weekly update of new job postings. The site does not maintain a résumé database; you send your résumé to employers directly.

Fort McMurray Jobs

www.ftmcmurray.net/jobs.htm

A must-visit site if you're thinking of heading out west: So you heard Fort McMurray, Alberta, was the place to go for a high-paying job. This site lists jobs in the city and provides links to company Web sites. It also has contact information for employment agencies in Fort McMurray.

Sask Jobs

www.sasknetwork.gov.sk.ca

Jobs in Saskatchewan's private and public sector: A great site sponsored by Saskatchewan's provincial government. It has a wealth of postings and includes resources for job hunters. You can post your résumé on the site for review by potential employers. A word of caution, however: once posted, your résumé becomes visible to anyone online. Employers do not have to subscribe or pay a fee to view posted résumés — all it takes is a simple search and anyone can do it.

International sites

All the U.K. Job Sites on One Page

www.job-page.co.uk

Quick and easy access to popular job banks in the United Kingdom: This site has links to numerous U.K. job banks and recruitment sites. There's a section for new grads. It also has links to job banks outside the U.K., providing they have a British component.

America's Job Bank

www.ajb.dni.us

★★ ★★

Over 1 million jobs posted on this U.S. job bank: America's Job Bank (AJB) is a government-run job bank that has tonnes of jobs all over the United States. You can create and post your résumé online. It has a great search function that allows you to search by job title, by category, or even by distance from a specific zip code. The keyword search function is one of the best I have seen and allows you to use keywords to search specific components of jobs, such as title, educational degree required, and location.

CareerMag.com

www.careermag.com

A U.S.-based job bank with a wealth of resources: If you're looking for a job south of the border, this is a good place to start. CareerMag.com is affiliated with numerous other sites, so it's able to offer services in addition to the basics of searching job postings. From here, you can access other international job banks, résumé-builder sites, and even business start-up sites. Other features include articles to help you find and land a job, employer profiles, a great search engine, and a job agent that alerts you to new job postings.

EuroJobs

http://eurojobs.com

Apply directly to jobs in Europe: Job postings are grouped according to country. You can apply for jobs with an electronic version of your résumé directly from the site. A great-looking site that's easy to navigate.

HotJobs.com

www.hotjobs.com

★★ ★★

A one-stop career resource centre: HotJobs.com offers advanced privacy features, numerous career tools — including industry-specific chat and newsletters — as well as a comprehensive relocation centre. The site boasts thousands of national and international jobs posted by corporate hiring managers, staffing firms, and executive recruiters. One of the key benefits of using HotJobs.com is that jobs posted by staffing agencies or executive recruiters are clearly marked as such, giving you the power of choice when conducting a job search or applying for a job.

Idealist.org

www.idealist.org

Opportunities with non-profit organizations around the world: Hey, all you newly minted graduates, are you looking for international volunteer opportunities to help kick-start your career and give you the opportunity to see other countries? Idealist.org has more than 6,000 international volunteer opportunities, 1,800 internships, and 1,600 paying jobs around the world listed in its job bank. The site has a career centre and multiple resources. Anyone can post to the site, so you have to be prepared to weed through a lot of stuff before you find what you are looking for. The site does not have a search engine but is pretty well organized. You can sign up to receive e-mail updates when postings related to your interests appear.

iJive.com/Flipdog.com

http://ijive.careers.flipdog.com

This puppy posts jobs in pretty well every populated country on the planet — of course, with some countries better represented than others: FlipDog gets its job postings by crawling all over the Web and copying jobs from job banks and company Web sites around the world. The site posts a large number of jobs at any give time, and access is fast and user-friendly. Search by keyword or by location. Sign up for the Job Hunter service, and have FlipDog e-mail you when it finds jobs that match your criteria.

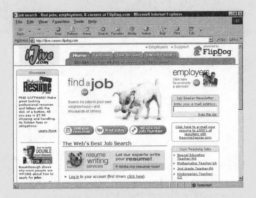

International Job Links

www.joblinks.f2s.com/index_eng.htm

Check out this site if you're looking for an overseas opportunity: This site isn't so much a job bank as a collection of links — more than 600 of them — to international job banks you can visit. You can focus your job search by country or geographic area. You also have access to country-specific visa and job-hunting information. A handy tip: The site uses numerous icons, which can be confusing, so be sure to print them out so you can find your way around. The ideal starting point for your overseas job hunt.

Planet Recruit

www.planetrecruit.com

More than 58,000 international jobs posted at any given time: The site has a great search engine that allows you to narrow your search by keyword, occupation, or country. It even has a section exclusively for new graduates. Register to receive immediate Job Alerts via e-mail when new jobs are posted that match your job-hunting criteria.

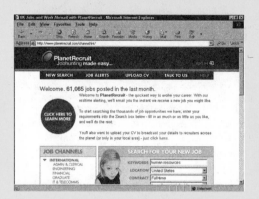

TopJobs.net

www.topjobs.net

TopJobs.net is a great place to start looking for that job overseas: TopJobs.net is a European job bank that offers job posting and search services for jobs in Germany, the United Kingdom, Ireland, Switzerland, Norway, Sweden, Austria, Spain, Poland, and Thailand.

Vault

www.vault.com

This job bank has an internship job board to help students and new grads find summer positions: Based in the U.S., Vault is a great all-around job-hunting resource. You can access sample résumés and cover letters, sample interview questions, message boards, and a job bank with more than 35,000 U.S. jobs posted. In addition to its own content, Vault partners with several other sites to provide one-stop shopping for career planning, company information, and career management. A cool site with thought-provoking quotes sprinkled throughout that will inspire you.

Government job banks

Public Service Commission of Canada
http://jobs.gc.ca/home_e.htm

Alberta
www.pao.gov.ab.ca/jobs/index.html

British Columbia
www.postings.gov.bc.ca

Manitoba
www.gov.mb.ca/csc/06access.html

New Brunswick
www.gov.nb.ca/0163/employ-e.asp

Newfoundland & Labrador
www.gov.nf.ca/psc

Northwest Territories
www.gov.nt.ca/utility/jobs

Nova Scotia
www.gov.ns.ca/psc/employ

Nunavut
http://www.gov.nu.ca/Nunavut/English/jobs/

Ontario
www.gojobs.gov.on.ca

Prince Edward Island
www.gov.pe.ca/jobs

Quebec
www.gouv.qc.ca/Informations/Emploi/Emploi_en.html

Saskatchewan
www.gov.sk.ca/psc/jobs/jobs.htm

Yukon
http://employment.gov.yk.ca

(Other) Job-Hunting Books

In addition to other . . . *For Dummies* books about jobs and careers that I refer to throughout this book, here are a few other shelf references you might want to check out.

The Complete Idiot's Guide to Getting the Job You Want, 2nd Edition
Marc Dorio, Alpha Books

What Color is Your Parachute?
Richard Nelson Bolles, Ten Speed Press
(Updated annually)

The Everything Get-A-Job Book
Steven Grager, Adams Media Corporation

The Overnight Job Search Strategy
Donald Asher, Ten Speed Press

The Overnight Résumé
Donald Asher, Ten Speed Press

The Complete Idiot's Guide to the Perfect Cover Letter
Susan Ireland, Alpha Books

201 Killer Cover Letters
Sandra Podesta & Andrea Paxton, McGraw-Hill Trade

The Guide to Internet Job Searching
Margaret Riley, N.T.C. Publishing

Résumé and Cover Letter Tools

Check out some of these sites that help you put together a résumé, offer samples to look at, or even review your résumé for free.

About.com: Job Search

http://jobsearchtech.about.com/careers/
jobsearchtech/library/weekly/
aa092997.htm

Find useful links on this site: This site is part of the About.com directory and is a series of articles providing cover letter tips and links to other cover letter, résumé, and job search sites.

Campus Access.com

www.campusaccess.com/campus_web/
career/c3job_res.htm

A great site for new grads: The résumé section of this site for new graduates has tips on how to make your résumé look good, and read even better. A useful feature is a list of action words you can include to give your résumé that added punch.

Career City: Cover Letters

www.careercity.com/content/cvlttr/
index.cfm

Write an effective cover letter: Most sites that give information on cover letters only have a single page that tells you how to write the letter. This site takes you further and gives you sample cover letters, blunders to avoid, tips on content and action words, and other useful tips on making your cover letter effective.

JobStar Central

http://jobstar.org/tools/resume/index.cfm

Résumé and cover letter basics and beyond: This site is a great resource to help you write your résumé and cover letter. It includes a section on choosing a résumé style, sample résumés and cover letters, and other résumé resources. It covers the basics of résumé writing and then goes a step further to offer examples you can look at.

Quintessential Careers.com

www.quintcareers.com/resume_tutorial/

Helpful tutorials found on this site: This Web site has both a basic and an advanced résumé tutorial that walks you through constructing your résumé. You will also find answers to most of your résumé-related questions on this site.

Rebecca Smith's eRésumés and Resources

www.eresumes.com

★ ★
★ ★

First aid for your electronic résumé: A well-known and highly recommended site to help you design an electronic résumé. You can also view many different samples of résumés on this site at www.erésumés.com/gallery_rezcat.html.

Resumania

www.resumania.com

A humorous site dedicated to real-life résumé mistakes: Check it out for a good laugh, plus some practical tips on what *not* to do with your résumé.

Résumé Tutor

www1.umn.edu/ohr/ecep/résumé/

This site has a great résumé template: It will not put it together for you but walks you through the process of developing one.

Salary Stuff

Wondering what salary you should be asking for, or how to negotiate salary? Here are a few sites that can help you out.

The Career Services Center Guide to Negotiating Salary and Benefits

www.usfca.edu/usf/career/salary.html

More money talk: For additional information to help you negotiate your salary and on fielding salary-related interview questions, be sure to check out this site. There are no links to other sites, as this is just an information page.

monsterTrak

www2.jobtrak.com/help_manuals/jobmanual/salary.html

Check out this page on JobTrak's Web site for tips on the sensitive issue of negotiating salary: You might want to check out some of the other features of this site, like the sample résumés, too.

D-26 Self-Assessment Tools

SalaryExpert.com

www.salaryexpert.com

A must-visit when negotiating salaries or making relocation decisions: A site dedicated to helping you find out what you need to know about salaries and the cost of living in both the U.S. and in Canada. It breaks down salaries by occupation and location. You can also access international salary information on this site.

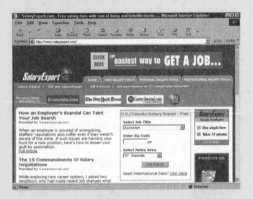

Self-Assessment Tools

The Web sites I profile in this section have a variety of self-assessment tests and tools to help you identify your personality type and your aptitudes. Try one if you're seeking help in choosing a job or career that really suits you.

Advisor Team

www.advisorteam.com/user/ktsintro1.asp

Are you an Artisan? A Guardian? Maybe an Idealist? On this site, you are invited to take the free Keirsey Temperament Sorter II —

the fun, interesting, and revealing questionnaire that tells you if you're an Artisan, Guardian, Rational, or Idealist. This is the same test used in career development programs at Fortune 500 companies and in counseling centres and career placement centres at major universities. You can view a summary of your test results for free but need to pay to purchase the entire 10-page report.

Human Resources Development Canada Worksearch

www.worksearch.gc.ca

★ ★
★ ★

Self-assessment tools and much more: This is a subsite of HRDC that provides career assessment tools. It guides you through the process, from deciding what you want to do to helping you write your résumé and search for a job. It has tips on developing a strategy, upgrading skills, and even managing your money when you are out of work.

Monster Self-Assessment Centre

http://assessment.monster.ca

★ ★
★ ★

Take the entrepreneurial assessment quiz on this section of Monster.ca to see whether you've got what it takes to go it alone in business: This fun yet informative page is part of the mega-Canadian Monster site. You will find personality and interest quizzes, self-assessment tools and links, even an entrepreneurial assessment on this site. You also have access to Monster's job bank and résumé posting at the click of a button. Articles, resources, and links to help with your job hunt can also be accessed from this page.

University of Waterloo Career Services

www.cdm.uwaterloo.ca

  ★★
★★

Check out the University of Waterloo's Career Development eManual: You don't have to download anything, though — it is all available on the Web site. The self-assessment tools on this site are fantastic. You are led through a series of steps to analyze and identify your pride experiences, personality, values, skills, interests, knowledge and learning, and self-employment aptitude — and the site actually tells you how to tie it all together and make it mean something to you.

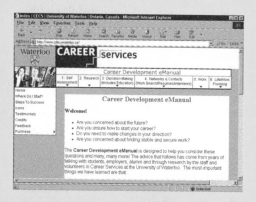

Staffing and Temp Agencies

One option you have is to work as a temp or sign on with a staffing agency for a while to gain experience, make connections, impress the right people, and hopefully (with a little luck thrown in) land a permanent job. In this section I profile some of the larger staffing and temp agencies across Canada.

Accountemps.com

www.accountemps.com

Like to crunch numbers and balance those books? Accountemps is a recruitment firm that specializes in filling temporary financial, accounting, and bookkeeping positions. Accountemps is actually a division of Robert Half International, a well-known staffing firm, and has over 325 offices in Canada, the U.S., Europe, and Australia. You can register online to view jobs but must be interviewed in person to become an Accountemps professional. Locate the office nearest you at `www.accountemps.com/Office Locations`. Accountemps has offices all across Canada in major cities. A bonus on this site is the wealth of job search articles and information they have posted.

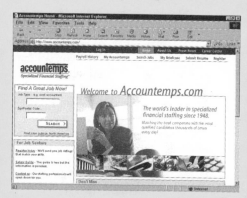

Alumni-Network

www.alumni-network.com

Are you an engineering or e-commerce graduate? Based in Oakville, Ontario, Alumni Network specializes in placement of university graduates in the U.S., Canada, and internationally. They are an online placement agency with a focus on ERP, e-commerce, and engineering graduates. To apply for a posted job, you have to submit your résumé by e-mail and recruiters will match it to potential positions.

The Directory of Canadian Recruiters

www.directoryofrecruiters.com

Get access to recruitment firms across the country: The Directory of Recruiters book is a listing complete with company information, a range of services, and contact information for recruiters all across Canada. From the Web site, you can access listings of recruiters (without contact information) and you can link directly to some of the recruiter sites. If you know the name of the recruitment firm, this Web site is worth a visit to find out more.

Kelly Services

www.kellyservices.ca

Kelly Services recruits for a wide variety of industries: Once well-known for clerical temporary staffing placements, Kelly Services is now an international player in temp and permanent recruitment in the science, finance and accounting, technical and professional, office, manufacturing, electronic assembly, call centre, and merchandising industries. Check out this page for branch locations across Canada: `www.kellyservices.ca/solutions/index.html`. You can register online as a preferred candidate to receive e-mail notification of jobs, but you are required to go through an extensive pre-screening process before being placed in a position.

Michael Page International

www.michaelpage.com

Michael Page International operates in 15 countries with more than 100 offices worldwide: If you are looking for a job on the international scene and at a higher level,

this is a good place to start. Applying for the jobs is very easy — you just submit your résumé online. Interview and résumé tips are a bonus on the site, but unfortunately the Salary Wizard on the site is U.S.-based only. You can sign up for JobStreamer — a weekly e-mail notification of news and hot career opportunities.

RHI Consulting (Technology Professionals)

www.rhic.com

Looking for a tech job? RHI Consulting specializes in placement of employees in the technology field. Owned by Robert Half International Inc., the company has more than 100 offices all over North America, Europe, and Australia. For an office near you, check out this page: `www.rhic.com/OfficeLocations`. Once you register and apply for a position, a recruiter will call you directly and set up an in-person meeting. RHI has offices in major cities across Canada.

Robert Half International Inc.

www.rhii.com

A twist on traditional staffing agencies: This mega-staffing company has seven staffing divisions, all of which run separate offices and act independently of one another. Three of these divisions, Accountemps (`www.accountemps.com`), Robert Half (`www.roberthalf.com`), and RHI Management Resources (`www.rhimr.com`), place temporary, full-time, and contract employees in the finance and accounting industries. The OfficeTeam (`www.officeteam.com`) division provides temporary office and administrative support, RHI Consulting (`www.rhic.com`) is the tech division, while The Affiliates (www.affiliates.com) places attorneys, paralegals, and legal support personnel. The last division is The Creative Group (www.creativegroup.com), which works with creative, advertising, marketing, and Web design professionals.

Each division of Robert Half is well represented internationally, as well as in North America, and the registration procedure for job hunters is the same for each division. You either register online or call the nearest office directly, and you will have an in-person interview to determine where you fit and what your goals are. They will then match you with a position, or you can apply for jobs directly online from their online database. This differs somewhat from the traditional staffing agency in that you actually get to see what jobs are available and request to be placed in one — rather than wait for the recruiter to match you.

Working Outside Canada

These Web sites point the way out of Canada and into a great job abroad.

Department of Foreign Affairs and International Trade (DFAIT)

www.dfait-maeci.gc.ca

Flying the maple leaf abroad: The Department of Foreign Affairs and International Trade (DFAIT) represents Canada abroad through a network of embassies and offices around the world. On this site, you will find information that you will need if you are planning on working abroad, including information on Canadian consulates in different countries and other foreign country–related issues. Information on work-abroad youth programs can be found here.

Department of Foreign Affairs and International Trade — Travel Reports

**http://voyage.dfait-maeci.gc.ca/
destinations/menu_e.htm**

Log on before you leave: This is the site to check out if you are looking for foreign country–specific information. It also has direct links to Consular Affairs to provide assistance for Canadians who are abroad, direct links to the passport office, and travel reports advising Canadians of the safety of different areas.

Homestore.com

www.homefair.com

Wondering what it takes to move abroad? Looking for information to help you make the decision to relocate to the U.S.? This site has everything you could be looking for. Explore this site. I can't begin to tell you everything that's on it. One feature I really like is a great free salary calculator that allows you to compare international, Canadian, and U.S. salaries.

Ogletree, Deakins

www.odnss.com

Looking for an immigration lawyer in the U.S. to help you with your visa or entry into the U.S.? Ogletree, Deakins provides assistance to job seekers and employers seeking temporary business visas and foreign nationals seeking permanent residence.

Part V
Exploring Other Options

The 5th Wave
By Rich Tennant

"I couldn't get this 'job skills' program to work on my PC, so I replaced the mother-board, upgraded the BIOS and wrote a program that links it to my personal database. It told me I wasn't technically inclined and should pursue a career in sales."

In this part . . .

You discover that there are lots of other ways to get your foot in the door of a full-time job if you lack experience or have special circumstances. Hey, you might just decide that you *prefer* one of these alternative employment options — contract work, temping, or working part-time — so much so that you decide to leave the 9-to-5 rat race behind for good. This part also covers starting your own business and working abroad.

Chapter 20

Finding Another Way In

. . . .

In This Chapter

▶ Freelancing your way to full-time work

▶ Researching your grant eligibility

▶ Linking up with a mentor

▶ Accepting a job you're overqualified for

▶ Looking at temping as an option

▶ Exploring the wonderful world of volunteering

. . . .

*M*ost job hunters agree that the toughest part of finding a job is just getting your foot in the door. You know you are qualified for the job, and if you were just given a chance you'd be able to show them all how well you could do it. The good news is that there are other ways of landing your dream job — less traditional ways. You have to be willing to work at it (and possibly work for nothing), but it could be worthwhile in the long run.

I describe several nontraditional forms of work in this chapter. If you go this route, here's what you might encounter:

✔ **You might not get a regular paycheque.** Heck, you might not even get a paycheque if you're interning or volunteering.

✔ **You probably won't have a benefits package.** Non–full-time employees often have to provide their own health benefits.

✔ **You might have to face a little uncertainty and lack of security.** You'll be responsible for your own savings and investments in lieu of a company pension or investment program.

✔ **You will have to open your mind and try something different.** This could be something you'd never dreamed of doing. (I don't mean anything bad, folks, just different — like working for free.)

But despite this, there are real benefits and opportunities to be gained from taking on one of these forms of work and finding another way in to a full-time gig. Hey, you might enjoy it so much that you decide not to look for a full-time job. One option you have is to go into business for yourself, which I discuss in Chapter 21.

Freelancing Your Way In

Freelancing is a great way to gain experience in your field and make valuable contacts at the same time. Some people choose to be a freelancer as a part-time solution to finding full-time employment, while others decide it's something they want to do full-time. You are a *freelancer* if you work for yourself and have a variety of clients and projects. Employers sometimes refer to freelancers as *contractors* or *consultants*.

The current trend toward downsizing corporate offices in both the private and public sectors has created opportunities for freelance or contract workers to fill the gap left behind, because there's still the same amount of work to do — but fewer employees left to do it. I used to work for a government department that employed over 3,000 people. Ten years later, this department had downsized to 750 people. It still provided the same services, but the majority of these were now contracted out because it was cheaper and more efficient to hire contractors, consultants, and freelancers. Interestingly enough, often the same people who had actually been doing the job for the department started up their own businesses and were awarded the contracts to provide the service.

Freelancing can help you break into a field and can also give you something to put on your résumé. And who knows? You may decide freelancing is something you really like. Then again, you may decide you prefer the security of a single employer and a regular paycheque at the end of the month.

Getting a Grant

Not too long ago, I was recruiting for an entry-level computer programmer position and was intrigued by one applicant whose cover letter stated that if we were to hire him, we would be eligible to have a large portion of his wages covered by a grant. He gave the specifics of the grant he had applied for and been awarded, and even volunteered to do the paperwork to set it up. I was intrigued and gave the applicant a call.

A *grant* is monies paid out of a government program for a specific purpose. There are several grants available that provide students currently enrolled in a post-secondary institution with the opportunity to gain experience in their chosen field. The money from these grants is used to reimburse the employer — up to a certain amount. It's a win–win situation for employee and employer. Generally, you must meet specific criteria in order to qualify for a grant.

Fiona goes to Central America

Fiona had recently graduated with a bachelor of science degree (BSc), and, not being able to find a job in her chosen occupation, was working as a research technician. There was an internship in Central America that she was interested in applying for. She knew someone who had received funding under a Human Resources Development Canada (HRDC) grant program to help underemployed people increase their skills and get them working at a level they should be. After visiting their Web site (www18.hrdc-drhc.gc.ca), she contacted the local HRDC office, but was told there was no such grant. Knowing there was, Fiona did her homework — picked the brain of her friend who had received a similar grant, searched the Web site for hints, and used her network by calling her little brother's friend's mother (seriously!) who worked for HRDC. She found the description of the program and showed it to the local agents, who were then (miraculously!) open to receiving her application.

She had also discovered the key to a successful application was to make sure that the internship for which she was trying to get funding would reflect the goals of the funding program.

Then she ran up against the stumbling block that the internship she wanted training for was in Central America — HRDC normally did not fund for out-of-country work experience if that experience could be obtained in Canada. This meant she had to do additional research to show that she could not get the training anywhere in Canada at that time of year. And she finally persuaded them to fund her internship in Central America. She got the green light two weeks before she was supposed to leave.

If Fiona had not persevered and done her research — finding the grant, applying for it, and making a case for actually gaining her training out of the country, she would have missed a once-in-a-lifetime opportunity.

There are grants available for students to help them gain experience between school terms, as well as for new grads to help them kick-start their careers. There are also grants for other job hunters — not just students or recent grads. For example, there are grants for *underemployed* people (people working in a position for which they are overqualified, such as someone with a law degree who works as an assistant). Other grants are administered by specific industries or by provinces and municipalities to attract employees to work in that given industry or move to that given location. You need to do your research to find out what grants are available and whether you fit the criteria. Then you have to go out and find an employer that also matches the grant criteria. See the sidebar "Fiona goes to Central America" for a real-life example of someone who did just that.

To find a list of grants administered by Human Resources Development Canada (HRDC), check out their Web site at www18.hrdc-drhc.gc.ca.

Finding a Mentor

A *mentor* is an individual, usually older, always more experienced, that helps and guides another individual's development. A mentor provides guidance and is a sounding board to bounce ideas off. A good mentor is one of the most valuable assets you can have for your career. How can a mentor help you find a job? Well, generally the purpose of a mentor is to guide you in your career path. When it comes time to change jobs or try for that promotion, your mentor may have an impact on whether you actually land the job.

Your mentor may be a professor or college instructor, someone who graduated ahead of you in the same program, someone you currently work with, or even someone you meet through a related professional association. To really be effective as a mentor, she should ideally work in the same occupation as you, though not necessarily in the same company.

You may be able to link up with a mentor through a professional or trade organization to which you belong or that you can join. For example, I belong to a professional association called the Periodical Writers Association of Canada (PWAC) (www.pwac.ca). PWAC has a program that links new writers up with mentors to help them break into the industry.

Taking a Job You're Overqualified For

When you're pursuing a job, remember that the first thing you need to do is get your foot in the door. If you can get a job — any job — with your dream employer, that may be the "in" you need. Don't worry if the job is an assistant or receptionist position. Entry-level jobs can be your way in. For example, a computer programmer can start out on the help desk to become familiar with the company's software.

Don't worry if the job starts out as part-time, contract, or casual work. Once you are working there, you will have the opportunity to impress the employer with your eagerness, intelligence, and willingness to work — and that could eventually lead to a full-time job.

Here are some ways to get noticed by your employer and move up one (or a few) rungs on the ladder:

- ✔ **Ask questions and learn as much as you can about the company and its products.** Employers like it when you show an active interest.
- ✔ **Propose ideas.** Keep it low-key, though, in the form of suggestions.

Dave's research pays off

Always be on the lookout for ways to increase your odds of getting hired. Ask people for ideas. Talk to suppliers, customers, and competitors of your target company. Do your research. Dave did.

Dave joined the navy right out of high school and remained there for four years. When he left, he had tonnes of hands-on experience as an electrician, but no formal training. He made a list of all the equipment on the ship that he had repaired, and researched the companies that made the products. He struck gold — one company happened to be located near his hometown. He sent them his résumé and included a reference letter specifically praising his repair work on the company's products. His cover letter detailed the various repairs he had made, as well as what he liked about the equipment and what he felt could be improved. Not only did they offer him the job, but they took his four years of experience into account in his starting salary.

- ✔ **Punch in early and punch out late.** One of the best tactics I learned for getting noticed is to show up at least five minutes before your boss and leave five minutes later. This shows that you are a hard worker and prepared to put in longer hours.

- ✔ **Read what comes across your desk.** You might see a memo complaining about lack of help or resources in an area where you can offer assistance.

- ✔ **Volunteer for projects that go beyond your entry-level duties.** Most companies are involved in some kind of charity work — walkathons, food drives, and the like. Go ahead and sign up. It's a great way to meet people throughout the organization.

Sometimes people work at jobs for which they are overqualified just to pay the bills until something else comes along. Remember, whatever the job is, you should do it to the *best* of your ability. Employers do check references and, if you are not performing in a job, the reference your employer gives you may end up costing you that dream job when it does come along.

Temping Your Way In

Working as a temp can provide you with insights into both the work and the organization. At one time, temporary jobs primarily helped companies with their excess clerical work. Today, many organizations and industries use temporary staff to help alleviate short-term work fluctuations or for expertise on special projects. Temping is a great way of making inroads, and also provides an opportunity for you to showcase your skills and work ethic. Often the temporary jobs you may be assigned are not your ultimate career goal, but they do allow you to work in either your field or the company of your choice. If you work hard, your work *will be* noticed.

Some companies use temp agencies as a way to screen candidates, and offer full-time jobs to the best temps. They say the fee they pay to the agency is less than the cost of recruiting.

Temporary work has its advantages:

- ✔ It helps pay the bills so you don't go without a paycheque for too long.
- ✔ It provides networking opportunities.
- ✔ It lets you add to your repertoire of skills.
- ✔ It is something you can put on your résumé to fill time gaps when you are not working full-time or when you're going to school.
- ✔ Employers are likely to think more highly of someone who worked as a temp while looking for a job than someone who did nothing.

There are a few things you should be aware of when you sign on with a temp agency. For one thing, the agency takes a fee off the top of your wage — it could be as much as $2 or $3 per hour. In addition, to ensure that the agency doesn't lose its best assets (good employees), there's often a contract provision between the agency and the employer specifying that the employer cannot hire you for a certain length of time after you stop working for the agency. If they do want to hire you, they must pay a *buyout fee* (a commission) to the agency, which is sometimes as much as three times your monthly salary! Does this mean that employers are loath to use temp agencies to recruit? Not really. In fact, many employers feel that the money they save from not having to advertise for the position is roughly equivalent to the buyout fee. An added bonus is that someone who's already worked for you (even as a temp) will know his way around a lot better than someone hired fresh. Shorter learning curves translate into lower training costs for employers.

Check the section on recruitment agencies in the yellow-paged Landing a Job For Canadians For Dummies Directory of Job Resources or some of these temp agencies on the Web to help you get started:

- ✔ **Adecco** (www.adecco.com)**:** A worldwide, full-service recruitment firm, Adecco also offers temporary staffing services. You can do a job search by geographic location.
- ✔ **Kelly Services** (www.kellyservices.ca)**:** A well-known name in the temping field, Kelly Services also has offices across Canada and posts its jobs online.

✔ **Net Temps** (www.net-temps.com): An online recruitment site that specializes in matching temps with jobs. It lists jobs in both Canada and the United States.

Volunteering Your Way In

Volunteering is not just something that makes you feel good about helping others — there are some side benefits that can come out of volunteering as well:

✔ You can enhance your work experience.

✔ You learn valuable skills.

✔ You fill time gaps on your résumé.

✔ Your network grows as you develop contacts in the profession that you can use to your advantage later.

✔ You gain a reference for future jobs.

✔ If you're a new grad with limited work experience, you have something tangible to put on your résumé.

For fresh grads especially, the ultimate benefit of volunteering is a job itself. Even if you're still in school while you volunteer (maybe in the summer or even during the school year), you'll have the inside track on available positions when you graduate.

What field are you interested in?

Your volunteer work can be in a number of different areas — all of which can help you in your job hunt. You can gain an edge by doing volunteer work in a field that interests you. For example, if you are interested in the medical profession, you can volunteer at a local hospital or extended care centre. You will learn more about the profession and the career options available, which will in turn help you decide whether you really want a career in the field. If you have completed your training and are looking for a job, volunteering is one way of showing the prospective employer what you are made of.

Offer to work for free

I am serious! This does work — can you imagine an employer saying no to someone who offers to work for free? If you have applied for a job and the employer is hedging, or if you have a dream employer you want to work for, you can volunteer to work for them for free for, say, a month. Take this approach: Tell them that there's no obligation to hire you, but you would like to gain experience and also show them what you can do. This will, at least, give you something you can put on your résumé. At best, you may land a job offer. This is sometimes called a *practicum* or an *internship*.

I have personally witnessed this work, many times. Once, I was recruiting for telecommunications technicians. I had a very enthusiastic young fellow apply for the job. While his attitude was good, my client was a little concerned about his technical skills — I had several other applicants who had higher-level skills in this area. He was interviewed but wasn't offered a position. He called the manager of the company directly (a great strategy is to bypass the HR person) to follow up on what he could do better next time (another great strategy) and offered his services for free for two weeks. It turned out that he was technically competent and he ended up being offered a full-time job. They even paid him for his volunteer time.

Another client, a software development company, was looking for an experienced developer and was really overwhelmed by the number of applications. Rather than shortlist and interview, they took on a recent graduate who offered to work in a practicum capacity for free for a month. He also ended up getting a full-time job.

Volunteer for a board or an association

You can also volunteer for the board of directors for a non-profit association. This can be a great career move for you if you want to work in the field; you are then in the know when a job comes up *and* it is quite likely that everyone on the hiring committee is also on the board of directors with you. In addition, being on a board helps you network. Board members are usually from a broad spectrum of businesses and industries, and getting to know them could eventually lead to a referral or a job offer.

Don't have the time to commit to being a board member? Volunteering for committees in associations can also give you great networking contacts and the inside edge on upcoming jobs. You don't have to be on the board, but you can volunteer to help with the newsletter or sit on a conference planning committee. These are great ways to meet new people in your field, network to get job leads, and potentially meet your future employer.

In your community

Community volunteer work can include working in your kid's school, coaching sports teams, helping out with the recycling program, joining a service club such as the Rotary, or a community-based program such as Block Parents.

Karen strikes gold at a Halloween party

Karen, a biologist, had just finished her bachelor of science degree and was working on a two-month contract down near Long Point, Ontario, for the fall, looking at pest problems in apple orchards. One day, her boss suggested they go check out the bird-banding station that the Long Point Bird Observatory ran down near an apple orchard on her route. She was completely enthralled and asked the young guy banding a bird how she could get involved. He suggested she come down in the evenings as they were banding owls and could use a hand. That was the start of a month of working all day in the apple orchards, then making the 40-minute drive to the banding station to band owls until about 2 a.m., and then driving back home to go to bed, and start this again the next day!

The banding station closed up about the same time as her contract ended, and Karen did not know what her next job would be. She went to a Halloween party down at the banding station and met the executive director of Long Point. He asked her about her plans and said if she was interested she could live at the banding station as a caretaker during the evenings and drive to the main office during the day to do office work on a volunteer basis. They would give her a place to live (the banding station) and a $25-a-week food allowance (which she actually managed to live on!). She worked in the office doing data entry and other menial tasks, but once the spring arrived and funding was secured she had the choice of *two* jobs.

In Karen's case, being a volunteer, showing enthusiasm, and being willing to live very, very cheaply eventually landed her a job and kick-started her career as biologist.

Chapter 21

Starting Your Own Business

• •

In This Chapter

▶ Evaluating your entrepreneurial I.Q.

▶ Weighing the good, the bad, and the ugly of being your own boss

▶ Getting your business off the ground

▶ Financing your business

▶ Enriching your solo business with other resources

• •

*Y*ou may be considering starting your own business for a number of reasons. It may be your dream to be your own boss. Perhaps you have a great product or service idea that you want to market and sell yourself. Maybe you've been downsized and are thinking about marketing your services to your old employer and clients as an *independent contractor* (you are self-employed rather than employed by someone else). Maybe you have something you are skilled at or that interests you — bookkeeping, gardening, house-keeping — that others don't like to do, don't have the time to do themselves, and are willing to pay for.

Lots of people leave the corporate, full-time workforce for one reason or another and discover that they actually *prefer* being that little bit removed from the rat race. Then again, maybe you're a fresh graduate with this groovy idea for a business that just burned a hole into your head during all those calculus lectures at university, and you want to try it out.

Whatever the reasons, starting your own business can sure be exciting — but it can also be overwhelming. Being your own boss isn't for everyone — you have to possess certain characteristics and skills in order to be any good at it. And there are outside forces to consider, too, which will have an effect on your business one way or the other. You have choices to make regarding the structure and financing of your business. This chapter discusses the benefits and liabilities of running your own business, tells you about the different types of business you can operate under law, and reviews the many different and varied financing options available to you as a prospective small business owner (there are lots of them). I finish off by pointing you in the direction of some very comprehensive and helpful small business resources. So dive in!

What It Takes to Be Your Own Boss

Your business can take many forms. You could be a colony of one, flying solo, or overseeing a flock of many (a small business is defined as any organization that employs 100 people or less). But do you have what it takes to be your own boss? In Chapter 2, I take you through a self-assessment exercise that gives you a better idea of your wants and needs as they apply to your job or career. After going through the 26 questions, you should have a pretty good idea whether being your own boss, among other things, is something that appeals to you. (Yes, there are 26 questions, but they don't take all that long to answer! If you haven't given it a try, head back to Chapter 2 and do so. It's fun!) But back to the topic at hand: self-employment. There are some particular skills and characteristics you should possess to be your own boss, whether you want to be an independent contractor or operate your own small business complete with employees — call these attributes your *entrepreneurial I.Q.* While personality *traits or* characteristics tend to be pretty hard to acquire — you're born the way you're born, aren't you? — the good news is that you *can* acquire the skills needed to be a successful entrepreneur.

Here is a list of personality traits that make a successful entrepreneur. See if you recognize yourself in more than four of them.

- ✔ **You are a self-starter:** Successful entrepreneurs must be hard workers and able to follow through on projects. You must be self-motivated and enjoy being in control.

- ✔ **You are willing to ask for help in areas that are not your strength:** In owning your own business, you'll have to wear many hats: the sales hat, the marketing hat, the finance hat, the production hat, the administrative hat, and the people-managing hat. Clearly you're talented in a lot of these areas (or you wouldn't be thinking about starting your own business), but I have yet to encounter the business equivalent of the Bionic Man or Woman who can pull *all* of this off. Chances are, you're going to need some help.

  You may want to consider teaming up with a partner (perhaps even your spouse) who brings a different skill set to the table. Another option is to take some courses to bone up on the requisite areas, delaying your opening until you are better prepared. Are you willing to do this?

- ✔ **You are decisive:** As the boss, you need to make decisions. You are comfortable making the call, and you do so based on a combination of gut instinct and thorough research.

- ✔ **You have a strong sense of self-confidence and self-worth:** You're not the type to get easily discouraged. Positive thinking is a prerequisite for those striking out on their own — you cannot dwell on setbacks. You focus on success rather than the possibility of failure.

✔ **You have the right motivation:** Successful entrepreneurs are usually motivated by a strong desire to achieve and attain financial success. You are determined to succeed in this venture.

✔ **You have all the time in the world and the patience of a saint:** Okay, I don't know anyone who fits this description, but time and patience still come into play here. Starting a business requires careful planning and preparation. Are you prepared to work long hours and make sacrifices such as not being able to play on weekends or having to buy a new photocopier instead of going to Disneyland?

✔ **You have a pretty high tolerance for risk:** While there may be potential for impressive and sizeable earnings if you start your own business, there's also the potential for acute and sizeable financial loss if your venture doesn't succeed. You are willing to take this risk.

Now we move on to skills you need to start and run your own business. Remember, you can acquire these skills if you need to, unlike the personality traits in the list above.

✔ **You can clearly articulate your dreams and goals in writing:** Some people who start their own business don't take the time and energy to go through this exercise, and, as a result, the whole thing can get derailed. You have a clear idea of where you want to take your business and how you are going to get it there.

✔ **You are able to *multi-task,* do many things at one time:** Coordinating and managing different types of responsibilities simultaneously is key to being a successful entrepreneur.

✔ **You are organized:** You are able to organize the resources of your business in order to make it run in the most efficient manner possible.

If organization is not your strength, you can hire someone to help you out. You may also have a spouse or partner who has strengths in this area.

Finally, there are a couple of additional prerequisites for starting your own business that have to do with your lifestyle.

✔ **You are in good health and are a whiz at handling stress:** None of us are all-powerful wizards when it comes to stress management, but some of us are better than others. You are prepared for the long hours and hard work involved in starting up and operating your own business.

✔ **You are able to balance starting your own business with personal and family commitments:** Making a profit and earning income may take some time. You may have to support yourself (and perhaps your family) while you get your business up and running, and your energy and time may have to be redirected for months — possibly even years.

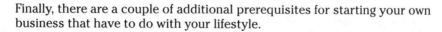

Perhaps most important, does the idea for your business reflect your passions? You'll be spending time and money to make your idea work — having a true passion for the business makes it a lot easier.

Your success in business is not only a result of your own motivation and skills, though they play an important part. Many a savvy entrepreneur has been helped (and, on occasion, hindered) by external forces beyond her control. For example, interest rates can affect your costs — especially if you have to borrow money and have heavy financing obligations. A market downturn can also affect the demand for your product — if demand for printed business cards is replaced by cards printed on people's home computers, a printer might feel the crunch. Some of the questions you need to consider (and will consider as part of your business plan — see later in this section) include these:

- Is there a demand for the product or service you are offering?
- Can you offer the product or service at a competitive rate?

Pros and cons of being da' boss

Many people in business for themselves love it! Others just aren't cut out to be self-employed. Before you decide to go into business for yourself, weigh the pros and cons of self-employment.

Pros of self-employment:

- You get to be your own boss. You are accountable to yourself rather than to an employer.

- The hard work and long hours you put in directly benefit *you*, rather than increasing profits for someone else.

- You control your company's direction, earnings, and growth potential.

- There are many tax advantages, such as being able to write off portions of your household expenses, office space, and claiming mileage on your personal vehicle if you use it for business.

- Running a business provides endless variety, challenge, and opportunities to learn.

- You can actually earn money by doing something you are passionate about!

Cons of self-employment:

- It is hard work and involves long hours.

- You may have to make personal and financial sacrifices.

- The learning curve can be steep and can seem overwhelming at first.

- The ups and downs of the business cycle can cause anxiety and stress.

- There is a risk of losing everything you have invested if your venture does not succeed.

- You are ultimately responsible for resolving problems and making decisions.

- It is easy to get distracted, and you may not end up putting in the time you should.

- If you are feeling unmotivated, there is no one (like a boss) to make you go in to the office. You need to motivate yourself.

- You have to look after your own medical coverage, benefits, payroll remittances, and pension.

✔ Is it cost-efficient to produce the product or service?

✔ Do you have the resources available to produce the product or service (labour, raw materials, and finances)?

If you go into business with the appropriate mindset and skills and you have evaluated your product and market, you are much more likely to meet with success. Have a friend go through the lists in this section with you. You're sure to get a valuable second opinion.

Launching Your Business

To increase your chances of success, you need to take some time before springing into a business venture, to evaluate your goals, your business idea, and the potential market. There are two very important things you have to have under your belt before you launch your business:

✔ You need to know which of three business structures is the right one for you.

✔ You need to develop a sound business plan.

You need a structure

There are three types of legal business structure. Selecting the right structure for your business depends upon a variety of issues, such as tax implications and the amount of personal financial risk you're prepared to take.

The business structures are these:

✔ A sole proprietorship

✔ A partnership

✔ A corporation.

A sole proprietorship

A *sole proprietorship* is the simplest of business structures, one that is usually owned by one person (known as the proprietor) and can be operated under that person's name or a registered trade name. For example, I could operate under Dawn McCoy Consulting if I wanted to, or, if I chose to, I could register a *company name,* also known as a *trade name,* which allows me to make sure that no one else can use my company name. The proprietor owns the business entirely — there is no legal separation between the owner's personal assets and those of the company. Come tax time, your business income is classified as personal income and you claim it all on your personal income tax. Business expenses are claimed on your personal tax return, as well.

A partnership

A *partnership* is when two or more individuals form an association or relationship for the purpose of operating a trade or business for profit. A partnership, whether there is a written agreement or not, is a legally binding relationship in which each partner is liable for the actions of the other partners. There is no difference legally between a proprietorship and a partnership, except that in a partnership, the partners share the liabilities and the profits. Partners include their share of income or losses on personal or corporate income tax returns.

When you enter a partnership, no matter how much you like or even love your partner, it is important to have a legal partnership agreement in place. Get a lawyer or an accountant to help you put this together. Even in the best partnerships, things can turn sour. Remember, this is a business deal and you need to do it right.

A corporation

If the words *Limited (Ltd.)*, *Incorporated (Inc.)*, or *Corporation (Corp.)* are included in the name of a company, you know you are dealing with a *corporation*, or a *limited company*. When you incorporate your business, you create a legal entity that is separate from the owner of the business.

Why would you want to incorporate your business? It costs a lot more to incorporate a company than it does to just register yourself as a sole proprietorship. There are a few benefits from a legal perspective, however:

✔ In a sole proprietorship, if someone sues your business and wins, your personal savings and assets can be taken to pay the bill. In a corporation, if you are sued, you are not on the hook personally, but only for whatever the business owns. So your home and personal savings account, for example, are protected.

✔ If your sole proprietorship or partnership goes out of business and owes a whole bunch of people money, you are personally responsible for those debts. In a corporation, you are not responsible — your company is. Again, your own savings account and personal assets are protected. (One exception is if you take out a bank loan and sign a personal guarantee for it, which means that you agree to take personal responsibility to pay back the loan.)

Consult a lawyer or an accountant to help you determine the best structure for your business.

You need a plan

In the excitement of starting a new business or in the haste to take advantage of an opportunity, many entrepreneurs skip the vital step of developing a *business plan,* a document that describes what you plan to do in your business and how you plan to do it. Proper planning for your business, from a financial, operational, marketing, and managerial perspective, is key to turning your idea into reality.

A business plan helps you set your business's vision and goals, and acts as an operational plan, or blueprint, for achieving them. It is also a prerequisite for receiving financing of any kind — from pretty much any kind of financial organization. When deciding whether to lend you money, the bank asks to look at your business plan. Later in the chapter, under the heading "Financing Your Business," I discuss different and creative ways to get start-up funds for your business. Your business plan can be as detailed or as informal as you decide. Think of your business plan as a tool to help you chart the course for your company. It's a road map that shows other concerned parties, such as the bank, your partners, potential customers, even your family, where your business is going and how it will get there.

Here's what you should detail in your business plan:

- A description of the product(s) or service(s) you're offering and an explanation of how it meets the needs of your potential customers
- An analysis of your target market, including who your customers are, their buying patterns, and the location of your customers
- The management and ownership structure of your business

- The materials and resources you'll need to start and operate your business
- The potential strengths and weaknesses of your company. Be honest here — it is best to identify weaknesses up front
- A description of your company's short-term goals (up to one year after its inception) and long-term goals (5, 10, and 25 years down the road)
- A competitive analysis of the industry into which your business is directed (including suppliers, customers, competitors, threats — such as an economic downturn or an increase in interest rates — and opportunities)
- Sample marketing, sales, and production plans
- An analysis of your company's *operating costs* (what it will cost to actually operate and run your business)
- The amount of money your business requires to get off the ground, the type(s) of financing it requires, and potential sources of this money, including personal resources you may need to tap into
- Sample sales and cash flow forecasts

Banks recognize that small businesses are a driving force in the Canadian economy. Most of the large Canadian banks have dedicated portions of their Web sites to informing prospective small business owners about everything they're about to get into — the rewards and the risks. Check out the following Web sites. They have sample business plans you can look at before embarking on your own. (Of course, they hope you'll come to them for financing after using their site to develop your plan. I'll leave that decision up to you.)

- **Bank of Montreal** (`www.bmo.com/business`)**:** Answering the questions will help you prepare a comprehensive business plan. This is not a fill-in-the-blanks site, but it is easy to access and walks you through the business planning process in easy steps.

- **Canadian Imperial Bank of Commerce (CIBC)** (`www2.cibc.com/english/business_services/small_business`)**:** This site is more of an overview of what should be in a business plan rather than the detailed help you get on the other sites.

- **RBC Financial Group** (`www.royalbank.com/sme`)**:** Shown in Figure 21-1, this is a first-rate site for helping you to prepare a business plan. It leads you through what is needed in every section of your business plan, provides sample plans, and helps you get organized.

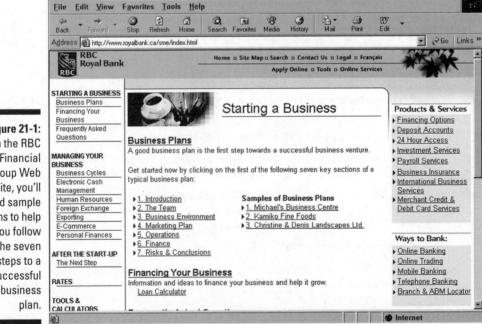

Figure 21-1: On the RBC Financial Group Web site, you'll find sample plans to help you follow the seven steps to a successful business plan.

✔ **Scotiabank (**www.scotiabank.com/cda/content**):** You can download the Scotia*business*™ Plan Writer from this site for help in preparing your business plan and financial forecasts.

✔ **TD Canada Trust (**www.tdcanadatrust.com/smallbusiness**):** This is a fill-in-the-blanks site where you complete a business plan by filling in the blanks in response to questions. It guides you through the financial as well as the business planning aspects of starting your business.

Strategis (www.strategis.gc.ca), an Industry Canada Web site, has an award-winning Business Start-up Assistant that guides you through preparing a business plan. It contains all the forms and information you need to register your company with the Canada Customs and Revenue Agency (CCRA) and to incorporate federally. You can also check out the Canada Business Service Centres site (www.cbsc.org/ibp/home) for a great interactive business planner. The Business Development Bank of Canada (www.bdc.ca) has information on grants available for business start-ups, plus a free business plan booklet that includes forms to help you develop your business plan.

There is nothing mysterious about preparing a business plan. You may use the assistance of an accountant, a lawyer, or another advisor or businessperson. Ultimately, however, the plan should reflect your own thinking — you need to

What about a franchise?

Everybody knows McDonald's and Tim Hortons. These are *franchises*. A franchise is not a unique business structure, but a method of distributing goods or services. At least two levels of people are involved in the franchise system: the *franchisor,* who lends her trademark or trade name and a business system, and the *franchisee,* who pays a royalty and often an initial fee for the right to do business under the franchisor's name and system. The franchisee benefits from using the franchisor's name, methods, and trademarks.

People purchase a franchise because it is often a successful company with a well-known brand name. Statistics also show that 80 percent of franchises are successful versus the rather dismal success statistics for other business start-ups. In fact, Statistics Canada (www.statcan.ca) reports that at least half of new companies

in Canada go out of business before their third anniversary, and only one-fifth of them survive a decade.

Though you may own the franchise, however, you do not have the same autonomy that you would in your own independent business venture. You gain benefits in being part of the overall franchise network, but you give up control and have to adhere to the franchise rules, including such things as the products you are allowed to carry or must carry, reporting procedures, dress codes, hours, and, overall, how you run your business. You may also have to buy your products directly from the parent company (which may prohibit you from getting the best prices). You have to pay an initial franchise fee and, in most cases, also pay a percentage of your monthly gross sales back to the parent company.

go through the process of understanding and planning for all aspects of your business. It is an important term of reference for you at the outset and on an ongoing basis. Business planning is a continuous process.

Financing Your Business

Money is a critical factor in starting a business — both for start-up and for operating expenses. Before you embark on your search for financing, you will have completed your business plan and will therefore know how much money you need to raise. But where to find it?

Surprisingly, in more places than you might think. This is a list of common sources of financing:

- ✔ **Angel investors:** An *angel investor* is someone who is interested in becoming a partner in a business. Angel investors are often retired business owners or executives with money to invest in promising small businesses. Usually, they want to play an active role in the business and, for start-ups, this type of investor can provide a great deal of experience and guidance.

- ✔ **Banks and other lending institutions:** Banks remain the foundation of small business financing. A well thought-out business plan is essential to gaining funding from a traditional bank. The Business Development Bank of Canada (www.bdc.ca) markets itself as Canada's small business bank. Other provincially based companies, such as the Alberta Opportunity Company (www.aoc.gov.ab.ca), also provide financing for small business. For more information and links to business resources in each province in Canada, check out this page from the Canada Business Service Centre Web site: (http://bsa.cbsc.org/scdt/startup/interface2.nsf/engdoc/14.html).

  Each of the "Big Five" Canadian banks offers resources for prospective small business owners. I discuss these earlier in the chapter, under the heading "Launching Your Business."

- ✔ **Credit cards or personal lines of credit:** For very small firms or home-based businesses, your credit card can be a ready means of obtaining small-scale funds for start-up, expansion, or operating expenses. Bear in mind, however, that credit cards traditionally have high interest rates and spending limits. Banks also offer *personal lines of credit* for certain classes of professionals, giving you ready access to funds if you need them, and only charging you interest when you use them. It may be the right option for you. Check with your bank, because the costs and benefits of personal lines of credit vary widely.

- ✔ **Government assistance:** There may be government grants available for specific industries or in some geographic locations. Check out these Web sites:

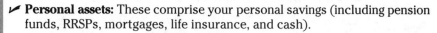

- **Business Gateway site of the Government of Canada** (`http://businessgateway.ca/`): You can find information regarding individual provinces on this site.

- **Strategis** (`http://strategis.ic.gc.ca/sc_mangb/sources`): You can also find specific government grant information on the Strategis site.

✔ **Love money:** Friends and relatives often invest in businesses owned by family members, associates, and friends. Love money is one of the most frequent sources of capital, beyond banks.

Be careful using the money of friends and relatives — it can put a strain on your personal and professional relationships.

✔ **Personal assets:** These comprise your personal savings (including pension funds, RRSPs, mortgages, life insurance, and cash).

When you approach potential lenders and investors, they will expect that you are prepared to invest in your company using your own resources, or assets. Why should they invest in you if you won't invest in yourself?

✔ **Self-financed/Part-time:** Some entrepreneurs start their businesses part-time or after hours, while still working at salaried jobs. If you have a business partner, perhaps one of you can run the new business, while the other retains his or her job and works part-time in the new business. This way, you have more security while waiting for your business to get off the ground.

✔ **Venture capital:** Venture capitalist companies give you start-up money in exchange for owning part of your firm. While they don't involve themselves in the day-to-day operation of your business, venture capitalists will nevertheless take an active position within your business and will expect a say in terms of significant longer-term decisions. Venture capital is a long-term investment, with investors expecting to be involved in the firm for at least three to seven years and then selling their share of the business back to you.

Some Additional Resources

There are many sources of information and assistance available to people interested in starting a business. I list a few worthy Web sites below. Each of these sites has links to related sites, if you need additional or specialized information.

✔ **Business Development Bank of Canada** (`www.bdc.ca`): Shown in Figure 21-2, the BDC is wholly owned by the government of Canada and classifies itself as Canada's small business bank. You can research financing options as well as access their business tools, including business plan help, a self-assessment quiz for wannabe entrepreneurs, and tools to help you with financial calculations. High-tech and e-businesses will be interested in the IT-specific tools on this site.

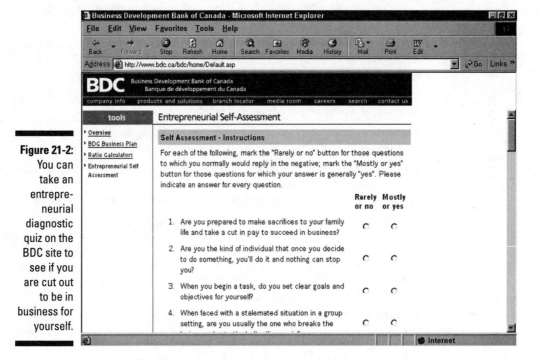

Figure 21-2: You can take an entrepreneurial diagnostic quiz on the BDC site to see if you are cut out to be in business for yourself.

✔ **Canada Business Service Centres** (www.cbsc.org): This comprehensive federal government–run Web site asks you a series of questions to help you decide if starting your own business is for you, and then guides you through the start-up process. Many of the required forms are available on the site. Links to province-specific information are also helpful.

✔ **CanadaOne** (www.canadaone.com): Another very good resource for business information, this site includes an online magazine (*CanadaOne Magazine*) and a directory of 550 Canadian-specific businesses and resources. This site also has a great tool, called Toolkit, which links you to other resources that are helpful in starting up your business.

✔ **Pan Canadian Community Futures** (www.communityfutures.ca): Community Futures Development Corporation offices (CFDC) are located in close to 300 communities across Canada. These offices are entrepreneurial development centres, and one of their mandates is to help small businesses start up and prosper in smaller communities. They provide business financing and training to rural entrepreneurs. Check out this site to see if there is an office in your community — and, if there is, be sure to check out the resources there.

Investigating business opportunities

Let your imagination wander for hours and you'll probably still not run out of ideas for opening a business. Business ideas often stem from a person's education, experience, and hobbies. By considering your natural talents, skills, and the sources of enjoyment in your life, you may discover a great business idea. If your interests coincide with what others don't like to do for themselves, don't have time to do, and are willing to pay for, you have a ready market.

Ideas can also come from observing trends, forecasting what people or businesses might want or need in the future, or simply seeing a potential opportunity. In other words, a need in the marketplace that no one is satisfying.

Don't limit yourself by thinking that your experience restricts you to starting a business in a particular field. For instance, if you've worked in a hotel for years, you may believe your business must be hospitality-related. But don't rule out applying your acquired skills in a variety of ways. While there's always a learning curve, good management and customer service skills can be transferred to virtually any business. Usually, the best business for you is the one in which you are most skilled and interested. As you review your options, you may wish to consult local experts about the growth potential of various businesses in your area. Matching your background with the local market will also increase your chance of success.

Chapter 22

Working Outside Canada

According to Government of Canada statistics, about 1.5 million Canadians currently live and work abroad. Working abroad, whether in the United States or elsewhere in the world, can be an exciting and enriching experience, and with the increased accessibility to information these days, it's far easier than it used to be to locate a job in a different country and to find out what you need to know to make a move. The world is at your doorstep!

And wow, do you have options! You have access to a wide variety of international work opportunities, including paid employment, volunteer work, and even new business ventures. If you want to light out for new and different territories, this chapter points you in the right direction. In this chapter, I give you the basics on finding a U.S.-based or overseas job. I also discuss other important stuff, including work visas, tax issues, and the cost of living.

Who Is Eligible to Work Abroad?

Finding a job abroad may be reasonably easy. *Qualifying* to work abroad can be the tough part. Different countries naturally have their own requirements regarding foreign workers (that would be you). Some of the things you need to be concerned with are visas, passports, immigration laws, time restrictions, and other country-specific issues.

When you look for a job abroad, you do so from two potential starting positions:

- **You have dual citizenship in the country you want to work in.** Lucky you! If you hold *dual* or *multiple citizenship* (when more than one country recognizes you as a citizen), you will likely be able to work in all the countries where you have citizenship. If you hold Irish citizenship along with Canadian citizenship, you can get a European Union passport and work throughout the EU. Depending on your personal circumstances, you may be able to find a job in one country more readily than in another.

- **You have your humble (but proud!) Canadian citizenship only.** If this is the case, a company abroad that wants to hire you is going to have to sponsor you as an employee. If you do not have dual citizenship in a country where you would like to work, you will have to work within the laws of that country in order to obtain a job and relocate there.

The word on dual (or multiple) citizenship

Dual citizenship means that a person is a citizen of two countries simultaneously. A person with *multiple citizenship* is a citizen of more than two countries at the same time.

While the rules governing dual citizenship are country-specific, there are only a couple of ways you can obtain this status, and they're standard across national borders:

- **Country of birth:** You are a citizen of the country in which you are born but, depending on the citizenship of your parents, you may also share their citizenship. For example, if you are born in Canada to parents who are United States citizens, you hold dual Canadian and U.S. citizenship. If you are born in Canada to Canadian parents, who were themselves born to Canadian parents (your Canadian grandparents), then boy, are you ever boring! (Just kidding.) Seriously, you're just proudly (and thoroughly) Canadian. And Canadian citizenship is the only citizenship you hold.

- **Naturalization:** You emigrate to another country from Canada and become a permanent resident there. So, you hold dual citizenship with Canada and the country you now call home.

    Note that, when you immigrate to Canada, some countries allow you to hold on to the citizenship of the country of your birth, while others require you to give it up.

Each country makes its own decisions regarding its citizens. You should be aware that if you choose to work and live in another country where you have citizenship, you may have both the rights *and* obligations that go with being a citizen. Whenever you are physically in a country that recognizes you as a citizen, its laws take priority over the laws of any other country of which you are a citizen. There may be laws in a country to which a foreign traveler is not subject, but which apply to you as a citizen of that country — for example, restrictions on exit, compulsory military service, and special taxes, or even financial compensation for services received in the past, including educational costs.

While it sounds like a great idea, having dual (or multiple) citizenship may not necessarily mean you can work in the other country of which you are a citizen. To be sure of your status, contact the embassy or consulate of the second country and ask for a decision about your status (in writing!). In some cases, you may have inadvertently given up your other citizenship when you obtained Canadian citizenship. Your country of original citizenship may, for example, have a rule that you cannot have dual citizenship and you *automatically* give yours up when you become a citizen of another country. The laws that apply to your case are generally the ones in force at the time of the event that affects your citizenship (your birth or marriage or your parents' birth or marriage, for example). This is why determining your current citizenship status can be a difficult and lengthy process.

To get more information on your citizenship status in a given country, you can call the country's embassy or consulate in Canada. Check out DocuWeb (`www.docuweb.ca/EmbassiesOttawa/members.html`) for a list of embassies and contact information.

Humble but proud Canadian seeking work abroad

Landing a job abroad sounds thrilling, but it can also be a daunting logistical challenge. The documentation you need varies between countries, but usually includes an offer of employment from an employer willing to sponsor you, a working visa, and any number of other requirements. This means lots of red tape to wade through for the company hiring you, so, if you are in this situation, you need to make yourself extra-attractive to them; they are going to have to move heaven and earth to hire you (in comparison with simply hiring someone with citizenship in that country).

To be granted permission to work in a different country, you will likely require a written offer of employment, obtained before you arrive there. In some countries, you can visit for a certain amount of time — and look for a job while there. But of course time inevitably runs out, and if you don't have a job offer and permission from the country's government to work there, you get summarily booted out. Permission to work in a country usually takes the form of a *work visa* or *work permit* (temporary authorization, usually for a specified period of time, allowing you to work or live in the country). The work visa is one way the government of the other country has of keeping track of foreign workers.

If you're lucky, your new employer abroad will provide assistance with, or even take full responsibility for, obtaining your work visa. If he does take this on for you, make sure that all the arrangements are legitimate and consistent with the requirements of the country concerned. The Department of Foreign Affairs and International Trade (DFAIT) has a Web site with country-specific requirements and information. Log on to http://voyage.dfait-maeci.gc.ca/destinations/menu_e.htm.

Getting the Necessary Documentation

You may require certain documents to work outside Canada:

- ✔ **Alien Registration Card:** When you arrive in your *host country* (the country where you will be working as a foreign worker), you may also need to register with the country's immigration department, for taxation and tracking purposes. In such a case, you will likely be assigned an *Alien Registration Card,* an official identification card issued by the government of your host country, which you are required to have in your possession at all times for identification purposes and as proof of your status.

- ✔ **Employment contract:** Ask your new employer for an employment contract in addition to the written offer of employment. It is definitely to your advantage to have the terms and conditions of your employment outlined in detail. It is never a good idea to accept a job abroad without finalizing the details prior to your arrival. Examine the terms of your contract carefully and have it reviewed by a lawyer in order to make sure that the financial and other conditions of the offer are carefully detailed and that you fully understand them. Employment contracts are covered in more detail in Chapter 18.

- ✔ **Passport:** All Canadian citizens must have a valid passport before taking up residence abroad. Once you are living internationally, you should continue to maintain a valid passport, just in case you need or want to return home, or travel. Application forms are available online through the Canadian Passport Office Web site (www.dfait-maeci.gc.ca/passport), as well as at passport offices, post offices, and Canadian government offices abroad.

  If you submit the appropriate documents with your completed passport application, you can usually get your passport within five working days (allow several weeks if it has to be mailed to you, however).

- ✔ **Visa:** If you aren't a citizen of the country in which you're looking for work, you can still hang out there for a specified period of time while you try to find a job. You may require special permission to do this, however, from the government of the host country. The document you need is called a *visitor's visa.* This permission may be as simple as an endorsement or stamp placed in your passport by immigration officials when you enter the country, or it may require tonnes of paperwork and documentation.

Tax matters

Check with the Canada Customs and Revenue Agency (CCRA) (www.ccra-adrc.gc.ca) before you kiss Canada goodbye. The CCRA publication *Canadian Residents Abroad* provides excellent information for individuals working outside of Canada. It's available online at www.ccra-adrc.gc.ca/E/pub/tg/t4131eq/t4131-01-e.pdf.

You may also wish to consult a private financial planner, who can provide advice and guidance on such matters as contributing to your Registered Retirement Savings Plan (RRSP) and the Canada Pension Plan (CPP) while you are abroad.

All countries also require you to obtain special permission or status — usually called a *work visa* or *work permit* — when you plan to work in that country. Getting a work visa/permit can be difficult, as most countries want to fill jobs with their own citizens before hiring outside the country. For this reason, to get permission to work in some countries you may have to leap tall buildings in a single bound. Also, you will likely require a valid, written offer of employment before you can apply for a work visa/permit.

For information about visa requirements, check the Country Travel Reports published by Canada's Department of Foreign Affairs and International Trade (DFAIT), available online at http://voyage.dfait-maeci.gc.ca/destinations/menu_e.htm. For more details, you can also contact the embassy or consulate of the country you are heading for. DocuWeb (www.docuweb.ca/EmbassiesOttawa/members.html) has contact information for embassies located in Ottawa.

Be sure to apply far in advance of your departure from Canada for your work visa/permit. And remember, you require a valid passport before you can apply for a visa.

Rules and visa requirements for Canadians working in the U.S. have been relaxed since 1989, so Canadians rarely need an actual visa to work there. Instead, you need to qualify for a temporary worker status, which is easier to get and for which you can apply at the Canada–U.S. border. Check out the section "Canadians Working in the United States" for more on the various types of temporary workers allowed in the U.S.

Canadians Working in the United States

Canada and the United States have had an agreement in place for some years that allows citizens of one country to work in the other with fewer restrictions than exist between other countries. Since Canada and the United States entered into the North American Free Trade Agreement (NAFTA) in 1989, the options for Canadians wanting to work in the U.S. have increased. You still need permission (primarily so the U.S. government can keep track of you), but the processing time has decreased substantially.

Everyone legally working and living in the United States fits into one of three categories:

- **Citizens:** These are people who were either born in the U.S. or who have immigrated there and become U.S. citizens. They have all the rights and privileges of employment in the U.S.

- **Immigrants:** Landed immigrants have permanent residency status in the U.S. and the same rights as citizens. They do not require work visas to hold employment in the U.S.

- **Non-immigrants:** Unless you plan to apply for permanent residency in the U.S., you will be classified as a *non-immigrant*. Non-immigrants usually require a work visa (or a *temporary work status,* in the case of Canadians) to work legally in the U.S. There are numerous visas or types of work status available, depending on the type of job, your own credentials, and the term of your position.

Non-immigrant temporary status

As a non-immigrant, you need to have a job to go to, in order to be granted status to work in the United States. As a Canadian, however, you do have several options when it comes to working in the U.S. — depending on your qualifications and the job you're applying for. For more information on these visas, including how to apply, check out the Web site of the American law firm Ogletree, Deakins (www.ogletreedeakins.com). The U.S. Department of State also has a Web site that provides detailed information on visas and other travel-related issues, at http://travel.state.gov/visa_services.html. Another great source of information is individual U.S. embassy Web sites. The URL of the Web site for the U.S. embassy in Canada is www.ins.usdoj.gov/graphics/services/tempbenefits/index.htm.

In this section, I give you a brief summary of the temporary work classifications/status in the United States for which Canadians may be eligible.

B-1 status: Temporary Visitor for Business

The B-1 classification applies only to persons employed by a Canadian business who visit the U.S. to perform services on behalf of their Canadian employer. This is a good visa for businesspeople who do not have professional accreditation (such as a university degree), which is required for other temporary permits. Under NAFTA, B-1 status is only good for one year, and the type of work that can be done in the U.S. is limited.

Usually, a Canadian-employed person who is just traveling to the U.S. for business periodically will use B-1 status.

H-1B status: Temporary Professional Worker

A privileged group of non–U.S. citizens, including Canadians, can obtain H-1B status, even if U.S. workers are available to do their types of jobs. H-1B non-immigrant status may be issued to individuals for temporary entry in a specialty occupation as a professional. Some examples include accountant, computer analyst, engineer, financial analyst, scientist, architect, or lawyer. Unlike the TN status (see below), there is no specific list of eligible professions, and a university degree may not be required if you have the equivalent in experience and education.

The H-1B non-immigrant category is for temporary employment only. It is not necessary for the actual position to be temporary — employers only need to show that the placement of the non–U.S. citizen in that position is to be temporary. An H-1B can be approved for an initial period of up to three years and a total of six years. The U.S. employer has to pre-apply to the U.S. government Department of Immigration and Naturalization Service (INS) for approval for you to be admitted under H-1B status. To be admitted to the country, you bring the approval with you to the border.

The United States has placed a quota of 195,000 on the number of H-1B classifications it will issue in the next three years, to be reduced to 65,000 in the fourth year. As such, it will become increasingly difficult to obtain this type of status. The good news for Canadians, though, is that most of the Canadians eligible for H-1B status are also eligible for TN status (see below).

Spouses of H-1B status employees are not eligible to work in the U.S. unless they qualify for status on their own.

TN status: Free Trade Professional

Under NAFTA, certain professionals have been awarded special employment status and are now eligible for a temporary non-immigrant status called the TN (*T* for Trade, *N* for NAFTA). TN status can be obtained, with no application form and the appropriate paperwork, within minutes of arriving at a port of entry into the United States. You require the following:

✔ A letter requesting TN status

✔ A copy of your university or college degree and your employment records establishing that you're qualified for the prospective job

✔ A letter from your U.S. or Canadian employer (on company letterhead) offering you the job in the United States.

To access a list of professions that are eligible for this status, log on to www.usvisa.com/tn_list.htm.

While the process sounds easy, I recommend having an immigration lawyer draft the letter requesting TN status, and give you a checklist to follow — so you don't get turned back at the border because you are missing something important. For example, you want to make sure your specific job title appears on the TN eligibility list, or you risk being refused entry.

The TN status is good for one year and can be renewed any number of times, but it will only be granted if the period of stay is temporary. One thing to consider if you are married: Unless your spouse also qualifies for TN status, she/he will be classified as a dependent, and will be unable to work in the U.S. Further, if you are in the process of applying for permanent residency, your TN status renewal or application could be denied — you would be better off applying for H-1B status.

L-1 status: Intra-Company Transferee

L-1 status allows a Canadian to live and work in the U.S. for a maximum of seven years. Here's what you need to qualify for an L-1 visa:

✔ You must be a management-level or specialized-knowledge employee of a Canadian company, and must have been employed by this company for at least one year.

✔ The U.S. position must be of a comparable level.

✔ Your company must have a U.S. branch or subsidiary of which it is at least 50-percent owner.

✔ The U.S. branch must actually have an office (with a lease or deed to prove it).

An example would be if you are a manager at IBM Canada and are transferred to IBM U.S. to work for several years.

A recent law passed in the U.S. allows spouses of L-1 status holders to receive work authorization in the U.S., unlike in the cases of H-1B and TN status.

E-2 status: Investor Temporary Work Visa

If you are a Canadian citizen and invest a substantial dollar amount in a U.S. business or enterprise (the rule of thumb is US$100,000 or more), you can apply for an E-2 visa, which allows you to work and run your business in the U.S. This is the only temporary work classification that requires you to apply to the U.S. embassy for a visa, and approval can take a few months. If you already have temporary worker status, such as TN status, you can apply to have this status changed — the processing time is much shorter. Your managers and essential personnel can also apply to work for you in the U.S. under E-2 status. Visas are issued for five-year terms, with no limit on the number of times they can be renewed.

You can help your new U.S. employer out by knowing exactly what temporary work classification you are eligible for and how to acquire it *before* you apply for a job across the border. You will make it much easier for a U.S.-based company to make the decision to hire you — you have already worked out the cross-border details for them.

Immigrant status

If you plan on relocating to the United States and working there on a permanent basis, you should consider becoming a permanent resident, the U.S. equivalent to Canadian landed immigrant status. This process can be time-consuming and is full of legal hurdles and issues, but it's easier than having to reapply for temporary status every few years.

The alternative to temporary working status is *permanent resident status,* of which the most common is a Green Card. Permanent resident status allows a person from another country to live and work in the United States with no time limitation.

In order to get a Green Card, you need to have one of the following: an offer of permanent employment from a U.S. employer, *sponsorship* from a U.S. relative (they sign a document stating they will not allow you to become a public charge), or an investment of over US$1 million in the U.S. that creates jobs for Americans. (Yes, folks, you can buy your way in, but if you have a million dollars, you probably don't really need a job, right?) This differs from the E-2 visa described above, in that you can actually get a Green Card if you have a million bucks to invest. With the E-2, you are investing less and only get a temporary visa.

Oh yes, there is one other way. The United States makes available 55,000 Green Cards through the DV Lottery Program each year. (DV stands for Diversity Visa.) The purpose of this lottery is to give people living in countries that don't have a high level of representation in the U.S. an opportunity to get their Green Cards. You are not eligible if you are Canadian-born, but if you are a Canadian citizen born in a different country you may be eligible to enter the lottery. Check out the eligibility requirements at `http://travel.state.gov/ visa_services.html`. Applicants are selected in a random, computer-generated draw.

Landing a U.S.-based job

So, just how difficult is it to land a job in the United States? Well, it depends on how you conduct your job hunt and how prepared you are. As a Canadian looking for a U.S.-based job, you'll likely focus primarily on Internet postings, networking, headhunters, or employment agencies. Log on and visit a search engine like Yahoo! (`www.yahoo.com`), Google (`www.google.com`), or Dogpile (`www.dogpile.com`) and type in "U.S. jobs." You will get dozens of hits.

Some U.S.-based online job banks are worth checking out:

- ✔ **HotJobs.com** (`www.hotjobs.com`): HotJobs.com is a one-stop career resource centre that offers advanced privacy features, numerous career tools — including industry-specific chat and newsletters — as well as a comprehensive relocation centre. The site boasts thousands of national and international jobs posted by corporate hiring mangers, staffing firms, and executive recruiters. One of the key benefits of using HotJobs.com is that jobs posted by staffing agencies or executive recruiters are clearly marked as such, giving you the power of choice when conducting a job search or applying for a job.

- ✔ **Monster.com** (`www.monster.com`): This fun and easy-to-use site offers the ability to search for jobs, research companies, read career-related articles, and customize your search using the site's MyMonster feature.

Canadians Working Overseas

While the United States is our closest neighbour and may be one of the easier "foreign" countries for Canadians to land a job in (especially in certain occupations), your employment options extend far beyond North America, providing you are willing to do the legwork to find the job, land it, and ensure your documentation is all in order before you depart. Again, permissions, visas, and paperwork vary by country, so check the requirements for each country that you are considering. You can check out the Department of Foreign Affairs and International Trade's (DFAIT) Web site for country-specific information at `http://voyage.dfait-maeci.gc.ca/destinations/menu_e.htm`.

Landing an overseas job

When you are searching for international employment, you literally have a world of opportunities open to you! You can apply to different countries, industries, and occupations. You can work in a volunteer or a paid position. You can apply for long- or short-term positions. If you are unsure about the length of time you want to work abroad, you can go for short-term projects, such as youth exchanges, internships, professional exchanges, or even working holidays. A short-term placement may give you the experience and background you need to decide whether you want to work abroad for an extended period. Lots of fresh grads take a year off after school to work abroad — it's a great experience.

Where you gonna look?

Going online is the easiest way to kick-start your international job hunt. Here are just a few of the many Web sites that will help you locate a job:

✔ **About.com** (www.about.com): This directory has excellent resources. Do a keyword search on their site for "International Jobs."

✔ **Monster.co.uk** (www.monster.co.uk): Monster has over 1 million jobs worldwide listed on this site, including almost 20,000 in the United Kingdom and over 60,000 in the rest of Europe. You can search for a job on every continent! The site offers features similar to the Canadian affiliate site, Monster.ca (www.monster.ca), including an e-mail update when jobs are posted, a career centre full of great articles, job-hunting tools and information, and a template for creating your résumé online.

✔ **Monster's Global Gateway** (http://international.monster.co.uk): This is a great site if you are looking for a job in a specific country. Pick the country of your choice and click your way directly to Monster's job bank in that country.

✔ **OverseasJobs.com** (www.overseasjobs.com): This site posts international job opportunities in many occupations and countries. They specialize in finding employees to fill overseas job openings or for U.S.-based companies willing to provide work visas for out-of-country employees.

✔ **TopJobs.co.uk** (www.topjobs.co.uk): This U.K.-based job bank allows you to sign up for e-mail updates when a job is posted in a field you're interested in. It has an especially great list of career tips and jobs for new graduates. Easy to navigate, you can search for jobs by job category, geographic region, or keyword.

In addition to the online job banks, weekend editions of the national papers, such as *The Globe and Mail,* the *National Post,* and the *Financial Post* advertise overseas job openings. Many companies also use recruitment agencies to fill their overseas positions. Check out Yahoo! Canada (www.yahoo.ca), Dogpile.com (www.dogpile.com), or Google (www.google.ca) and do a search for "international recruitment specialists" to find specific agencies related to your field of work.

Canada's Department of Foreign Affairs and International Trade (DFAIT) coordinates two programs for young Canadians interested in working abroad:

- **The International Youth Exchange Program (IYEP):** The IYEP provides a wealth of information concerning opportunities in more than 60 programs in over 20 countries. Call 1-800-267-8376 or (613) 992-6142, or consult DFAIT's Web site (www.dfait-maeci.gc.ca/123go).

- **The Youth International Internship Program (YIIP):** The YIIP provides paid internships with organizations operating in other countries. Call 1-800-559-2888 or (613) 944-2413, or visit www.dfait-maeci.gc.ca/interns.

Cost of living comparisons

Cost of living figures provide a general idea of the salary you would need to maintain the lifestyle to which you are accustomed in Canada. The figures indicate the price of a "basket" of goods and services used by the typical household in locations throughout the world.

Here are a few online calculators you can use to calculate cost of living differences between Canada and other countries:

- **ACCRA** (www.accra.org/costofliving/index.cfm): A pay-per-use site, but it does cost-of-living comparisons for Canadian cities.

- **Homestore.com** (www.homefair.com/homefair/calc/salcalc.html): Salary comparisons for U.S. cities, with links to foreign countries.

- **Living Abroad** (www.livingabroad.com/profiles/index.html): Another pay-per-use site, but with cost-of-living comparisons for foreign countries.

For a great free salary calculator that allows you to compare international, Canadian, and U.S. salaries, check out Homestore.com (www.homefair.com) or SalaryExpert.com (www.salaryexpert.com).

Be wary, though, about using an across-the-board cost of living comparison when you are relocating to a country with an entirely different culture and therefore a very different basket of goods and services. You might not be comparing apples to apples.

For example, the cost of utilities would be weighed quite heavily in Canada, but much less so in a country that doesn't have the dreaded winters we do.

In some countries where it's prevalent, the cost of a live-in housekeeper is factored into the cost of living figures.

Taking some time to review possible cost of living differences might make a difference in your decision to relocate to another country.

If you are offered a job overseas by an organization or company, it can be very exciting — but, at the same time, it is important that you investigate the company and the offer carefully before you accept. The first step is to find out as much as you can about the organization or company that is offering you a job. You can ask for references from previous or current employees, government agencies they deal with, or other Canadian corporations with which they do business. You can also visit their Internet site, look up the company on www.strategis.gc.ca/corporations, or even call your local Better Business Bureau (if the organization or company is Canadian-owned) to get information.

Part VI
The Part of Tens

The 5th Wave   By Rich Tennant

@RICHTENNANT

"Well, so much for my lucky hat! I've worn it to five interviews and not ONE call-back!"

In this part . . .

You read about 10 blunders, blips, and other missteps not to make during your job hunt. Read them twice, to sear them into your memory. You also read about 10 soft skills that go the distance in helping you stand out from the other applicants and get hired. The best thing about these soft, or transferable skills, is that you probably don't realize you already have them. Surprise! You also read about 10 little tricks you can practise to keep your head up and your spirits humming as you make your way along the road to gainful employment.

Chapter 23

Ten Big Job-Hunting Blunders

· ·

Landing a job is tough enough, but job hunters often make the task even tougher through easy-to-avoid mistakes that land their résumé in the discard pile. Sometimes, one mistake is all it takes to get passed over for a job. This chapter outlines some of the most common blunders that pretty well guarantee you will *not* land that job.

Being disorganized

Keeping yourself organized is very important to your success. If an employer or recruiter contacts you, and you can't remember what job they're talking about, let alone any details about the company, you might as well kiss the job goodbye — not to mention the embarrassment factor. When I phone a candidate whose first question is, "What company is this again?" or "What job is this for?" I not only question how detail-oriented they are, but also, more important, how interested they are in the job.

Use a binder as a daily log with reminders of which companies you applied to and for which positions (in case you get a surprise telephone inquiry). In the same binder, keep a copy of the job ad, if there was one, and a copy of the résumé and cover letter you sent. Also, make notes of whom you talked to in the company, what follow-up you have done, and when you plan on calling to follow up again.

Disregarding detail

Pay close attention to your résumé and cover letter. Spelling errors, wrong or misspelled names, wrong job (oops, forgot to change the subject line!) may stop your résumé from progressing any further. Other mistakes include being unclear in your Objective, pointing out your own weaknesses or not stressing your strong points, using the wrong style of résumé (if you have no job experience, don't use a chronological style), and not highlighting transferable skills. Remember, quantity is not quality! Don't just send out hundreds of résumés without taking the time to personalize each.

Doing half the job

One of the most common mistakes job hunters make is not taking their job search seriously — only doing half the job. You should treat your job hunt the way you would an actual job, and do it to the best of your ability. You wouldn't only half complete a job you were getting paid for, would you? A waitress doesn't just take your order and then not bring your food. Just sending out résumés and then kicking back won't land you a job . . . unless you have incredible luck.

Here are some of the most common areas where job hunters fall short:

- **Sending an incomplete application package:** Your job application is incomplete when you do not include a cover letter or don't tailor your résumé to the job you are applying for.

- **Assuming your credentials will speak for themselves:** What a silly assumption to make. Considering that you'll likely be up against a large number of other applicants, you need to find a way to stand out. There are many techniques to help you do so, including tailoring your résumé and cover letter to a specific job, showing enthusiasm in your cover letter, letting the employer know you have researched the organization, phoning to see if your résumé has arrived, making connections with someone in the company who can help you, and sending a thank-you note after an interview.

- **"Forgetting" to research the company:** Showing up at an interview without having done any research into the company is likely to get your résumé nixed! Employers want to know that you are really interested in the job *and* the company.

- **Neglecting your networks:** Put out feelers when you are looking for a job. Cultivate and look after your network — it will come in very handy during a job hunt. If you don't know anyone in your *target company* (the company you're applying to), head down to the office, ask to speak to the recruiter or supervisor, and get a general feel for the place. See if you can swing an information interview with a potential co-worker you feel comfortable with. You'd be surprised how helpful people can be. Find out who supervises the position you're applying for, and as much as you can about that person's working style. Don't take everything you learn too seriously, however. You may inadvertently interview someone who is dissatisfied with his job and get a skewed picture.

- **Neglecting to follow up:** Following up after an interview can improve your chances of landing a job. You can send an e-mail or a handwritten note to thank the interviewer for taking the time to talk to you. You can also phone several days after the interview to find out your status. Following up distinguishes you from the competition.

Forgetting to ask questions

Making yourself stand out is very important not only in landing an interview but also in excelling in that interview. Smart questions can show interviewers not only that you've done your homework, but also that you are sincerely interested in the company. You can even use questions to direct the interview toward your strengths.

Forgetting to think about fit

This blunder has two parts: First, you need to make sure you really want to work for this company and why, before you even go for the interview (or before you apply!). Second, you need to market yourself to the company, not just in terms of what your accomplishments are and what you have done, but how you can apply this experience to the particular employer.

If you believe you fit with the company, this will come across in your cover letter and interview. You will be more enthusiastic about the company and the job, and the information you learn about the employer from your research can do nothing but help you in an interview!

Marketing yourself is far easier when you have researched the job and the company. You can determine what it is about you and your experience that is a good fit, and you can tell the employer, in your cover letter and interview, what you can do for them if they hire you.

Getting in the recruiter's face

While most recruiters don't mind if you call them to get a little more information about a job or to follow up on the status of your application, some people carry this too far.

I received an e-mail from a fellow inquiring about the status of his application. I responded, telling him that it was good to follow up and that I was in the process of shortlisting, and that I'd be in touch if he made the short list. He then proceeded to call me at home — at midnight, no less — getting me out of bed! Now that's what I call "in your face"!

Aside from calling at all hours of the night, which I don't recommend, calling too often or being too pushy turns off a recruiter as well.

Having the wrong attitude

This doesn't mean just having a bad attitude — you know, the person who believes the company should be lucky to have *him* for an employee! The wrong attitude also includes getting depressed during your job hunt or coming across as desperate to land a job. You need to find ways to help you stay positive, focused, and to not take rejection, or even lack of acknowledgement, personally.

Most employers are interested in self-confidence and a positive attitude. Whatever you do, don't come across as being desperate for a job, no matter how badly you want it — or need it.

Mistaking quantity for quality

Job hunters who send out dozens of résumés and apply to almost any job that looks remotely interesting clearly don't know what they want to do when they grow up! Strive to get a clear idea of the kind of work you want to do, then seek out jobs directly, or closely, related to it.

Putting your job search on hold to pursue a hot lead

You have finally landed an interview! Or, an employer calls you to get more information! It's a great accomplishment, and I don't want to burst your bubble, but . . . only one person is going to get that job and there are still several steps in the process. The odds are small that one hot lead actually turns into a job offer.

Continue to follow up on and create other job leads. If the hot lead doesn't pan out, then you may have unnecessarily prolonged your job hunt. This can lead to the kind of setback that, if it happens a few times, might discourage you altogether. Try to have at least six warm leads at all times.

Stretching the truth

What is the harm of misrepresenting the truth — just a little? The most common forms of misrepresentation on résumés include lying about job titles, responsibilities, credentials, or length of employment. Unfortunately for the job hunter, most employers today do background checks, so if you lie, there is a good chance you'll be found out. Also, if you get the position and are later discovered to have lied, even if you do prove to be a good employee, you are likely to lose the job. Most employers will not tolerate dishonesty from an employee.

One of the biggest complaints I've heard from employers is about applicants who exaggerate their abilities or accomplishments in a résumé or application and then try to fudge their way through the interview. It's good to market yourself to a company, but it's equally important to be honest about your limitations. Most employers can see through misrepresentations. It's better to assess what the employer's needs are and then communicate, as honestly as you can, how well you can meet those needs.

Chapter 24

Ten Soft Skills to Help Land That Job

• •

*Y*ou have two important, yet very different, sets of skills when it comes to employment. These are your technical skills, often called hard skills, that you need to perform the job, and transferable skills, or soft skills, that you have developed as a result of your life experiences: jobs you've held, classes you've taken, and projects you've worked on. Other experiences contribute to your set of soft skills, such as parenting, hobbies you're involved in, sports you play, and so on. Soft skills and hard skills are often complementary, but, when two applicants both have the necessary technical skills, it is often the soft skills that tip the balance in favour of one over the other.

You acquire *hard skills* through education and on-the-job learning (also known as trial by fire). If you are a mechanic, you have specific skills when it comes to troubleshooting and repairing machinery or vehicles. As a computer programmer, you have the technical skills to program in different computer languages. Teachers have the knowledge of their subject matter and the skills to impart this knowledge to their students.

Soft skills, on the other hand, are the ones that make you a better employee. They can go a long way to convincing an employer to hire you. This is true if your technical skills are somewhat lacking, or if you are up against someone with the same technical skills as you, and it's especially true if you're a younger or an inexperienced job hunter. A recent study reports that a positive attitude and reliability (both soft skills that I discuss in this chapter) are the two qualities that employers identify as most important when hiring someone for entry-level work.

Your soft skills fall into the following four categories:

✔ **Communication skills:** In an era of information technology, it is an absolute requirement that you have the ability to express, transmit, and interpret knowledge and ideas in both verbal and written form. Good communication skills will help you in just about any job. If you have these skills, make sure the employer knows you have them.

✔ **Interpersonal skills:** You have to work with people in almost every job, although some interpersonal skills are more job-specific than others. Your skills in working with, relating to, and helping people are very important. In manager positions or team environments, your interpersonal skills will be key to your success.

✔ **Management and leadership skills:** To be an effective leader you need skills in supervising, directing, and guiding people. Organizational skills will help you in any position, and leadership/management skills are very important in managerial and supervisory roles. Team environments also benefit from having team members with leadership and organizational skills.

✔ **Research and planning skills:** Research and planning skills are also something you will use in many different jobs. You need to know where to find information and what to do with that information when you find it. In most jobs, planning and the ability to see the impact of an event or decision on the overall organization are also sought-after skills.

In this chapter, I give you my take on 10 soft skills from these categories that will help you get hired. The best part is, you probably have several of them already, maybe without even knowing it. Harness your soft skills, be confident in them, and go knock somebody's socks off.

You can speak

Okay, so I know most people have the ability to speak — but to speak well, without tripping over your tongue, and to be able to articulate your thoughts is a skill that many people do not have. The good news is that you can learn to speak better. You can join public speaking clubs like Toastmasters (www.toast masters.org/index.htm) or service clubs like the Rotary (www.rotary.org) where you have the opportunity to practise public speaking.

You should also be able to speak well in the language the company to which you are applying uses to do business. In other words, if the employer uses English predominantly, your verbal English skills can make or break your chances at a job. Again, you can improve your language skills simply by practising or taking classes. If you are trying to learn English language skills, most communities offer English as a second language (ESL) courses. French courses are also offered in many communities.

You can write

So you think you can write, do you? There is a big difference between being able to write and being able to get your point across clearly and succinctly in writing. Written communication skills are important in most jobs. Whether you need to write reports, memos, or just e-mails, it is crucial to be able to put the words together in a way that makes your message clear. Again, you need to be able to write in the language your employer uses — being Canada, this is probably French or English, but it may involve other languages if the employer does business outside of Canada. Being able to communicate, both verbally and in writing, in another language can open many doors for job hunters.

The Web site called English Page.com (www.englishpage.com) provides an online opportunity to enhance your English writing skills and may be worth checking out if you do not have a classroom program available in your area.

You can listen

Most of us can hear but we may have a hard time actually listening to what others are saying. Listening skills are important in a work setting when it comes to understanding what is expected of you and interpreting instructions. Have you ever heard someone say, "How many times do I have to tell you?"

Improving your listening skills all goes back to BERPing. (If you have no idea what I am talking about here, you should check out Chapter 17, "Acing the Interview.") BERPing is a straightforward technique to help you improve your listening skills. In Chapter 17, I apply it specifically to the interview process, but you can make use of it in virtually any situation that requires you to be a good listener. When BERPing, you focus on having an active and alert body posture (that's the "B"), maintaining eye contact ("E"), responding to the speaker by asking questions and clarifying points ("R"), and remembering the purpose of the conversation ("P").

You can cooperate with others

Seems like an obvious skill, doesn't it. However, the old you-can-play-in-my-sandbox-if-I-can-play-in-yours scenario doesn't always apply when we grow up. Somewhere along the line, the ability to cooperate and work together — our teamwork skills — often gets lost. It could be because we learn early that competition is good and that the fastest and the best usually get the biggest cookies when the job is done. Many employers today have recognized that teamwork is often the most efficient and effective way to complete tasks and, as such, promote teamwork in the workplace. If you work better or prefer to work on your own, you might want to think twice about applying to an ad that says teamwork skills are essential. The good news, again, is that like most soft skills, you can acquire the ability to cooperate with others and work in a team. Check out your local colleges for interpersonal skills seminars that focus on teamwork.

You have a positive attitude

I talk about the importance of having a positive attitude throughout this book, but I want to restate it here because it is so important. A positive attitude will make the difference between who gets the job and who doesn't. An employer will choose someone with a positive attitude and who requires a little training over a person who is a sourpuss but requires no training, any day. It all goes back to the six things an employer wants to know (see Chapter 16) — one of these being "Will you do the job?" If you show a positive outlook and enthusiasm in everything from your cover letter, to follow-up calls, to the interview, you show the employer that yes, you are willing to do the job. You have the right attitude — and that counts for a lot.

You have a strong work ethic and are reliable

What exactly is a strong work ethic? A person who gives whatever job they have their best effort, who shows up on time and puts in an honest day's work, has a strong work ethic. Sometimes, if you take a job that is below the level or salary you want to start at, or if you are just killing time at a job until something better comes along, you may feel that it is not worth putting in a lot of effort. Remember, however, that any job worth doing is worth doing right! Your work ethic will follow you through your career and is something that employers will check when doing references. You alone have control over your work ethic.

An employer needs to know that you will be a reliable employee — someone who can be counted on to do the job and to do it right. Reliability also means showing up for work when scheduled and putting in a full day's work. If you tend toward the lazy side and take shortcuts or unplanned days off, you may be surprised to find out that you are not really classified as a reliable employee. Reliability is a skill that you can work on if you make it a priority, and I suggest you should. References that attest to your reliability can be invaluable in landing you that next job.

You are willing to learn

Employers don't expect you to come into their organization knowing everything about the job you will be doing. They expect you to have certain base skills, but they also know they will have to train you. They want employees that are willing to learn and adapt to the employer's way of doing things. If new systems are introduced, they want to know you will be willing and able to learn them and use them as part of your job. Ability to learn quickly is a great soft skill to have on your résumé.

You can motivate others

Okay, so now I am telling you it is not enough to have a great attitude and be motivated yourself, but that you also need to motivate others? This is an important soft skill to have if you aspire to be a group leader or manager. Being able to motivate others is a key skill in leadership positions and, luckily, it is also one that can be learned. There's a multitude of motivational techniques you can use and courses you can take to help you develop these motivational skills. Check out the Internet (do a search on Dogpile (www.dogpile.com) for "motivational techniques") or your local college or university for seminars.

You are creative

Can you think outside the box? Can you come up with new and innovative ideas? This skill is highly valued in today's workforce, and people who have this ability are in great demand. Most jobs require some problem-solving abilities and many go beyond just simple problem solving and encourage employees to come up with new ideas and suggestions for improvement. This highly valued skill comes naturally to some people, while others have some difficulty expressing their creative thoughts. You may not think you are creative, but, under the right circumstances, you may be surprised. Working in an atmosphere that is non-threatening and encourages people to voice their opinions can bring out a creative side you may not have known you possessed.

You are organized

Being able to organize data (information), people, or things (everything that is not information or human falls into this category — like inventory), is a highly valued skill in most jobs. In today's workplace, where employees are expected to multitask (be able to do more than one thing at the same time), staying organized is far more important than ever before. You may be called upon to find information quickly and in a format that you can immediately use. Also, with the multitude of inputs (e-mail, voice mail, written instructions, verbal instructions) into a job today, you need a method to organize these to ensure everything that needs to be done actually gets done (and also that there is some record of it having been done). Can you learn to be organized? The good news is, yes, you can learn organizational techniques. Good thing, too! Being organized comes more naturally to some of us than to others. If you have good organizational skills — which, by the way, can be obvious by the way you conduct your job hunt — you may have the edge over other candidates with similar technical skills. See Chapter 4 for tips on organizing your job hunt.

Chapter 25

Ten Ways to Stay Motivated During Your Job Hunt

• •

*Y*ou've either just graduated, have been laid off, are re-entering the workforce, or have decided that it's time to change jobs. In any case, you are quite likely highly motivated when you start your job hunt. If you don't achieve results in the first few weeks, however, chances are your motivation will take a dip. You may begin to get discouraged and find it difficult to stay on track. Staying motivated is a job hunter's most difficult task. Rejections, unanswered application packages, and unsuccessful interviews can affect your attitude, and in consequence, lower your motivation. This chapter discusses ways to keep your morale up and remain positive during your job hunt.

Build a support network

Sometimes, job hunters need a little additional support (or a little prodding!) to just keep at it. Who is better qualified to take this on than your family and friends? It's easy to get discouraged during your job hunt. Defend yourself from this by enlisting the help of a support group of friends and family who understand that it's their job to help you get back on track if you fall off. Sign them up *before* you start your job hunt, as it's sometimes difficult to recognize that you're losing motivation once you're on that downward slope.

Keep in touch with specific members of your support network on an ongoing basis and let them know what your game plan is. You can pick out one person in particular who you speak to each day (try to make it a local call!), and tell them what you're up to. Think of it as a daily strategy session. The rationale behind this is that when you vocalize an idea, it tends to become more real to you, and you'll feel compelled to act on it.

Another way of using a support network is to join or even start a job-hunting group, so you can connect with other positive and motivated job hunters (just like you, right?) to discuss what you are doing. These groups can be great networking opportunities, too. You may hear about a hot lead for yourself, or hear about one you may be able to tip someone else off about. See Chapter 14 for more networking advice. In today's super-charged era of high technology, it would be all too easy to conduct your job hunt exclusively from home. Just tune in, turn on, and poof, you're online and nobody sees you for days. This may seem great (think how productive I'll be, you think to yourself) but maintaining contact with the outside world is especially important when you're involved in a demanding process like job hunting. Try to get out of the house and meet at least one person every day — whether it be a friend or a potential employer. Tell your support group to encourage you to do so!

Celebrate small successes

Set small, realistic, achievable goals to propel you through your job hunt, and celebrate achieving them. For example, set a goal of making five new quality contacts daily and following up on five existing ones. At the end of a week, you could potentially make as many as 50 contacts. Celebrate achieving this goal. Take Saturday off! Go out for dinner or spend the day with your family.

Measure your progress in a different way. Remember, a job offer is not the only sign of success. It may be just landing an interview. Just think about it: There may be 200 applicants for a given job, and you get an interview. Celebrate this! You are at the head of the pack. Even if you don't get a job offer, you at least had enough going for you to get an interview. That is success!

Celebrate getting a telephone interview or having an employer return your call. Share your success with your support network so they can celebrate with you.

Have a couple of kids and get a mortgage

Let me explain. Responsibility can be a great motivator! The person who has kids and a mortgage is much more likely to stay motivated when looking for a job than someone with lesser obligations. I don't recommend acquiring these just to motivate yourself during your job hunt, however!

Keep busy

If your job hunt drags on for a long time and you find yourself in need of something to help keep you occupied, try doing some volunteer work in your community, or even in your chosen field or occupation. If money is also a concern, try doing some contract work, temping, or finding a part-time job. As I discuss in Chapter 20, all of these types of work can open the door to a full-time gig. Finding something to occupy your mind will give you a break from your job hunt, and will also help you get motivated again. It can also present more great networking opportunities.

Stay on track

It's so easy to wander off track when you are looking for a job. You may find that you develop a sudden affinity for housework when you're job-hunting, coming up with all sorts of chores that need to be done — laundry, dishes, cleaning out the eavestroughs, sorting through old boxes. . . . Or you may be researching accounting jobs online, for example, when you come across a link to one of your favourite hobbies: fly-fishing. Before you know it, you've pointed and clicked your way to the home page of the premier fly-fishing resort in British Columbia, and you can't even remember whether you had been looking at accounting sites or actuarial sites. You look at your watch. It's been half an hour since you first laid eyes on that fly-fishing link. See what I mean? (Check out Chapter 12 for ways to steer clear of the pitfalls of the Internet so you can use it effectively in your job hunt.) Keep a daily journal of what you've done in the past weeks, as well as what you intend to do in the coming weeks and months. Writing down a plan makes it more likely that you'll actually follow through. Your job-hunting journal can be as formal as a workbook, as fancy as a spreadsheet program on your computer, or as simple as a large wall calendar — as long as you can record your progress and plan your next move.

Set (and write down) your goals for the week and for each day. Reward yourself for achieving these goals. Revisit your job-hunting strategy on occasion and see if there is anything else you should be doing on a daily basis to keep yourself on track.

Remember to keep your eyes on the horizon instead of on the ground in front of you. You should always have 5 or 6 leads that you are following up on. If you've only got one and it doesn't pan out, you'll end up a week behind in your job hunt.

It's useful to think of your job hunt in terms of a strategic game such as chess — be thinking three or four moves into the future. You should never count on your current task being your last. You should always be strategizing and planning for your next move, until you achieve your goal.

Take a break for you

Another hurdle you'll face during your job hunt is finding the time to do everything that job-hunting books tell you to do! Books and resources can give you so much information that you might feel overwhelmed by the amount of work involved and by the time commitment. Finding a balance between your job hunt and your priorities in your life — family, friends, hobbies — is important to help you stay motivated in your job hunt.

So, it's important to take a break every once in a while and do something just for you. It can be going for a walk, going for lunch with a friend, or even going shopping. Anything *not* related to your job hunt is A-okay.

Build 30 minutes of physical activity into each and every day — take a walk, work out, go for a swim — whatever it takes to increase those endorphins that help you keep up that positive attitude.

Treat your job hunt as a job

Yes, that's exactly what I mean. Treat your job hunt as a job in itself, and take it seriously, as you would any other job. There's a direct correlation between the amount of effort you put into your job hunt and your success — just as there is in any regular job.

Set aside a space in your home and conduct your job hunt from there. I like to think of this area as Mission Control, or my job-hunting headquarters. Get up every morning and plan your day. Keep regular hours, and take breaks for lunch and coffee. If you stay focused and organized, and follow your plan, you'll establish a routine that will help keep you motivated. For more tips on how to transform that chosen space in your home into your job-hunting headquarters, see Chapter 3.

Try to keep an upbeat attitude

The operative word here is *try*! Your job-hunting success depends on the way you look at things — just as with every experience in life. You can either see the glass as half empty or half full. The many tasks in your job hunt can either drain your energy or enhance it — it all depends on your attitude. If you make the decision to try to stay upbeat, chances are you will.

So stay positive. Don't give up. I know this is easier said than done, but staying positive during your job hunt is important. Your positive attitude will come through in how you approach employers, in the tone of your cover letters, and in your voice during interviews. It will influence how much you get done in a day and the quality of the leads you dig up in your research.

Here are a few tips to help you keep your attitude positive:

- ✔ Keep away from people with negative attitudes.
- ✔ Realize that being rejected for a job is not a rejection of you as a person.
- ✔ Use your support network to help you stay optimistic.
- ✔ Celebrate small successes.

- ✔ Set daily goals that are realistic and achievable.

- ✔ Think of your job hunt as a learning experience. Just think of the skills you are developing. You are becoming a skilled researcher, networker, and interviewer. Add your new skills to your résumé!

- ✔ Accept that your feelings of stress, and possibly panic, are normal. Then put them aside. You can't control your subconscious mind — even if your conscious mind knows you are doing all you can and that things will eventually work out. Don't deny what you're going through.

- ✔ Seek professional assistance if depression or anxiety are affecting you.

- ✔ Read a self-help book, like this one. You can also check out *Résumés For Dummies, Cover Letters For Dummies*, and *Job Interviews For Dummies,* all by Joyce Lain Kennedy, all published by John Wiley & Sons Ltd.

Upgrade your skills

If you find that you are not having success with your job hunt, it could be because you need to upgrade your skills. Or perhaps you want to expand the horizons of your job hunt — be it going for a higher salary, a better position, or a different location — and you need to acquire a few new skills to do so. In any case, taking a course or reading a self-help book (like this one!) can help you acquire new skills that will benefit you in your job search and help keep you motivated along the way. You could even read a book on staying motivated!

Use professional resources

Getting some professional help with your job hunt can also help you stay motivated. Career counselors and coaches are trained to recognize when a client's motivation needs a boost, and have the tools to help keep you on track. If you find that motivation is not your only problem and you are beginning to get depressed, you may want to consider seeking medical help or visiting a psychologist.

Index

FIND THE ROLE OF YOUR LIFE

At a nationwide casting call just for you. Search by company, city or keyword.

Choose from thousands of jobs at hundreds of companies.

Hand pick your audience - you choose who sees your résumé and who doesn't.

Step into the spotlight and find your fit.

hotjobs.ca®

a YAHOO! service

ONWARD. UPWARD.

FREE PASS TO YOUR FUTURE

Sign up for a MyHotJobs account and search for thousands of jobs quickly and easily.

Then check back everyday for new listings.

Step 1 : Go to www.HOTJOBS.ca

Step 2 : Select the myHOTJOBS tab

Step 3 : Create your confidential account.

The limelight awaits.

ONWARD. UPWARD.